Accounting for Non-Accounting Students

J R Dyson

Department of Accounting and Law, Napier Polytechnic of Edinburgh

Second edition

PITMAN
PUBLISHING

Pitman Publishing
128 Long Acre, London WC2E 9AN

A Division of Longman Group UK Limited

First published in 1987
Second edition 1991

© J. R. Dyson 1987, 1991
Reprinted 1991, 1992, 1993

British Library Cataloguing in Publication Data
Dyson, J. R. (John Richard) 1939–
    Accounting for non-accounting students.-2nd. ed.
    1. Accountancy
    I. Title
    657

ISBN 0 273 03439 1

Printed in England by Clays Ltd, St Ives plc

Contents

To Auntie Clarice

Preface to the first edition

This is a book for non-accountants. It is intended primarily for students who are required to study accounting as part of a non-accounting degree or professional studies course. It should also be of value to those working in commerce, government or industry who find that their work involves them in dealing with accounting information. It is hoped that the book will help to explain why there is a need for such information.

Non-accounting students (such as engineers, personnel managers, purchasing officers, and sales managers) are sometimes unable to understand why they are required to study accounting. This is often found to be the case when they have to take an examination in the subject, and they are then presented with a paper of some considerable technical rigour.

Accounting books written specifically for the non-accountant are also often extremely demanding. The subject needs to be covered in such a way that non-accounting students do not become confused by too much technical information. They do not require the same detailed analysis that is only of relevance to the professional accountant. Some accounting books specially written for the non-accountant go to the opposite extreme. They outline the subject so superficially that they are of no real practical help either to examination candidates or to those non-specialists requiring some guidance on practical accounting problems.

The aim of this book is to serve as a good introduction to the study of accounting. The subject is not covered superficially. In parts, the book goes into considerable detail, but only where it is necessary for a real understanding of the subject. It is appreciated that non-accountants are unlikely to be involved in the *detailed* preparation of accounting information such as, for example, in the compilation of a company's annual accounts. However, if such accounts are to provide the maximum possible benefit to their users, it is desirable that users should have a good knowledge of how they are prepared and how to extract the maximum possible information from them.

This concept is analogous to that of driving a car. It is perfectly possible to drive a car without knowing anything about how it works. However, to get the best possible performance from the car, it is useful to know something about the engine. It is not necessary to know as much about the car as a motor mechanic. All that is required is just sufficient knowledge to be able to drive the car so that it operates at its maximum efficiency. Similarly, it is not absolutely necessary to know how to prepare accounts to be able to use them, but they will mean a great deal more if the user knows something about their construction.

The background to the book

Many colleges and polytechnics now run a number of degree and diploma courses which include accounting as a compulsory subject. Whilst the syllabuses for such courses have usually to be approved by external bodies (such as by the CNAA or by a number of various professional associations and institutes), the detailed contents of such syllabuses are often left to the individual college lecturer to decide. This book has been written with that type of course especially in mind.

The material contained in the book has been designed so that it can be covered in about 90 class contact hours. If more time is available, there will be an opportunity for students to tackle additional exercises in the classroom under the general supervision of their lecturer, but if less class contact time is available, it will probably be necessary for students to work largely unsupervised.

The book is divided into four parts. Part 1 puts the subject of accounting into context. Part 2 deals with financial accounting, and Part 3 with cost and management accounting. It is possible that most students will more readily identify with Part 3 of the book, since cost and management accounting probably relates more directly to their current day-to-day responsibilities. It might seem more logical, therefore, to begin by studying that branch of accounting, but experience suggests that students find it very difficult to understand cost and management accounting if they have not first studied financial accounting. Part 4 of the book outlines the contents of a limited liability company's annual report. Some lecturers may prefer to cover this part of the book before moving on to cost and management accounting. It would then be possible to link directly and immediately the material covered in Chapter 8 on the interpretation of accounts with the information contained in a company's annual report.

However, the section on annual reports has been placed at the end of the book for two main reasons:

1 The contents may not be of immediate interest to most non-accounting students until they become senior officers in their respective companies;
2 This subject requires an almost unlimited amount of class contact hours, so that it is perhaps best left to the end of the course when lecturers will know how much spare time they have available.

How to use the book

Lecturers will have their own way of introducing the various subjects. It is to be hoped, however, that they will still use the various exhibits in the book to demonstrate particular accounting procedures. It is believed that lecturers spend far too much time photocopying questions for use in lectures. The students then spend their time in lectures trying to take down what the lecturer is writing on the blackboard without really listening to what he/she is saying.

If this book is used as it is intended, it is not necessary for lecturers to photocopy additional exhibits and answers. The book contains sufficient exhibits for most one year courses, and every exhibit is followed by a detailed solution. Thus there is no need for students to copy answers that have been written on the blackboard: they should be able to listen to the lecturer as each point is demonstrated step by step.

Most chapters are also followed by a number of tutorial exercises. Since detailed solutions for these questions are contained in Appendix 3, lecturers will also be spared having to provide solutions of their own.

A word to students

If you are using this book as part of a formal course, your lecturer will provide you with a work scheme which will outline just how much of the book you are expected to cover each week. In addition to the work done in your lecture, you will probably have to read each chapter two or three times. As you read a chapter work through each exhibit, and then have a go at doing it without reference to the solution.

You are also recommended to attempt as many of the questions that follow each chapter as you can, but avoid looking at the solutions until you are absolutely certain that you do not know how to do the question. The more questions that you attempt, the more confident you will be that you really do understand the subject matter. However, you must not spend all your time studying accounting, so make sure that you put enough time into your other subjects.

Many students study accounting without having the benefit of attending lectures. If you fall into this category, it is suggested that you adopt the following study plan:

1 Organize your private study so that you have covered every topic in your syllabus by the time of your examination. You will probably need to allow for extra time to be spent on Chapters 3, 4, 8, 13 and 15.
2 Read each chapter slowly, being careful to work through each exhibit. Do not worry if you do not immediately understand each point: read on to the end of the chapter.

3 Read the chapter again, this time making sure that you do understand each point. Try doing each exhibit without looking at the solution.
4 Attempt as many questions at the end of the chapter as you can, but do not look at the solutions until you have finished or you are certain that you cannot do the question.
5 If you have time, re-read the chapter.

One word of caution. Accounting is not simply a matter of elementary arithmetic. The solution to many accounting problems often calls for a considerable amount of personal judgement, and hence there is bound to be some degree of subjectivity attached to the solution.

The problems demonstrated in this book are not readily solved in the real world, and the suggested answers ought to be subject to a great deal of argument and discussion. It follows that non-accountants ought to be severely critical of any accounting information that is supplied to them, although it is difficult to be constructive in your criticism unless you have some knowledge of the subject matter.

By the end of this book, you should have a sufficient knowledge of accounting to be able to examine critically and constructively much of the accounting information that you are likely to meet. In addition, if you have to take an examination in accounting, you should be able to pass it with flying colours!

Preface to the second edition

The first edition of this book has proved very popular, and I am grateful to all those lecturers and students who have contacted me to say just how much they like it. I am especially grateful to those correspondents who also had ideas for improving the book. In preparing the second edition, I have tried to take into account all of the various suggestions that have been made. The main changes are as follows:

1   Each chapter begins with a statement of learning objectives.
2   Some additional questions have been added to most chapters. As requested, the answers to these questions have not been included in the book. Instead, they have been included in a separate *Solutions Manual*, which is available at no cost to *bona fide* lecturers on application to the publishers.
3   The contents have been brought up to date.
4   Numerous improvements have been made to the text, and various errors have been corrected.
5   A further reading list has been added.

Some lecturers would have liked some additional material included in the book. In particular, it was suggested that there should be extra chapters on local authority accounting and on process costing. After careful consideration, it was decided not to include such chapters. There were two main reasons for coming to this decision: 1 This is meant to be a book about accounting *principles*. It is aimed primarily at a non-accounting audience (although there is no reason why it cannot be used by first-year and foundation-level accounting students). Local authority accounting and process costing are rather specialized topics, and it was felt inappropriate to introduce them into a basic text for non-accountants. 2 Additional chapters would have added to the size and cost of the book. Both the author and the publishers are extremely conscious that students operate on a very tight budget, and that it would be unfair to put the book beyond the reach of most students.

For extra tutorial material, lecturers may find the companion volume *Case Studies in Basic Accounting* (Pitman, 1990) a useful supplement. The case studies are aimed at a general accounting audience, and they are quite suitable for non-accounting students.

Acknowledgements

Like most authors, I could not have written this book without the help of a considerable number of other people. Many of them have contributed directly to the ideas that have gone into the writing of the book, whilst in other cases I know that I have absorbed their views without being conscious of doing so.

I am indebted to far too many people for me to name them individually, but it would be remiss of me if I did not at least place on record my thanks to Douglas Sievewright of the Napier Polytechnic of Edinburgh. I am grateful to Douglas for reading an earlier draft of the manuscript, and for making very many valuable suggestions for improving it. Most of his recommendations have been incorporated into the final draft. There will, no doubt, still be very many imperfections in it for which I am, of course, entirely responsible.

I have always found that my students are usually extremely tolerant of any mistakes that I make (often unintentional, sometime deliberate) in my attempts to teach them something about accounting. I can only hope that my readers will be just as tolerant!

In presenting the second edition, I must add my thanks to all those lecturers and students who have found the book useful and who have been kind enough to tell me so!

Part 1
Introduction to accounting

1 The accounting world

Learning objectives_____

1 describe the nature and purpose of accounting;

2 understand why non-accountants should study accounting;

3 detail the main branches of accounting;

4 summarize the basic structure of the accountancy profession; and

5 compare and contrast various types of business entities.

This chapter is an introduction to the world of accounting. It begins with an explanation of the nature and purpose of the subject, and then outlines the relevance of accounting to non-accountants. Modern accounting has now developed into a considerable number of specialisms, and these are briefly described in a subsequent section. An outline of the structure of the accountancy profession then follows. The final section describes the major types of organizations covered in the book.

Nature and purpose of accounting

The word *account* in everyday language is often used as a substitute for an *explanation* or a *report* of certain actions or events. Employees may, for example, have to account for how they have been spending their time, or managers of a business may be asked to report upon its progress. In order to do so it is necessary, of course, for them to remember what they have done or to know what has happened. This may come entirely from personal observation or because someone has supplied them with the necessary information. As it is difficult, even in the smallest of businesses, to remember everything of importance for very long, it is usually necessary to write down those events that may need to be reported. Such records can be said to form the basis of a rudimentary accounting system.

In a primitive sense, man has always been involved in some form of accounting. It may have gone no further than measuring wealth by (say) counting the number of cows a farmer owned, but the advent of the monetary system enabled a more sophisticated system to be developed. It then became possible not only to calculate much more meaningfully the increase or decrease in individual wealth over a period of time, but also to assess whether a farmer with (say) ten cows was wealthier than one with fifty sheep.

It took a very long time for formal recording systems to develop on any scale, although it is possible to trace the origins of modern book-keeping as far back as the twelfth century. It was from about then that traders began to adopt a system of recording information that we now refer to as *double-entry book-keeping.* By the end of the fifteenth century, double-entry was widely used in business, especially by the Venetian merchants of that time. The first known book on the subject was published in 1494 by an Italian mathematician called Pacioli. Modern book-keeping systems are still based on the principles of double-entry book-keeping first established in medieval times and as outlined by Pacioli.

Put at its simplest, such systems supply managers and proprietors with the answers to three basic questions which can be summarized as follows:

1   What profit has the business made?
2   How much does the business owe?
3   How much is owed to it?

In a small business, a basic double-entry book-keeping system still provides sufficient information to be able to answer these three questions. In larger and more complex business enterprises this is not the case.

Following the industrial revolution, many enterprises grew at an enormous rate, as well as becoming much more complex. It also became quite common for ownership to become divorced from managership. In such situations, it became almost impossible for managers (still less owners) to exercise day-to-day control based largely on personal observation and intervention. It became apparent that if businesses were to be controlled effectively, managers needed to be supplied with more detailed information. As a traditional double-entry book-keeping system was not designed for this purpose, it became necessary to convert the traditional form of recording information into a form that met the requirements of management.

In summary, therefore, it can be argued that modern accounting is now primarily concerned with meeting the demand for information from two main sources:

1   from business owners who want to monitor the progress of their investment − this is known as *financial* accounting; and

2 from the internal management of the company who want information so that they can plan and control the activities of the
business − this is known as *management* accounting.

Whilst it is useful to categorize accounting into financial and
management accounting, the subject covers an enormously wide range
of information supply that ranges far beyond that required by just
business managers and proprietors. Other interested parties include
creditors, employees, central and local government, investors, journalists,
financial analysts and the general public.

This book is mainly concerned with the supply of information to
proprietors and business managers. The importance of the subject in that
context is examined in the next section.

Accounting and the non-accountant

Some types of business organizations (such as limited liability companies)
have a statutory obligation to publish a certain amount of information
about their affairs. In order to ensure that the required information is
available for publication, a considerable amount of data has to be
collected, collated and summarized. This process was referred to in the
last section as *financial* accounting.

It is unlikely that non-accountants will be directly involved in the
preparation of financial accounts unless they are at a very senior level.
They may, however, be required to provide some information for eventual
incorporation into them. It is more likely that non-accountants will be
involved in supplying information for management purposes, that is,
as part of the *management* accounting function. The main purpose of
management accounting is to provide management with information for
planning and control purposes. Besides supplying information, the non-
accountant may also *receive* a great deal of management accounting data.
As a result of having more information on which to base plans and
monitor their progress, non-accountants should be able to do their job
far more effectively.

Employees at all levels are increasingly asked to supply a great deal
of information to senior employees. These requests are often directed
through the accounting function, but it is not always apparent why such
information is required. It may be because it forms part of the annual
reporting system, or it may be because it is part of the information-for-
management system. Such requests can be highly irksome to those
employees who are asked for the information, especially if they do not
understand why it is wanted.

Companies must publish their annual financial accounts, but there is
no legislation requiring them to publish management accounts.
Consequently, it is sometimes very difficult to see why it is necessary

to collect a vast amount of data simply for internal consumption. Thus if the job is to be done properly, it is very important that employees are made aware of the purpose and the need for such information. Unfortunately, many management accounting information systems are largely ineffective because they are not properly explained to those employees who are involved in them.

More information does not necessarily mean, of course, that managers take better decisions, since there is no comparative test that can be applied to decisions that might have been taken in the absence of additional information. The test has to be a fairly subjective one. If managers *feel* that they have made a better decision as a result of having more information, then it has probably been worthwhile supplying it to them. This point helps to explain why accounting is such an important subject for non-accountants to study. Until they know something about accounting, it is difficult for them to judge whether accounting information can help them, and if it can, what form it should take.

In brief, therefore, it is suggested that non-accountants need to know something about accounting for two main reasons:

1   in order to ensure that their organizations comply with statutory disclosure requirements; and
2   to ensure that information supplied to them can help them do a far better job.

The purpose of this book is to explain how accounting can be of assistance to the non-accountant. By the end of it, conscientious students should have a sound grasp of basic accounting techniques. The knowledge acquired should be sufficient for them to judge the importance and relevance of much accounting information that they come across.

As modern accounting systems embrace a considerable number of specialisms, it may be helpful to outline some of the major branches of accounting that non-accountants may meet during their careers. These are briefly reviewed in the next section.

Branches of accounting

The work which accountants now undertake ranges far beyond that of simply collating data in order to assess business profitability and liquidity. Although this work is still very important, accountants have gradually extended the scope of their responsibilities. Other disciplines (such as operational research and work study) have similarly evolved in order to satisfy an ever-increasing demand for information.

At one time, some observers expected accounting to be superseded by the newer and more scientifically based disciplines. As yet this has not happened, although many accountants now work in those areas, whilst others have absorbed the methods into the solution of accounting problems.

Accountants have always been well placed in this respect, since specialist techniques have to be translated into a language that everyone can understand if any benefit is to be obtained from them. The accountant uses money as his language, and since the language of money is generally understood by everyone, accountants have always been at an advantage.

A brief explanation of the main branches of accounting is given in the following sub-sections.

Accountancy and accounting

The accountancy profession is engaged in the collection, collation and distribution of information as an aid towards the control of resources and as a contribution towards decision-making. Many writers use accountancy and accounting as synonymous terms, but in this book *accountancy* will be used to refer to the profession and *accounting* to the subject.

Auditing

Auditing forms a most important branch of the accountancy profession. Once accounts have been prepared they may be checked in order to ensure that they do not present a distorted picture. Such a process is known as *auditing*. Not all businesses have their accounts audited, but for some organizations, such as limited liability companies, it is compulsory.

Auditors are usually accountants acting under another title. If they are appointed from outside the organization they are sometimes referred to as the *external* auditors. In the case of a limited liability company, they are appointed by the shareholders and not by the company's management. Their job is to protect the interests of the shareholders, and as such, they are answerable to the shareholders. This contrasts with *internal* auditors who are employees of the company, and therefore answerable to the management of the company.

Internal auditors perform routine tasks and undertake detailed checking of the company's accounting and management procedures. In practice, external and internal auditors usually work very closely together, but the distinction made between their respective employers is an important one.

Whilst internal auditors expect to be given a great deal of freedom in performing their duties and to be free from direct interference, they are still employees of the company. Ultimately, therefore, they have to report to the company's senior management. By contrast, external auditors *should* be completely independent, but as the directors of the company normally make a recommendation to the shareholders about the appointment of the auditors, even external auditors may be subject to some indirect pressure. It may be suggested to them, for example, that the directors are considering another firm of auditors. It is not always easy for external auditors to appeal directly to the shareholders, although this is sometimes done when the auditors feel that their freedom is being jeopardized.

Bankruptcy, liquidation and receivership

The work involved in dealing with bankruptcy, liquidation and receivership is all very similar. Individuals and businesses are said to be insolvent if they cannot pay their debts when they are asked to do so. If individuals cannot pay their debts, a legal procedure known as *bankruptcy* may be instituted. Their assets may be sold to pay off as many of the debts as possible, and they are then given the chance to begin a new life not burdened by their former debts. They may be subject, however, to some very severe legal restrictions before they are allowed to take on new debts.

In a similar way, a company unable to pay its debts may have to be liquidated; in other words, it will be wound-up and it will go out of existence. Those parties who are owed money either by a bankrupt individual or by a liquidated company may lose all or most of what is owed to them.

The treatment of the affairs of a bankrupt individual or that of a company going into liquidation is very complex. The aim is to ensure that the assets are realized in such a way that everyone who is involved is treated in the fairest possible manner.

Those companies that are in financial difficulties sometimes anticipate that they may have to go into liquidation by calling in a *receiver*. Sometimes a receiver may be appointed by the creditors or by some other group who is owed money by the company. The receiver's task is to ascertain whether it is possible to reorganize the company in such a way that it can continue to operate. If it can continue to operate, then the receiver will try to ensure that at least some (if not all) of the client's debts are settled. It follows that a company is not always put into liquidation when a receiver is called in.

Bankruptcy, liquidation and receivership work is a highly specialist accounting and legal function. It also involves a great deal of business and managerial expertise. Few accountants have much experience of this type of work, and it is usually left to a small number of specialist firms of practising accountants.

Book-keeping

Book-keeping is a mechanical task involving the collection of basic information and the entry of it in special records known as *books of account*. At the end of an agreed period of time, the data are extracted and summarized. This is usually in the form of a periodic statement, known as a *profit and loss account*, and a statement of assets and liabilities, known as a *balance sheet*.

The book-keeping function ends when the periodic statements have been prepared. At that stage, the specific *accounting* function takes over. Although accounting is a generic term, covering almost anything to do with the collection and supply of information, it should be more properly applied to the use and conversion of that information once it has been extracted from the books of account. Book-keeping is a routine operation, whilst accounting requires the ability to assess a problem from certain facts obtained from, *inter alia*, the books of account.

Cost book-keeping, costing and cost accounting

These branches of accounting deal with the collection, collation and supply of *detailed* information, mainly for management purposes. The object is to have sufficient information available in order to help management control the resources of the entity and to provide information for decision-making.

The difference between costing (or cost accounting) and accounting is only one of degree: a costing system requires a great deal more information to be collected. The difference between cost book-keeping and cost accounting is very similar to that between book-keeping and accounting. The collection and storage of information is known as cost book-keeping, whilst the use of it for planning and decision-making is known as cost accounting. A cost book-keeping system contains much more information than a financial book-keeping system and hence the accounts have to be re-adapted to deal with the additional information.

Executorship and trusts

Executorship work involves dealing with the affairs of deceased persons. The deceased may, for example, have left a will which requires the estate to be disposed of in a certain way. A solicitor would normally deal with the legal disposition of the assets and settling of any debts, but an accountant may be responsible for looking after any investments and the calculation and distribution of any income on them in accordance with the will. It is possible that the estate will not be wound-up for many years, and an accountant may act in this capacity for some time.

An accountant may also be involved in administering the affairs of a minor. The minor may be a beneficiary of an estate, but minors may not be able to control what has been bequeathed until of a certain age. Until that time, a trustee will look after the minor's affairs in strict accordance with both trustee law and the conditions laid down by the person setting up the trust.

Executorship and trustee work is another highly specialist accounting function, and few accountants will have had any experience of it.

Financial accounting

Financial accounting is the more specific term applied to the publication of periodic financial data. Such information is usually prepared for the owner of the business, but it may also be used by management for control and decision-making purposes. Other interested parties may include creditors, employees, central and local government, financial analysts, investors, journalists, and the general public.

Management accounting

Management accounting is another all-embracing term. It was suggested earlier that cost book-keeping deals with the routine collection and summary of information for internal management purposes, whilst cost accounting is more orientated towards supplying information for control and decision-making. Management accounting covers any type of information provided for management. It often necessitates using cost accounting data and adapting it for highly specific decisions which management may be called upon to make. A management accounting system can, therefore, incorporate *all* types of information. Such information may be obtained from a wide range of sources which stretch far beyond those used in a conventional accounting system.

Taxation

Taxation is a highly complex and technical branch of accounting. Accountants involved in tax work are responsible for computing the amount of tax payable both by business entities and by individuals. Neither companies nor individuals need pay more tax than is lawfully demanded, and so tax experts spend much of their time trying to reduce their clients' tax bills. If this is done strictly in accordance with the law, it is known as tax *avoidance*. Tax avoidance is a perfectly legitimate exercise. Tax lawfully due but not paid is known as tax *evasion*, and it is a very serious offence. The borderline between tax avoidance and tax evasion is a fairly narrow one.

The major accounting specialisms outlined above illustrate the many diverse jobs in which an accountant may be involved. Some are highly specialist functions and most accountants will have had little experience of them. Accountants in practice, for example, are usually specialists in auditing, financial accounting and taxation. Although many accountants in industry also work in these areas, their major specialism tends to be in management accounting. This book is mainly concerned with financial and management accounting.

As it is likely that the non-accountant will be in contact with members of the different accountancy bodies, it may be helpful to describe briefly the organizational structure of the accountancy profession. This is outlined in the next section.

The accountancy profession

Anyone can practise in the United Kingdom as an accountant. Irrespective of training and experience, there is almost complete freedom to perform accounting work. Some work is, however, legally restricted, especially that relating to the audit of limited liability companies.

Accountants are sometimes described as being *qualified*. A qualified accountant is generally regarded as someone who has been admitted to membership of one of the major accountancy bodies, but many non-qualified accountants would strongly dispute that they also were not 'qualified', and hence unable to act in a professional capacity.

The accountancy profession within the United Kingdom is very diverse. There are, in fact, *six* major professional accountancy bodies. They are as follows:

1 the Institute of Chartered Accountants in England and Wales;
2 the Institute of Chartered Accountants in Ireland;
3 the Institute of Chartered Accountants of Scotland;
4 the Chartered Association of Certified Accountants;
5 the Chartered Institute of Management Accountants; and
6 the Chartered Institute of Public Finance and Accountancy.

Chartered accountants (that is, categories 1, 2 and 3) have to undergo most of their training in practice (like solicitors), much of their time being spent on auditing and taxation work. After qualifying, many chartered accountants move out of a practitioner's office and go to work in industry, commerce or government. Certified accountants may also obtain their training in practice, but relevant experience elsewhere counts towards their training. Management accountants usually train and work mainly in industry, while public sector accountants specialize almost exclusively in central and local government work, the nationalized industries and other quasi-government entities (such as health authorities and water undertakings).

Apart from the six major bodies, there are a number of important, although less well known, smaller accountancy associations and institutes. There is also another organization known as the *Association of Accounting Technicians*. The Association was formed in 1980 especially for those who *assist* qualified accountants in the preparation of accounting information. In order to become an accounting technician, it is necessary to take (or be exempt from) the Association's examinations. The examinations are, however, less technically demanding than those of the major accountancy bodies.

It is clear from this brief outline of the accountancy profession that there are a bewildering number of individuals who may call themselves accountants. Many such accountants are employed in commerce, industry and government, and non-accountants are likely to meet a considerable number of them. The accountants that they do meet may perhaps all be members of different accountancy bodies, but they will all have one thing in common: their job is to help the *non*-accountant perform more effectively. Accountants are employed to provide a service. They have much to offer to non-accountants, and it is up to them to make the best use of their services.

This book will help to explain what assistance an accountant can provide. Before moving on, however, it would be helpful to examine the main *types* of organizations which will be encountered in the book. These are reviewed in the next section.

Types of organizations

In a book of this nature it is not possible to consider *all* the types of organizations in which non-accountants might be working, but the main ones used as examples in this book are examined in the following sub-sections.

Sole traders

Like much else in accounting, the term 'sole trader' is misleading. The term refers to an organization owned and controlled by one individual, although the owner may employ many other people to help operate it.

Similarly, the term is not restricted to *trading* organizations. It can be used to refer to any type of organization regardless of whether it is a manufacturing, a trading, a service or a not-for-profit-making entity (such as a charity). The main requirement is that it should be owned by one individual.

Sole trader organizations usually operate on an informal basis, and the private affairs of the proprietor may be difficult to distinguish from those of the entity.

Chapters 3, 4 and 5 of this book are primarily concerned with sole trader organizations. As this is the simplest form of organization, the procedures involved in recording and extracting accounting information are much easier to follow than is the case with other types of entities.

Partnerships

A partnership exists where two or more individuals share the ownership and control of an entity. It is often the case, for example, that an individual may form a business. After some time, it is realized that the business is short of funds or of managerial expertise. The individual may then be willing to let someone else come into the business as a partner. Each partner becomes a joint owner of the business (although they may not necessarily be *equal* partners). It is also not unusual to find that new businesses are formed immediately as partnerships, partly to help finance the business and partly to share the burden of running it.

The precise arrangements between the partners (such as over the sharing of profits) should be agreed between them. In the absence of any formal agreement, the provisions of the Partnership Act 1890 are deemed to apply. Otherwise, partnerships are not covered by any specific legislation.

The accounting procedures involved in dealing with partnerships are similar to those that apply to sole trader organizations, and they will not be covered in very much detail in this book.

Companies

A limited liability company is a much more formal type of organization than that of either a sole trader or a partnership. By law, a company is regarded as a *being* quite separate from its owners. As such, therefore, the operation of a company is bound by some extremely severe legal restrictions on how it may be operated. These restrictions are now largely contained within the Companies Act 1985 (as amended by the Companies Act 1989).

Company accounts will be examined in Chapter 6. The chapters that then follow will be mainly concerned with this type of organization.

Other organizations

Besides sole traders, partnerships and companies, there are, of course, many other types of organizations, such as charities, local authorities and voluntary organizations. There are also specialist types of organizations which the layman might regard as being a form of company, for example, banks, building societies, and unit trusts. This book will not be dealing with these types of organizations, since its main purpose is to deal with *basic* accounting practices. These basic practices apply to almost any type of organization, although some specific changes may be necessary depending upon the precise nature and size of the organization's operations.

Conclusion

The aim of this chapter has been to introduce the non-accountant to the world of accounting. The chapter has emphasized that the main objective of accounting is to supply information to those parties that have a need for it.

Information must be of benefit to those for whom it is intended. Non-accountants are often reluctant to question the value of some accounting information because they are not quite sure either what it means or what purpose it serves. By the end of this book, the non-accountant should have sufficient knowledge to be able to judge the value of almost any accounting information that is encountered.

Now that the world of accounting has been outlined, it is time to turn to the detailed subject matter, and the first task is to learn the basic rules of accounting. These rules are explained in the next chapter.

Questions

1.1 State briefly the main reasons why a company may employ a team of accountants.

1.2 Why does a limited liability company have to engage a firm of external auditors, and for what purpose?

1.3 Why should a non-accountant study accounting?

1.4 Are there any statutory obligations requiring the preparation of management accounts?

1.5 Are there any statutory obligations supporting the publication of financial accounts?

1.6 Describe briefly the nature and purpose of accounts.

Additional questions (without answers)

1.7 Assume that you were a personnel officer in a manufacturing company, and that one of your employees was a young engineering manager called Joseph Sykes. Joseph has been chosen to attend the local Polytechnic's Business School to study for a diploma in management.

Joseph is reluctant to attend the course because it will include a subject called 'financial management'. As an engineer, he thinks that it will be a waste of time for him to study such a subject.

Required:
Draft an internal memorandum addressed to Joseph Sykes explaining why it would be of benefit to him to study financial management.

1.8 Clare Wong spends a lot of her time working for a large local charity. The charity has grown enormously in recent years, and the trustees have been advised to overhaul their accounting procedures. This would involve its voluntary workers in more book-keeping, and there is a great deal of resistance to this move. The staff have said that they are there to help the needy, and not to get involved in book-keeping.

Required:
As the financial consultant to the charity, prepare some notes that you could use in speaking to the voluntary workers in order to try and persuade them to accept the new proposals.

2 Accounting Rules

Learning objectives_____

1   understand why it is necessary to formulate a number of basic
    accounting rules;

2   identify and classify the main accounting rules into broad
    groupings;

    and

3   outline the nature and purpose of each major accounting rule.

It was suggested in Chapter 1 that accountancy is a profession engaged in the supply of information to a wide range of interested parties. In fact, the amount of information that is available is so enormous that it is necessary to place some limit on what is to be supplied.

Modern accounting systems have evolved over a long period of time. They have not been developed out of any sort of theoretical model, but out of practical necessity. As a result, a number of basic procedures have been developed. These procedures may perhaps best be described as the *basic rules of accounting*. Some authors refer to them under a variety of other names, the most common being: assumptions, axioms, concepts, conventions, postulates, principles and procedures.

In preparing and presenting information, accountants have considerable freedom over which rules to adopt and how to interpret them. Since 1971, the accountancy profession has tried to restrict the room for manoeuvre by issuing a series of accounting guides. These guides are known as Statements of Standard Accounting Practice (SSAPs), and qualified accountants are supposed to use them when preparing accounting statements. It is impossible, however, to lay down totally rigid rules, because information is only useful if it has been prepared to suit individual circumstances, and individual circumstances may vary enormously. Consequently, accountants are still able to use a great deal of discretion in the preparation and presentation of accounting information.

It is possible, of course, to ignore all of the generally recognized accounting rules and to prepare accounts in an entirely novel way. This would be like trying to play football under different rules than the ones laid down by the Football Association. If the accepted rules were abandoned, any match played under entirely new rules would result in a game that would be incomprehensible to most of the spectators.

The same situation would apply in accounting if the conventional rules were abandoned. These rules govern the amount and type of information to be collected and the length of the accounting period. They are practical rules, like those in football covering the size of the pitch and the length of the match. Other accounting rules are more of an ethical nature. The rules should be applied consistently, for example, and information should not be presented in a deliberately distorted fashion. These rules may again be compared with those in football that prohibit the ball being handled and an opponent being kicked.

The basic accounting rules will be outlined in subsequent sections. For convenience, they have been classified as follows:

1 boundary rules;
2 measurement rules; and
3 ethical rules.

This classification is largely arbitrary. It has been chosen in order to help examine some of the more important accounting rules more clearly. There are something like 150 recognized accounting rules, but there are only some 14 rules that are of particular relevance to non-accountants.

Boundary rules

In small businesses proprietors can probably obtain all the information that they need from personal observation. In larger organizations this is much more difficult, so it is necessary for some formal reporting procedure to be implemented. In order to restrict the amount of information that it would be possible to collect, a number of accounting rules have been devised. These rules may be classified as *boundary* rules.

There are four main boundary rules, and they will be examined in the following sub-sections.

Entity

There is so much information available that accountants start by drawing a boundary around what is known as an *entity*. An entity could be a profit-making business, such as a shop buying and selling goods, or a firm of solicitors offering a service. Such businesses are usually referred to as *profit-making* entities. A profit-making entity may be organized in the form of a sole trader, a partnership or a limited liability company.

However, an entity might well be a *not-for-profit* entity, such as a charity or a local authority. The primary purpose of such organizations is to provide a service to the public, the profit motive being either irrelevant or of secondary consideration.

The accountant tries to restrict the amount of information to that of the entity itself. This is sometimes very difficult, especially in small businesses as there is often no clear distinction between the affairs of the business and the private affairs of the proprietor. It is quite common for proprietors to finance their household expenditure through the business, and they might also pay for some business transactions out of their private bank account. In such a situation, their accountant has to decide what are the business transactions and what are the private transactions of the proprietor. He has then to establish exactly what the business owes the proprietor and what the proprietor owes the business. Accountants will, however, only be interested in recording the effect on the *business* and not on the proprietor's private affairs.

It would be an entirely different exercise if the accountant did deal with the private affairs of the proprietor. In effect, he would be accounting for a different entity. That entity would be considered to be quite distinct from that of the business, although there would obviously be a very close link between them.

Periodicity

Most entities have an unlimited life. They are usually started in the expectation that they will operate for an indefinite life, but it is clearly impractical for interested parties to wait until the entity eventually ceases before a report is received on its progress. Such parties almost certainly wish to receive regular reports at frequent intervals.

If an entity has an unlimited life, any report must be prepared at the end of what is inevitably an arbitrary period of time. In practice, accounting statements are usually prepared for a period of twelve months. Such a time period has arisen largely as a matter of custom, although in the westernized agrarian world it does reflect the four seasons. There is also a natural tendency to compare recent events with those of a year ago. Where entities have an unlimited life, the preparation of annual accounts presents considerable problems in relating specific transactions to appropriate accounting periods.

Apart from custom, there is no reason why an accounting period could not be shorter or longer than twelve months. Indeed, management accounts are often prepared more frequently than once every twelve months, while in the construction industry, for example, a very long accounting period may be adopted because of the time that it takes to complete a contract. Nonetheless, current legislation requires limited liability companies to prepare annual accounts, and as tax computations are also calculated on a twelve months basis, it would not be possible for an entity to ignore altogether the conventional twelve months period. In any case, it must be appreciated that given the unlimited life of most entities, *any* period must be somewhat arbitrary irrespective of how carefully a particular entity tried to relate its accounting period to the nature of its business.

Going concern

The periodicity rule requires a regular period of account to be established regardless of the life of the entity and of the arbitrary nature of the accounting period. The going concern rule arises out of the periodicity rule. Unless there is information to the contrary, if an arbitrary accounting period is adopted, it is assumed that the entity will continue in existence for the foreseeable future. It is important to make absolutely certain that the entity's existence is assured for the immediate future since different measurement rules are used in preparing accounts for entities that have a limited life.

Quantitative

Accounting information is usually restricted to information that is easily quantifiable. If a company uses a fleet of vans in the operation of its business, for example, it is normally very easy to count them and to check their ownership. Similarly, it is usually very easy to count the number of employees employed by a company. They may also be very *skilled* employees, but skill is a concept which is hard to quantify. Such a concept is normally ignored, therefore, in preparing a traditional set of accounts.

Measurement rules

The boundary rules state *what* should be included in an accounting system, whereas the measurement rules explain *how* that information should be recorded. There are six main measurement rules, and they are outlined in the following sub-sections.

Money measurement

It would be very cumbersome to record information simply in terms of quantifiable amounts. It would also be impossible to make any fair or meaningful comparisons between different types of assets or different types of transactions. In order to do so, it is necessary to convert the information that has been quantified into a common and recognizable measure. It was argued in the first chapter that the monetary unit has been used for this purpose for many centuries. The monetary unit enables meaningful comparisons to be made between different events and different types of transaction.

Money is an ideal means of converting accounting data into a common unit, and since most quantifiable information is capable of being translated into monetary terms, there is usually no difficulty in adopting the monetary measurement rule.

Historic cost

The historic cost rule is an extension of the money measurement rule. It requires transactions to be recorded at their *original* cost, so subsequent changes in prices or values are usually ignored. Increased costs may arise because of a combination of an improved product and changes in the purchasing power of the monetary unit, that is, as a result of inflation.

Over the last 20 years there have been numerous attempts in the United Kingdom to change the method of accounting in order to allow for the effect of inflation in preparing financial statements. There has been so much disagreement on what should replace historic cost accounting (HCA) that no new method has been acceptable. In this book the historic cost rule will be adopted, alhough in Chapter 20 the problems involved in preparing inflation adjusted accounts will be briefly examined.

Realization

One of the problems of putting the periodicity rule into practice is that it is often difficult to relate a particular transaction to a specific period. A business may order some goods in period 1, for example, receive them in period 2 and pay for them in period 3. It is not easy to decide in which period the goods were actually *purchased*. In conventional accounting, it would be most unusual to include them in the accounts for period 1, because the business at that stage has not got a legal title to them. They could be included in period 3's accounts when the cash has been received. This method is not uncommon; it is known as *cash flow accounting*, transactions only being entered in the books of account when a cash exchange has taken place.

It is customary to enter most transactions in the books of account when the legal title of the goods has been transferred from one party to another and when there is an obligation to pay for them, that is, when they have been *realized*.

The realization rule applies not only to sales of goods to customers, but also to the receipt of other incomes.

It can produce some rather misleading results. A company can, for example, treat some goods as being realized in one period, only to find in a subsequent period that the customer cannot pay for them. This means that if the sales have been included in the earlier period, the profit for that period has been overstated (by the amount of profit on the sales). When the bad debt becomes certain, the profit for that period will be reduced, because the bad debt will have to be charged against that year's profit. As it happens, there is an accounting technique that enables the effect of these distortions to be smoothed. The procedure is examined in Chapter 4.

Matching

The realization rule applies largely to the purchase and sale of goods and services, but a similar procedure can be adopted for other incomes and expenses. This procedure is covered by what is known as the *matching* rule.

An unfair comparison could be made if cash received during a period was simply matched against the cash paid out during the same period. The exact period in which the cash was either received or paid may bear no relationship to the period in which the transactions took place, so accountants normally adjust cash received and cash paid on to what is known as an *accruals* and a *prepayments* basis. An accrual is an amount owed at the end of a period for services supplied during that period. A prepayment is an amount paid or received in advance for services expected to be supplied during a future period.

The conversion of cash received and cash paid on to an accruals and a prepayments basis at a period end often involves a considerable amount of arithmetical adjustment. An allowance has to be made for accruals and prepayments calculated at the end of the previous period (that is, for *opening* accruals and prepayments), as well as for accruals and prepayments at the end of the current period (that is, for *closing* accruals and prepayments. The subject of accruals and prepayments will be dealt with in Chapter 4.

An accruals and prepayments system of accounting enables a much fairer comparison to be made between one accounting period and another. It enables the incomes of one period to be matched against the costs of the same period. The comparison is not distorted by the accidental timing of cash receipts and payments. However, the matching rule does require the accountant to estimate the accruals and prepayments at the end of a period, and a degree of subjectivity is, therefore, built into the system.

Dual aspect

The dual aspect rule is a useful practical rule, although it really only states what is a truism. Every type of transaction that the entity is engaged in has a two-fold effect. If the amount of cash in the business is increased, for example, then someone must have provided the money for it to be increased. Similarly, if the business pays out some money, then it must be giving it to someone. In other words, every time something is given, someone else must be receiving it.

It was explained in Chapter 1 that this two-fold effect was recognized many centuries ago. It gave rise to the system of recording information known as double-entry book-keeping. This system of book-keeping is still widely used, and even computerized recording systems are based on it. Double-entry book-keeping is a most convenient system to adopt, because it provides accessible information about an entity's profitability and liquidity. It also provides a double-check on the accuracy of the transactions that have been entered into the system, thereby enabling errors to be traced more speedily.

There is no real necessity to adopt the dual aspect rule in recording information, but experience has shown that is a convenient way of storing much basic data. The incorporation of the dual aspect rule into an accounting system is considered in detail in the next chapter.

Materiality

Strict application of the various accounting rules may not always be practical. It could involve a considerable amount of work that may be out of all proportion to the information that is eventually obtained. The materiality rule permits other rules to be ignored if the effects are not considered to be significant. Hence the materiality rule avoids the necessity to follow other accounting rules to the point of absurdity. Normally it would be considered unnecessary, for example, to value the closing stock of small amounts of stationery, or to maintain detailed records of inexpensive items of office equipment. Immaterial items may, therefore, be treated in the accounting system quite different from material items, even if they are of a similar nature.

Ethical rules

There is an old story in accounting about the company chairman who asks his chief accountant how much profit the company had made. The chief accountant replied by asking how much profit the chairman would like to make. Accountants recognize that there is some truth in this story. In calculating profit, it is quite possible that if a number of accountants used the same basic data, they would produce entirely different levels of profit.

It might be thought that by obeying all the same accounting rules, it would be impossible to arrive at different levels of profit. Unfortunately, this is not the case, since all of the main accounting rules are capable of wide interpretation. As has been seen in an earlier section, the matching rule, for example, involves making an estimate of accruals and prepayments, whilst the materiality rule allows the accountant to decide what is material. Both rules involve an element of subjective judgement, and no two accountants are likely to agree precisely on how these rules should be applied in specific instances.

In order to limit the room for individual manoeuvre, a number of other rules have been evolved. These rules are somewhat ethical in nature, and indeed some authors refer to them as accounting *principles* (while other authors may refer to *all* of the basic accounting rules as principles). The ethical rules requires accountants to follow not just the letter, but the spirit of the basic rules.

Prudence

The prudence rule (which is sometimes known as *conservatism*) arises out of the need to make a number of estimates in preparing periodic accounts. Business managers and proprietors are often naturally over-optimistic about future events. As a result, there is a tendency to be too confident about the future, and not to be altogether realistic about the entity's prospects. There may be, for example, some undue optimism over the creditworthiness of a particular customer.

Such optimism may result in a gross over-estimation of profit, because insufficient allowance is made for the level of doubtful debts. The prudence rule is sometimes expressed in the form of a simple maxim:

If in doubt, overstate losses and understate profits.

Consistency

As has been seen, the preparation of traditional accounting statements necessitates a considerable amount of discretion in the application of the basic accounting rules. The consistency rule requires that once the various accounting rules have been adopted, they should be followed in all subsequent accounting periods.

It would be considered quite unethical to change those rules just because they were unfashionable, or because alternative ones gave better results. Once adopted, the rules ought to be *consistent*, unless circumstances change which make it necessary to adopt new ones. If the rules are consistently followed, the users of the accounts can be confident that fair and undistorted comparisons can be made between different accounting statements.

If new rules are adopted, then the effect of any changes must be clearly highlighted, and any comparative figures adjusted accordingly.

Objectivity

Accounts should be prepared with the minimum amount of bias. This is not an easy task, since individual judgement is required in interpreting the rules and adapting them to suit particular circumstances. Proprietors may want, for example, to adopt a policy that would result in higher profit figures or to disguise poor results.

If optional policy decisions are possible within the existing rules, it is advisable to fall back on the prudence rule. Indeed, the prudence rule tends to be an overriding one. If in doubt about which rule to adopt (or how it should be interpreted), the prudence rule should always take precedence.

It should be recognized, however, that if the prudence rule is always adopted as the easy way out of a difficult problem, accountants could be accused of a lack of objectivity. In other words, they must not use this rule to avoid making a difficult decision. Indeed, it is just as unfair to be excessively cautious as it is to be widely optimistic. Extremism of any kind suggests a lack of objectivity, and both over-caution and over-optimism should be avoided.

Relevance

The amount of information that could be supplied to any interested party is practically unlimited. If too much information is disclosed, it becomes very difficult to absorb, so it should only be presented if it is relevant.

The selection of relevant information requires much experience and judgement, as well as calling for a great understanding of the user's requirements. It needs to be designed in such a way that it meets the *objectives* of specific user groups. If too much information is given it may be thought to be an attempt to mislead the users. As a result, the information may be rejected altogether.

In this context, accountants try to present accounts in such a way that they represent 'a true and fair view'. In fact, the Companies Act 1985 (as amended by the Companies Act 1989) requires company accounts to reflect this precise criterion. The Act does not define what is meant by 'true and fair', but it is assumed that accounts will represent a true and fair view if a company has followed the rules laid down in statements of standard accounting practice (SSAPs).

Accounting standards are formulated by an Accounting Standards Board (ASB), and professionally qualified accountants are expected to follow its recommendations contained within SSAPs. By 1990, 25 standards had been issued (although three had been withdrawn). Such statements are considered to represent the most authoritative view of how certain matters should be dealt with in 'financial statements whose purpose is to give a true and fair view of the financial position and of the profit or loss for the period' (as the SSAP's explanatory foreword puts it). This is perhaps rather a strange way of requiring compliance with the standards, because it suggests that some accounts are not meant to give a true and fair view!

The standards cover such diverse subjects as the accounting policies adopted by an entity, and the treatment of depreciation, taxation and stock valuations. Although professionally qualified accountants are required to follow the recommendations contained within the standards, they still leave room for considerable individual interpretation. Indeed, some accountants ignore them, but as yet no disciplinary action has been taken against anyone for doing so.

Summary

It may be convenient at this stage to summarize the basic accounting rules outlined in the previous section, since a summary will be useful to refer back to when studying later chapters. In brief, therefore, the basic accounting rules may be summarized as follows:

Boundary rules

1 *Entity*. Accounting information must be restricted to the entity itself. It should not be extended to the private affairs of those individuals connected with it.
2 *Periodicity*. Accounts should be prepared at the end of a defined period of time. This period should be adopted as the regular period of account.
3 *Going concern*. The accounts should be prepared on the assumption that the entity will continue in existence for the foreseeable future.
4 *Quantitative*. Only information that is capable of being easily quantified should be included in an accounting system.

Measurement rules

1 *Money measurement*. Quantifiable information must be translated into monetary terms before being included in an accounting system.

2 *Historic cost*. Transactions should be recorded in the books of account at their historic cost, that is, at their original purchase cost.

3 *Realization*. Transactions should be entered in the books of account when the legal title to them has been transferred from one party to another party, irrespective of when the cash settlement takes place.

4 *Matching*. Cash received and cash paid during a particular accounting period should be adjusted in order to match the cost of sales against the sales revenue for the same period.

5 *Dual aspect*. All transactions should be recorded in a double-entry format so that the giving and the receiving effect of each transaction is reflected within the accounting system.

6 *Materiality*. The basic accounting rules must not be rigidly applied if the treatment of some transactions would be out of all proportion to the results obtained by adopting an inflexible interpretation of the rules.

Ethical rules

1 *Prudence*. If there is some doubt over the treatment of a particular transaction, income should be underestimated and expenditure overestimated, so that losses are more likely to be overstated and profits understated.

2 *Consistency*. Accounting rules should not be amended unless there is a fundamental change in circumstances that necessitates a reconsideration of the original rules.

3 *Objectivity*. Personal prejudice must be avoided in the interpretation of the basic accounting rules.

4 *Relevance*. Accounting statements should not include information that prevents the user from obtaining a true and fair view of the information being communicated to him.

Conclusion

Fourteen basic accounting rules have been identified in this chapter. These rules are commonly adopted in the preparation of accounting statements. Four of the rules have been described as boundary rules, six as measurement rules and four as ethical rules. It has been argued that the boundary rules limit the amount and type of information that is traditionally collected and stored in an accounting system. The measurement rules provide some guidance on how that information should be recorded, and the ethical rules lay down a code of conduct on how all the other rules should be interpreted.

The exact number, classification and description of accounting rules is subject to much debate amongst accountants. Most entities can, in fact, adopt what rules they like, although limited liability companies are expected to adopt the going concern, matching, prudence, and consistency rules. In fact, most companies will also adopt the other ten accounting rules. It should also be noted that the Companies Act 1985 requires companies to adopt another rule. This rule has not been covered in this chapter. It is known as the non-aggregation rule. This means that assets and liabilities should be shown separately, and not netted off.

The next chapter deals with the practical application of the dual aspect rule. This rule is at the heart of double-entry book-keeping and most modern accounting systems are based upon it.

Questions

In questions 2.1, 2.2 and 2.3 you are required to state which accounting rule the accountant would most probably adopt in dealing with the problem.

2.1 (1) Electricity consumed in period 1 and paid for in period 2. *Matching*

     (2) Equipment originally purchased for £20,000 which would now cost £30,000. *Hist convention*

     (3) The company's good industrial relations record. *Quantitative*

     (4) A five year construction contract. *Period*

     (5) A customer who might go bankrupt owing the company £5,000. *Prudence*

     (6) The company's vehicles which would only have a small scrap value if it goes into liquidation.

2.2 (1) A demand by the company's chairman to include every detailed transaction in the presentation of the annual accounts.

     (2) A sole-trader business which has paid the proprietor's income tax based partly on the business profits for the year.

     (3) A proposed change in the method of valuing stock.

     (4) The valuation of a gallon of petrol in one vehicle at the end of accounting period 1.

     (5) A vehicle which could be sold for more than its purchase price.

     (6) Goods which were sold to a customer in period 1, but for which the cash was only received in period 2.

2.3 (1) The proprietor who has supplied the business capital out of his own private bank account.

     (2) The sales manager who is always very optimistic about the credit-worthiness of prospective customers.

     (3) The managing director who does not want annual accounts prepared as the company operates a continuous 24 hours a day, 365 days a year process.

     (4) At the end of period 1, it is difficult to be certain whether the company will have to pay legal fees of £1,000 or £3,000.

     (5) The proprietor who argues that the accountant has got a motor vehicle entered twice in the books of account.

(6) Some goods were purchased and entered into stock at the end of period 1, but they were not paid for until period 2.

2.4 The following is a list of problems which an accountant may well meet in practice:
(1) The transfer fee of a footballer.
(2) Goods sold in one period, but the cash for them is received in a later period.
(3) The proprietor's personal dwelling house has been used as security for a loan which the bank has granted to the company.
(4) What profit to take in the third year of a five year construction contract.
(5) Small stocks of stationery held at the accounting year end.
(6) Expenditure incurred in working on the improvement of a new drug.

Required:
State:
(a) which accounting rule the accountant would most probably adopt in dealing with each of the above problems; and
(b) the reasons for your choice.

Additional questions (without answers)

2.5 The Companies Act 1985 lists five prescribed accounting principles, while SSAP 2 (Disclosure of accounting policies) refers to four fundamental accounting concepts.

Required:
Write a report for your managing director comparing and contrasting the five accounting principles laid down in the Companies Act 1985 with the four fundamental accounting concepts outlined in SSAP 2. (Note: before preparing your report, you are advised to consult both the Act and the standard.)

2.6 The adoption of the realization and matching rules in preparing financial accounts requires a great deal of subjective judgement.

Required:
Write an essay examining whether it would be fairer, easier, and more meaningful to prepare financial accounts on a cash flow basis.

Part 2

Financial accounting

3 Recording accounting information

Learning objectives_____

1   comprehend the two-fold nature of all transactions;

2   identify debit and credit entries;

3   select appropriate accounts in which to enter some typical business transactions;

4   enter such transactions in some basic ledger accounts;

5   balance the ledger accounts and extract a trial balance as at the end of a given accounting period;

6   locate any errors within the ledger accounting system;

    and

7   outline the main types of book-keeping errors not revealed by preparing a trial balance.

In the last chapter a number of basic accounting rules were outlined. In this chapter one of those rules, the dual aspect rule, will be examined in more depth.

Most modern book-keeping systems adopt the dual aspect rule, irrespective of whether they are handwritten, mechanized or computer based. Whilst it is unlikely that non-accountants will be involved in the detailed recording of accounting information they may well be presented with summaries of it. Such summaries are often prepared in a format that presupposes some knowledge of double-entry book-keeping.

This chapter has been specially designed to introduce the *non-accountant* to the subject of double-entry book-keeping. The chapter contains a number of book-keeping examples, and whilst it might seem unnecessary for a non-accountant to work through them, you are recommended to do so for two main reasons:

1   it will help you to become familiar with accounting terminology; and
2   a knowledge of the methods used in collating accounting information

will help you to assess its *usefulness* in whatever context you are going to use it, for example, in decision-making.

You are advised that this will not be an easy chapter to work through. Indeed, it is essential that it is *worked*, instead of being merely read. Most sections in the chapter contain an exhibit which illustrates the book-keeping procedure being examined in that particular section. These exhibits must be studied most carefully. To help you work through this chapter, you are recommended to adopt the following approach:

1   Read the descriptive material in each section very carefully.
2   Make sure that you understand the requirements of each exhibit.
3   Examine the answer to each exhibit, paying particular attention to the following points:
    (a)   the way in which it has been presented, i.e. its format; and
    (b)   how the data in the exhibit have been converted in response to the requirements of the question.
4   Once you have worked through the answer, try and do the question on your own without reference to the printed answer.
5   If you get the wrong answer, or you find that you do not know how to do the question, re-read the earlier parts of the chapter and then have another attempt at the question.

A detailed study of the dual aspect rule is outlined in the next section.

The dual aspect rule

The dual aspect rule arises from a recognition that every time a transaction takes place, there must always be a double-sided effect *within* the entity itself. A few examples may help to establish the point.

1   If the proprietor pays £10,000 into a business bank account out of his private resources, the business bank account will go *up* by £10,000, but the amount owed by the business to the proprietor will also go *up* by £10,000.
2   If the business owes Jones £3,000 and it sends him a cheque for £2,000, the amount that it owes Jones will go *down* by £2,000, but its bank account will also go *down* by £2,000.
3   If a business receives £1,000 in cash from someone who owes it some money, its cash will go *up* by £1,000, but the amount that it is owed will go *down* by £1,000.
4   If the business pays £5,000 in cash for a motor car, then the total value of its motor cars will go *up* by £5,000, but the amount of cash that it has available will go *down* by £5,000.

Transaction 1 results in an *up/up* effect. Transaction 2 results in a *down/down* effect. Transactions 3 and 4 result in an *up/down* effect. Thus although some transactions result in a consequent movement in the same direction, other transactions cause a movement to take place in the opposite direction. Nonetheless, there is *always* a two-fold effect: there are *no* exceptions to this phenomenon. It can be stated quite categorically that *within* an entity any transaction results in a corresponding and equal effect taking place elsewhere within the entity: the effect is always two-fold.

It is this recognition of the two-fold effect of all transactions that has given rise to the system of recording information that is known as double-entry book-keeping. The main objective of double-entry book-keeping is very simple: it is to record the dual nature of all transactions. The method that has evolved to record information in this way is deceptively simple: all that it requires is for each transaction to be recorded *twice* within the system.

The recording is achieved by classifying all transactions into appropriate groupings. These are then stored separately in what are known as *accounts*. An account is simply a history or a record of a particular type of transaction. Accounts used to be kept in bound books known as ledgers. Nowadays, many entities store information in mechanized or in computer-based systems, although old-fashioned recording methods are still to be found.

The effect of a particular transaction on an account is to cause the balance on the account either to go up or to go down. In other words, the monetary value of the transaction could either *increase* the total value of all transactions contained within the account, or it could have the opposite effect and *decrease* them. The account can, therefore, *receive* an extra amount, or it can *give* (or release) something that it already contains. It is this receiving and giving effect that has given rise to two terms used in accounting, and with which you must become familiar. The two terms are as follows:

- *Debit:* from the Latin meaning to receive or value received; and
- *Credit:* also from the Latin meaning to give or value given.

Accountants judge the two-fold effect of all transactions on particular accounts from a receiving and giving point of view, and each transaction is recorded on that basis. Thus when a transaction takes place, it is necessary to ask the following questions:

1 which account should *receive* this item, i.e. which account should be debited? and
2 which account has *given* it, i.e. which account should be credited?

Accounts have been designed to keep the debit entries separate from

Exhibit 3.1: Example of a ledger account

DATE	DESCRIPTION	FOLIO	AMOUNT £	DATE	DESCRIPTION	FOLIO	AMOUNT £
	DEBIT SIDE				CREDIT SIDE		

Tutorial notes

1 The columnar headings would normally be omitted.
2 The description of each entry is usually limited to the *title* of the corresponding account in which the equal and opposite entry may be found.
3 The folio column is used to refer to the folio (or page) number of the corresponding account.
4 This example of a ledger account may nowadays only be found in a fairly basic handwritten book-keeping system. Computerized and mechanized systems of recording information usually necessitate an alternative format.

the credit entries, thereby emphasizing the opposite (although equal) effect of each transaction. The separation is achieved by recording the *debit* entries on the *left*-hand side of the account, and the *credit* entries on the *right*-hand side. In a handwritten system, each account is normally kept in a *book of account* on separate pages (a page is referred to as a *folio*). If there are a lot of entries in one account, it may be necessary to keep several books of account. A book of account is also sometimes known as a *ledger*, and hence accounts are often referred to as ledger accounts. The format of a typical handwritten ledger account is illustrated in Exhibit 3.1.

There is no logical reason why debits should be entered on the left-hand side of an account, and credits on the right-hand side. It is purely a matter of custom, just as in some countries motorists drive on the left-hand side of the road, while in others they drive on the right-hand side.

The way in which particular transactions are recorded in ledger accounts is examined in the next section.

Recording information

It would not be helpful to record information haphazardly, and so what has evolved is a systematic method of capturing the two-fold nature of all transactions in separate accounts. The book-keeper has first to choose the two accounts in which to record the respective transactions. This procedure is examined in detail in the following sub-sections.

Choice of accounts

As it happens, most transactions can be relatively easily grouped into appropriate categories without too much difficulty. The exact number and type of account will depend upon the amount of detail that the proprietors wish to extract from the system. They might be interested, for example, in having a separate analysis for both salaries and wages, or it might be thought that just one account would be sufficient. In practice, there are a number of accounts that are common to most entities, but if there is any doubt about which account to use, the following rule should be adopted:

If in doubt, open another account.

If an account becomes superfluous, it can always be combined with other accounts at a later stage in the analysis.

Whilst some accounts are common to most entities, it will not always be clear from their description what type of transaction they are supposed to record. A brief summary of the main types of account is listed below.

Capital	The capital account records what the proprietor has contributed (or given) to the entity out of his private resources in order to start the business and to keep it going.
Cash at bank	The bank account records what money the entity keeps at the bank. It shows what has been paid in (usually in the form of cash and cheques) and what has been taken out (usually by cheque payments).
Cash in hand	The cash account works on similar lines to that of the bank account, except that it records the physical cash received, such as notes, coins and cheques, before it is paid into the bank. The cash may be used to purchase goods, and services, or it may be paid straight into the bank. From a control point of view, it is best not to pay for purchases directly from such cash receipts, but to

draw an amount out of the bank specifically for sundry purchases.

Creditors

Creditors accounts record what the entity owes its suppliers for goods or services purchased by or supplied on credit.

Debtors

Debtors accounts record what is owed to the entity for goods or services sold to its customers on credit.

Discounts allowed

Discounts allowed are cash discounts granted to the entity's customers for the prompt settlement of any debts due to the entity. As a result, the amount of cash received from debtors who claim a cash discount will be less than the total amount for which they will have been invoiced.

Discounts received

Discounts received relate to cash discounts given by the entity's suppliers for the prompt payment of any amounts due to them. As a result of claiming a cash discount, the amount paid to the entity's creditors will be less than the amounts stated on their respective invoices.

Drawings

The description *drawings* is a special term used in accounting. The drawings account is used to record what cash (or goods) the proprietors have withdrawn from the business for their own personal use during a particular accounting period.

Petty cash

The petty cash account works like the bank and the cash accounts. It is usually limited to the recording of minor cash transactions, such as bus fares and small items of office expenses. The cash used to finance this account will either be transferred out of the main cash account or withdrawn from the bank account.

Purchases

The term *purchases* has a restricted meaning in accounting. It relates to those goods that are bought primarily with the intention of selling them (usually at a higher price). The purchase of a motor car, for example, would not usually be recorded in the purchases account if it had not been bought with the intention of selling it to a customer. Goods not bought for resale are usually recorded in separate accounts of their own. It should be noted that purchases may require further work to be done on them, or they may be sold exactly in the same form that they were bought.

Sales	The sales account records the value of goods sold to customers during a particular accounting period. The account includes both cash and credit sales. It does not include, for example, receipts from the sale of a motor car originally purchased for use within the business.
Stock	Stock includes the value of goods which had not been sold at the end of the accounting period. In accounting terminology, this is referred to as *closing* stock. The closing stock at the end of one period becomes the *opening* stock at the beginning of the next period.
Trade creditors	Trade creditors accounts are similar to creditors accounts except that they relate specifically to amounts owing to suppliers for goods purchased on credit terms.
Trade debtors	Trade debtor accounts are similar to debtors accounts except that they relate specifically to amounts owing by customers for goods sold to them on credit terms.
Trade discounts	Trade discounts are a form of special discount given, for example, for large orders or to special customers. They result in a reduction of the purchase price or the selling price of goods bought or sold. Trade discounts are not recorded in books of account.

Once the book-keeper has chosen the accounts in which to record all the transactions that have taken place during a particular accounting period, a decision has to be taken as to which account to debit and which account to credit. This problem is examined in the next sub-section.

Entering transactions in accounts

There is one simple rule to follow in entering transactions in their relevant accounts. It can be summarized as follows:

Debit the account which receives
and
credit the account which gives.

The application of this rule is illustrated below with some common ledger account entries:

1   The proprietor contributes some cash to the business.

   Debit: Cash account   *Credit:* Capital account

Reason: The cash account receives some cash given to the business by the proprietor. The capital account is the giving account and the cash account is the receiving account.

2 Some cash-in-hand is paid into a business bank account.

Debit: Bank account: *Credit:* Cash account
Reason: The cash account is the giving account because it is releasing some cash to the bank account.

3 A van is purchased for use in the business; it is paid for by cheque.

Debit: Van account *Credit:* Bank account
Reason: The bank account is giving some money in order to pay for a van, so the bank account must be credited since it is the giving account.

4 Some goods are purchased for cash.

Debit: Purchases account *Credit:* Cash account
Reason: The cash account is giving up an amount of cash in order to pay for some purchases. The cash account is the giving account and it must be credited.

5 Some goods are purchased on credit terms from Fred.

Debit: Purchases account *Credit:* Fred's account
Reason: Fred is supplying the goods on credit terms to the business. He is, therefore, the giver and his account must be credited.

6 Some goods are sold for cash.

Debit: Cash account *Credit:* Sales account
Reason: The cash account receives the cash from the sale of goods, the sales account being the giving account.

7 Some goods are sold on credit terms to Sarah.

Debit: Sarah's account *Credit:* Sales account
Reason: Sarah's account is debited because she is receiving the goods, and the sales account is credited because it is supplying (or giving) them.

It is not easy for beginners to identify correctly the receiving and giving effect of each transaction. Furthermore, it is especially easy to get them mixed up and reverse the entries. In transactions 6 and 7, for example, it is difficult to understand why the sales account should be credited. Why is the sales account the giving account? Surely it is *receiving* an amount and not giving anything? In fact the sales account is a giving account because it is releasing something to another account.

If you find this concept difficult to understand, think of the effect on the *opposite* account. A cash sale, for example, results in a receipt of cash. The cash account must, therefore, be the receiving account, and it must be debited. It follows that the corresponding entry must be *credited*, in this case to the sales account.

Most students find it easier to work out the double-entry effect of respective transactions by relating them to the movement of cash, and you might find it useful to remember the following procedure:

Either *Debit:*   the cash (or bank) account
        Credit: the corresponding account
        if the entity *receives* some cash;

Or   *Debit:*   the corresponding account
        Credit: the cash (or bank) account
        if the entity *gives* some cash.

If a movement of cash is not involved in a particular transaction, work out the effect on the corresponding account on the assumption that one account *is* affected by a cash transaction. In the case of credit sales, for example, the account that benefits from the *receipt* of the goods must be that of an individual, so that individual's account must be debited (instead of the cash account). The corresponding entry must, therefore, be *credited* to some other account. In this example it will be the sales account.

Before leaving this section, it would be useful to summarize a general rule used in double-entry book-keeping:

For every debit there must be a credit
and
for every credit there must be a debit.

There are no exceptions to this rule. As this chapter develops, more practice will be obtained in deciding which account to debit and which account to credit. After some time, it becomes largely a routine exercise, and you will find yourself making the correct entries automatically.

The entry of a number of transactions in specific accounts is illustrated in the next section.

A ledger account example

This section illustrates the procedure adopted in entering various transactions in ledger accounts. The section brings together the basic material covered so far in this chapter and demonstrates the types of account to be adopted, and the effect of each transaction in terms of debit and credit.

The example given in Exhibit 3.2 and its answer below relates to a sole trader entity. Most non-accountants will not be involved in sole trader entities, but this type of entity has been chosen in order to illustrate the principles of double-entry book-keeping. If a more involved form of entity was used, those principles would become somewhat obscured.

The example is also confined to a business that purchases and sells goods on cash terms. Businesses that buy and sell goods on credit terms will be a feature of later examples.

Exhibit 3.2: Joe Simple: A sole trader

The following information relates to Joe Simple who started a new business on 1 January 19X1:

1	1.1.X1	Joe started the business with £5,000 in cash.
2	3.1.X1	He paid £3,000 of the cash into a business bank account.
3	5.1.X1	Joe bought a van for £2,000 paying by cheque.
4	7.1.X1	He bought some goods, paying £1,000 in cash.
5	9.1.X1	Joe sold some of the goods, receiving £1,500 in cash.

Required:
Enter the above transactions in Joe's ledger accounts.

The answer to this exhibit is shown below. Work through the solution making sure that you understand the treatment of each transaction. If you are not sure why a transaction has been treated in a particular way, refer back to the earlier sections of this chapter.

Answer to Exhibit 3.2

Joe Simple's books of account:

Cash Account

		£			£
1.1.X1	Capital (1)	5,000	3.1.X1	Bank (2)	3,000
9.1.X1	Sales (5)	1,500	7.1.X1	Purchases (4)	1,000

Capital Account

	£			£
		1.1.X1	Cash (1)	5,000

Bank Account

		£			£
3.1.X1	Cash (2)	3,000	5.1.X1	Van (3)	2,000

Van Account

		£		£
5.1.X1	Bank (3)	2,000		

Purchases Account

	£		£
7.1.X1 Cash (4)	1,000		

Sales Account

	£		£
		9.1.X1 Cash (5)	1,500

Tutorial notes

1 The numbers in brackets after each entry refer to the exhibit notes; they have been inserted for tutorial guidance only.
2 The narration relates to that account in which the equal and opposite entry may be found.

It is unnecessary for the non-accountant to spend too much time on detailed ledger work, but before moving on to the next section you are recommended to work through Exhibit 3.2 without reference to the answer. This exercise will help you to familiarize yourself with the dual aspect rule and so help you to understand the rest of the book much more clearly.

After entering all the transactions for a particular period in the ledger accounts, the next stage in the exercise is to calculate the balance on each account at the end of each accounting period. This procedure is outlined in the next section.

Balancing the accounts

During a particular accounting period, some accounts (such as the bank and cash accounts) will contain a great many entries on both sides of the account. Other accounts may contain largely debit entries (for example, the purchases account), whilst other accounts may contain largely credit entries (for example, the sales account). It would be extremely cumbersome to allow the entries (whether they are all debit entries, all credit entries or a mixture of both) to build up without occasionally obtaining a total balance. Indeed, the proprietor will almost certainly want to know not just the detailed composition of each account, but also its overall or *net* balance, so it is necessary to balance the accounts at regular intervals. Balancing the accounts requires the book-keeper to add up all the respective debit and credit entries in each account, take one total away from the other, and arrive at a net balance for each account.

Accounts may be balanced extremely frequently (for example, once a week, or once a month), although some entities only balance their books once a year prior to the preparation of the annual accounts. For control purposes, however, it is useful to balance the books fairly regularly. The frequency will depend upon the size of the organization, but once a month is probably sufficient for most entities.

The balancing of the accounts is part of the double-entry procedure, and the method is quite formal. The balancing of an account with a *debit* balance (that is, when its total debit entries exceed its total credit entries) is illustrated in Exhibit 3.3.

Exhibit 3.3: Balancing an account with a debit balance

		Cash Account			
		£			£
1.1.X1	Sales (1)	2,000	10.1.X1	Jones (1)	3,000
15.1.X1	Rent received (1)	1,000	25.1.X1	Davies (1)	5,000
20.1.X1	Smith (1)	4,000			
31.1.X1	Sales (1)	8,000	31.1.X1	Balance c/d (2)	7,000
	(3)	£15,000		(3)	£15,000
1.2.X1	Balance b/d (4)	7,000			

Note: The number shown after each narration relates to the tutorial notes below.

Tutorial notes

1   The total debit entries equal £15,000 (£2,000 + £1,000 + £4,000 + £8,000). The total credit entries equal £8,000 (£3,000 + £5,000). The net balance on this account, therefore, at 31 January 19X1 is a *debit* balance of £7,000 (£15,000 − £8,000). Until both the debit entries and the credit entries have been totalled, of course, it will not usually be apparent whether the balance is a debit one or a credit one. However, it should be noted that there can never be a credit balance in a cash account, because it is impossible to pay out more cash than has been received.

2   The debit balance of £7,000 is inserted on the *credit* side of the account at the time that the account is balanced (in the case of Exhibit 3.3 at 31 January 19X1). This then enables the total of the credit column to be balanced so that it agrees with the total of the debit column. The abbreviation 'c/d' means carried down. In this exhibit the debit balance is carried down in the account in order to start the new period on 1 February 19X1.

3   The £15,000 shown as a total in both the debit and the credit columns demonstrates that the columns balance (they do so, of course, because £7,000 has been inserted in the credit column to make them balance). The totals are double-underlined with the currency sign placed in front of them in order to signify that they are a final total.

4   The balancing figure of £7,000 is brought down ('b/d') in the account to start the new period on 1 February 19X1. The double-entry has been completed because £7,000 has been debited *below* the line (i.e. below the £15,000 debit total), and the £7,000 balancing figure credited *above* the line (i.e. above the £15,000 total).

Exhibit 3.4 illustrates how an account with a *credit* entry is balanced.

Exhibit 3.4: Balancing an account with a credit entry

Scott's Account

		£			£
31.1.X1	Bank (1)	20,000	15.1.X1	Purchases (1)	10,000
31.1.X1	Balance c/d (2)	5,000	20.1.X1	Purchases (1)	15,000
	(3)	£25,000		(3)	£25,000
			1.2.X1	Balance b/d (4)	5,000

Note: The number shown after each narration relates to the tutorial notes below.

Tutorial notes

1 Apart from the balance, there is only one debit entry in Scott's account: the bank entry of £20,000. The total credit entries amount to £25,000 (£10,000 + £15,000). Scott has a *credit* balance, therefore, in his account as at 31 January 19X1 of £5,000 (£10,000 + £15,000 − £20,000). With many more entries in the account it would not always be possible to tell immediately whether the balance was a debit one or a credit one.

2 The credit balance of £5,000 at 31 January 19X1 is inserted on the *debit* side of the account in order to enable the account to be balanced. The balance is then carried down (c/d) to the next period.

3 The £25,000 shown as the total for both the debit and the credit columns identifies the balancing of the account. This has been made possible because of the insertion of the £5,000 balancing figure on the debit side of the account.

4 The balancing figure of £5,000 is brought down (b/d) in the account in order to start the account in the new period beginning on 1 February 19X1. The double-entry has been completed because the debit entry of £5,000 *above* the £25,000 line on the debit side equals the credit entry *below* the £25,000 line on the credit side.

Exhibits 3.3 and 3.4 demonstrate the importance of always obeying the cardinal rule of double-entry book-keeping:

For every debit there must be a credit
and
for every credit there must be a debit.

This rule must still be followed even if the two entries are made in the same account (as is the case when an account is balanced). If this rule is ignored, the accounts will not balance. This could mean that a lot of time is spent looking for the error, or it could even mean that some incorrect information is supplied to the proprietor (since there is bound to be a mistake in at least one account).

After balancing each account, the next stage in the procedure is to check that the double-entry has been completed throughout the system. This is done by compiling what is known as a *trial balance*. This procedure is examined in the next section.

The trial balance

A trial balance is a statement compiled at the end of a specific accounting period listing all of the ledger account debit balances and all of the ledger account credit balances. The preparation of a trial balance is a convenient method of checking that the double-entry has been satisfactorily completed.

Once all the debit balances and credit balances have been listed, the total of all the debit balances must be compared with the total of all the credit balances. If the two totals agree, the book-keeper can be reasonably confident that the double-entry has been completed.

It should be noted that a trial balance is a working paper: it does not form part of the double-entry process.

The preparation of a trial balance is illustrated in Exhibit 3.5 which also gives more examples of how transactions are entered in ledger accounts.

Exhibit 3.5: Edward — Compilation of a trial balance

Edward started a new business on 1 January 19X1. The following transactions took place during his first month in business:

19X1
1.1   Edward commenced business with £10,000 in cash.
3.1   He paid £8,000 of the cash into a business bank account.
6.1   He bought a van on credit from Perkin's garage for £3,000.
9.1   Edward rented shop premises for £1,000 per quarter; he paid for the first quarter immediately by cheque.
12.1 He bought goods on credit from Roy Limited for £4,000.
15.1 He paid shop expenses amounting to £1,500 by cheque.
18.1 Edward sold goods on credit to Scott and Company for £3,000.
21.1 He settled Perkin's account by cheque.
24.1 Edward received a cheque from Scott and Company for £2,000; this cheque was paid immediately into the bank.
27.1 Edward send a cheque to Roy Limited for £500.
31.1 Goods costing £3,000 were purchased from Roy Limited on credit.
31.1 Cash sales for the month amounted to £2,000.

Required:
(a) Enter the above transactions in appropriate ledger accounts, balance off each account as at 31 January 19X1, and bring down the balances as at that date; and
(b) extract a trial balance as at 31 January 19X1.

The answer to Exhibit 3.5 is shown below. Before moving on to part (b) of the exhibit, make sure that you can do part (a). Follow through the transactions, checking that you understand the respective debit and credit entries. Note carefully how each account has been balanced. When you are confident that you can do part (a), move on to part (b).

Answer to Exhibit 3.5(a)
Edward's accounts:

Cash Account

		£			£
1.1.X1	Capital (1)	10,000	3.1.X1	Bank (2)	8,000
31.1.X1	Sales (12)	2,000	31.1.X1	Balance c/d	4,000
		£12,000			£12,000
1.2.X1	Balance b/d	4,000			

Capital Account

		£			£
			1.1.X1	Cash (1)	10,000

Bank Account

		£			£
3.1.X1	Cash (2)	8,000	9.1.X1	Rent payable (4)	1,000
24.1.X1	Scott and		15.1.X1	Shop expenses (6)	1,500
	Company (9)	2,000	21.1.X1	Perkin's garage (8)	3,000
			27.1.X1	Roy Limited (10)	500
			31.1.X1	Balance c/d	4,000
		£10,000			£10,000
1.2.X1	Balance b/d	4,000			

Van Account

		£		£
6.1.X1	Perkin's Garage (3)	3,000		

Perkin's Garage Account

		£			£
21.1.X1	Bank (8)	3,000	6.1.X1	Van (3)	3,000

Rent Payable Account

		£		£
9.1.X1	Bank (4)	1,000		

Purchases Account

		£			£
12.1.X1	Roy Limited (5)	4,000			
31.1.X1	Roy Limited (11)	3,000	31.1.X1	Balance c/d	7,000
		£7,000			£7,000
1.2.X1	Balance b/d	7,000			

Roy Limited Account

		£			£
27.1.X1	Bank (10)	500	12.1.X1	Purchases (5)	4,000
31.1.X1	Balance c/d	6,500	31.1.X1	Purchases (11)	3,000
		£7,000			£7,000
			1.2.X1	Balance b/d	6,500

Shop Expenses Account

		£		£
15.1.X1	Bank (6)	1,500		

Sales Account

		£				£
			18.1.X1	Scott & Company (7)		3,000
31.1.X1	*Balance* c/d	5,000	31.1.X1	Cash (12)		2,000
		£5,000				£5,000
			1.2.X1	*Balance* b/d		5,000

Scott and Company Account

		£			£
18.1.X1	Sales (7)	3,000	24.1.X1	Bank (9)	2,000
			31.1.X1	Balance c/d	1,000
		£3,000			£3,000
1.2.X1	Balance b/d	1,000			

Tutorial notes

1 The number shown after each narration has been inserted for tutorial guidance only in order to illustrate the insertion of each entry in the appropriate account.
2 There is no need to balance an account and carry down the balance when there is only a single entry in one account (for example, Edward's Capital Account).
3 Note that some accounts have no balance in them at all as at 31 January 19X1 (for example, Perkin's Garage Account).

When you have completed part (a) of the question, move on to part (b). Note the format of the trial balance, and the listing of all those accounts that have balances on them as at 31 January 19X1.

Answer to Exhibit 3.5(b)

Trial Balance at 31 January 19X1

	Dr	Cr
	£	£
Cash	4,000	
Capital		10,000
Bank	4,000	
Van	3,000	
Rent Payable	1,000	
Purchases	7,000	
Roy Limited		6,500
Shop Expenses	1,500	
Sales		5,000
Scott and Company	1,000	
	£21,500	£21,500

Tutorial notes

1 The total debit balance agrees with the total credit balance, and therefore the trial balance balances. This confirms that the transactions appear to have been entered in the books of account correctly.
2 The total amount of £21,500 shown in both the debit and credit columns of the trial balance does not have any significance, except to prove that the trial balance balances.

Once the trial balance has been balanced, it is possible to be reasonably confident that the double-entry procedures have been made correctly throughout the system. However, there are some errors that do not affect the balancing of the trial balance. They may be summarized as follows:

1 *Omission.* A transaction could have been completely omitted from the books of account.
2 *Complete reversal of entry.* A transaction could have been entered in (say) Account A as a debit and in Account B as a credit, when it should have been entered as a credit in Account A and as a debit in Account B.
3 *Principle.* A transaction may have been entered in the wrong *type* of account; for example, the purchase of a new delivery van may have been debited to the purchases account, instead of the delivery vans account.
4 *Commission.* A transaction may have been entered in the correct type of account, but in the wrong *personal* account, for example in Bill's Account instead of in Ben's Account.
5 *Compensating.* An error may have been made in (say) adding the debit side of one account, and an identical error in adding the credit side of another account, the two errors thereby cancelling each other out.
6 *Original entry.* A transaction may be entered incorrectly in both accounts, for example, as £291 instead of as £921.

Even allowing for the types of errors listed above, the trial balance still serves a useful purpose. It has three main functions:

1 it enables the general accuracy of the accounts to be checked;
2 it provides a summary of the balance on each account; and
3 it serves as a basis for the preparation of the annual accounts.

The next chapter illustrates how the trial balance may be used to prepare the annual accounts.

Conclusion

It is most unlikely that non-accountants will become involved in entering transactions in ledger accounts, so this chapter has avoided going into too much detail about double-entry book-keeping. However, as part of their managerial role, non-accountants will almost certainly be supplied with information that has been extracted from such a system. In order to assess its real value, it is most important that they should know something about where it has come from, what it means, and what reliability can be placed on it. Before leaving this chapter, therefore, it is recommended that you make absolutely sure that you are familiar with the following features of a double-entry book-keeping system:

● the types of account generally used in practice;
● the meaning of the terms *debit* and *credit*;
● the meaning of the terms *debtor* and *creditor*;
● the way in which transactions are entered in ledger accounts;
● the balancing of accounts; and
● the significance of the trial balance.

This chapter has attempted to provide the basic information necessary to become familiar with the six features listed above. If you are reasonably confident that you now have a basic grasp of double-entry book-keeping, you can move on to an examination of how financial accounts are prepared, but before doing so, you are recommended to test your knowledge of the contents of this chapter by attempting some of the questions that now follow.

Questions

3.1 Adam has just gone into business. The following is a list of his transactions for the month of January 19X1:
  1 Cash paid into the business by Adam.
  2 Goods for resale purchased on cash terms.
  3 Van bought for cash.
  4 One quarter's rent for premises paid in cash.
  5 Some goods sold on cash terms.
  6 Adam buys some office machinery for cash.

Required:
State which account in Adam's books of account should be debited and which account should be credited.

3.2 The following is a list of Brown's transactions for February 19X2:
  1 Transfer of cash to a bank account.
  2 Cash received from sale of goods.
  3 Purchase of goods paid for by cheque.
  4 Office expenses paid in cash.
  5 Cheques received from customers from sale of goods on cash terms.
  6 A motor car for use in the business paid for by cheque.

Required:
State which account in Brown's books of account should be debited and which account should be credited.

3.3 Corby is in business as a retail distributor. The following is a list of his transactions for March 19X3:
1 Goods purchased from Smith on credit.
2 Corby introduces further capital in cash into the business.
3 Goods sold for cash.
4 Goods purchased for cash.
5 Cash transferred to the bank.
6 Machinery purchased, paid for in cash.

Required:
State which account in Corby's books of account should be debited and which account should be credited.

3.4 Davies buys and sells goods on cash and credit terms. The following is a list of his transactions for April 19X4:
1 Capital introduced by Davies paid into the bank.
2 Goods purchased on credit terms from Swallow.
3 Goods sold to Hill for cash.
4 Cash paid for purchase of goods.
5 Dale buys goods from Davies on credit.
6 Motoring expenses paid by cheque.

Required:
State which account in Davies' books of account should be debited and which account credited.

3.5 The following is a list of Edgar's transactions for May 19X5:
1 Goods purchased on credit from Gill.
2 Goods sold on credit to Ash.
3 Goods sold for cash to Crosby.
4 Goods purchased in cash from Lowe.
5 Cheque sent to Gill.
6 Cash received from Ash.

Required:
State which account in Edgar's books should be debited and which account should be credited.

3.6 Ford buys and sells goods on cash and credit terms. The following is a list of his transactions for June 19X6.
1 Goods sold on cash terms to Orange.
2 Goods purchased from Carter on credit.
3 Goods sold to Holly on credit.
4 Goods bought on cash terms from Apple.

5 Holly returns some of the goods.
6 Goods returned to Carter.

Required:
State which account in Ford's books should be debited and which account should
be credited.

3.7 The following transactions relate to Gordon's business for the month of
July 19X7:
1 Bought goods on credit from Watson.
2 Sold some goods for cash.
3 Sold some goods on credit to Moon.
4 Sent a cheque for half the amount owing to Watson.
5 Watson grants Gordon a cash discount.
6 Moon settles most of his account in cash.
7 Gordon allows Moon a cash discount that covers the small amount owed
by Moon.
8 Gordon purchases some goods for cash.

Required:
State which accounts in Gordon's books of account should be debited and which
account should be credited.

3.8 Harry started a new business on 1 January 19X8. The following
transactions cover his first three months in business:
1 Harry contributed an amount in cash to start the business.
2 He transferred some of the cash to a business bank account.
3 He paid an amount in advance by cheque for rental of business premises.
4 Bought goods on credit from Paul.
5 Purchased a van paying by cheque.
6 Sold some goods for cash to James.
7 Bought goods on credit from Nancy.
8 Paid motoring expenses in cash.
9 Returned some goods to Nancy.
10 Sold goods on credit to Mavis.
11 Harry withdrew some cash for personal use.
12 Bought goods from David paying in cash.
13 Mavis returns some goods.
14 Sent a cheque to Nancy.
15 Cash received from Mavis.
16 Harry receives a cash discount from Nancy.
17 Harry allows Mavis a cash discount.
18 Cheque withdrawn at the bank in order to open a petty cash account.

Required:
State which accounts in Harry's books of account should be debited and which
account should be credited.

3.9 The following is a list of transactions which relate to Ivan for the first month that he is in business:

1.9.X9	Started the business with £10,000 in cash.
2.9.X9	Paid £8,000 into a business bank account.
3.9.X9	Purchased £1,000 of goods in cash.
10.9.X9	Bought goods costing £6,000 on credit from Roy.
12.9.X9	Cash sales of £3,000.
15.9.X9	Goods sold on credit terms to Norman for £4,000.
20.9.X9	Ivan settles Roy's account by cheque.
30.9.X9	Cheque for £2,000 received from Norman.

Required:
Enter the above transactions in Ivan's ledger accounts.

3.10 Jones has been in business since 1 October 19X1. The following is a list of his transactions for October 19X1:

1.10.X1	Capital of £20,000 paid into a business bank account.
2.10.X1	Van purchased on credit from Lang for £5,000.
6.10.X1	Goods purchased on credit from Green for £15,000.
10.10.X1	Cheque drawn on the bank for £1,000 in order to open a petty cash account.
14.10.X1	Goods sold on credit for £6,000 to Haddock.
18.10.X1	Cash sales of £5,000.
20.10.X1	Cash purchases of £3,000.
22.10.X1	Miscellaneous expenses of £500 paid out of petty cash.
25.10.X1	Lang's account settled by cheque.
28.10.X1	Green allows Jones a cash discount of £500.
29.10.X1	Green is sent a cheque for £10,000.
30.10.X1	Haddock is allowed a cash discount of £600.
31.10.X1	Haddock settles his account in cash.

Required:
Enter the above transactions in Jones' ledger accounts.

3.11 The transactions listed below relate to Ken's business for the month of November 19X2:

1.11.X2	Started the business with £15,000 in cash.
2.11.X2	Transferred £14,000 of the cash to a business bank account.
3.11.X2	Paid rent of £1,000 by cheque.
4.11.X2	Bought goods on credit from the following suppliers:

	Ace	£5,000
	Mace	£6,000
	Pace	£7,000

10.11.X2	Sold goods on credit to the following customers:

	Main	£2,000
	Pain	£3,000
	Vain	£4,000

15.11.X2	Returned goods costing £1,000 to Pace.
22.11.X2	Pain returned goods sold to him for £2,000.

25.11.X2 Additional goods purchased from the following suppliers:

Ace	£3,000
Mace	£4,000
Pace	£5,000

26.11.X2 Office expenses of £2,000 paid by cheque.

27.11.X2 Cash sales for the month amounted to £5,000.

28.11.X2 Purchases paid for in cash during the month amounted to £4,000.

29.11.X2 Cheques sent to the following suppliers:

Ace	£4,000
Mace	£5,000
Pace	£6,000

30.11.X2 Cheques received from the following customers:

Main	£1,000
Pain	£2,000
Vain	£3,000

30.11.X2 The following cash discounts were claimed by Ken:

Ace	£200
Mace	£250
Pace	£300

30.11.X2 The following cash discounts were allowed by Ken:

Main	£100
Pain	£200
Vain	£400

30.11.X2 Cash transfer to the bank of £1,000.

Required:

Enter the above transactions in Ken's ledger accounts.

3.12 The following transactions relate to Pat's business for the month of December 19X3:

1.12.X3 Started the business with £10,000 in cash.

2.12.X3 Bought goods on credit from the following suppliers:

Grass	£6,000
Seed	£7,000

10.12.X3 Sold goods on credit to the following customers:

Fog	£3,000
Mist	£4,000

12.12.X3 Returned goods to the following suppliers:

Grass	£1,000
Seed	£2,000

15.12.X3 Bought additional goods on credit from Grass for £3,000 and from Seed for £4,000.

20.12.X3 Sold more goods on credit to Fog for £2,000 and to Mist for £3,000.

24.12.X3 Paid office expenses of £5,000 in cash.

29.12.X3 Received £4,000 in cash from Fog and £6,000 in cash from Mist.

31.12.X3 Pat paid Grass and Seed £6,000 and £8,000 respectively in cash.

Required:

(a) Enter the above transactions in Pat's ledger accounts.

(b)   Balance off the accounts as at 31 December 19X3.
(c)   Bring down the balances as at 1 January 19X4.
(d)   Compile a trial balance as at 31 December 19X3.

3.13   Vale has been in business for some years. The following balances were
brought forward in his books of account as at 31 December 19X2:

	£ Dr	£ Cr
Bank	5,000	
Capital		20,000
Cash	1,000	
Dodd		2,000
Fish	6,000	
Furniture	10,000	
	£22,000	£22,000

During the year to 31 December 19X3 the following transactions took place.
1   Goods bought from Dodd on credit of £30,000.
2   Cash sales of £20,000.
3   Cash purchases of £15,000.
4   Goods sold to Fish on credit for £50,000.
5   Cheques sent to Dodd totalling £29,000.
6   Cheques received from Fish totalling £45,000.
7   Cash received from Fish amounting to £7,000.
8   Office expenses paid in cash totalling £9,000.
9   Purchase of delivery van costing £12,000 paid by cheque.
10   Cash transfers to bank totalling £3,000.

Required:
(a)   Compile Vale's ledger accounts for the year 31 December 19X3, balance
off the accounts and bring down the balances as at 1 January 19X4.
(b)   Extract a trial balance as at 31 December 19X3.

3.14   Brian started in business on 1 January 19X4. The following is a list of
his transactions for his first month of trading:
1.1.X4   Opened a business bank account with £25,000 obtained from private
resources.
2.1.X4   Paid one month's rent of £2,000 by cheque.
3.1.X4   Bought goods costing £5,000 on credit from Linda.
4.1.X4   Purchased motor car from Savoy Motors for £4,000 on credit.
5.1.X4   Purchased goods costing £3,000 on credit from Sydney.
10.1.X4   Cash sales of £6,000.
15.1.X4   More goods costing £10,000 purchased from Linda on credit.
20.1.X4   Sold goods on credit to Ann for £8,000.
22.1.X4   Returned £2,000 of goods to Linda.
23.1.X4   Paid £6,000 in cash into the bank.
24.1.X4   Ann returned £1,000 of goods.
25.1.X4   Withdrew £500 in cash from the bank to open a petty cash account.

26.1.X4 Cheque received from Ann for £5,500; Ann also claimed a cash discount of £500.
28.1.X4 Office expenses of £250 paid out of petty cash.
29.1.X4 Sent a cheque to Savoy Motors for £4,000.
30.1.X4 Cheques sent to Linda and Sydney for £8,000 and £2,000 respectively. Cash discounts were also claimed from Linda and Sydney of £700 and £100 respectively.
31.1.X4 Paid by cheque another month's rent of £2,000.
31.1.X4 Brian introduced £5,000 additional capital into the business by cheque.

Required:
(a) Enter the above transactions in Brian's ledger accounts for January 19X4, balance off the accounts and bring down the balances as at 1 February 19X4.
(b) Compile a trial balance as at 31 January 19X4.

3.15 The following balances have been extracted from Field's ledger accounts as at 28 February 19X5:

	£
Bank	13,000
Cash	2,000
Capital	15,000
Creditors	4,000
Debtors	10,000
Drawings	5,000
Electricity	4,000
Furniture	7,000
Office expenses	3,000
Purchases	50,000
Sales	100,000
Wages	25,000

Required:
Compile Field's trial balance as at 28 February 19X5.

3.16 An accounts clerk has compiled Trent's trial balance as at 31 March 19X6 as follows:

	Dr £	Cr £
Bank (overdrawn)	2,000	
Capital	50,000	
Discounts allowed		5,000
Discounts received	3,000	
Dividends received	2,000	
Drawings		23,000
Investments		14,000
Land and buildings	60,000	
Office expenses	18,000	
Purchases	75,000	

Sales		250,000
Suspense (unexplained balance)		6,000
Rates		7,000
Vans	20,000	
Van expenses		5,000
Wages and salaries	80,000	
	£310,000	£310,000

Required:
Compile Trent's corrected trial balance as at 31 March 19X6.

3.17 The following balances have been extracted from Severn's books of account as at 30 April 19X7:

	£000
Purchases	300
Cash	8
Discounts received	2
Rents received	5
Wages	44
Discounts allowed	5
Creditors	12
Telephone	3
Sales	500
Capital	100
Sales returns	20
Bank interest received	1
Furniture and fittings	18
Bank (deposit)	50
Advertising	14
Motor cars	22
Bank (current)	5
Purchases returns	15
Land and buildings	40
Debtors	30
Plant and equipment	37
Drawings	45
Fees received	10
Motor car expenses	4

Required:
Compile Severn's trial balance at 30 April 19X7.

Additional questions (without answers)

3.18 Donald's transactions for the month of March 19X9 are as follows:

	£
Cash receipts	
Capital contributed	6,000
Sales to customers	3,000

Cash payments

Goods for sale	4,000
Stationery	500
Postage	300
Travelling	600
Wages	2,900
Transfers to bank	500

Bank receipts
Receipts from trade debtors:

Smelt	3,000
Tait	9,000
Ure	5,000

Bank payments
Payments to trade creditors:

Craig	2,800
Dobie	5,000
Elgin	6,400
Rent and rates	3,200
Electricity	200
Telephone	100
Salaries	2,000
Miscellaneous expenses	600

Other transactions
Goods purchased from:

Craig	3,500
Dobie	7,500
Elgin	7,500
Goods returned to Dobie	400

Goods sold to:

Smelt	4,000
Tait	10,000
Ure	8,000
Goods returned by Ure	900

Discounts allowed:

Smelt	200
Tait	500
Ure	400

Discounts received:

Craig	50
Dobie	100
Elgin	200

Required:
(a) Enter the above transactions in appropriate ledger accounts;
(b) balance each account as at 31 March 19X9;

and

(c)   extract a trial balance as at that date.

3.19   The following trial balance was extracted from Ryan's books of account as at 30 June 19X2:

	£ Dr	£ Cr
Bank		1,500
Capital		61,500
Cash	100	
Trade creditors:		
Arnot		2,000
Bain		3,000
Croft		4,000
Trade debtors:		
Xram	11,200	
Yousif	12,300	
Zlot	13,400	
Vehicles	35,000	
	£72,000	£72,000

During July 19X2, the following transactions took place:

(1)   Cash and bank

	Receipts			Payments	
	Cash £	Bank £		Cash £	Bank £
Watt (sales)	2,000	4,000	Arnot		1,800
Xram		9,000	Bain		3,000
Yousif		10,000	Croft		2,500
Zlot		12,000	Ducat		
			(purchases)		6,000
Sales		1,500	Drawings	1,200	
			Heat and		
			light		750
			Wages and		
			salaries		3,400
			Office		
			expenses		550
			Purchases	1,000	

(2)   Other transactions

	Purchases	Purchases Returns	Sales	Sales Returns	Discounts
	£	£	£	£	£
Arnot	3,000	500			150
Bain	4,500	1,500			250
Croft	6,000	700			200
Ducat	7,000	600			100
Watt			9,000	300	450
Xram			8,000	400	50
Yousif			22,000	2,000	350
Zlot			26,000	1,000	650

Required:
(a)   Enter the above transactions in appropriate ledger accounts;
(b)   balance each account as at 31 July 19X2;
      and
(c)   extract a trial balance as at that date.

4 Basic financial statements

Learning objectives_____

1 make adjustments for a number of typical post-trial balance transactions;

2 prepare a simple trading, profit and loss account, and balance sheet relating to a sole trader entity;

3 understand the nature of accounting profit;

4 assess its limitations;

and

5 criticize the traditional method of preparing financial statements.

In Chapter 1 it was suggested that business proprietors want to know the answers to three fundamental questions:

1 What profit has the business made?
2 How much does the business owe?
3 How much is owed to it?

The last chapter included an illustration of how a trial balance may be constructed. The trial balance not only provides a check on the accuracy of the double-entry book-keeping, but it also enables some *basic financial statements* to be prepared. It is from such statements that the three questions posed by business proprietors can be answered. The preparation of the basic financial statements forms the subject of this chapter.

The measurement of profit

Before examining the preparation of basic financial statements in detail, it would be useful to determine what accountants mean by *profit*.

Proprietors often try to measure business profit (that is, how well the business has done) by comparing how much cash the business had at the beginning of a period with how much cash it had at the end. This is not usually what accountants mean by profit.

As was argued in Chapter 2, accounts are normally prepared by adopting a certain number of accounting rules. It will be recalled that two of these rules (the realization and matching rules) require the matching of the cost of sales against the sales revenue for a particular period irrespective of whether the respective transactions have been settled in cash during that period. It follows that the difference between cash received during a period and the cash paid out during the same period is not the same as accounting profit. Cash transactions may relate to earlier or later periods, whereas incomes and expenditure (as defined in accounting) try to measure the *precise* activity which has occurred during a determined period of time.

There are great problems, of course, in trying to measure income and expenditure rather than cash receipts and cash payments. Some expenditure, for example, may provide a benefit in more than one time period. Thus if the entity purchases a machine, and it is estimated to have a life of 20 years, how should the cost of the machine be matched against the sales revenue earned during each year of the life of that machine?

To cope with this problem, accountants classify expenditure into *capital* and *revenue*. Capital expenditure is regarded as being expenditure that provides a benefit in more than one accounting period. Revenue expenditure is expenditure that relates only to one accounting period. Since basic financial statements are normally prepared on an annual basis, revenue expenditure can be regarded as being virtually synonymous with annual expenditure. During the next period the service will have to be re-ordered or renewed if it is to be obtained.

Examples of revenue expenditure include goods purchased with the intention of resale, electricity charges, expenditure on business rates, and wages and salaries. Examples of capital expenditure include land and buildings, plant and machinery, motor vehicles, and furniture and fittings. Such items are described as *fixed assets*, because they are intended for long-term use within the business. It is also possible to classify income into capital and revenue, although the terms *capital income* and *capital revenue* are not commonly adopted. Income of a revenue nature would include the revenue from the sale of goods to customers, and rents received. Income of a capital nature would include the proprietor's capital, and loans made to the business (such as a long-term bank loan).

In practice, it is not always easy to distinguish between capital and revenue items, and the distinction is often an arbitrary one. Some items of expenditure are particularly difficult to distinguish, although most transactions fall into recognizable categories.

The distinction between capital and revenue items is very important, because accounting profit is essentially the difference between revenue income and revenue expenditure. If capital and revenue items are not classified accurately, therefore, a misleading level of accounting profit would be reported.

The calculation of accounting profit is examined in the next section.

Preparation of basic financial statements

It is now possible to examine how basic financial statements are prepared. It may be assumed that a trial balance has been prepared and that the books balance. There are two main stages in preparing such statements, and each stage will be dealt with separately.

The trading and profit and loss account stage

The first stage in compiling basic financial statements is to prepare a profit and loss account. In a trading organization, this stage will first require the preparation of a *trading* account before preparing the actual profit and loss account. In order to compile such accounts, it is necessary to extract all the revenue income and expenditure items from the trial balance. These are then matched against each other in the form of a statement called a *trading and profit and loss account*. By deducting income balances from the total of revenue expenditure balances, the level of the accounting profit (or loss) for the period can be determined. There are two important points to note. These are as follows:

1　It is customary for the trading account to come before the profit and loss account. The trading account matches the sales revenue against the cost of goods sold (mainly the cost of purchasing goods). The difference between the sales revenue and the cost of goods sold is known as *gross profit*. The gross profit is then transferred to the profit and loss account where it is added to the other revenue incomes of the business, the total then being matched against all the other expenses of the business (such as heat and light, and wages and salaries). The difference between the gross profit plus other non-trading incomes, less the other expenses is known as *net profit* (or net loss). In other words:

$$(\text{Gross profit} + \text{Other revenue incomes})$$
$$- \text{Revenue expenditure} = \text{Net profit (or net loss)}$$

2　Both the trading account and the profit and loss account are accounts in their own right. This means that any transfer to them forms part of the double-entry system, and so a corresponding and equal entry has to be made in some other account.

The balance sheet stage

Once all the trading account and profit and loss account balances have been extracted, the second stage in the preparation of basic financial statements is to summarize all the balances that remain in the trial balance. These are listed in the form of a statement called a *balance sheet*. Unlike the trading and profit and loss accounts, a balance sheet does not form part of the double-entry: it is merely a listing of balances.

It would be helpful at this stage to illustrate the preparation of basic financial statements with a simple example; this is done in the next section.

An illustration of basic financial statements

Exhibit 4.1 illustrates how to prepare a trading account, a profit and loss account, and a balance sheet.

Exhibit 4.1

The following trial balance has been extracted from Bush's books of account as at 30 June 19X7:

Name of account		Dr £	Cr £
Bank (1)		5,000	
Capital (at 1 July 19X6) (2)			11,000
Cash (3)		1,000	
Drawings (4)		8,000	
Motor vehicle at cost (5)		6,000	
Motor vehicle expenses (6)	(R)	2,000	
Office expenses (7)	(R)	3,000	
Purchases (8)	(R)	30,000	
Trade creditors (9)			4,000
Trade debtors (10)		10,000	
Sales (11)	(R)		50,000
		£65,000	£65,000

Note: There were no opening or closing stocks.

Required:
(a) Prepare Bush's trading and profit and loss account for the year to 30 June 19X7; and
(b) a balance sheet as at that date.

The answer to the exhibit is shown below. Note that account numbers have been inserted in the trial balance to help you trace the entries through the respective financial statements. The symbol 'R' (meaning revenue) has also been inserted to help show you those balances that relate to the trading account and the profit and loss account.

Work through the solution, noting in particular two main features:

1 which balance goes in which statement; and
2 the format of the respective statements.

Answer to Exhibit 4.1(a)

BUSH

Trading, profit and loss account for the year to 30 June 19X7

	£		£
Purchases (8)	30,000	Sales (11)	50,000
Gross profit c/d	20,000		
	£50,000		£50,000
Motor vehicle expenses (6)	2,000	Gross profit b/d	20,000
Office expenses (7)	3,000		
Net profit c/d	15,000		
	£20,000		£20,000
		Net profit b/d	15,000

Tutorial notes

1 The number shown in brackets after each narration refers to the account number of each balance extracted from the trial balance.
2 Both the trading account and the profit and loss account cover a period of time. In this exhibit it is for the year *to* (or alternatively, *ending*) 30 June 19X7.
3 It is not customary to keep the trading account totally separate from the profit and loss account. The usual format is the one shown above whereby the trading account balance (that is, the gross profit) is carried down straight into the profit and loss account.
4 Note that the proprietor's drawings (account (4)), are not an expense of the business. They are treated as an *appropriation,* i.e. amounts withdrawn by the proprietor in advance of any profit that the business might have made.

Now that part (a) of the question has been completed it is possible to move on to part (b).

Answer to Exhibit 4.1(b)

BUSH

Balance sheet at 30 June 19X7

	£	£		£	£
Capital			*Fixed assets*		
Balance at 1 July			Motor vehicle at		
19X6 (2)		11,000	cost (5)		6,000
Add: Net profit					
for the year*	15,000		*Current assets*		
Less: Drawings					
(4)	8,000	7,000	Trade debtors		
			(10)	10,000	
c/f		18,000	c/f	10,000	6,000

b/f	18,000		b/f	10,000	6,000
		Bank (1)		5,000	
		Cash (3)		1,000	16,000

Current liabilities
Trade creditors
(9)

4,000	
£22,000	£22,000

*This balance has been obtained from the profit and loss account.

Note: The number in brackets shown after each narration refers to the account number of each balance listed in the trial balance on p. 61.

Tutorial notes

1   The balance sheet is prepared *at* a particular moment in time. It depicts the balances as they were at a specific date. In this example, the balances are shown as at 30 June 19X7.

2   The format of this balance sheet shows the capital and liability balances on the left-hand side of the page, and the asset balances on the right-hand side.

3   The left-hand side of the balance sheet is divided into two main sections:
   (a)   the capital section shows how the business has been financed (usually from combination of the original capital contributed by the proprietor and the profit that has been left in the business); and
   (b)   the current liabilities section shows the amounts owed to various parties outside the entity and due for payment within 12 months.

4   As far as the capital section is concerned, the net profit obtained from the profit and loss account must be added to it, because it is a remaining balance within the ledger system. In effect, it is a summary balance: it is merely a *net* balance obtained after matching the revenue income and expenditure balances. It is preferable to deduct any drawings that the proprietor may have made from the net profit for the year in order to show how much profit has been left in the business out of that year's profits.

5   The current liabilities should be listed in the order of those that are going to be paid last being placed before those that are going to be paid first, e.g. creditors should come before a bank overdraft.

6   The right-hand side of the balance sheet is also divided into two main sections:
   (a)   the fixed assets section includes those assets that are intended for long-term use within the business; and
   (b)   the current assets section includes assets that are constantly being turned over, for example stocks, debtors and cash.

7   Fixed assets are usually shown at their original, i.e. at their *historic* cost. The fact that they are stated at cost should be noted on the balance sheet.

8   Both fixed assets and current assets should be listed with the least liquid (or realizable) asset being placed first, e.g. property should come before machinery, and stocks before debtors.

9   The total of fixed assets and current assets is known as *total assets*.

You are now recommended to work through Exhibit 4.1 again, but this time without reference to the answer.

Format of accounts

In Exhibit 4.1, the *horizontal* format was adopted for both the trading and profit and loss accounts, and for the balance sheet. In the United Kingdom, it is now more fashionable to prepare such statements in a *vertical* format so that the information can be read down the page on a line-by-line basis.

There are three good reasons for adopting this format:

1 It is believed that the vertical format is more helpful than the horizontal format for those users who are untrained in double-entry book-keeping since it does not presuppose any knowledge of double-entry book-keeping.
2 It highlights the various sections more clearly.
3 It is easier to read down a page than across it.

As you are probably more likely to meet financial statements prepared in the vertical format (although you will still come across examples of the horizontal format), the vertical format will be adopted throughout the rest of this book.

Exhibit 4.2 represents the answer to Exhibit 4.1 using the vertical format.

Exhibit 4.2

BUSH

Trading and profit and loss account for the year to 30 June 19X7

	£	£
Sales		50,000
Less: Cost of goods sold:		
Purchases		30,000
Gross profit		20,000
Less: Expenses:		
Motor vehicle expenses	2,000	
Office expenses	3,000	5,000
Net profit for the year		£15,000

BUSH

Balance sheet at 30 June 19X7

	£	£
Fixed assets		
Motor vehicle at cost		6,000
Current assets		
Trade debtors	10,000	
Bank	5,000	
Cash	1,000	
	16,000	
Less: Current liabilities:		
Trade creditors	4,000	12,000
		£18,000

Financed by:
Capital

Balance at 1 July 19X6		11,000
Add: Net profit for the year	15,000	
Less: Drawings	8,000	7,000
		£18,000

Study Exhibit 4.2 carefully, noting how the information shown in Exhibit 4.1 has been rearranged. There are very few changes, except that the information now reads downwards, rather than across the page. The exhibits that have been used so far to illustrate the preparation and format of basic financial statements have been made deliberately simple. In practice, major complications may arise in the preparation of these statements, and these are considered in the next section. There is quite a lot of difficult material contained in the section, so take your time over it.

Post trial balance adjustments

After a trial balance has been prepared, it is usually necessary to make a number of last minute adjustments to the accounts. The normal procedure is to calculate a *provisional* balance for each account and then to prepare the trial balance. Any errors will be located at the provisional trial balance stage. Once the books have been balanced, any necessary further adjustments will be made, and it is at that stage that the final accounts will be prepared. Such adjustments will only be entered into the ledger accounts when the financial statements have been finalized. The ledger accounts will then be balanced and the balances carried down to the next period.

There are four main types of year-end adjustments that are normally required after a provisional trial balance has been extracted. They may be summarized as follows:

1 stock adjustments;
2 depreciation adjustments;
3 accruals and prepayments adjustments; and
4 adjustments for bad debts and provisions for doubtful debts.

These adjustments will be considered in some detail in the following subsections.

Stock adjustments

It is most unlikely that all of the purchases that have been made during a particular period will have been sold by the end of it. It is almost certain that some purchases will still be in store at the period end. In accounting terminology, purchases still on hand at the period end are referred to as *stock*.

In calculating the gross profit for the period, therefore, it is necessary to make some allowance for closing stock in order to match the cost of goods actually sold (and not the cost of all those goods purchased) with the sales revenue earned for the period. Consequently, the quantity of stock on hand at the end of the accounting period has to be checked, and then some value put on it. In practice, this is an extremely difficult exercise, and it will be examined in more detail in Chapter 10. Most examples used in this part of the book assume that the value of the closing stock is readily available.

There is also another problem in dealing with stock. Closing stock at the end of one period becomes the *opening* stock at the beginning of the next period. In calculating the cost of goods sold, therefore, an allowance has to be made for opening stock. In fact, the cost of goods sold can be quite easily calculated by adopting the following formula:

Cost of goods sold = (Opening stock + Purchases) − Closing stock

The book-keeping entries are not quite so easy to understand, but they may be summarized as follows:

1   Transfer the opening stock to the trading account:
    Required: *Debit:* Trading account   *Credit:* Stock account
    with the value of the opening stock as estimated at the end of the previous period (this should have been brought down as a debit balance in the stock account at the beginning of the current period).

2   Estimate the value of the closing stock:
    Required: *Debit:* Stock account   *Credit:* Trading account
    with the value of the closing stock as estimated at the end of the current period.

By making these adjustments the trading account should now appear as in Exhibit 4.3.

Exhibit 4.3: Example of a trading account with stock adjustments

	£		£
Opening stock	1,000	Sales	4,000
Purchases	2,000	Closing stock	1,500
Gross profit c/d	2,500		
	£5,500		£5,500

Note: This format does not show clearly the cost of goods sold, so it is customary to deduct the closing stock from the total of opening stock and purchases, as shown below:

	£			£
Opening stock	1,000	Sales		4,000
Purchases	2,000			
	3,000			
Less: Closing stock	1,500			
	1,500			
Gross profit c/d	2,500			
	£4,000			£4,000

Study this amended format very carefully, because it will be encountered frequently in subsequent examples.

Depreciation adjustments

Expenditure that covers more than one accounting period has been defined in a previous section as *capital* expenditure. Capital expenditure is not included in either the trading account or the profit and loss account. It would be misleading, however, to exclude it altogether from the calculation of profit.

Expenditure on fixed assets (such as plant and machinery, motor vehicles and furniture) is presumably necessary in order to help provide a general service to the business. The benefit received from the purchase of fixed assets must (by definition) extend beyond at least one accounting period. Nonetheless, the benefit is just as much a charge against profit as that expenditure that provides a benefit for just one accounting period. The only difference is that it is difficult to know how much of the cost of fixed assets should be charged to each accounting period. In accounting terminology, such a charge is known as *depreciation*.

There is also another reason why fixed assets should be depreciated. By *not* charging each accounting period with a proportion of the cost of fixed assets, the level of profit in each period would be correspondingly higher. Thus the proprietor would be able to withdraw a higher level of the profit from the business. If this were the case, insufficient funds may be left in the business, and it may not be possible to finance the replacement of stocks and fixed assets in order to continue operating at the same level as it had experienced in the past.

In practice, it is not easy to measure the benefit provided in each accounting period by respective fixed assets. Most depreciation methods are very simple. The one most commonly adopted is known as *straight-line* depreciation. This method charges an equal amount of depreciation to each accounting period that benefits from the service that the fixed asset provides. The annual depreciation charge is calculated as follows:

Annual depreciation charge =

$$\frac{\text{Original cost of the asset} - \text{estimated residual value}}{\text{Estimated life of the asset}}$$

In order to calculate the annual depreciation charge, it is necessary to work out how long the asset is likely to last, and what it can be sold for when its useful life is ended.

Although it is customary to include fixed assets at their historical cost in the balance sheet, some fixed assets (such as property) may be revalued. If this is the case, then the depreciation charge will be based on the revalued amount, and not on the historic cost. It should be noted that even if the asset is depreciated on the basis of its revalued amount, there is no guarantee that it will be replaced at that amount. A combination of inflation and obsolescence may mean that its eventual replacement cost is far in excess of either its revalued amount or its historic cost. It follows that when the fixed assets eventually come to be replaced, there could well be a short-fall of funds.

Besides straight-line depreciation, there are other methods that may be adopted. One other depreciation method that is sometimes preferred (although it is far less common than straight-line) is known as the *reducing balance* method. This method is similar to straight-line in that it is based on the historic cost of the asset. It also requires an estimate to be made of the life of the asset, and of its estimated residual value. The depreciation rate is usually expressed as a percentage, and the rate is then applied to the *reducing* balance of the asset, i.e. after the depreciation charge in previous years has been deducted.

Suppose, for example, that an asset costs £1,000, and that the depreciation rate is 50% of the reducing balance. The depreciation charge per year would then be as follows:

Year		£
1. 1.X1	Historic cost	1,000
31.12.X1	Depreciation charge for the year (50%)	500
	Reduced balance	500
31.12.X2	Depreciation charge for the year (50%)	250
	Reduced balance	250
31.12.X3	Depreciation charge for the year (50%)	125
	Reduced balance	125

.. and so on, until the asset has been written down to its estimated residual value.

The reducing balance depreciation rate may be found by formula, viz.:

$$r = 1 - \sqrt[n]{\frac{R}{C}}$$

where: r = the depreciation rate to be applied;
          n = the estimated life of the asset;
          R = its estimated residual value;
          C = its historic cost.

The reducing balance method results in a much higher level of depreciation in the first few years of the life of an asset, and a much lower charge in later years. It is a more suitable method to adopt in depreciating vehicles, for example, because vehicles tend to have a high depreciation rate in their early years, and a low rate towards the end of their life. In addition, maintenance costs tend to be low initially, and become greater as the vehicles become older. Consequently, the combined depreciation charge plus the maintenance costs produce a more even pattern of *total* vehicle costs than is the case if the straight-line method of depreciation is used.

There are other methods of depreciating fixed assets, but since they are rarely used, they are considered beyond the scope of this text.

The ledger account entries for depreciation are quite straightforward. The annual charge for depreciation will be entered into the books of account as follows:

Debit: Profit and loss account *Credit:* Accumulated depreciation account with the depreciation charge for the year.
Note: Each group of fixed assets will normally have its own accumulated depreciation account.

As far as the balance sheet is concerned, it is customary to disclose the following details for each group of fixed assets:

1 gross book value (either historic cost or revalued amount);
2 accumulated depreciation; and
3 net book value (i.e. 1 less 2).

Exhibit 4.4 illustrates the balance sheet presentation.

Exhibit 4.4 shows how the accumulated depreciation is deducted from the original cost for each group of assets, thereby arriving at the respective net book value for each group. The total net book value £88,000 in Exhibit 4.4) forms part of the balance sheet total. The total cost of the fixed assets and the total accumulated depreciation are shown purely for information. Such totals do not form part of the balancing process.

Exhibit 4.4: Balance sheet disclosure of fixed assets

Fixed assets	Cost	Accumulated depreciation	Net book value
	£	£	£
Buildings	100,000	30,000	70,000
Equipment	40,000	25,000	15,000
Furniture	10,000	7,000	3,000
	£150,000	£62,000	88,000
Current assets			
Stocks		10,000	
Debtors		8,000	
Cash		2,000	
			20,000
			£108,000

Accruals and prepayment adjustments

In Chapter 2, the requirement to make adjustments for accruals and prepayments at the end of a particular accounting period was briefly outlined. This procedure will now be examined in a little more detail.

Accruals

An *accrual* is an amount outstanding at the end of an accounting period for a service rendered during that period. The amount outstanding will be settled in cash in a subsequent period. The entity may, for example, have settled the last quarter's electricity bill one week before the year end. In its accounts for that year, therefore, it needs to allow (or *accrue*) for the amount it will owe for the electricity that it has consumed during the last week of its accounting year (since it is unlikely that it will be invoiced for it until the next period).

The accrual will be based on an estimate of the likely cost of a week's supply of electricity, or if it is preparing its accounts after the next quarter's invoice has been received, on an apportionment of that quarter's invoice.

The ledger account entries are reasonably straightforward. It is not normal practice to open a separate account for accruals, the double-entry being completed within the same account. Exhibit 4.5 illustrates the procedure.

It will be noted from Exhibit 4.5 that at 31 March 19X2 an amount is transferred to the profit and loss account for the cost of electricity consumed during that year. The ledger account entries are as follows:

Debit: Profit and loss account   *Credit:* Electricity account
with the electricity charge for the year.

Exhibit 4.5: Accounting for accruals

Electricity Account

		£			£
1.4.X1	Bank	400	1.4.X1	Balance b/d*	400
1.7.X1	Bank	300			
1.9.X1	Bank	100			
1.1.X2	Bank	500			
31.3.X2	Balance c/d**	600	31.3.X2	Profit and	
				loss account	1,500
		£1,900			£1,900
			1.4.X2	Balance b/d	600

*This balance is assumed to be an accrual made in the year to 31 March 19X1.
**This amount is an accrual for the year to 31 March 19X2.

The double-entry has been completed for the accrual by debiting it to the electricity account for the year to 31 March 19X2 (i.e. above the line), and crediting it in the following year's account (i.e. below the line). The accrual of £600 will be shown on the balance sheet at 31 March 19X2 in the current liabilities section under the subheading 'accruals'.

Prepayments

A prepayment is an amount settled in cash during an accounting period for a service or a benefit that is to be received in a subsequent period. If a company, for example, buys a van half way through Year 1 and pays for 12 months tax on it, half of the tax will relate to Year 1 and half to Year 2. It is necessary, therefore, to adjust Year 1's accounts so that only half of the tax is charged to that year's accounts. The other half will eventually be charged to Year 2's accounts. The procedure is illustrated in Exhibit 4.6.

Exhibit 4.6: Accounting for prepayments

Van Tax Account

		£			£
1.1.X1	Balance b/d*	40			
1.7.X1	Bank	100			
			31.12.X1	Profit and loss account	90
			31.12.X1	Balance c/d**	50
		£140			£140
1.1.X2	Balance b/d	50			

*This balance is assumed to be a prepayment arising in the previous period.
**This amount is assumed to be a prepayment for the year to 31 December 19X1.

It will be noted from Exhibit 4.6 that at 31 December 19X1, an amount is transferred from the van tax account to that year's profit and loss account. The double-entry procedure is as follows.

Debit: Profit and loss account   *Credit:* Van tax account
with the annual cost of the
tax on the van.

The double-entry has been completed by debiting the prepayment in next year's accounts (i.e. below the line) and crediting it to this year's accounts (i.e. above the line).

The prepayment of £50 made at 31 December 19X1 will be shown in the balance sheet at that date in the current assets section under the subheading 'prepayments'.

Adjustments for bad debts and provisions for doubtful debts

The fourth main series of adjustments that need to be made in preparing the basic financial statements are those relating to bad debts and provisions for bad debts.

In Chapter 2 it was explained that the realization rule allows profits to be claimed on goods sold even if the cash for them is not received until a future accounting period. This means that a risk is taken in claiming the profit earlier in the period, because if the customer defaults the proprietor might already have taken the profit out of the business. By that time, if it is found that the debt is bad, it is usually too late to do anything about the miscalculation of profit in the earlier period. In order to allow for a possible miscalculation of profit, it is possible to build in an allowance in case any of the trade debtors do default.

The accounting treatment for both bad debts and possible bad debts is outlined below.

Bad Debts

Once it is absolutely certain that a debt is bad, then it must be written off immediately. If credit for the sale has been taken in an earlier period, the bad debt has to be charged against the current profit, even though it relates to an earlier period.

It is considered impractical to revise accounts that may have been prepared some years ago.

The double-entry procedure for writing off bad debts is quite straightforward. The entries are as follows:

Debit: Profit and loss account   *Credit:* Trade debtor's account
with the amount of the bad
debt to be written off.

As far as the balance sheet is concerned, trade debtors will be shown net of any bad debts that have been written off to the profit and loss account.

The provision for doubtful debts account

The profit in future accounting periods will be severely distorted if a number of bad debts occur. It appears prudent, therefore, to allow for the possibility that profit could be overstated if some debtors do subsequently default. This is achieved by setting up what is called a 'provision for doubtful debts account'.

An estimate is made of the likely level of bad debts. The estimate will be based on past experience, and it is usual to express it as a percentage of the outstanding trade debtors as at the period end. The double-entry procedure is as follows:

Debit: Profit and loss account   *Credit:* Provision for doubtful debts
account

with the amount of the provision needed to meet the expected level of bad debts.

The procedure is illustrated in Exhibit 4.7.

Exhibit 4.7: Accounting for doubtful debts

You are presented with the following information for the year to 31 March 19X3:

	£
Trade debtors at 1 April 19X2	20,000
Trade debtors at 31 March 19X3 (including £3,000 of specific bad debts)	33,000
Provision for doubtful debts at 1 April 19X2 5% x 20000	1,000

Note: A provision for doubtful debts is maintained equivalent to 5% of the trade debtors as at the end of the year.

Required:
(a) Calculate the increase required in the doubtful debts provision account for the year to 31 March 19X3; and
(b) show how both the trade debtors and the provision for doubtful debts account would be featured in the balance sheet at 31 March 19X3.

Answer to Exhibit 4.7

(a)	£
Trade debtors as at 31 March 19X3	33,000
Less: Specific bad debts to be written off to the profit and loss account for the year to 31 March 19X3	3,000
	30,000

Provision required: 5% thereof	1,500
Less: Provision at 1 April 19X2	1,000

Increase in the doubtful debts provision account to be
charged to the profit and loss account for the year to
31 March 19X3
500

Tutorial note

The balance on the provision for doubtful debts account will be higher at 31 March
19X3 that it was at 1 April 19X2. This arises because the level of trade debtors
is higher at the end of 19X3 than it was at the end of 19X2. The required increase
in the provision of £500 will be *debited* to the profit and loss account. If it had
been possible to reduce the provision (because of a lower level of trade debtors
at the end of 19X3 compared with 19X2), the decrease would have been *credited*
to the profit and loss account.

(b) Balance sheet extract at 31 March 19X3

	£	£
Current assets		
Trade debtors	30,000	
Less: Provision for doubtful debts	1,500	
		28,500

The treatment of bad debts and doubtful debts in ledger accounts is a
fairly technical and complicated matter. However, as a non-accountant
it is important for you to grasp just two essential points:

1   A debt should never be written off until it is absolutely certain that
    it is bad (because once written off, probably no further attempt may
    be made to recover it).
2   It is prudent to allow for the possibility of some doubtful debts,
    although it is rather a questionable decision to reduce profit in such
    an arbitrary manner.

A great deal of technical matter has been covered in this chapter. It
would now be helpful to bring all the material together in the form of
a comprehensive example; this is done in the next section.

A comprehensive example

In this section the procedures outlined in the chapter in preparing basic
financial statements are examined in Exhibit 4.8. This example is a fairly
detailed one, so take your time in working through it.

Exhibit 4.8

Wayne has been in business for many years. His accountant has extracted the
following trial balance from his books of account as at 31 March 19X5:

	£	£
Bank	1,200	
Capital		33,000
Cash	300	
Drawings	6,000	
Insurance	2,000	
Office expenses	15,000	
Office furniture at cost	5,000	
Office furniture: accumulated depreciation at 1 April 19X4		2,000
Provision for doubtful debts at 1 April 19X4		500
Purchases	55,000	
Salaries	25,000	
Sales		100,000
Stock at 1 April 19X4	10,000	
Trade creditors		4,000
Trade debtors	20,000	
	£139,500	£139,500

Notes: The following additional information is to be taken into account:

1 Stock at 31 March 19X5 was valued at £15,000.
2 The insurance included £500 worth of cover which related to the year to 31 March 19X6.
3 Depreciation is charged on office furniture at 10% per annum of its original cost (it is assumed not to have any residual value).
4 A bad debt of £1,000 included in the trade debtors balance of £20,000 is to be written off.
5 The provision for doubtful debts is to be maintained at a level of 5% of outstanding trade debtors as at 31 March 19X5, i.e. after excluding the bad debt referred to in note 4 above.
6 At 31 March 19X5, there was an amount owing for salaries of £1,000.

Required:
(a) Prepare Wayne's trading, and profit and loss account for the year to 31 March 19X5; and
(b) a balance sheet as at that date.

Answer to Exhibit 4.8

(a) WAYNE
Trading and profit and loss account for the year to 31 March 19X5

	£	£	*Source of entry)*
Sales		100,000	(TB)
Less: Cost of goods sold:			
Opening stock	10,000		(TB)
Purchases	55,000		(TB)
	65,000		
Less: Closing stock	15,000		(QN 1)
		50,000	
	c/f	50,000	

	£	£	
	b/f	50,000	
Gross profit			
Less: Expenses:			
Insurance (£2,000 – £500)	1,500		(Wkg.1)
Office expenses	15,000		(TB)
Depreciation: office furniture	500		(Wkg.2)
Bad debt	1,000		(QN 4)
Increase in provision for doubtful debt	450		(Wkg.3)
Salaries (£25,000 + £1,000)	26,000		(Wkg.4)
		44,450	
Net profit for the year		£5,550	

(b)

WAYNE

Balance sheet at 31 March 19X5

Fixed assets	£ Cost	£ Accumulated depreciation	£ Net book value	(Source of entry)
Office furniture	5,000	2,500	2,500	(TB & Wkg.5)
Current assets				
Stock		15,000		(QN 1)
Trade debtors (£20,000 – £1,000)	19,000			(Wkg.3)
Less: Provision for doubtful debts	950	18,050		(Wkg.3)
Prepayment		500		(QN 2)
Cash at bank		1,200		(TB)
Cash in hand		300		(TB)
		35,050		
Less: Current liabilities				
Trade creditors	4,000			(TB)
Accrual	1,000			(QN 6)
		5,000	30,050	
			£32,550	
Financed by:				
Capital				
Balance at 31 March 19X4			33,000	(TB)
Add: Net profit for the year		5,550		(P&L A/c)
Less: Drawings		6,000	(450)	
			£32,550	

Key:

TB = from trial balance.

QN = extracted straight from the question and related notes.

Wkg. = workings (see below).

P&L A/c = balance obtained from the profit and loss account.

Workings

		£
1	Insurance:	
	As per the trial balance	2,000
	Less: Prepayment (QN 2)	500
	Charge to the profit and loss account	£1,500
2	Depreciation:	
	Office furniture at cost	£5,000
	Depreciation: 10% of the original cost	£500
3	Increase in provision for doubtful debts:	
	Trade debtors at 31 March 19X5	20,000
	Less: Bad debt (QN 4)	1,000
		19,000
	Provision required: 5% thereof	950
	Less: Provision at 1 April 19X4	500
	Increase in provision: charge to profit and loss	£450
4	Salaries:	
	As per the question	25,000
	Add: Accrual (QN 6)	1,000
		26,000
5	Accumulated depreciation:	
	Balance at 1 April 19X4 (as per TB)	2,000
	Add: Depreciation for the year (Wkg.2)	500
	Accumulated depreciation at 31 March 19X5	£2,500

After you have worked through Exhibit 4.8 as carefully as you can, try and do the question without referring to the answer.

Estimating accounting profit

Before leaving this chapter, it may be helpful to summarize the major defects inherent in the traditional historic cost model used in calculating accounting profit.

As a non-accountant, it is most important that you appreciate one vital fact: the traditional method results in an *estimate* of what the accountant thinks that the profit should be. You must not, therefore, place too much reliance on the *absolute* level of accounting profit. Accounting profit can only be as reliable and as accurate as the assumptions upon which it is based. If you regard it as a reasonable estimate (and you accept the assumptions adopted in measuring it), you will not go too far wrong in using the information for decision-making purposes.

Listed below is a summary of the main reasons why you should not place too much reliance on accounting profit:

1   Goods are treated as being sold when the legal title to them changes hands, and not when the customer has paid for them in cash. In practice, the cash for some sales may never be received.
2   Purchases are also regarded as having been purchased when the legal title to them is exchanged, even though some of them may be returned to the supplier.
3   Goods that have not been sold at the period end have to be quantified and valued. This procedure involves a considerable amount of subjective judgement.
4   There is no clear distinction between capital and revenue items.
5   Estimates have to be made in order to allow for accruals and prepayments.
6   The cost of fixed assets is shared out amongst respective accounting periods using methods that are fairly simplistic and highly questionable.
7   Arbitrary reductions in profit are made to allow for doubtful debts.
8   Historic cost accounting makes no allowance for inflation. In a period of inflation, for example, the *value* of £100 at the beginning of a period is not the same as £100 at the end of the period.

The above disadvantages of historic cost accounting are extremely serious, but to date accountants have not been able to recommend any better model. If at this stage, therefore, you do not feel to have much confidence in accounting information, then take comfort in the old adage that 'it is better to be vaguely right than precisely wrong'!

Conclusion

The construction of basic financial statements has been examined in some detail in this chapter. You should now be in a far better position to assess the relevance and reliability of any accounting information that you come across.

The material that has been covered so far in this book provides a broad foundation for all the remaining chapters. It is essential that before moving on to the other chapters, you satisfy yourself that you really do understand the mechanics behind the preparation of basic financial statements. To test your understanding of this subject, you are recommended to work through all of the exhibits once again, and then to attempt some of the following exercises.

Questions

4.1 The following trial balance has been extracted from Ethel's books of account as at 31 January 19X1:

	Dr £	Cr £
Capital		10,000
Cash	3,000	
Creditors		3,000
Debtors	6,000	
Office expenses	11,000	
Premises	8,000	
Purchases	20,000	
Sales		35,000
	£48,000	£48,000

Required:
Prepare Ethel's trading, and profit and loss account for the year to 31 January 19X1, and a balance sheet as at that date.

4.2 Marion has been in business for some years. The following trial balance has been extracted from her books of account as at 28 February 19X2.

	Dr £000	Cr £000
Bank	4	
Buildings	50	
Capital		50
Cash	2	
Creditors		24
Debtors	30	
Drawings	55	
Heat and light	10	
Miscellaneous expenses	25	
Purchases	200	
Sales		400
Wages and salaries	98	
	£474	£474

Required:
Prepare Marion's trading and profit and loss account for the year to 28 February 19X2 and a balance sheet as at that date.

4.3 The following trial balance has been extracted from the books of Garswood as at 31 March 19X3.

	Dr	Cr
	£	£
Advertising	2,300	
Bank	300	
Capital		55,700
Cash	100	
Discounts allowed	100	
Discounts received		600
Drawings	17,000	
Electricity	1,300	
Investments	4,000	
Investment income received		400
Office equipment	10,000	
Other creditors		800
Other debtors	1,500	
Machinery	20,000	
Purchases	21,400	
Purchases returns		1,400
Sales		63,000
Sales returns	3,000	
Stationery	900	
Trade creditors		5,200
Trade debtors	6,500	
Wages	38,700	
	£127,100	£127,100

Required:
Prepare Garswood's trading, and profit and loss account for the year to 31
March 19X3, and a balance sheet as at that date.

4.4 The following information has been extracted from Lathom's books of
account for the year to 30 April 19X4:

	£
Purchases	45,000
Sales	60,000
Stock (at 1 May 19X3)	3,000
Stock (at 30 April 19X4)	4,000

Required:
(a) Prepare Lathom's trading account for the year to 30 April 19X4; and
(b) state where the stock at 30 April 19X4 would be shown on the balance
      sheet as at that date.

4.5 Rufford presents you with the following information for the year to 31 March 19X5:

	£
Purchases	48,000
Purchases returns	3,000
Sales	82,000
Sales returns	4,000
Stock at 1 April 19X4	4,000

He is not sure how to value the stock as at 31 March 19X5. Three methods have been suggested. They all result in different closing stock values, viz.:

Method 1	£8,000
Method 2	£16,000
Method 3	£4,000

Required:
(a) Calculate the effect on gross profit for the year to 31 March 19X5 by using each of the three methods of stock valuation; and
(b) other things being equal, state the effect on gross profit for the year to 31 March 19X6 if method 1 is used instead of method 2.

4.6 Standish has been trading for some years. The following trial balance has been extracted from his books of account as at 31 May 19X6:

	Dr £	Cr £
Capital		22,400
Cash	1,200	
Creditors		4,300
Debtors	6,000	
Drawings	5,500	
Furniture and fittings	8,000	
Heating and lighting	1,500	
Miscellaneous expenses	6,700	
Purchases	52,000	
Sales		79,000
Stock (at 1 June 19X5)	7,000	
Wages and salaries	17,800	
	£105,700	£105,700

Note: Stock at 31 May 19X6: £12,000.

Required:
Prepare Standish's trading, and profit and loss account for the year to 31 May 19X6, and a balance sheet as at that date.

4.7 Witton commenced business on 1 July 19X6. The following trial balance was extracted from his books of account as at 30 June 19X7:

	Dr	Cr
	£	£
Capital		3,000
Cash	500	
Drawings	4,000	
Creditors		1,500
Debtors	3,000	
Motor car at cost	5,000	
Office expenses	8,000	
Purchases	14,000	
Sales		30,000
	£34,500	£34,500

Additional information:
1   Stocks at 30 June 19X7: £2,000.
2   The motor car is to be depreciated at a rate of 20% per annum on cost; it was purchased on 1 July 19X6.

Required:
Prepare Witton's trading, and profit and loss account for the year to 30 June 19X7, and a balance sheet as at that date.

4.8   Croxteth has been in the retail trade for many years. The following is his trial balance as at 31 July 19X8:

	Dr	Cr
	£	£
Bank	2,000	
Capital		35,000
Creditors		4,800
Delivery vans at cost	40,000	
Depreciation:		
Delivery vans (at 1 August 19X7)		12,000
Shop equipment (at 1 August 19X7)		2,400
Drawings	8,000	
Purchases	70,000	
Sales		85,000
Shop equipment at cost	8,000	
Shop expenses	7,200	
Stock (at 1 August 19X7	4,000	
	£139,200	£139,200

Additional information:
1   Stock at 31 July 19X8: £14,000.
2   Depreciation on delivery vans at a rate of 30% per annum on cost, and on shop equipment at a rate of 10% per annum on cost.

Required:
Prepare Croxteth's trading, and profit and loss account for the year to 31 July 19X8, and a balance sheet as at that date.

4.9 The following is an extract from Barrow's balance sheet at 31 August 19X8:

Fixed Assets	Cost	Accumulated depreciation	Net book value
	£	£	£
Land	200,000	—	200,000
Buildings	150,000	60,000	90,000
Plant	55,000	37,500	17,500
Vehicles	45,000	28,800	16,200
Furniture	20,000	12,600	7,400
	£470,000	£138,900	331,100

Barrow's depreciation policy is as follows:

1 a full year's depreciation is charged in the year of acquisition, but none in the year of disposal;
2 no depreciation is charged on land;
3 buildings are depreciated at an annual rate of 2% on cost;
4 plant is depreciated at an annual rate of 5% on cost after allowing for an estimated residual value of £5,000;
5 vehicles are depreciated on a reduced balance basis at an annual rate of 40% on the reduced balance;
6 furniture is depreciated on a straight-line basis at an annual rate of 10% on cost after allowing for an estimated residual value of £2,000.

Additional information:
1 During the year to 31 August 19X9, new furniture was purchased for the office. It cost £3,000 and it is to be depreciated on the same basis as the old furniture. Its estimated residual value is £300.
2 There were no additions to or disposals of any other fixed assets during the year to 31 August 19X9.

Required:
(a) Calculate the depreciation charge for each of the fixed asset groupings for the year to 31 August 19X9; and
(b) show how the fixed assets would appear in Barrow's balance sheet as at 31 August 19X9.

4.10 Pine started business on 1 October 19X1. The following is his trial balance at 30 September 19X2:

	£	£
Capital		6,000
Cash	400	
Creditors		5,900
Debtors	5,000	
Furniture at cost	8,000	
General expenses	14,000	
Insurance	2,000	
c/f	29,400	11,900

		£	£
b/f		29,400	11,900
Purchases		21,000	
Sales			40,000
Telephone		1,500	
		£51,900	£51,900

The following information was obtained after the trial balance had been prepared:

1 Stock at 30 September 19X2: £3,000.
2 Furniture is to be depreciated at a rate of 15% on cost.
3 At 30 September 19X2, Pine owed £500 for telephone expenses, and insurance had been prepaid by £200.

Required:
Prepare Pine's trading, and profit and loss account for the year to 30 September 19X2, and a balance sheet as at that date.

4.11 Dale has been in business for some years. The following is his trial balance at 31 October 19X3:

	Dr	Cr
	£	£
Bank	700	
Capital		85,000
Depreciation (at 1 November 19X2):		
Office equipment		14,000
Vehicles		4,000
Drawings	12,300	
Heating and lighting	3,000	
Office expenses	27,000	
Office equipment, at cost	35,000	
Rates	12,000	
Purchases	240,000	
Sales		350,000
Stock (at 1 November 19X2)	20,000	
Trade creditors		21,000
Trade debtors	61,000	
Vehicles at cost	16,000	
Wages and salaries	47,000	
	£474,000	£474,000

Additional information (not taken into account when compiling the above trial balance) is as follows:
1 Stock at 31 October 19X3: £26,000.
2 Amount owing for electricity at 31 October 19X3: £1,500.
3 At 31 October 19X3, £2,000 had been paid in advance for rates.

4 Depreciation is to be charged on the office equipment for the year to 31 October 19X3 at a rate of 20% on cost and on the vehicles at a rate of 25% on cost.

Required:
Prepare Dale's trading, and profit and loss account for the year to 31 October 19X3, and a balance sheet as at that date.

4.12 The following information relates to Astley for the year to 30 November 19X4:

Item	Cash paid during the year to 30 November 19X4 £	As at 1 December 19X3 Accruals/ Prepayments £	£	As at 30 November 19X4 Accruals/ Prepayments £	£
Electricity	26,400	5,200	—	8,300	—
Gas	40,100	—	—	—	4,900
Insurance	25,000	—	12,000	—	14,000
Rates	16,000	—	4,000	6,000	—
Telephone	3,000	1,500	—	—	200
Wages	66,800	1,800	—	—	—

Required:
(a) Calculate the charge to the profit and loss account for the year to 30 November 19X4 for each of the above items.
(b) Demonstrate what amounts for accruals and prepayments would be shown in the balance sheet as at 30 November 19X4.

4.13 Duxbury started in business on 1 January 19X3. The following is his trial balance as at 31 December 19X3:

	Dr £	Cr £
Capital		40,000
Cash	300	
Delivery van, at cost	20,000	
Drawings	10,600	
Office expenses	12,100	
Purchases	65,000	
Sales		95,000
Trade creditors		5,000
Trade debtors	32,000	
	£140,000	£140,000

Additional information:
1 Stock at 31 December 19X3 was valued at £10,000.
2 At 31 December 19X3, an amount of £400 was outstanding for telephone expenses, and the rates had been prepaid by £500.

3   The delivery van is to be depreciated at a rate of 20% per annum on cost.
4   Duxbury decides to set aside a provision for doubtful debts equal to 5% of trade debtors as at the end of the year.

Required:
Prepare Duxbury's trading, and profit and loss account for the year to 31 December 19X3, and a balance sheet as at that date.

4.14   Beech is a retailer. Most of his sales are made on credit terms. The following information relates to the first four years that he has been in business:

Year:	19X4	19X5	19X6	19X7
Trade debtors as at				
31 January:	£60,000	£55,000	£65,000	£70,000

The trade is one which experiences a high level of bad debts. Accordingly, Beech decides to set aside a provision for doubtful debts equivalent to 10% of trade debtors as at the end of the year.

Required:
(a)   Show how the provision for doubtful debts would be disclosed in the respective balance sheets as at 31 January 19X4, 19X5, 19X6 and 19X7; and
(b)   calculate the increase/decrease in provision for doubtful debts transferred to the respective profit and loss accounts for each of the four years.

4.15   The following is Ash's trial balance as at 31 March 19X5:

	Dr £	Cr £
Bank		4,000
Capital		20,500
Depreciation (at 1 April 19X4): furniture		3,600
Drawings	10,000	
Electricity	2,000	
Furniture, at cost	9,000	
Insurance	1,500	
Miscellaneous expenses	65,800	
Provision for doubtful debts (at 1 April 19X4)		1,200
Purchases	80,000	
Sales		150,000
Stock (at 1 April 19X4)	10,000	
Trade creditors		20,000
Trade debtors	21,000	
	£199,300	£199,300

Additional information:
1 Stock at 31 March 19X5: £15,000.
2 At 31 March 19X5 there was a specific bad debt of £6,000. This was to be written off.
3 Furniture is to be depreciated at a rate of 10% per annum on cost.
4 At 31 March 19X5, Ash owes the electricity board £600, and £100 had been paid in advance for insurance.
5 The provision for doubtful debts is to be made equal to 10% of trade debtors as at the end of the year.

Required:
Prepare Ash's trading, and profit and loss account for the year to 31 March 19X5, and a balance sheet as at that date.

4.16 Elm is a wholesaler. The following is his trial balance at 30 June 19X6:

	Dr £	Cr £
Advertising	3,000	
Bank	400	
Capital		73,500
Cash	100	
Depreciation (at 1 July 19X5):		
furniture		1,800
vehicles		7,000
Discounts allowed	400	
Discounts received		500
Drawings	10,000	
Electricity	3,200	
Furniture, at cost	12,000	
General expenses	28,900	
Interest on investments		800
Investments, at cost	5,000	
Provision for doubtful debts		
(at 1 July 19X5)		2,300
Purchases	645,000	
Purchases returns		2,000
Rates	6,000	
Sales		820,000
Sales returns	4,000	
Stock (at 1 July 19X5)	47,000	
Telephone	1,300	
Trade creditors		13,000
Trade debtors	42,000	
Vehicles, at cost	35,000	
Wages and salaries	77,600	
	£920,900	£920,900

Additional information:
1 Stock at 30 June 19X6: £50,000.
2 The provision for doubtful debts is to be made equal to 5% of trade debtors as at 30 June 19X6.
3 Furniture is to be depreciated at a rate of 15% on cost, and the vehicles at a rate of 20% on a reducing balance basis.
4 At 30 June 19X6 amount owing for electricity, £300, rates paid in advance £1,000.

Required:
Prepare Elm's trading, and profit and loss account for the year to 30 June 19X6, and a balance sheet as at that date.

4.17 Lime's business has had liquidity problems for some months. The following trial balance was extracted from his books of account as at 30 September 19X7:

	Dr £	Cr £
Bank		15,200
Capital		19,300
Cash from sale of office equipment		500
Depreciation (at 1 October 19X6):		
office equipment		22,000
Drawings	16,000	
Insurance	1,800	
Loan (long-term from Cedar)		50,000
Loan interest	7,500	
Miscellaneous expenses	57,700	
Office equipment, at cost	44,000	
Provision for doubtful debts		
(at 1 October 19X6)		2,000
Purchases	320,000	
Rates	10,000	
Sales		372,000
Stock (at 1 October 19X6)	36,000	
Trade creditors		105,000
Trade debtors	93,000	
	£586,000	£586,000

Additional information:
1 Stock at 30 September 19X7: £68,000.
2 At 30 September 19X7, accrual for rates of £2,000 and insurance prepaid of £200.
3 Depreciation on office equipment is charged at a rate of 25% on cost. During the year, office equipment costing £4,000 had been sold for £500. Accumulated depreciation on this equipment amounted to £3,000. Lime's depreciation policy is to charge a full year's depreciation in the year of

acquisition, and none in the year of disposal.

4 Specific bad debts of £13,000 are to be written off.

5 The provision for doubtful debts is to be made equal to 10% of outstanding trade debtors as at 30 September 19X7.

Required:

Prepare Lime's trading, and profit and loss account for the year to 30 September 19X7, and a balance sheet as at that date.

4.18 Teak has extracted the following trial balance from his books of account as at 31 December 19X8:

	Dr £	Cr £
Building society deposit	20,000	
Capital		66,500
Cash at bank and in hand	400	
Depreciation:		
Plant and equipment		
(at 1 January 19X8)		30,000
vehicles (at 1 January 19X8)		16,000
Dividends received (interim)		100
Interest received from building society		700
Interest received from Gray		500
Investments at cost	5,000	
Loan to Gray (repayable 1 October 19X9	10,000	
Office expenses	39,000	
Plant and equipment at cost	50,000	
Purchases	83,000	
Sales		164,000
Stock (at 1 January 19X8)	2,800	
Trade debtors/trade creditors	13,200	22,200
Vehicles at cost	64,000	
Vehicle expenses	12,600	
	£300,000	£300,000

Additional information:

1 Stock at 31 December 19X8: £15,800.

2 During the year to 31 December 19X8, Teak had used some goods (purchased through the business) for his own personal consumption. At cost price these were estimated to be worth £6,000. No entries had been made in the books of account to record this transaction.

3 At 31 December 19X8 there was an amount owing for office expenses of £1,200. At the same date Teak was due to receive interest from the building society of £800, and a final dividend of £600 from a company in which he had some investments.

4 Depreciation is to be charged on plant and equipment at a rate of 30% per annum on cost, and on vehicles at a rate of 25% on the reduced balance.

5   Office expenses include Teak's drawings for the year of £9,000.

Required:
Prepare Teak's trading, and profit and loss account for the year to 31 December 19X8, and a balance sheet as at that date.

Additional questions (without answers)

4.19   Daly's book-keeper has extracted the following trial balance as at 31 January 19X1:

	Dr	Cr
	£000	£000
Administrative expenses	63	
Capital		252
Cash at bank and in hand	9	
Creditors		8
Debtors	1	
Drawings	18	
Furniture and fittings at cost	200	
:accumulated depreciation (at 1 February 19X0)		90
Motor vehicles at cost	800	
:accumulated depreciation (at 1 February 19X0)		480
Purchases	500	
Rent, rates, heat and light	9	
Sales		760
Stock (at 1 February 19X0)	35	
Trade creditors		170
Trade debtors	70	
Wages and salaries	55	
	£1,760	£1,760

Additional information:
1   Stock at 31 January 19X1: £40,000.
2   Depreciation is charged on the fixed assets as follows:
      Furniture and fittings: 15% on cost;
      Motor vehicles: 60% on the reduced balance.
3   A trade debt of £10,000 is to be written off.
4   A provision for bad and doubtful debts is to be established equivalent to 5% of outstanding trade debtors as at the end of the year.

Required:
Prepare Daly's trading and profit and loss account for the year to 31 January 19X1, and a balance sheet as at that date.

4.20 Patsy Chan has been in business for several years. The following trial balance was extracted from her books of account as at 30 September 19X9:

	Dr £000	Cr £000
Bad debt	15	
Capital		653
Carriage inwards	10	
Carriage outwards	34	
Cash at bank and in hand	7	
Discounts allowed	18	
Discounts received		27
Dividends received		2
Drawings	12	
Investments at cost	20	
Motor vehicles at cost	600	
:accumulated depreciation (at 1 October 19X8)		300
Office expenses	35	
Plant and equipment at cost	240	
:accumulated depreciation (at 1 October 19X8)		144
Provision for bad and doubtful debts (at 1 October 19X8)		3
Purchases	570	
Salaries	105	
Sales		900
Stock (at 1 October 19X8)	200	
Trade creditors		71
Trade debtors	160	
Wages	74	
	£2,100	£2,100

Additional information:
1 Stock at 30 September 19X9: £180,000.
2 Depreciation is charged as follows:
     Motor vehicles: 25% on cost;
     Plant and equipment: 30% on cost.
3 Wages owing at 30 September 19X9: £2,000.
4 Business rates paid in advance at 30 September 19X9: £5,000.
5 A provision for bad and doubtful debts is maintained equivalent to 2½% of outstanding trade debtors as at the end of the year.

Required:
Prepare Patsy Chan's trading and profit and loss account for the year to 30 September 19X9, and a balance sheet as at that date.

5 Manufacturing accounts

Learning objectives_____

1 explain the nature and purpose of a manufacturing account;

2 prepare a simple manufacturing account;

   and

3 incorporate such an account into a set of financial statements.

The two previous chapters have dealt almost entirely with trading entities. It has been assumed that when goods have been purchased, no further work has been necessary to put them into a saleable condition before they were eventually sold at a profit.

There are of course many businesses whose main purpose is simply to buy *finished* goods, and then to sell them to someone else at a profit. These types of businesses are known as *trading* entities. There are, however, other types of businesses who *manufacture* their own products. They may buy materials that require further work to be done on them before they can be sold. Such materials are known as *raw* materials.

In compiling a trading account for manufacturing entities, it is not possible to add purchases to the opening stock and then to deduct the closing stock. The entity will purchase raw materials and further work will need to be done on them before they can be put in their *finished* goods state. It may well be that in manufacturing entities, a considerable amount of work needs to be done to the raw materials before they can be sold to customers. The cost of such work is usually shown in a *manufacturing* account.

Manufacturing accounts form the subject of this chapter. They are similar to trading and profit and loss accounts in three respects:

1 they form part of the double-entry system;
2 they are used as summary statements at the end of the financial period, and
3 they can be presented in either the horizontal or the vertical format.

The chapter falls into two main parts. The first part illustrates the contents of a manufacturing account, and the second part explains how such an account is constructed.

Contents

A manufacturing account mainly records manufacturing costs, and it is unlikely that any income will form part of such an account. The costs which are debited to the account can be divided into two important categories. These are as follows:

1 direct costs (i.e. direct to the product, such as materials and labour); and
2 indirect costs (i.e. indirect to the product, such as canteen expenses and factory management).

Direct and indirect costs may be defined as follows:

- A direct cost is a cost which is easily identifiable with a particular department or product.
- An indirect cost is a cost which is *not* easily identifiable with a particular department or product.

The manufacturing account is usually broken down into three main sections. They are as follows:

1 direct materials.
2 direct labour; and
3 indirect costs.

These sections are sometimes known as the *elements of cost*, and Exhibit 5.1 illustrates the format of a basic manufacturing account classified in such a way. The account is shown in the vertical format. As explained in the last chapter, the vertical format is considered easier to follow for non-specialists unused to double-entry book-keeping. A detailed explanation of the items in the account follows the exhibit.

Exhibit 5.1: Format of a basic manufacturing account

	£000	£000
Direct costs (1)		
Direct material (2)	20	
Direct labour (3)	70	
Other direct expenses (4)	5	
Prime cost (5)		95
Manufacturing overhead (6)		
Indirect material cost (7)	3	
Indirect labour cost (7)	7	
Other indirect expenses (7)	10	
Total manufacturing overhead incurred (8)		20
Total manufacturing costs incurred (9)		115
	c/f	115

	b/f	115
Work-in-progress (10)		
Opening work-in-progress	10	
Closing work-in-progress	(15)	(5)
Manufacturing cost of goods produced (11)		110
Manufacturing profit (12)		11
Market value of goods produced transferred to the trading account (13)		£121

Notes:

1 The number shown after each item refers to the tutorial notes (see below). The amounts have been inserted purely for illustrative purposes.
2 The term 'factory' or 'work' is sometimes substituted for the term *manufacturing.*

Tutorial notes

1 *Direct costs.* The exhibit relates to a *company's* manufacturing account. It is assumed that the direct costs listed for materials, labour and other expenses relate to those expenses which have been easy to identify with the specific products that the company manufactures.
2 *Direct materials.* The charge for direct materials will be calculated as follows:

Direct material cost = (Opening stock of raw materials + purchases of raw materials) – Closing stock of raw materials

The total of direct material cost is sometimes referred to as *materials consumed.* Direct materials will include all the raw material costs and component parts which have been easy to identify with particular products.
3 *Direct labour.* Direct labour will include all those employment costs that have been easy to identify with particular products.
4 *Other direct expenses.* Besides direct material and direct labour costs, there are sometimes other direct expenses that are easy to identify with particular products, for example, the cost of hiring a specific machine. Such expenses are relatively rare.
5 *Prime cost.* The total of direct material costs, direct labour costs and other direct expenses is known as prime cost.
6 *Manufacturing overhead.* Overhead is the collective term given to represent the total of all indirect costs, so any manufacturing costs that are not easy to identify with specific products will be classified separately under this heading.
7 *Indirect material cost, indirect labour cost and other indirect expenses.* Manufacturing overhead will probably be shown separately under these three headings.
8 *Total manufacturing overhead incurred.* This item represents the total of indirect material cost, indirect labour cost and other indirect expenses.
9 *Total manufacturing costs incurred.* The total of prime cost and the total of total manufacturing overhead incurred equals the total manufacturing costs incurred.
10 *Work-in-progress.* Work-in-progress represents the estimated cost of incomplete work that is not yet ready to be transferred to finished stock. There will usually be some opening and closing work-in-progress.

11 *Manufacturing cost of goods produced.* The manufacturing cost of goods produced equals the total manufacturing costs incurred plus (or minus) the difference between the opening and closing work-in-progress.

12 *Manufacturing profit.* The manufacturing cost of goods produced is sometimes transferred to the finished goods stock account without any addition for manufacturing profit. If this is the case the double-entry effect is as follows:

Debit: Finished goods stock account   *Credit:* Manufacturing account
with the manufacturing cost of goods produced.

The finished goods stock account is the equivalent of the purchases account in a trading organization.

Sometimes, however, a manufacturing profit is added to the manufacturing cost of goods produced before it is transferred to the trading account. The main purpose of this adjustment is to enable management to compare more fairly the company's total manufacturing cost inclusive of profit with outside prices (since such prices will also be normally inclusive of profit). The profit added to the manufacturing cost of goods produced may simply be an appropriate percentage, or it may represent the level of profit that the industry generally expects to earn. Any profit element added to the manufacturing cost (irrespective of how it is calculated) is an internal book-keeping arrangement, as the profit has not been *realized* or earned outside the business. The double-entry is effected as follows:

Debit: Manufacturing account   *Credit:* Profit and loss account
with the manufacturing profit.

13 *Market value of goods produced.* As explained in 12 above, the market value of goods produced is the amount which will be transferred (that is, debited) to the trading account.

You are now recommended to study Exhibit 5.1 most carefully, along with the accompanying tutorial notes. Once you are clear about its structure, you can move on to the next section.

Construction

The construction of a manufacturing account can best be observed by reference to a simple example. This is illustrated in Exhibit 5.2.

Exhibit 5.2

The following balances, *inter alia*, have been extracted from the books of the Wren Manufacturing Company as at 31 March 19X5:

	Dr £
Carriage inwards (on raw materials)	6,000
Direct expenses	3,000
Direct wages	25,000
Factory administration	6,000
Factory heat and light	500
Factory power	1,500
Factory rent and rates	2,000

Factory supervisory costs	5,000
Purchase of raw materials	56,000
Raw materials stock (at 1 April 19X4)	4,000
Work-in-progress (at 1 April 19X4)	5,000

Additional information:
1 The stock of raw materials at 31 March 19X5 was valued at £6,000.
2 The work-in-progress at 31 March 19X5 was valued at £8,000.
3 A profit loading of 50% is added to the total cost of manufacture.

Required:
Prepare Wren's manufacturing account for the year to 31 March 19X5.

The answer to the exhibit is shown below. You are recommended to work through it very slowly, paying particular attention to its format. To help you understand how it has been constructed, some tutorial notes have been added to the solution.

Answer to Exhibit 5.2

Wren Manufacturing Company
Manufacturing account for the year to 31 March 19X5

	£	£	£
Direct materials			
Raw material stock at 1 April 19X4		4,000	
Purchases	56,000		
Carriage inwards (1)	6,000	62,000	
		66,000	
Less: Raw material stock at 31 March 19X5		6,000	
Cost of materials consumed			60,000
Direct wages			25,000
Direct expenses			3,000
Prime cost			88,000
Other manufacturing costs (2)			
Administration		6,000	
Heat and light		500	
Power		1,500	
Rent and rates		2,000	
Supervisory		5,000	
Total manufacturing overhead expenses			15,000
Total manufacturing costs incurred			103,000
Work-in-progress			
Add: Work-in-progress at 1 April 19X4		5,000	
Less: Work-in-progress at 31 March 19X5		(8,000)	(3,000)
Manufacturing cost of goods produced			100,000
Manufacturing profit (50%) (3)			50,000
Market value of goods produced (4)			£150,000

Tutorial notes

1   Carriage inwards (i.e. the cost of transporting goods to the factory) is normally regarded as being part of the cost of purchases. 2   Other manufacturing costs include production overhead expenses. In practice, there would be a considerable number of other manufacturing costs. 3   A profit loading of 50% has been added to the manufacturing cost (see Note 3 of the question). The manufacturing profit is a debit entry in the manufacturing account. The corresponding credit entry will eventually be made in the profit and loss account. 4   The market value of goods produced will be transferred to the finished goods stock account.

You are now recommended to work through Exhibit 5.2 again, but this time without reference to the answer.

A comprehensive example

In Exhibit 5.2 the manufacturing account was dealt with in isolation. In order to understand how the manufacturing account complements the trading account, the profit and loss account and the balance sheet, it is necessary to work through a comprehensive example. This is done in Exhibit 5.3. Once again, you are recommended to study the solution along with the tutorial notes.

Exhibit 5.3

The following trial balance has been extracted from the books of account of the Knight Manufacturing Company as at 31 December 19X3:

	Dr £	Cr £
Bank overdraft		2,500
Capital		24,000
Direct wages	75,000	
Discounts allowed	3,000	
Discounts received		1,000
Drawings	8,000	
Finished goods stock (at 1 January 19X3)	15,000	
Long-term loan		5,000
Long-term loan interest	500	
Manufacturing expenses (administration and supervisory)	35,000	
Motor van at cost	5,000	
Motor van: depreciation (at 1 January 19X3)		2,000
Motor van expenses	850	
Office expenses	1,650	
Plant and equipment at cost	28,000	
Plant and equipment: depreciation (at 1 January 19X3)		14,000
Purchases of raw materials	50,000	
Raw material stock (at 1 January 19X3)	6,000	
Sales		250,000
c/f	228,000	298,500

		£	£
	b/f	228,000	298,500
Salaries (administration)		29,000	
Salaries (selling and distribution)		14,000	
Trade creditors			12,500
Trade debtors		30,000	
Work-in-progress (at 1 January 19X3)		10,000	
		£311,000	£311,000

Additional information:
1 Stocks at 31 December 19X3 were valued as follows:

	£
Raw materials	7,000
Work-in-progress	12,000
Finished goods	18,000

2 Depreciation is to be charged on the motor van at a rate of 20% on cost, and on the plant and equipment at a rate of 25% on cost.
3 There were no accruals or prepayments at the end of the year.
4 A manufacturing profit of 20% should be added to the manufacturing cost of goods produced.
5 The motor van is used entirely for the delivery of goods to customers.

Required:
(a) Prepare Knight's manufacturing, trading and profit and loss account for the year to 31 December 19X3; and (b) a balance sheet as at that date.

This looks to be a formidable question, but remember that you have dealt with most of the items in the previous chapter. Only the manufacturing account details are new.

Now here is the solution. Take your time in working through it.

Answer to Exhibit 5.3

(a) Knight Manufacturing Company
Manufacturing, trading and profit and loss account for the year to
31 December 19X3

	£	£	£	£
Sales (1)				250,000
Less: Cost of goods sold:				
Finished stock at				
1 January 19X3			15,000	
Market value of finished				
goods produced (2):				
Direct materials				
Raw material stock at				
1 January 19X3		6,000		
Purchases of raw materials		50,000		
		56,000		
c/f		56,000	15,000	250,000

	£	£	£	£
	b/f	56,000	15,000	250,000
Less: Raw material stock at 31 December 19X3		7,000		
Cost of materials consumed		49,000		
Direct wages		75,000		
Prime cost		124,000		
Other manufacturing costs:				
Administration and supervisory	35,000			
Pland and equipment depreciation	7,000			
		42,000		
Total manufacturing costs incurred		166,000		
Work-in-progress:				
Add: Work-in-progress at 1 January 19X3	10,000			
Less: Work-in-progress at 31 December 19X3	(12,000)	(2,000)		
Manufacturing costs of goods produced		164,000		
Manufacturing profit (20%)		32,800	196,800	
			211,800	
Less: Finished stock at 31 December 19X3			18,000	193,800
Gross profit (3)				56,200
Add: Other incomes (4):				
Manufacturing profit			32,800	
Discounts received			1,000	33,800
				90,000
Less: Other expenses (4):				
Administration				
Office expenses			1,650	
Salaries			29,000	30,650
Selling and distribution:				
Motor van depreciation			1,000	
Motor van expenses			850	
Salaries			14,000	15,850
Finance				
Discounts allowed			3,000	
Loan interest			500	3,500
				50,000
Net profit for the year				£40,000

(b)

Knight Manufacturing Company
Balance sheet at 31 December 19X3

	£	£	£
Fixed assets (5)	Cost	*Accumulated depreciation*	*Net book value*
Plant and equipment (6)	28,000	21,000	7,000
Motor van (7)	5,000	3,000	2,000
(8)	£33,000	24,000	9,000
Current assets			
Stocks: Raw materials (9)	7,000		
Work-in-progress (9)	12,000		
Finished goods (9)	18,000	37,000	
Trade debtors		30,000	
		67,000	
Less: Current liabilities:			
Trade creditors	12,500		
Bank overdraft	2,500	15,000	52,000
			£61,000
Financed by:			£
Capital			
Balance at 1 January 19X3			24,000
Add: Net profit for the year		40,000	
Less: Drawings		8,000	32,000
Proprietor's capital (10)			56,000
Loan (11)			5,000
			£61,000

Tutorial notes

1 Notice that with the vertical format the account begins with sales.
2 A detailed explanation is then given of how the manufacturing cost of goods produced has been arrived at. This part of the manufacturing account is similar to the one used in Exhibit 5.2.
3 At the gross profit stage both the manufacturing account and the trading account have been effectively completed.
4 If the information permits, it is customary to sectionalize other incomes and expenses into appropriate categories. Thus in this example the other expenses have been classified into administration, selling and distribution, and finance expenses.
5 As explained in the last chapter, the fixed assets should be analysed into different classes of assets. The cost, accumulated depreciation, and the net book value for each group of fixed asset should also be shown.
6 The accumulated depreciation of £21,000 for plant and equipment has been obtained from the trial balance by taking the accumulated depreciation of £14,000 as at 1 January 19X3 and adding the £7,000 depreciation charge for the year to 31 December 19X3 to it. The question states that depreciation is to be charged for that year at a rate of 25% on the cost of the machinery (i.e. 25% × £28,000).

7 The accumulated depreciation charge on the motor van has been calculated by taking the accumulated depreciation balance of £2,000 as at 1 January 19X3 from the trial balance, and adding it to the £1,000 depreciation charge for the year. The question states that depreciation is to be charged on the motor van at a rate of 20% of its cost (i.e. 20% × £5,000).

8 The total net book value for all classes of fixed assets is required for balancing purposes.

9 Details for the different categories of stock should be disclosed.

10 It is useful to disclose separately the total amount of capital invested by the proprietor in the business.

11 The question states that the loan is a long-term loan. It should be shown separately as part of the capital section, and not as part of the proprietor's capital.

Exhibit 5.3 is quite a complicated example. You should now work through it again, but without reference to the solution.

Conclusion

A manufacturing account needs to be prepared for those business entities that undertake further work on goods purchased before they are ready to be sold to customers. Manufacturing accounts are normally prepared annually along with all the other basic financial statements.

Some entities may try to prepare a manufacturing account more frequently than once a year, but the traditional double-entry book-keeping system is not really designed to cope with very frequent reporting requirements. As explained in Chapter 1, a cost and management system helps to overcome some of the disadvantages of financial accounting. Those entities that operate a cost and management accounting system will not normally find it necessary to prepare a manufacturing account.

Cost and management accounting forms Part 3 of this book. In the meantime, some further and important aspects of financial accounting will be covered in the next three chapters.

Questions

5.1 The following information relates to Megg for the year to 31 January 19X1:

	£000
Stocks at 1 February 19X0:	
Raw material	10
Work-in-progress	17
Direct wages	65
Factory: Administration	27
Heat and light	9
Indirect wages	13
Purchases of raw materials	34
Stocks at 31 January 19X1:	
Raw material	12
Work-in-progress	14

Required:
Prepare Megg's manufacturing account for the year to 31 January 19X1.

5.2   The following balances have been extracted from the books of account of Moor for the year to 28 February 19X2:

	£
Administration expenses	33,000
Direct wages	50,000
Factory indirect wages	27,700
Purchase of raw materials	127,500
Sales	250,000
Selling and distribution expenses	10,200
Stocks at 1 March 19X1:	
Raw materials	13,000
Work-in-progress	8,400
Finished goods	24,000
Stocks at 28 February 19X2:	
Raw materials	15,500
Work-in-progress	6,300
Finished goods	30,000

Required:
Prepare Moor's manufacturing, trading, and profit and loss account for the year to 28 February 19X2.

5.3   The following balances have been extracted from the books of Stuart for the year to 31 March 19X3:

	Dr £000	Cr £000
Administration: Factory	230	
General	112	
Bank	7	
Capital at 1 April 19X2		264
Creditors		335
Debtors	184	
Direct wages	330	
Miscellaneous expenses	16	
Plant and machinery: At cost	594	
Accumulated depreciation at 31 March 19X3		199
Purchases of raw materials	1,123	
Sales		1,932
Stock at 1 April 19X2:		
Raw material	38	
Work-in-progress	29	
Finished goods	67	
	£2,730	£2,730

Additional information:

Stocks at 31 March 19X3:	£000
Raw materials	44
Work-in-progress	42
Finished goods	65

Required:

Prepare Stuart's manufacturing, trading, and profit and loss account for the year to 31 March 19X3, and a balance sheet as at that date.

5.4 The following balances have been extracted from the books of the David and Peter Manufacturing Company as at 30 April 19X4.

	Dr £000	Cr £000
Administration salaries	76	
Capital at 1 May 19X3		218
Cash	18	
Creditors		102
Debtors	116	
Direct wages	70	
Drawings	26	
Factory equipment: At cost	360	
Accumulated depreciation at 1 May 19X3		180
General factory expenses	13	
General office expenses	9	
Heat and light (factory 3/4; general 1/4)	52	
Purchase of raw material	100	
Sales		420
Stocks at 1 May 19X3:		
Raw materials	12	
Work-in-progress	18	
Finished goods	8	
Rent and rates (factory 2/3; general 1/3)	42	
	£920	£920

Additional information:

1 Stocks at 30 April 19X4:

	£000
Raw material	14
Work-in-progress	16
Finished goods	22

2 The factory equipment is to be depreciated at a rate of 15% per annum on cost.

Required:

Prepare the David and Peter Manufacturing Company's manufacturing, trading, and profit and loss account for the year to 30 April 19X4, and a balance sheet as at that date.

5.5 Jeffrey is in business as a manufacturer. He has extracted the following trial balance from his books of account as at 31 May 19X5:

	Dr £000	Cr £000
Bank	6	
Capital		58
Creditors		156
Debtors	89	
Drawings	15	
Factory expenses:		
Direct wages	200	
General expenses	60	
Office equipment:		
At cost	30	
Accumulated depreciation at 1 June 19X4		9
Office expenses	127	
Plant:		
At cost	160	
Accumulated depreciation at 1 June 19X4		70
Purchases of finished goods	55	
Purchases of raw materials	180	
Sales		693
Stocks at 1 June 19X4:		
Raw materials	17	
Work-in-progress	21	
Finished goods	26	
	£986	£986

Additional information:
1 Stocks at 31 May 19X5: £000
   Raw materials 20
   Work-in-progress 30
   Finished goods 29
2 Goods manufactured by Jeffrey are transferred to finished stock at the cost of manufacture plus 20%.
3 Office equipment is to be depreciated at a rate of 10% per annum on cost, and plant at a rate of 20% per annum on cost.

Required:
Prepare Jeffrey's manufacturing, trading, and profit and loss account for the year to 31 May 19X5, and a balance sheet as at that date.

5.6 Clarico is a small manufacturing company. The following trial balance has been extracted from the books of account as at 30 June 19X6:

	Dr £000	Cr £000
Administration expenses	39	
Capital		252
Carriage inwards	22	
Cash	7	
Delivery vans:		
At cost	36	
Accumulated depreciation at 1 July 19X5		18
Delivery van expenses	12	
Drawings	110	
Electricity	16	
Plant:		
At cost:	110	
Accumulated depreciation at 1 July 19X5		40
Provision for doubtful debts (at 1 July 19X5)		55
Purchases:		
Raw materials	450	
Finished goods	30	
Rent and rates	70	
Sales		1,570
Sales expenses	56	
Stocks at 1 July 19X5:		
Raw materials	120	
Work-in-progress	40	
Finished goods	48	
Trade creditors		265
Trade debtors	800	
Wages:		
Factory direct	142	
Factory indirect	48	
Administration	26	
Sales	18	
	£2,200	£2,200

Additional information:

1   Stocks at 30 June 19X6   £000

      Raw materials   102

      Work-in-progress   74

      Finished goods   76

2   Manufactured goods are transferred to finished goods stock at cost plus 10%.

3   Provision is to be made for the following amounts owing at 30 June 19X6:

                         £000

      Electricity   4

      Rent   15

      Delivery van expenses   3

4   The following expenses had been paid in advance at 30 June 19X6:

	£000
Rates	25
Delivery van licences	2

5 The bad debts provision is to be made equal to 10% of outstanding trade debtors as at 30 June 19X6.

6 Depreciation for the year is to be charged as follows:
   Plant: 20% on cost
   Delivery vans: 25% on cost

7 Expenses are to be apportioned as follows:

	Factory	Administration
	%	%
Electricity	80	20
Rent and rates	60	40

Required:

Prepare Clarico's manufacturing, trading, and profit and loss account for the year to 30 June 19X6, and a balance sheet as at that date.

Additional questions (without answers)

5.7 Joan Petrie owns a small manufacturing company. The following trial balance has been extracted from her books of account as at 30 September 19X9:

	Dr £000	Cr £000
Advertising	40	
Capital		3,500
Cash at bank and in hand	16	
Discounts allowed	25	
Discounts received		15
Drawings	32	
Factory: Direct expenses	13	
Indirect expenses	262	
Wages and salaries	2,900	
Fixed assets at cost	5,000	
Accumulated depreciation (at 1 October 19X8)		1,500
Office expenses	1,552	
Purchases of raw materials	729	
Rent, rates, heat and light	40	
Sales		8,087
Stocks at 1 October 19X8:		
Raw materials	80	
Work-in-progress	70	
Finished goods	50	
Trade creditors		121
c/f	10,809	13,223

		£000	£000
	b/f	10,809	13,223
Trade debtors		820	
Wages and salaries (administration 50%,			
distribution 50%)		1,594	
		£13,223	£13,223

Additional information:

1   Stocks at 30 September 19X9:

	£000
Raw materials	95
Work-in-progress	54
Finished goods	65

2   Depreciation is charged on fixed assets at a rate of 10% per annum on cost. It is apportioned as follows:

	%
Factory	75
Administration and distribution	25
	100

3   Rent, rates, heat and light apportioned 50% to the factory and 50% to the office.

4   A profit loading of 30% is added to the manufactured cost of goods.

Required:
Prepare Joan Petrie's manufacturing, trading and profit and loss account for the year to 30 September 19X9, and a balance sheet as at that date.

5.8   Dunk's accountant has extracted the following trial balance as at 31 October 19X1:

		Dr	Cr
		£000	£000
Advertising		9	
Bank overdraft			17
Capital			418
Carriage inwards		5	
Carriage outwards		37	
Delivery vans at cost		200	
Accumulated depreciation (at 1 November 19X0)			100
Direct factory expenses:			
General		7	
Raw materials		198	
Wages and salaries		530	
Discounts allowed		50	
	c/f	1,036	535

		£000	£000
	b/f	1,036	535
Discounts received			11
Distribution costs		60	
Drawings		42	
Indirect factory expenses:			
General		4	
Materials		10	
Wages and salaries		13	
Office: General expenses		8	
Lighting and heating		6	
Rent and rates		23	
Wages and salaries		46	
Plant and equipment at cost		600	
Accumulated depreciation (at 1 November 19X0)			360
Provision for bad and doubtful debts (at 1			
November 19X0)			3
Sales			1,300
Salesmen's salaries and expenses		76	
Stocks at 1 November 19X0:			
Raw materials		22	
Work-in-progress		70	
Finished goods		130	
Trade creditors			33
Trade debtors		96	
		£2,242	£2,242

Additional information:

1 Stocks at 31 October 19X1:

	£000
Raw materials	10
Work-in progress	91
Finished goods	70

2 Depreciation:

| Delivery vans: | 25% on cost |
| Plant and machinery (all factory): | 20% on cost. |

3 Accruals at 31 October 19X1:

	£000
Indirect factory expenses	2
Office rent	7

4 Prepayments at 31 October 19X1:

	£000
Telephone	1
Salesmen's expenses	4

5   A profit loading of 10% is added to the cost of manufactured goods.
6   A bad debt of £16,000 is to be written off.
7   A provision for bad and doubtful debts is maintained equivalent to 5% of outstanding trade debtors as at the end of each year.

Required:
Prepare Dunk's manufacturing, trading and profit and loss account for the year to 31 October 19X1, and a balance sheet as at that date.

6 Partnership and company accounts

Learning objectives_____

1 outline the structure of a set of partnership accounts;

2 understand the concept of limited liability;

3 distinguish between private and public limited liability companies;

4 compile a company's profit and loss account and balance sheet;

and

5 examine the usefulness of such statements.

The last three chapters have dealt mainly with the sole trader type of entity. As argued earlier, this term is not to be taken too literally. The term *sole* trader does not necessarily mean that the trader is working entirely alone, because some staff may be employed to help operate the business. What it means is that the entity is *owned* by one individual. The entity could, in fact, be a very large one, and many hundreds of employees may work for it. The term *trader* is also misleading. It is not restricted to trading entities, that is, those entities that buy and sell goods. It may be a manufacturing entity, or a business that offers a service, such as an accountant, a doctor or a solicitor.

Sole trader entities are quite common, especially amongst small businesses, but there are two other main types of entities that are perhaps just as common. These are partnerships and limited liability companies, and they form the subject of this chapter.

In order to form either a partnership or a company, at least two people are required. Almost any type of entity can be operated as a partnership. A partnership may simply involve two or more people getting together to form a business. A company may also be similarly formed, but the formation of a *limited liability company* is bound by some fairly severe legal restrictions.

As a result of its unique legal position, the accounts of limited liability companies present particular difficulties, but before dealing with such accounts, the partnership type of entity will be briefly examined.

Partnerships

A partnership entity is similar to that of a sole trader, except that a *partnership* is presumed to exist when two or more people get together in business with the objective of making a profit. This common form of business entity is considered in more detail in the following subsections.

Management

The law limits the total number of people who may get together to form a partnership. Apart from a few exceptions (such as firms of accountants and solicitors) a partnership may not consist of more than twenty partners. It is not necessary for partners to make a capital contribution to be a partner. If they are regarded as being partners, then it is assumed that they are partners.

The management of the partnership will be by agreement amongst the partners, but if there is no apparent agreement (either formal or informal), then it is presumed that the partnership will operate in accordance with the Partnership Act 1890. This Act lays down arrangements for dealing with such matters as the amount of capital to be contributed, the management of the business, and the apportionment of profit and loss among the partners.

If the partners have come to some agreement, then partnerships (like sole traders) may operate without much formal legal intervention.

Accounts

Partnership accounts are very similar to those of sole traders. There are just three essential differences.

1 The net profit for the year (as per the profit and loss account) is transferred to what is called the profit and loss *appropriation* account. This account shows how the profit is divided among the partners.
2 Details concerning the partners share of profits and their drawings are usually kept in *current* accounts (although not all partnerships keep them). Current accounts enable such details to be kept separate from the partners' capital accounts, thereby ensuring that amounts contributed as capital are not obscured by day-to-day transactions.
3 The capital section on the balance sheet shows the respective partners' capital and current accounts balances.

An example of partnership accounts is shown in Exhibit 6.1.

Exhibit 6.1: Illustration of partnership accounts

Duke & Luke
Profit and loss appropriation account for the year to 31 March 19X9

	£	£
Net profit (1)		20,000
Appropriation (2):		
Duke (70%)	14,000	
Luke (30%)	6,000	20,000

Duke & Luke
Balance sheet (extract) at 31 March 19X9

	£	£
Net assets (3)		24,500
Financed by:		
Capital accounts (4)		
Duke		10,000
Luke		5,000
		15,000
Current accounts (5)		
Duke	6,000	
Luke	3,500	9,500
		£24,500

Tutorial notes

1 Profit is calculated in exactly the same way as that for sole trader entities.
2 The exhibit assumes that the partners have agreed to share out the profit in the ratio 70:30, the double-entry effect being as follows:

    Dr Profit and loss appropriation account
        with £20,000
    Cr Duke's current account
        with £14,000
    Cr Luke's current account
        with £6,000

By making these transfers to the partners' current accounts, no balance remains in the profit and loss account.

3 It is assumed that the net assets of the partnership are £24,500.
4 The partners have contributed £15,000 in capital (Duke £10,000 and Luke £5,000). It should be noted that profit may not necessarily be apportioned in their capital sharing ratios; this is a matter for the partners to agree among themselves.
5 The partners' current accounts represent their respective net balances as at the end of the year (after allowing for the balance brought forward, the partner's share of the profit and any drawings that may have been made during the year).
6 The total of the capital account and the current account balances represent the total amount of capital invested in the business by the partners. The current account balances are, however, usually just a short-term source of finance, since the partnership agreement would probably allow the partners to withdraw from

their current accounts at any time. By using current accounts, the balances on the capital accounts will remain at their original levels, unless more capital is contributed or some withdrawn.

It should be noted that no matter what arrangements the partners make for the apportionment of profit among themselves (for example, to draw a salary, to allow for interest on their capital and current accounts, or for that matter, to charge interest on their drawings), such arrangements are all dealt with in the *appropriation* account. Such matters must *not* be entered in the profit and loss account, no matter how they are described. There is just one exception to this rule. Where a partner makes a specific *loan* to the partnership, and that loan lies outside the partnership agreement, then the interest on the loan *may* be charged to the profit and loss account.

The preparation of partnership accounts is a fairly routine accounting exercise, and it is unlikely that as a non-accountant you will be involved in their preparation.

It is now time, therefore, to move on to the most important type of business entity to be considered in this book: the *limited liability company* entity.

Limited liability companies

There is a great personal risk in operating a business as a sole trader or as a partnership. If the business runs short of funds, the proprietors may be called upon to settle the business debts out of their own private resources. This type of risk can have an inhibiting effect on the development of new businesses. Hence the need for a different type of entity that will neither make the owners bankrupt nor inhibit the growth of new businesses. This need became apparent in the nineteenth century as a result of the industrial revolution.

In order to finance the new and rapidly expanding industries (such as the iron and steel industry and the railways), enormous amounts of capital were required. These sorts of ventures were undertaken at great risk. By agreeing to become involved in them, investors often faced bankruptcy if (as seemed likely) the ventures were unsuccessful. It became apparent that the development of industry would be severely restricted unless some means could be devised of restricting the liability of prospective investors.

Hence the need for a form of limited liability. In fact, the concept of limited liability was not an innovation of the nineteenth century, although it did receive legal recognition for the first time in the Limited Liability Act of 1855. The Act only remained in force for a few months before it was repealed and incorporated into the 1856 Joint Stock Companies Act.

In accepting the concept of limited liability the 1855 Act effectively recognized the entity concept. By accepting that there could be a distinction between the private and public affairs of business proprietors, a new form of entity was created. Since that time, Parliament has passed a number of other companies acts (the most recent being the Companies Act 1989). All of them have continued to give legal recognition to the concept of limited liability.

The important point about a limited liability company is that it does not require its members to contribute more than a certain amount of capital, no matter what financial difficulties the company may get into. Thus the risk of members being called upon to contribute unlimited amounts of capital is removed, and they are less likely to find themselves being forced into bankruptcy.

The concept of limited liability is often very difficult for business proprietors to understand, especially if they have formed a limited liability company out of what was originally a sole trader or a partnership entity. Unlike such entities, in return for the privilege of limited liability, companies are bound by some fairly severe legal restrictions about how they are operated and managed.

The legal restrictions can be somewhat burdensome, but they are necessary for the protection of all those parties who might have dealings with the company (for example, creditors and employees). If a limited liability company runs short of funds, the creditors and employees might not get paid. It is only fair, therefore, to warn all those people who might have dealings with the company that its liability is limited, and there is a danger that their debts may not be settled. The law requires the company to be more open about its affairs, therefore, than it would have to be if it operated as a non-limited liability entity.

Structure and operation

In this section, the structure and operation of limited liability companies will be briefly examined. In order to make it easier to follow, the examination has been broken down into a number of subsections.

Share capital

Although the law recognizes that limited liability companies are separate beings (that is, separate from those individuals who collectively own the company), it also accepts that someone has to take responsibility for *promoting* the company, i.e. bringing it into being. Only two members are required to form a company. They agree to contribute to its capital by subscribing to shares in it. The capital of a company is known as its *share capital*. Although £1 shares are very common, the share capital may be divided into a number of shares of any monetary denomination. A member may hold just one share, or in very large companies, some shareholders may hold many thousands of shares.

When a company is formed, it must state its maximum amount of share capital. In other words, it must place a limit on the total amount of share capital that it wishes to issue. This is known as its *authorized* share capital.

Although a company has to state its authorized share capital, this does not mean that it will necessarily issue shares up to that amount. It will probably only issue sufficient capital to meet its immediate requirements. The amount of share capital that it has actually issued is known as the *issued* share capital. Sometimes when the capital is issued, the prospective shareholders are only required to contribute in instalments. If a share capital is described as being *fully paid*, it means that it has received all of the capital that it was due to be paid.

There are two main types of shares: *ordinary* shares and *preference* shares. Ordinary shares do not usually entitle the shareholder to any specific level of dividend, and the rights of other parties always take precedence over the rights of the ordinary shareholders, for example on the disposal of the assets when the company is wound up. Preference shareholders are normally entitled to a fixed level of dividend, and they take priority over the ordinary shareholders if the company is wound up. Sometimes the preference shares are classed as *cumulative*. This means that if the company cannot pay its preference dividend in one year, the amount due accrues until such time as the company has the profits to pay the accumulated dividend.

There are many other different types of shares, but for the purpose of this chapter, only ordinary and preference shares need be considered.

Types of companies

A prospective shareholder may invest in either a public company or a private company. A public company must have an authorized share capital of at least £50,000, and it must make its share capital available to the general public. This normally means that the shares will be listed on a stock exchange where the public can buy and sell the company's shares relatively easily.

As a warning to those parties who might have dealings with them, public limited liability companies must include that term (or its abbreviation 'plc') after their name.

Any company which does not make its shares available to the public is regarded as being a private company. Like public companies, private companies must also have an authorized share capital, although no minimum amount is prescribed. Otherwise, as far as their share capital requirements are concerned, they are very similar to public companies.

Private companies also have to warn the public that their liability is limited. They must do so by describing themselves as 'limited liability companies', and use that term (or its abbreviation 'ltd') after their name.

Loans

Besides obtaining finance from their shareholders, companies often borrow money in the form of *debentures*. A company may invite the public to loan it some money for a certain period of time (although the period can be unspecified) at a fixed rate of interest. The loans may be secured on specific assets of the company, or on its assets generally, or they might not be secured at all. If they are secured and the company cannot repay the loans on their due date, the debenture holders may sell the secured assets and settle the amount due to themselves out of the proceeds.

Debentures may be bought and sold freely on the Stock Exchange, exactly like shares. The nearer the redemption date for the repayment of the debentures, the closer the market price will be to their nominal value. Indeed, if they are to be redeemed at a premium, the market price may exceed the nominal value.

Debenture holders are not shareholders of the company and they do not have voting rights. Debenture interest is also an allowable expense for tax purposes, and so debentures are a popular way of raising extra funds.

Disclosure of information

It is necessary for both public and private companies to supply a minimum amount of information to their members. The detailed requirements are dealt with in Part 4 of this book. You might be surprised to learn that shareholders do not have a right to all the information that they might want, or a right of access to the company's premises. It would be clearly impractical to give all shareholders these rights, especially in large public companies where there might be hundreds of thousands of shareholders.

Instead, both private and public companies have to submit an annual report to their members (containing at least the minimum amount of information laid down by the Companies Act 1985, as amended by the Companies Act 1989), and to file the report with the Registrar of Companies at Companies House in Cardiff or in Edinburgh. This means that on payment of a small fee, the report is open for inspection to any member of the public. Some companies (defined as small or medium) are permitted to file abbreviated accounts with the Registrar, although they must still supply the more detailed report to their members.

Company accounts

The preparation of company accounts is very similar to that adopted for sole trader and partnership entities. Some modifications do, of course, have to be made because of the legal position that a company enjoys. Company accounts will be dealt with in more detail a little later on in the chapter.

Directors

A limited liability company is regarded as being a separate entity, that is, separate from those shareholders who own it collectively, and separate from anyone who is employed by it. This means that all those who work for it (no matter how senior) are employees. However, someone has to take responsibility for the management of the company on behalf of the shareholders. To look after their interests, shareholders usually appoint a number of *directors*.

Directors are the most senior level of management. They are responsible for the day-to-day running of the company on behalf of the shareholders. Directors are employees of the company, and any remuneration paid to them as directors is charged as an expense of the business. Directors may also be shareholders, and any dividends paid to them as shareholders are treated in exactly the same way as dividends paid to other shareholders.

The distinction between employees and shareholder-employees is an important one, although it is one that is not always understood, especially in small companies where all shareholders may also be employees. As has been seen, in law the company is regarded as being a separate entity. Even if there are just two shareholders who both work full-time for the company, the company is still treated as distinct from the two individuals who manage and own it.

They may take decisions that appear to affect no one else except themselves, but because they are operating the company under the protection of limited liability, they have certain obligations as well as rights. These obligations mean that they are not as free to operate the company as they might if they were a partnership.

Dividends

Profits are usually distributed to shareholders in the form of a *dividend*. A dividend is usually declared at so many pence per share. The actual dividend will depend upon the amount of net profit earned during the year and how much profit the company needs to retain for future investment.

A dividend may have been *paid* during the year as an *interim* dividend. In effect, an interim dividend is a payment on account, as the actual profit for the year on which the dividend should be based will only be known once the year is over. The directors may only *propose* to pay a dividend when preparing the annual accounts, because it has to be approved by the shareholders at their annual general meeting. The proposed dividend is usually referred to as the *final* dividend.

Taxation

Taxation is another feature which distinguishes a limited liability company from that of a sole trader or partnership entity.

Sole trader and partnership entities do not have tax levied on them as entities. Tax is charged on the profit which the proprietors or partners take out of the business. The tax that they pay is a private matter, and the entity is not responsible for it. Any tax that appears to have been paid by the entity on the proprietors behalf is treated as part of their drawings.

Companies are treated quite differently. The law recognizes them as being distinct entities in their own right. They are, therefore, charged with their own form of taxation: it is known as *corporation tax*. Corporation tax was introduced in 1965. All companies are due to pay their corporation tax nine months after the year end.

Corporation tax is based on a company's accounting profits, but the accounting profit has to be adjusted for certain items that are treated differently for tax purposes.

The corporation tax based on the accounting profits for the year will normally appear as a current liability on the balance sheet, since it will not be due for payment until nine months after the end of the financial year.

Some corporation tax, however, may have to be paid in advance. This is known as *advance corporation tax (ACT)*. ACT is payable if a company pays a dividend. The amount is based on the dividend, but any ACT paid goes to reduce the total amount of corporation tax eventually payable on the profits for the year. The net amount of corporation tax payable (the total amount due less any ACT paid) is known as *mainstream* corporation tax.

Now that the background to limited liability companies has been outlined, it is possible to examine their accounts. The next section deals with the profit and loss account.

The profit and loss account

As suggested earlier, the preparation of a company's manufacturing, trading, and profit and loss account is basically no different from that applicable to a sole trader entity. A similar format may be adopted, and it is only after the net profit stage that some differences become apparent.

Like partnership accounts, company accounts also include a profit and loss appropriation account (although no clear distinction is drawn between where the profit and loss account ends and the appropriation account begins). Exhibit 6.2 illustrates a company's profit and loss appropriation account.

Exhibit 6.2: Example of a company's profit and loss appropriation account

	£000
Net profit for the year before taxation	1,000
Taxation	(300)
Profit for the year after taxation	700
Dividends	(500)
Retained profit for the year	200
Retained profits brought forward	400
Retained profits carried forward	£600

As can be seen from Exhibit 6.2, the company's net profit for the year is used in three ways:
1 to pay tax;
2 to pay dividends; and
3 for retention within the business.

The balance sheet

The structure of a limited liability company's balance sheet is also very similar to that of a sole trader or of a partnership. The main differences arise because of the company's capital structure, but there are also some other features that are not usually found in non-company balance sheets.

The main features of a company's balance sheet are illustrated in Exhibit 6.3. Study this exhibit carefully, but note that the information has been kept to a minimum. The full details have not been given where there are no significant differences between a company's balance sheet and those for other entities.

Exhibit 6.3: Example of a company's balance sheet

Exhibitor Limited
Balance sheet at 31 March 19X1

	£000	£000	£000
Fixed assets			600
Investments (1)			100
Current assets		6,000	
Less: Current liabilities			
Trade creditors	2,950		
Accruals	50		
Corporation tax (2)	300		
Proposed dividend (3)	500	3,800	2,200
			£2,900

Financed by:		
Capital and reserves (4)	Authorized	Issued and fully paid
	£000	£000
Ordinary shares of £X each (5)	2,000	1,500
Preference shares of £X each (5)	500	500
	£2,500	2,000
Capital reserves (6)		200
Revenue reserves (7)		600
Shareholders' funds (8)		2,800
Loans (9)		100
		£2,900

Note: The number shown after each narration refers to the tutorial notes below.

Tutorial notes

1 *Investments.* This item usually represents long-term investments in the shares of other companies. Short-term investments (such as money invested in bank deposit accounts) would be included in current assets. The shares may be either in public limited liability companies or in private limited companies.
   It is obviously more difficult to buy shares in unlisted companies and to obtain current market prices for them. The market price of the investments should be stated, or where this is not available, a directors' valuation should be obtained.
2 *Corporation tax.* Corporation tax represents the tax due on the company's profits for the year. It is due for payment nine months after the company's year end, that is, in Exhibitor's case, on 1 January 19X2.
3 *Proposed dividend.* A proposed dividend will probably be due for payment very shortly after the year end, so it will usually be shown as a current liability.
4 *Capital and reserves.* Details of the authorized, issued and fully paid-up share capital should be shown.
5 *Ordinary shares and preference shares.* Details about the different types of shares that the company has issued should be shown.
6 This section may include several different reserve accounts of a capital nature, that is, amounts that are not available for distribution to the shareholders as

dividend. It might include, for example, a *share premium account,* i.e. the extra amount paid by shareholders in excess of the nominal value of the shares. This extra amount does not rank for dividend, but sometimes shareholders are willing to pay a premium if they think that the shares are particularly attractive. Another example of a capital reserve account is a *revaluation* reserve account. A fixed asset may have been revalued, and the difference between the original cost and the revalued amount will be credited to this account.

7 *Revenue reserves.* Revenue reserve accounts are amounts which are available for distribution to the shareholders. Sometimes profits which could be distributed to shareholders are put into general reserve accounts, although no real purpose is served in classifying them in this way.

8 *Shareholders' funds.* The total amount available to shareholders at the balance sheet date is equal to the share capital originally subscribed, plus all the capital reserve and revenue reserve account balances.

9 *Loans.* The loans section of the balance sheet will include all the long-term loans obtained by the company, i.e. those loans which do not have to be repaid for at least twelve months, such as debentures and long-term bank loans.

A comprehensive example

In this section the structure of company accounts will be examined in more detail. In Exhibit 6.4 it is assumed that the accounts are being prepared for internal management purposes. Accounts prepared for external-user purposes will be dealt with in Part 4 of the book.

Exhibit 6.4

The following information has been extracted from the books of Handy Limited as at 31 March 19X5:

	Dr £	Cr £
Bank	2,000	
Capital: 100,000 issued and fully paid ordinary shares of £1 each		100,000
50,000 issued and fully paid 8% preference shares of £1 each		50,000
Debenture loan stock (10%: repayable 19X9)		30,000
Debenture loan stock interest	3,000	
Discounts allowed	2,000	
Discounts received		5,000
Dividends received		700
Dividends paid: Ordinary interim	5,000	
Preference	4,000	
Freehold land at cost	200,000	
Investments (listed: market value at 31 March 19X5 was £11,000)	10,000	
Office expenses	15,000	
Office salaries	35,000	
c/f	276,000	185,700

		£	£
	b/f	276,000	185,700
Motor van at cost		15,000	
Motor van: accumulated depreciation at 1 April 19X4			6,000
Motor van expenses		2,700	
Purchases		220,000	
Retained profits at 1 April 19X4			9,000
Sales			300,000
Share premium account			10,000
Stocks at cost (at 1 April 19X4)		20,000	
Trade creditors			50,000
Trade debtors		27,000	
		£560,700	£560,700

Additional information:
1 The stocks at 31 March 19X5 were valued at cost at £40,000.
2 Depreciation is to be charged on the motor van at a rate of 20% per annum on cost. No depreciation is to be charged on the freehold land.
3 Corporation tax (based on profits for the year at a rate of 35%) has been estimated at £10,000.
4 The directors propose a final ordinary dividend of 10p per share.
5 The authorized share capital of the company is as follows:
   • 150,000 ordinary shares of £1 each; and
   • 75,000 preference shares of £1 each.

Required:
(a) Prepare Handy Limited's trading, profit and loss account for the year to 31 March 19X5; and
(b) a balance sheet as at that date.

The answer to the exhibit now follows. Work through it carefully making sure that you understand each step in its construction.

Answer to Exhibit 6.4

(a)

Handy Limited

Trading, profit and loss account for the year to 31 March 19X5

	£	£	£
Sales			300,000
Less: Cost of goods sold:			
Opening stocks		20,000	
Purchases		220,000	
		240,000	
Less: Closing stocks		40,000	200,000
Gross profit			100,000
Add: Incomes:			
Discounts received		5,000	
Dividends received		700	5,700
c/f			105,700

	£	£	£
b/f			105,700
Less: Expenditure:			
Debenture loan stock interest		3,000	
Discounts allowed		2,000	
Motor van depreciation (1)	3,000		
Motor van expenses	2,700	5,700	
Office expenses		15,000	
Office salaries		35,000	60,700
Net profit for the year			45,000
Less: Corporation tax (based on the profits for the year at a rate of 35%) (2)			10,000
			35,000
Less: Dividends (3):			
Preference dividend paid (8%)		4,000	
Interim ordinary paid (5p per share)		5,000	
Proposed final ordinary dividend (10p per share)		10,000	19,000
Retained profit for the year			16,000
Retained profits brought forward			9,000
Retained profits carried forward (4)			£25,000

(b)

Handy Limited
Balance sheet at 31 March 19X5

Fixed assets	£ Cost	£ Accumulated depreciation	£ Net book value
Freehold land (5)	200,000	—	200,000
Motor van (6)	15,000	9,000	6,000
	£215,000	£9,000	206,000
Investments			
At cost (market value at 31 March 19X5: £11,000) (7)			10,000
Current assets			
Stocks at cost		40,000	
Trade debtors		27,000	
Bank		2,000	
		69,000	
Less: Current liabilities			
Trade creditors	50,000		
Corporation tax (due for payment on 1 January 19X6) (8)	10,000		
Proposed ordinary dividend (9)	10,000	70,000	(1,000)
			£215,000

Financed by:

Capital and reserves	Authorized	Issued and fully paid
Ordinary shares of £1 each (10)	150,000	100,000
Preference shares of £1 each (10)	75,000	50,000
	£225,000	150,000
Share premium account (11)		10,000
Retained profits (12)		25,000
Shareholders' funds (13)		185,000
Loans (14)		
10% debenture stock (repayable 19X9)		30,000
		£215,000

Note: The number shown after each narration refers to the tutorial notes.

Tutorial notes

1 Depreciation has been charged on the motor van at a rate of 20% per annum on cost as instructed in question note 2.

2 Question note 3 requires £10,000 to be charged as corporation tax. Note that the corporation tax rate of 35% is applied to the taxable profit, and not to the accounting profit of £45,000. The taxable profit has not been given in the question.

3 A proposed ordinary dividend of 10p has been included as instructed in question note 4.

4 The total retained profit of £25,000 is carried forward to the balance sheet (see tutorial note 12 below).

5 Question note 2 states that no depreciation is to be charged on the freehold land.

6 The accumulated depreciation for the motor van of £9,000 is the total of the accumulated depreciation brought forward at 1 April 19X4 of £6,000 plus the £3,000 written off to the profit and loss account for the current year (see tutorial note 1 above).

7 Note that the market value of the investments has been disclosed on the face of the balance sheet.

8 The corporation tax charged against profit (question note 3) will be due for payment on 1 January 19X6 (to be precise, nine months plus one day after the year end). It is, therefore, a current liability.

9 The proposed ordinary dividend will be due for payment shortly after the year end, so it is also a current liability. The interim dividend and the preference dividend have already been paid, so they are not current liabilities.

10 Details of the authorized, issued and fully paid share capital should be disclosed.

11 The share premium is a capital account; it cannot be used for the payment of dividends. This account will tend to remain unchanged in successive balance sheets, although there are a few highly restricted purposes for which it may be used.

12 The retained profits become part of a revenue account balance that the company could use for the payment of dividends. The total retained profits of £25,000 is the amount brought in to the balance sheet from the profit and loss account.

13 The total amount of shareholders' funds should always be shown.
14 The loans are long-term loans. Loans are not part of shareholders' funds, and they should be shown in the balance sheet as a separate item.

You are now recommended to work through Exhibit 6.4 again without reference to the solution.

Conclusion

This chapter began with a brief outline of a partnership entity. It then briefly examined the background to company account legislation. This was followed by an explanation of how company accounts are prepared for *internal* purposes. The preparation of company accounts for *external* purposes will be examined in Part 4 of the book.

Although a great deal of information can be obtained from studying the financial accounts of a company, it is difficult to extract the most relevant and significant features. Some guidance is necessary, therefore, in making the best use of the accounting information presented to you as a non-accountant. That guidance is provided in the next two chapters.

Questions

6.1 The following balances have been extracted from the books of Margo Limited for the year to 31 January 19X1:

	Dr £000	Cr £000
Cash at bank and in hand	5	
Plant and equipment:		
At cost	70	
Accumulated depreciation (at 31.1.X1)		25
Profit and loss account (at 1.2.X0)		15
Profit for the financial year (to 31.1.X1)		10
Share capital (issued and fully paid)		50
Stocks (at 31.1.X1)	17	
Trade creditors		12
Trade debtors	20	
	£112	£112

Additional information:
1 Corporation tax based on the profits for the year is estimated at £3,000.
2 Margo Limited's authorized share capital is £75,000 of £1 ordinary shares.
3 A dividend of 10p per share is proposed (ignore advance corporation tax).

Required:
Prepare Margo Limited's profit and loss account for the year to 31 January 19X1 (in so far as the information permits), and a balance sheet as at that date.

6.2 Harry Limited was formed in 1980. The following balances as at 28 February 19X2 have been extracted from the books of account after the trading account has been compiled:

	Dr £000	Cr £000
Administration expenses	65	
Cash at bank and in hand	10	
Distribution costs	15	
Dividend paid (on preference shares)	6	
Furniture and equipment:		
At cost	60	
Accumulated depreciation at 1.3.X1		36
Gross profit for the year		150
Ordinary share capital (shares of £1 each)		100
Preference shares (cumulative 15% of £1 shares)		40
Profit and loss account (at 1.3.X1)		50
Share premium account		20
Stocks (at 28.2.X2)	130	
Trade creditors		25
Trade debtors	135	
	£421	£421

Additional information:
1 Corporation tax based on the profits for the year is estimated at £24,000.
2 Furniture and equipment is depreciated at an annual rate of 10% of cost and it is all charged against administrative expenses.
3 A dividend of 20p per ordinary share is proposed (ignore advance corporation tax).
4 All of the authorized share capital has been issued and is fully paid.

Required:
Prepare Harry Limited's profit and loss account for the year to 28 February 19X2, and a balance sheet as at that date.

6.3 The following balances have been extracted from the books of Jim Limited as at 31 March 19X3:

	Dr £000	Cr £000
Advertising	3	
Bank	11	
Creditors		12
Debtors	118	
Furniture and fittings:		
At cost	20	
Accumulated depreciation (at 1.4.X2)		9
c/f	152	21

		£000	£000
	b/f	152	21
Directors' fees		6	
Profit and loss account (at 1.4.X2)			8
Purchases		124	
Rent and rates		10	
Sales			270
Share capital (issued and fully paid)			70
Stock (at 1.4.X2)		16	
Telephone and stationery		5	
Travelling expenses		2	
Vehicles:			
At cost		40	
Accumulated depreciation (at 1.4.X2)			10
Wages and salaries		24	
		£379	£379

Additional information:
1 Stock at 31 March 19X3 was valued at £14,000.
2 Furniture and fittings and the vehicles are depreciated at a rate of 15% and 25% respectively on cost.
3 Corporation tax based on the year's profits is estimated at £25,000.
4 A dividend of 40p per share is proposed (ignore advance corporation tax).
5 The company's authorized share capital is £100,000 of £1 ordinary shares.

Required:
Prepare Jim Limited's trading, and profit and loss account for the year to 31 March 19X3, and a balance sheet as at that date.

6.4 The following trial balance has been extracted from Cyril Limited as at 30 April 19X4:

	Dr	Cr
	£000	£000
Advertising	2	
Bank overdraft		20
Bank interest paid	4	
Creditors		80
Debtors	143	
Directors' remuneration	30	
Freehold land and buildings:		
At cost	800	
Accumulated depreciation at 1.5.X3		102
General expenses	15	
Investments at cost	30	
Investment income		5
c/f	1,024	207

		£000	£000
	b/f	1,024	207
Motor vehicles:			
At cost		36	
Accumulated depreciation (at 1.5.X3)			18
Preference dividend paid		15	
Preference shares (cumulative 10% shares of £1 each)			150
Profit and loss account (at 1.5.X3)			100
Purchases		480	
Repairs and renewals		4	
Sales			900
Share capital (authorized, issued and fully paid ordinary shares of £1 each)			500
Share premium account			25
Stock (at 1.5.X3)		120	
Wages and salaries		221	
		£1,900	£1,900

Additional information:
1   Stock at 30 April 19X4 was valued at £140,000.
2   Depreciation for the year of £28,000 is to be provided on buildings and £9,000 for motor vehicles.
3   A provision of £6,000 is required for the auditors' remuneration.
4   £2,000 had been paid in advance for renewals.
5   Corporation tax based on the year's profits is estimated at £60,000.
6   The directors propose an ordinary dividend of 10p per share.
7   The market value of the investments at 30 April 19X4 was £35,000.
8   Ignore advance corporation tax.

Required:
Prepare Cyril Limited's trading, and profit and loss account for the year to 30 April 19X4, and a balance sheet as at that date.

6.5   Nelson Limited was incorporated in 1980 with an authorized share capital of 500,000 £1 ordinary shares, and 200,000 5% cumulative preference shares of £1 each. The following trial balance was extracted at 31 May 19X5:

		Dr	Cr
		£000	£000
Administrative expenses		257	
Auditor's fees		10	
Cash at bank and in hand		5	
Creditors			85
Debentures (12%)			100
	c/f	272	185

		£000	£000
	b/f	272	185
Debenture interest paid		6	
Debtors		225	
Directors' remuneration		60	
Dividends paid:			
Ordinary interim		20	
Preference		5	
Furniture, fittings and equipment:			
At cost		200	
Accumulated depreciation at 1.6.X4			48
Investments at cost (market value at 31.5.X5:			
£340,000)		335	
Investment income			22
Ordinary share capital (issued and fully paid)			400
Preference share capital			200
Profit and loss account (at 1.6.X4)			17
Purchases		400	
Sales			800
Share premium account			50
Stock at 1.6.X4		155	
Wages and salaries		44	
		£1,722	£1,722

Additional information:
1 Stock at 31 May 19X5 was valued at £195,000.
2 Administrative expenses owing at 31 May 19X5 amounted to £13,000.
3 Depreciation is to be charged on the furniture and fittings at a rate of 12½%
  on cost.
4 Salaries paid in advance amounted to £4,000.
5 Corporation tax based on the profit for the year is estimated at £8,000.
6 Provision is to be made for a final ordinary dividend of 1.25p per share.
7 Ignore advance corporation tax.

Required:
Prepare Nelson Limited's trading, and profit and loss account for the year to
31 May 19X5, and a balance sheet as at that date.

6.6 The following trial balance has been extracted from the books of Keith
Limited as at 30 June 19X6:

		Dr	Cr
		£000	£000
Advertising		30	
Bank		7	
Creditors			69
	c/f	37	69

		£000	£000
	b/f	37	69
Debentures (10%)			70
Debtors (all trade)		300	
Directors' remuneration		55	
Electricity		28	
Insurance		17	
Investments (quoted)		28	
Investment income			4
Machinery:			
At cost		420	
Accumulated depreciation at 1.7.X5			152
Office expenses		49	
Ordinary share capital (issued and fully paid)			200
Preference shares			50
Preference share dividend		4	
Profit and loss account (at 1 July 19X5)			132
Provision for doubtful debts			8
Purchases		1,240	
Rent and rates		75	
Sales			2,100
Stock (at 1.7.X5)		134	
Vehicles:			
At cost		80	
Accumulated depreciation (at 1.7.X5)			40
Wages and salaries		358	
		£2,825	£2,825

Additional information:

1 Stock at 30 June 19X6 valued at cost amounted to £155,000.
2 Depreciation is to be provided on machinery and vehicles at a rate of 20% and 25% respectively on cost.
3 Provision is to be made for auditor's remuneration of £12,000.
4 Insurance paid in advance at 30 June 19X6 amounted to £3,000.
5 The provision for doubtful debts is to be made equal to 5% of outstanding trade debtors as at 30 June 19X6.
6 Corporation tax based on the profits for the year of £60,000 is to be provided.
7 An ordinary dividend of 10p per share is proposed.
8 The investments had a market value of £30,000 at 30 June 19X6.
9 The company has an authorized share capital of 600,000 ordinary shares of £0.50 each and of 50,000 8% cumulative preference shares of £1 each.
10 Ignore advance corporation tax.

Required:
Prepare Keith Limited's trading and profit and loss account for the year to 30 June 19X6, and a balance sheet as at that date.

Additional questions (without answers)

6.7 Hanna and Weston are in partnership sharing profits and losses in the ratio 3 to 2. According to the partnership agreement, Hanna is allowed a salary of £7,000 per annum, and both partners are entitled to receive interest of 10% per annum on their capital account balances as at the beginning of each financial year.

The following trial balance has been extracted from their books of account as at 31 August 19X8:

	Dr £000	Cr £000
Administrative expenses	84	
Capital at 1 September 19X7:		
Hanna		120
Weston		80
Cash at bank and in hand	3	
Creditors		21
Debtors	70	
Delivery vans at cost	160	
Accumulated depreciation (at 1 September 19X7)		80
Distribution costs	34	
Drawings: Hanna	40	
Weston	30	
Plant and equipment at cost	100	
Accumulated depreciation (at 1 September 19X7)		60
Purchases	200	
Sales		400
Stock (at 1 September 19X7)	40	
	£761	£761

Additional information:
1   Stock at 31 August 19X8: £50,000.
2   Depreciation is to be charged as follows:
    Delivery vans: 25% on cost.
    Plant and equipment: 15% on cost.

Required:
Prepare Hanna and Weston's trading, profit and loss, and profit and loss appropriation account for the year to 31 August 19X8, and a balance sheet as at that date.

6.8 Muir Limited's trial balance for the year to 30 November 19X1 is shown below:

	Dr £000	Cr £000
Administrative expenses	210	
Called up share capital (£1 ordinary shares)		720
Cash at bank and in hand	40	
Distribution costs	580	
Dividends received		4
Fixed asset investments (at cost)	20	
Land and property at cost	200	
Accumulated depreciation (at 1 December 19X0)		16
Profit and loss account (at 1 December 19X0)		160
Purchases	1,360	
Sales		2,480
Stock (at 1 December 19X0)	260	
Trade creditors		120
Trade debtors	430	
Vans at cost	700	
:accumulated depreciation (at 1 December 19X0)		300
	£3,800	£3,800

Additional information:
1   Stock at 30 November 19X1: £250,000.
2   Depreciation is to be charged as follows:
        Property: 4% on cost (land at cost = £100,000)
        Vans: 25% on cost.
3   At 30 November 19X1:
        £10,000 was owing for office salaries
        £5,000 had been paid in advance for van licences.
4   Corporation tax based on the profit for the year at a rate of 35% is estimated to be £55,000.
5   The directors propose to pay an ordinary dividend of 10p per share.
6   Advance corporation tax may be ignored.

Required:
Prepare Muir's profit and loss account for the year to 30 November 19X1, and a balance sheet as at that date.

6.9   The following trial balance has been extracted from the books of account of McAdam Limited as at 31 December 19X2:

	Dr £000	Cr £000
Administrative expenses	2,370	
Bank overdraft		130
Called up share capital:		
Ordinary shares of £1 each		800
c/f	2,370	930

		£000	£000
	b/f	2,370	930
10% cumulative preference shares			200
Creditors			600
Debtors		570	
Deferred taxation			500
Distribution costs		900	
Fixed asset investments:			
Dividends received			120
Investments at cost		700	
Furniture and fittings at cost		100	
Accumulated depreciation (at 1 January 19X2)			40
Interim dividend paid (10p per ordinary share)		80	
Plant and equipment at cost		7,000	
Accumulated depreciation (at 1 January 19X2)			4,000
Preference dividend paid		10	
Profit and loss account			3,000
Purchases		8,000	
Sales			13,200
Share premium account			380
Stock at 1 January 19X2		2,000	
Trade creditors			980
Trade debtors		2,220	
		£23,950	£23,950

Additional information:

1   Stock at 31 December 19X2: £2,400,000.
2   Depreciation is to be charged as follows:
        Furniture and fittings: 10% on cost
        Plant and equipment (all relating to distribution activities): 50% on the
        reduced balance.
3   Corporation tax based on the profit for the year at a rate of 35%: £530,000.
4   The directors propose to pay a final ordinary dividend of 20p per ordinary
    share.
5   Advance corporation tax may be ignored.

Required:
Prepare McAdam's profit and loss account for the year to 31 December 19X2,
and a balance sheet as at that date.

7 Source and application of funds

Learning objectives_____

1 understand the relationship between accounting profit/loss and movements in cash/bank balances;

2 compile a statement of source and application of funds; and

3 assess the usefulness of such a statement.

In previous chapters, manufacturing, trading, and profit and loss accounts and balance sheets have been prepared in accordance with the accounting rules laid down in Chapter 2. Such accounts have provided some basic information about profitability, but they have not told the user very much about the entity's cash position, that is, about its *liquidity*.

Information about liquidity is vital, because an entity is technically insolvent if it cannot settle its debts as they fall due. It is unlawful to carry on trading if the management knows that it is in this position. The entity's cash balances can always be checked, of course, by examining its balance sheet, but this only gives the user the opening and closing cash position.

It is for these reasons that all entities are now encouraged to produce a *statement of source and application of funds* (or in short, a funds' statement) along with the traditional profit and loss account and balance sheet. The encouragement is so strong that it is mandatory for professional accountants to produce a funds statement for all those entities that have a turnover in excess of £25,000 per annum.

Funds' statements are a link between the profit and loss account and the balance sheet, and they form the subject of this chapter.

Accounting profit and liquidity

Experience has taught accountants that it is unwise to rely entirely upon the profit and loss account and the balance sheet to monitor an entity's liquidity position. The opening and closing cash and bank balances can be obtained from the balance sheet, but they do not relay any information about the movement of cash during the year. A great deal more information is needed if the entity's success in handling its cash is to be monitored. This is especially important when proprietors regard an increase in profit as being the same as an increase in cash.

If this is the view of the proprietor, then as long as the entity's accounting profit appears acceptable, very little attention may be paid to the cash position.

Indeed, it is not uncommon for an entity to be experiencing a boom in sales, and then to go suddenly into liquidation. This rather paradoxical situation is known as *overtrading*. It arises because too much attention has been given to selling goods, and not enough attention paid to managing cash resources.

It was suggested in an earlier chapter that proprietors want to know the answers to three basic questions, viz.:

1 What profit has the business made?
2 How much does the business owe?
3 How much is owed to it?

There ought, perhaps, to be a fourth question:

4 What is the cash position?

The answer might be to look at the cash and bank balances, but as has been suggested, the information from such sources does not enable it to be examined in detail.

If you have worked through the questions in the earlier chapters of this book, you will appreciate that accounting profit does not necessarily lead to an automatic increase in cash. In preparing the traditional accounting statements, the realization and matching rules are adopted. These rules require the adjustment of the cash received and the cash paid to reflect the trading *activity* of a particular accounting period. It follows, therefore, that neither sales (and other incomes) nor purchases (and other expenses) will necessarily cause an immediate increase or decrease in the cash position. Furthermore, non-profit and loss items (such as the purchase of fixed assets, and the issue of shares and debentures for cash) are not included in the calculation of accounting profit.

For these reasons, it is very difficult to assess the entity's cash position from the information normally disclosed in the traditional financial accounting statements. Another type of statement is needed that will give much more information about what has happened to the cash during an accounting period. A statement of source and application of funds is designed for that very purpose. Such a statement will be examined in the next section.

Format and contents

The information contained in a statement of source and application of funds can usually be summarized fairly briefly, but the non-accountant should be warned that funds' statements are not easy to construct. In fact, to be able to do so it is probably necessary to have a good grasp of double-entry book-keeping. Chapters 3 and 4 of this book provided you with the necessary knowledge. It is to your advantage to know how funds' statements are constructed because then you will understand a great deal more about what they are trying to tell you. In this section, the format and contents of a simple funds' statement will be examined. The next section will explain how it is constructed.

For the moment, you should assume that 'funds' are the same as cash and bank balances. With this assumption in mind, the modern funds' statement can be examined in some detail.

Exhibit 7.1 illustrates a statement of source and application of funds.

Exhibit 7.1: Example of a statement of source and application of funds

	£000	£000
Source of funds:		
Profit before taxation		2,000
Cash from issue of shares		100
Cash from sale of fixed assets		500
		2,600
Application of funds:		
Dividends paid	(200)	
Tax paid	(300)	
Purchase of fixed assets	(900)	(1,400)
		1,200
Increase in working capital:		
Increase in stocks	700	
Increase in debtors	250	
Decrease in creditors	200	
Increase in cash	50	1,200

You will see from Exhibit 7.1 that a funds' statement comprises three main sections, viz.:

1 a section showing the source of funds;
2 a section showing the application of funds; and
3 a summary of the working capital movements.

The *sources'* section lists the various sources from which the funds have come during a particular accounting period, for example from profits, from sales of fixed assets, and from the issue of shares for cash.

The *applications'* section explains what has happened to those funds. In other words, it lists all the ways in which the funds have been used during the same period.

If the sources' section is in excess of the applications' section, then there will have been a net increase in funds during the period. Alternatively, if the total applications are in excess of the total sources there will have been a decrease in funds.

The working capital section explains where that increase (or decrease) has gone. It might have been used to buy more stocks, for example, or it might simply have been left in the bank account.

It is at this point that difficulties begin. You were asked to assume that funds were the same as cash and bank balances. It seems sensible to make such an assumption. After all, the main purpose of a funds' statement is to give more information about the cash position. Unfortunately, Statement of Standard Accounting Practice 10 (which deals with funds' statements) defines the term 'funds' as being virtually the same as working capital. It is a pity that the standard defines funds in this way, because it causes much confusion. A statement presented in the recommended format is not really disclosing details about the movement of cash, but about the movement of working capital. Since the main purpose of a funds' statement is to inform the proprietor about the source and application of *cash*, it is a mystery why the profession recommends a statement showing the source and application of working capital.

However, it is recommended that you accept this definition of funds, because that is the one you are likely to meet. The *construction* of a funds' statement will be examined in the next section.

Construction

The easiest way to explain how a funds' statement is constructed is to work through a question that requires the preparation of such a statement. Exhibit 7.2 contains the details.

Exhibit 7.2

Ande forms a business on 1 June 19X1 with £10,000 in cash. During the year to 31 May 19X2, he bought some goods for cash costing £50,000. All of these goods were sold on cash terms during the year for £100,000. A few days after starting the business, he paid £8,000 for some machinery in cash. Ande did not keep a bank account.

Required:
Prepare Ande's statement of source and application of funds for the year to 31 May 19X2.

Answer to Exhibit 7.2

ANDE
Statement of source and application of funds for the year to 31 May 19X2 (1)

		£
Source of funds		
Profit (2)		50,000
Application of funds		
Purchase of machinery (3)		(8,000)
	(4)	42,000
Increase in working capital		
Increase in cash balance (5)		£42,000

Tutorial notes

1   The funds' statement is prepared for a period of time like a profit and loss account.
2   Ande's cash profit amounted to £50,000 (£100,000 – £50,000), so his cash position ought to have increased by that amount if he has not spent the cash on anything else.
3   In fact, Ande purchased some machinery for cash. This is an application of funds.
4   The net source (or application) is the difference between the total sources and the total applications.
5   The working capital section measures the difference between the opening working capital and the closing working capital. In Ande's case, the only working capital that he had was cash. The movement in his cash position can be reconciled as follows:

	£
Cash at 1 June 19X1	10,000
Add: Cash profit	50,000
	60,000
Less: Purchase of machinery	8,000
Cash at 31 May 19X2	£52,000

∴ The movement in cash during the year = £52,000 – £10,000 = £42,000.

Ande's statement of source and application of funds is a very simple one. There were not many transactions during the year, and they were all on cash terms. Exhibit 7.3 examines what happens if Ande buys and sells goods on *credit* terms.

Exhibit 7.3

Ande formed a business on 1 June 19X1 with £10,000 which he paid immediately into a business bank account. A few days after starting the business, he drew a cheque for £8,000 to pay for some machinery for use within the business.
    During the year to 31 May 19X2, he bought some goods on credit for £50,000, and at the end of the year he still owed his creditors for this amount. By the end

of the year he had sold all of the goods on credit for £100,000 and he was still owed for this amount at 31 May 19X2.

Required:
Prepare Ande's statement of source and application of funds for the year to 31 May 19X2.

Answer to Exhibit 7.3

ANDE

Statement of source and application of funds for the year to 31 May 19X2

	£	£
Source of funds:		
Profit (1)		50,000
Application of funds:		
Purchase of machinery		8,000
	(2)	42,000
Increase in working capital:		
Increase in debtors (3)	100,000	
(Increase) in creditors (4)	(50,000)	
(Decrease) in bank balance (5)	(8,000)	42,000

Tutorial notes

1 Ande's profit is still £50,000 (£100,000 – £50,000), even though he has not paid for his purchases, and none of his customers have settled their accounts.
2 His net source of funds remains at £42,000.
3 Ande's increase in debtors is £100,000 (from £0 at the beginning of the year, to £100,000 at the end).
4 His creditors have increased by £50,000 (from £0 at the beginning of the year to £50,000 at the end). Note that an *increase* in creditors reduces working capital, whereas a *decrease* in creditors increases working capital. If this point is not clear, remember:

Working capital = (Debtors + Stocks + Cash) – Creditors

5 By the end of the year his bank balance has gone down by £8,000 (from £10,000 at the beginning of the year, to £2,000 at the end of the year: a movement of £8,000).

Both Exhibits 7.2 and 7.3 show that Ande has made an accounting profit of £50,000. When he traded on cash terms (as in Exhibit 7.2), by the end of the year his cash position had improved by £42,000. However, when he traded on credit terms (as in Exhibit 7.3), his cash position had deteriorated by £8,000.

It should now be possible to see why it is necessary to supplement the traditional financial statements with a statement of source and application of funds. Although Exhibits 7.2 and 7.3 are very simple, they do make the point.

If Ande had relied on his profit and loss account and balance sheet, he would normally have been quite justified in withdrawing the £50,000 accounting profit that he had made. In Exhibit 7.2 there would have been no problem, because the profit had been realized in cash. In Exhibit 7.3 however, it would have been most unwise of him to try to withdraw the profit, because his profit had not been realized in the form of cash. In a more realistic example, it would be even more difficult to monitor the situation, because during the year there would be constant changes in his trade debtor and trade creditor position.

Before moving on to look at a more advanced example of a source and applicaation of funds statement, the recommended format must first be examined.

The recommended format

The format of a simple statement of source and application of funds was covered in an earlier section. In this section, the format recommended in SSAP 10 relating to a single entity will be examined (more complicated structures are covered in Chapter 19).

It should be noted that the format is not mandatory, and companies are free to design their own statements.

Exhibit 7.4 presents a slightly simplified version of the recommended format.

Exhibit 7.4: Recommended format of statement of source and application of funds

SINGLE COMPANY LIMITED
Statement of source and application of funds for the year to XX

	£000	£000	£000
Source of funds			
Profit before tax (1)			1,400
Adjustments for items not involving the movement of funds (2):			
Depreciation			<u>400</u>
Total generated from operations (3)			1,800
Funds from other sources (4):			
Issue of shares for cash			<u>100</u>
			1,900
Application of funds (5):			
Dividends paid		(400)	
Tax paid		(700)	
Purchase of fixed assets		(500)	(1,600)
			300
Increase in working capital (6):			
Increase in stocks (7)		100	
Increase in debtors (7)		200	
	c/f	300	300

	£000	£000	£000
	b/f	300	300
(Increase) in creditors—excluding taxation and proposed dividends (7)		150	
Movement in net liquid funds (8):			
Increase (decrease) in:			
Cash balances	50		
Short-term investments	(200)	(150)	300

Note: The statement would also show details of the previous year's results. The amounts have been included purely for illustrative purposes.

Tutorial notes

1 Notice that this is the profit *before* tax. This means that any appropriations of profit (such as tax and dividends) are ignored. In fact, as will be seen, only tax and dividends that have been *paid* are brought into a funds statement. Other tax and dividend adjustments (such as tax due and proposed dividends) are excluded altogether.

2 Adjustments for items not involving the movement of funds include such items as depreciation, and under- or over-depreciation on the sale of fixed assets. These items have to be added back (or deducted as the case may be) to accounting profit because they are what accountants call 'book entries'. Although they are a legitimate charge to the profit and loss account, they do not affect the movement of funds, i.e. cash does not either go up or go down as a result of making these entries, so a funds statement has to be adjusted to allow for them.

3 Funds obtained from operational activities (mainly from profit) should be shown separately from funds obtained from other sources.

4 Funds from other sources will include *cash* received from the sale of shares and debentures, and from the sale of fixed assets.

5 The application of funds section should only include amounts actually paid in cash. Thus tax due to be paid and any proposed dividend must *not* be included as an application of funds (see also tutorial note 1 above).

6 The working capital section illustrates the movement (i.e. the change) in working capital during the period. The movement is calculated simply by deducting the respective closing balances from the respective opening balances. Working capital is basically the difference between current assets and current liabilities, except that current liabilities do not include any tax payable or any proposed dividends. This definition of working capital is what SSAP 10 means by 'funds'.

7 It should be noted that changes in stocks, debtors and creditors *do* affect the movement of funds.

8 Movements in net liquid funds include cash and bank balances and those investments that could be turned into cash very quickly, such as cash invested in over-night deposit accounts.

Students usually find it very difficult to understand how a funds statement is constructed. There is usually particular difficulty in understanding how changes in working capital affect the movement of funds. Exhibit 7.5, therefore, summarizes the effect of working capital changes on cash flow.

Exhibit 7.5: Working capital movements: effect on cash flow

Item		Movement (Closing balance − opening balance		Effect on cash
Stocks	(i)	Increase	(i)	Down (more cash has been spent on stock)
	(ii)	Decrease	(ii)	Up (less cash has been spent on stock)
Debtors and prepayments	(i)	Increase	(i)	Down (less cash has been received)
	(ii)	Decrease	(ii)	Up (more cash has been received)
Creditors and accruals	(i)	Increase	(i)	Up (less cash has been spent)
	(ii)	Decrease	(ii)	Down (more creditors have been paid)

The next section outlines the construction of a comprehensive example, and you are recommended to work through it most carefully.

A comprehensive example

The example used in this section is a very much more complicated one than those illustrated earlier, and you will probably need to keep referring back to the previous exhibits as you work through it.

Exhibit 7.6

You are presented with the following summarized information for Martin Limited for the year to 31 March 19X8:

MARTIN LIMITED

Profit and loss account (extract) for the year to 31 March 19X8

	19X7 £000	19X8 £000
Net profit for the year before taxation	65	85
Taxation	30	35
Proposed dividend	35	50
	20	30
	15	20
Retained profits brought forward	10	25
Retained profits carried forward	£25	£45

MARTIN LIMITED
Balance sheet (extract) at 31 March 19X8

	19X7 £000	19X7 £000	19X8 £000	19X8 £000
Fixed assets				
Plant at cost		45		95
Less: Accumulated depreciation		18		25
		27		70
Current assets				
Stocks	51		67	
Debtors	110		170	
Bank	2		1	
	163		238	
Less: Current liabilities				
Creditors	15		28	
Taxation	30		35	
Dividends	20		30	
	65		93	
		98		145
		£125		£215
Financed by:				
Capital and reserves				
Ordinary shares of £1 each		100		150
Retained profits		25		45
Shareholders' funds		125		195
Loans				
Debenture stock		—		20
		£125		£215

Additional information:
1   There were no sales of fixed assets during the year.
2   During the year to 31 March 19X8, 50,000 ordinary shares of £1 each and £20,000 of debenture stock were issued for cash.

Required:
Prepare a statement of source and application of funds for the year to 31 March 19X8.

Answer to Exhibit 7.6

MARTIN LIMITED
Statement of source and application of funds for the year to 31 March 19X8

	£000	£000
Source of funds:		
Profit before tax (1)		85
Adjustment for items not involving		
the movement of funds:		
Depreciation (2)		7
Total generated from operations	c/f	92

		£000	£000
	b/f		92
Funds from other sources:			
Issue of shares for cash (3)		50	
Issue of debentures for cash (3)		20	70
			162
Application of funds:			
Dividends paid (4)		(20)	
Tax paid (4)		(30)	
Purchase of fixed assets (5)		(50)	(100)
	(6)		62
Increase in working capital (7):			
Increase in stocks		16	
Increase in debtors		60	
(Increase) in creditors		(13)	
Movement in net liquid funds:			
(Decrease) in cash balances (8)		(1)	£62

Tutorial notes

1 The funds' statement normally begins with the profit *before* tax. This is the direct link that a funds' statement makes with the profit and loss account.
2 Depreciation for the year has been calculated as follows:

	£000
Accumulated depreciation at 31 March 19X8 (as per the balance sheet)	25
Less: Accumulated depreciation at 31 March 19X7 (as per the balance sheet)	18
∴ Depreciation for the year	£7

It is possible to calculate the depreciation in this way because there were no sales of fixed assets during the year. The depreciation charge for the year would normally be obtained from the profit and loss account.
3 The question states that £50,000 of shares and £20,000 of debenture stock were issued for cash during the year.
4 Both the dividends paid and the tax paid relate to the items that were outstanding at 31 March 19X7. The 19X8 proposed dividend and the tax on the profits for the year will be paid during the year to 31 March 19X9, so they do not affect the 19X8's cash position.
5 The question states that there were no sales of fixed assets during the year. However, there were obviously some purchases of fixed assets because the plant at cost has increased from £45,000 in 19X7 to £95,000 in 19X8, an increase of £50,000.
6 Since the beginning of the year, the company has increased its funds by a net amount of £62,000 (£162,000 – 100,000). The working capital section shows where it has invested these funds.
7 The £62,000 of increased funds available to the business have been invested as follows:

Working capital at:	31.3.X7	31.3.X8	*Movement*
	£000	£000	£000
Stocks	51	67	16
Debtors	110	170	60
Bank	2	1	(1)
	163	238	75
Less: Creditors	15	28	13
Net working capital	£148	£210	£62

8 The net decrease in the closing bank balance can be reconciled as follows:

	£000	£000
Opening bank balance at 1 April 19X7		2
Add: Net sources of funds for the year		62
Reductions in amounts paid to creditors		13
		77
Less: Investment in stocks	16	
Reduction in receipts from debtors	60	76
Closing bank balance at 31 March 19X8		£1

You are now recommended to work through Exhibit 7.6 without reference to the solution.

Conclusion

The preparation of a statement of source and application of funds is a complex operation. As a non-accountant it is most unlikely that you will ever have to prepare your own funds' statement, but it is considered that in order to make the best possible use of such a statement it is necessary to know something about its construction. In this chapter you have been taught how to construct your own funds' statements, and in the process learn more about them.

A funds' statement links the profit and loss account and the balance sheet, and the changes that have taken place in the amount of funds available to the business during a particular accounting period. Such information is extremely valuable, because unlike the traditional financial statements, a funds' statement shows where the funds have come from and where they have gone to. Funds may be generated from operational sources or they may be raised outside the business. Funds may be disposed of either by spending them outside the business or by investing them in working capital.

This chapter is closely linked with the next which deals with the interpretation of accounts. The purpose of both chapters is threefold:

1 to enable the non-accountant to use the traditional financial statements to much greater effect;
2 to foster an awareness of their weaknesses; and

3 to be able to extract more meaningful information that might be useful in decision-making.

Questions

7.1 You are presented with the following information:

DENNIS LIMITED
Balance sheet at 31 January 19X2

	31 January 19X1 £000	31 January 19X1 £000	31 January 19X2 £000	31 January 19X2 £000
Fixed assets:				
Land at cost		600		700
Current assets:				
Stock	100		120	
Debtors	200		250	
Cash	6		10	
	306		380	
Less: Current liabilities:				
Creditors	180	126	220	160
		£726		£860
Capital and reserves:				
Ordinary share capital		700		800
Profit and loss account		26		60
		£726		£860

Required:
Prepare Dennis Limited's statement of source and application of funds for the year to 31 January 19X2.

7.2 The following balance sheets have been prepared for Frank Limited:

Balance sheets at:	28.2.X1 £000	28.2.X1 £000	28.2.X2 £000	28.2.X2 £000
Fixed assets:				
Plant and machinery at cost		300		300
Less: Depreciation		80		100
		220		200
Investments at cost		—		100
Current assets:				
Stocks	160		190	
Debtors	220		110	
Bank	—		10	
c/f	380	220	310	300

		£000	£000		£000	£000
b/f		380	220		310	300
Less: Current liabilities:						
Creditors		200			160	
Bank overdraft		20			—	
		220	160		160	150
			£380			£450
Capital and reserves:						
Ordinary share capital			300			300
Share premium account			50			50
Profit and loss account			30			40
			380			390
Shareholders' funds						
Loans:						
Debentures			—			60
			£380			£450

Additional information:
There were no purchases or sales of plant and machinery during the year.

Required:
Prepare Frank Limited's statement of source and application of funds for the year to 28 February 19X2.

7.3 You are presented with the following information:

STARTER
Profit and loss account for the year to 31 March 19X3

	£	£
Sales		10,000
Less: Cost of goods sold:		
Purchases	5,000	
Less: Closing stock	1,000	4,000
Gross profit		6,000
Less: Depreciation		2,000
Net profit for the year		£4,000

Balance Sheet at 31 March 19X3

		£	£
Van			10,000
Less: Depreciation			2,000
	c/f		8,000

		£	£
	b/f		8,000
Stock		1,000	
Trade debtors		5,000	
Bank		12,500	
		18,500	
Less: Trade creditors		2,500	16,000
			£24,000
Capital			20,000
Add: Net profit for the year			4,000
			£24,000

N.B. Starter commenced business on 1 April 19X2.

Required:
Compile Starter's statement of source and application of funds for the year to 31 March 19X3.

7.4 The following is a summary of Gregory Limited's accounts for the year to 30 April 19X4.

Profit and loss account for the year to 30 April 19X4

	£000
Net profit before tax	75
Taxation	25
	50
Dividend (proposed)	40
Retained profit for the year	£10

Balance sheet at 30 April 19X4

	30.4.X3		30.4.X4	
Fixed assets:	£000	£000	£000	£000
Plant at cost		400		550
Less: Depreciation		100		180
		300		370
Current assets:				
Stocks	50		90	
Debtors	70		50	
Bank	10		2	
	130		142	
Less: Current liabilities:				
Creditors	45		55	
Taxation	18		25	
Proposed dividend	35		40	
	98	32	120	22
		£332		£392

Capital and reserves:		
Ordinary share capital	200	200
Profit and loss account	132	142
	332	342
Loans	—	50
	£332	£392

Additional information:
There were no sales of fixed assets during the year to 30 April 19X4.

Required:
Prepare Gregory Limited's statement of source and application of funds for the year to 30 April 19X4.

7.5 The following summarized accounts have been prepared for Pill Limited:

Profit and loss account for the year to 31 May 19X5

	19X4	19X5
	£000	£000
Sales	2,400	3,000
Less: Cost of goods sold	1,600	2,000
Gross profit	800	1,000
Less: Expenses:		
Administrative expenses	310	320
Depreciation: Vehicles	55	60
Furniture	35	40
	400	420
Net profit	400	580
Taxation	120	150
	280	430
Dividends	200	250
Retained profits for the year	£80	£180

Balance sheet at 31 May 19X5

	31.5.X4		31.5.X5	
	£000	£000	£000	£000
Fixed assets:				
Vehicles at cost	600		800	
Less: Depreciation	200	400	260	540
Furniture	200		250	
Less: Depreciation	100	100	140	110
c/f		500		650

		£000	£000		£000	£000
	b/f		500			650
Current assets:						
Stocks		400			540	
Debtors		180			200	
Cash		320			120	
		900			860	
Less: Current liabilities:						
Creditors		270			300	
Corporation tax		170			220	
Proposed dividends		150			100	
		590	310		620	240
			£810			£890
Capital and reserves:						
Ordinary share capital			500			550
Profit and loss account			120			300
Shareholders' funds			620			850
Loans:						
Debentures (8%)			190			40
			£810			£890

Additional information:
There were no sales of fixed assets during the year to 31 May 19X5.

Required:
Compile Pill Limited's statement of source and application of funds for the year to 31 May 19X5.

7.6 The following information relates to Brian Limited for the year to 30 June 19X6.

Profit and loss account for the year to 30 June 19X6

	£000	£000
Gross profit		230
Administrative expenses	76	
Loss on sale of vehicle	3	
Increase in provision for doubtful debts	1	
Depreciation on vehicles	35	115
Net profit		115
Taxation		65
		50
Dividends		25
Retained profit for the year		£25

Balance sheet at 30 June 19X6

	19X5		19X6	
	£000	£000	£000	£000
Fixed assets:				
Vehicle at cost		150		200
Less: Depreciation		75		100
		75		100
Current assets:				
Stocks		60		50
Trade debtors	80		100	
Less: Provision for doubtful debts	4	76	5	95
Cash		6		8
		142		153
Less: Current liabilities:				
Trade creditors	60		53	
Taxation	52		65	
Proposed dividend	20	132	25	143
Net current assets		10		10
		£85		£110
Capital and reserves:				
Ordinary share capital		75		75
Profit and loss account		10		35
		£85		£110

Additional information:
1 The company purchased some new vehicles during the year for £75,000.
2 During the year the company sold a vehicle for £12,000 in cash. The vehicle had originally cost £25,000, and £10,000 had been set aside for depreciation.

Required:
Prepare a statement of source and application of funds for Brian Limited for the year to 30 June 19X6.

Additional questions (without answers)

7.7 The following summarized information relates to Weir Limited for the year to 30 September 19X9:

Profit and loss account

		£000
Profit before taxation		320
Taxation		100
Profit after taxation	c/f	220

		£000
	b/f	220
Dividends		80
Retained profit for the year		£140

Balance sheets at 30 September

	19X8	19X9
	£000	£000
Fixed assets:		
At cost	2,130	2,560
Less: Accumulated depreciation	740	930
	1,390	1,630
Current assets:		
Stocks	470	535
Trade debtors	540	620
Prepayments	45	40
	1,055	1,195
Current liabilities:		
Bank overdraft	(95)	(110)
Trade creditors	(145)	(180)
Accruals	(50)	(30)
Taxation	(200)	(50)
Dividends	(60)	(70)
	(550)	(440)
Debenture loans	(580)	(630)
	£1,315	£1,755
Capital and reserves:		
Called up share capital	350	615
Share premium account	15	30
Revaluation reserve	130	150
Profit and loss account	820	960
	£1,315	£1,755

Additional information:
1 A provision for bad and doubtful debts is maintained. At 1 October 19X8, the balance was £30,000, and at 30 September 19X9 it was £40,000.
2 During the year to 30 September 19X9, fixed assets originally costing £65,000 (and on which depreciation of £40,000 had been charged) were sold for £30,000 in cash.

Required:
Prepare Weir's statement of source and application of funds for the year to 30 September 19X9.

7.8 The following summarized information relates to Conway Limited:

Profit and loss account for the year to 31 October 19X9

	£000
Gross profit	2,400
Distribution costs	(190)
Administrative expenses	(900)
Profit before taxation	1,310
Taxation	(200)
Profit after taxation	1,110
Dividends	(170)
Retained profit for the year	£940

Balance sheets at 31 October

	19X8 £000	19X9 £000
Fixed assets:		
At cost	3,400	5,800
Less: Accumulated depreciation	1,400	2,100
	2,000	3,700
Current assets:		
Stocks	700	100
Trade debtors (net of provision)	2,000	6,000
Other debtors	200	250
Bank and cash	950	—
	3,850	6,350
Current liabilities:		
Bank overdraft	—	(400)
Trade creditors	(300)	(1,200)
Other creditors	(400)	(210)
Taxation	(350)	(450)
Dividend	(100)	(150)
	(1,150)	(2,410)
Long-term loans (15% debenture stock)	—	(2,000)
	£4,700	£5,640
Capital and reserves:		
Called up share capital	2,500	3,500
Share premium account	500	500
Profit and loss account	1,700	1,640
	£4,700	£5,640

Additional information:

1 During the year to 31 October 19X9, fixed assets originally costing £650,000 were sold for £300,000 in cash. The accumulated depreciation on these fixed assets was £400,000.
2 The company maintains a provision for bad and doubtful trade debtors. The provision at 1 November 19X8 was £100,000 and at 31 October 19X9 it was £500,000.
3 During the year to 31 October 19X9, a bonus issue of shares of two shares for every five shares held was made to the company's shareholders.

Required:

Prepare Conway's statement of source and application of funds for the year to 31 October 19X9.

8 Interpretation of accounts

Learning objectives

1 understand the need for and the importance of ratio analysis;

2 calculate a number of common accounting ratios;

3 interpret a set of accounts using a variety of different techniques;

and

4 prepare a report outlining the results of your investigation.

This chapter explains how the non-accountant can convert and interpret basic accounting information into a more meaningful form using what is known as *ratio analysis*.

Data are extracted from the traditional accounting statements and converted into statistics which can be used to compare the entity's results either with previous periods or with similar entities in the same industry. Such comparisons can be done on a percentage basis or by using simple factors. For convenience, these will be referred to as *ratios*.

Ratios are not usually very important when viewed in isolation, but they can be useful when they are used to *interpret* a set of accounts. Students often believe that if they calculate a great many ratios they have 'interpreted' the accounts. In fact, the calculation of a number of ratios is only a beginning. Ratio analysis forms part of a detailed investigation into the entity's results for the period. The results may then be compared with previous periods and with other similar entities.

The interpretation of a set of accounts enables the information to be put into context. This chapter is very important, therefore, because it will enable you as a non-accountant to get far more out of a set of accounts than by simply looking at the figures in isolation.

The need for ratios

In Chapter 1 it was suggested that a business proprietor wants to know the answers to three basic questions:

1 How much profit has the business made?
2 How much does the business owe?
3 How much is owed to the business?

Chapters 3 to 6 showed how an accountant would go about trying to answer these questions, but as has been seen, the method is far from satisfactory. It is only possible to calculate the *absolute* amount of profit, and the total amount of respective indebtedness. Even then, some highly arguable assumptions have to be used in trying to arrive at the answers.

If such results are used in isolation, the proprietor could be misled by the current liquidity position and by the apparent long-term trend of the profits. The debtor and creditor balances do not tell the user very much. Are they, for example, too high or too low? It is not really possible to know until they have been put into context. An outstanding debtors balance of £200,000 would appear to be a very large amount for a small business, but it might be a very small one for a large international company (although it is not possible to be certain until the matter has been gone into in much greater detail).

Ratio analysis is one way to do this. In any case, it is possible to produce hundreds of ratios, but for the purposes of this book it is sufficient to select just a few key ones. In any case, it is difficult to handle a great many ratios, and also it is not necessary to use a large number to demonstrate the basic principles of ratio analysis.

The main ratios will be examined in the following sections under four main headings: profitability, liquidity, efficiency, and investment.

Profitability ratios

Users of accounts will want to know how much profit a business has made so that it can be compared either with previous periods or with other entities. Unfortunately, it is difficult to compare meaningfully the absolute level of profit unless it is related to the size of the entity and the amount of capital invested in it.

Return on capital employed ratio

The best way of doing this is to calculate a ratio comparing the profit with the capital invested. This can be done by using a ratio known as the *return on capital employed* (ROCE) ratio. It can be expressed quite simply as follows:

$$\text{ROCE} = \frac{\text{Profit}}{\text{Capital}} \times 100$$

This ratio (like most other ratios) is expressed as a percentage.

As far as ROCE is concerned, there is, unfortunately, no common agreement about the definition of either profit or capital. As a result, different ROCE ratios can be produced by changing the definitions of both terms. Thus when comparing one ROCE ratio with another, it is important to make sure that the same definitions have been used. It should be noted that no matter how it is calculated, ROCE is a vital and most important ratio.

If profit is considered from the point of view of how successful the entity has been in using its resources, profit should mean the net profit before tax and dividends. The profit (as defined) must then be related to the amount of capital needed to generate it. It would seem appropriate, therefore, to relate profit to the shareholders' funds.

As there are several quite acceptable measures of ROCE, the choice will depend upon the use to which it is to be put. It could be argued, for example, that ordinary shareholders, will only be interested in the profit *after* tax and preference dividends, because their dividend will be based on what profit the company has available after providing for taxation and the preference dividend.

Since you may need to calculate ROCE for different purposes, the main methods of calculating this important ratio are summarized below:

1 $\dfrac{\text{Net profit before tax}}{\text{Shareholders' funds}} \times 100$

2 $\dfrac{\text{Net profit after tax and preference dividend but before extraordinary items}}{\text{Shareholders' funds less preference shares}} \times 100$

3 $\dfrac{\text{Profit before tax and interest}}{\text{Shareholders' funds plus long-term loans}} \times 100$

4 $\dfrac{\text{Profit after tax and before extraordinary items}}{\text{Shareholders' funds}} \times 100$

Note: Extraordinary items are items that are material in amount. They are not considered to be part of the ordinary activities of the business, and it is not expected that they will recur frequently or regularly. Extraordinary items are considered further in more detail in Chapter 19.

By calculating the return on capital employed, a far better measure of the entity's profitability can be achieved than by merely viewing the level of profit in isolation. By using ROCE, sweeping assertions can be avoided about (say) a profit of £500 million being high (it might be thought relatively low if the capital employed was £10,000 million), or a profit of £500 being low (it might be acceptable if the capital invested was £2,000). High and low in this context can only be viewed in an absolute sense.

Gross profit ratio

There are a number of other important profitability ratios that ought to be considered. The *gross profit ratio*, for example, enables the *trading* profitability of the entity to be established. It is calculated as follows:

$$\text{Gross profit ratio} = \frac{\text{Gross profit}}{\text{Total sales revenue}} \times 100$$

The gross profit ratio measures how much profit the entity is earning in relation to the amount of sales that it is making. The definition of gross profit does not usually cause any problems. Most entities adopt the definition that has been used in this book (that is, sales less the cost of goods sold), so meaningful comparisons can usually be made between different entities.

Mark-up ratio

The gross profit ratio complements another main trading ratio that for convenience may be termed the *mark-up ratio*. It is calculated as follows:

$$\text{Mark-up ratio} = \frac{\text{Gross profit}}{\text{Cost of goods sold}} \times 100$$

Mark-up measures the amount of profit added to the cost of goods sold [i.e. (Opening stock + Purchases) − Closing stock] to arrive at the selling price. The mark-up may be reduced to stimulate extra sales, but this will have the effect of reducing the gross profit. However, if extra goods are sold, the greater volume of sales compensates for the reduction in each unit's mark-up.

Net profit ratio

Proprietors sometimes like to compare the net profit with the sales revenue. This can be expressed in the form of the *net profit ratio*. It is calculated as follows:

$$\text{Net profit ratio} = \frac{\text{Net profit before tax}}{\text{Total sales revenue}} \times 100$$

It is difficult to make a fair comparison between different companies' net profit ratios. Individual circumstances vary so much that companies are bound to have different levels of expenditure, no matter how efficient one company is compared with another. Thus it may only be practicable to use a net profit ratio in making comparisons between different periods within the same entity. Over a period of time a pattern will emerge, and by plotting a trend it might be possible to draw some conclusions.

Liquidity ratios

Liquidity ratios measure the overall state of indebtedness of the entity. The total amount of trade debtors and trade creditors can be ascertained quite easily from the balance sheet, but the absolute amounts are not very meaningful. Liquidity ratios, therefore, help to put them into context. There are two main liquidity ratios: the *current assets ratio* and the *acid test ratio*.

Current assets ratio

This ratio is not usually expressed in the form of a percentage. It is calculated as follows:

$$\text{Current assets ratio} = \frac{\text{Current assets}}{\text{Current liabilities}}$$

In most circumstances, current assets will be in excess of current liabilities. If this is not the case, the entity may not have sufficient liquid resources to meet its short-term liabilities.

However, as the term *current* means receivable or payable within the next twelve months, the company may not always have to settle all of its current debts within the next week or month. Its corporation tax, for example, may not have to be paid for some nine months; in the meantime, cash may be received from its debtors. Some entities, such as supermarkets, do not do much trade on credit terms, and it is not uncommon for their current assets to be less than their current liabilities. This is not usually a problem, because as cash is coming in daily, it can always be used to satisfy any short-term indebtedness.

Acid test ratio

The second main liquidity ratio is known as the acid test (or quick) ratio. It is calculated as follows:

$$\text{Acid test ratio} = \frac{\text{Current assets} - \text{stocks}}{\text{Current liabilities}}$$

The acid test ratio is probably a better measure of the entity's real liquidity than is the current assets ratio. If the current assets less stocks are *less* than the current liabilities, the entity's liquidity position may not be critical because (as explained above) the current liabilities may not be due for payment for some time. Nonetheless, it is a situation that must be examined most carefully.

Efficiency ratios

Traditional accounting statements do not measure the *efficiency* of an entity, that is, they do not show how successful the management has been in using the resources of the entity. As argued above, even the net profit does not give any real measure of efficiency when it is viewed in isolation. As a result, a number of efficiency ratios must be calculated that help to put the results into context. There are many different types of efficiency ratios, but in this book only the more common ones will be examined. These are summarized below.

Stock turnover ratio

$$\text{Stock turnover ratio} = \frac{\text{Cost of goods sold}}{\text{Average stock}}$$

The average stock can be calculated as follows:

$$\frac{\text{Opening stock} + \text{Closing stock}}{2}$$

The sales revenue may be substituted for the cost of goods sold if the accounts do not disclose the cost of goods sold. Sales revenue should not be used if it can be avoided, however, since it contains a profit loading which can cause the ratio to be distorted. Instead of using a simple average, many accountants also prefer to use a more sophisticated method of calculating the average stock held during a particular period, especially if goods are purchased irregularly. Sometimes it is also useful to compare the closing stock with the cost of sales in order to gain a clearer idea of what the stock position is like at the end of the year, although this can be misleading if the year-end falls when stocks are abnormal.

The greater the stock turnover (it is not usually expressed as a percentage), the more efficient the entity would appear to be in purchasing goods and selling them quickly to its customers. A stock turnover of 2 for example, would suggest that the entity has about six months of sales in stock which (in most circumstances) would appear to be high, whereas a stock turnover of (say) 12 would mean that the entity only kept about a month's normal sales in stock.

Fixed assets turnover ratio

Another important area to examine from the point of view of efficiency relates to fixed assets. Fixed assets enable the business to function more efficiently, so an investment in fixed assets ought eventually to generate more sales. This can be checked by calculating a ratio known as the *fixed assets turnover* ratio. It is calculated as follows:

$$\text{Fixed assets turnover ratio} = \frac{\text{Total sales revenue}}{\text{Fixed assets at net book value}}$$

This ratio may also be expressed as a percentage.

The fixed assets turnover ratio is really only useful if it is calculated as part of a trend. In isolation, it does not mean very much; for example, is a turnover of 5 good, and 4 poor? All that can be suggested is that if the trend is upwards, then the investment in fixed assets is beginning to pay off, at least in terms of increased sales.

Trade debtor collection period ratio

Generating extra sales revenue is not going to be very helpful if the entity's trade debtors do not settle their debts very promptly. It might be possible to generate extra sales by a combination of lowering selling prices and by offering generous credit terms. In the meantime, the entity has to finance its operational activities, and if it is slow at turning its sales into cash, it might easily run into a short-term liquidity problem. It is important, therefore, for it to have tight control over its trade debtors.

Its success may be checked by calculating an *average trade debtor collection period* ratio. It is calculated as follows:

$$\text{Average trade debtor collection period} = \frac{\text{Average trade debtors}}{\text{Total credit sales}} \times 365$$

The average trade debtors are usually a simple average of opening and closing trade debtors, i.e. ½ (Opening trade debtors + Closing trade debtors). The closing trade debtors are sometimes substituted for the average trade debtors. This is acceptable provided that the closing trade debtors are representative of the period as a whole.

It is important to relate trade debtors to *credit* sales, and not to include any cash sales in the calculation. The method shown above for calculating the ratio would relate the average trade debtors to so many *days'* sales, but it would be possible to substitute weeks or months. It is not customary to express the ratio as a percentage.

A typical debtor collection period cannot be identified, as much depends upon the type of trade in which the company is engaged. Some companies expect settlement within 28 days of either delivery of the goods, or on receipt of the invoice. Other companies might expect settlement within 28 days following the end of the month in which the goods were delivered. On average, therefore, this adds another 14 days (half a month) to the overall period of 28 days. In these circumstances a company would appear to be highly efficient in collecting its debts if the average debtor collection period was about 42 days.

Like most of the other ratios, however, it is important to establish a trend, and if the trend is upwards, then it might suggest that the company's credit control was beginning to weaken.

Trade creditor payment period ratio

A similar ratio can be calculated for the average trade creditor payment period. The formula is as follows:

$$\text{Average trade creditor payment period} = \frac{\text{Average trade creditors}}{\text{Total credit purchases}} \times 365$$

The average trade creditors may again be a simple average of the opening and closing balances, although it is quite customary to substitute the closing trade creditors. The trade creditors must be related to *credit* purchases, and weeks or months may be substituted for the number of days. Like the trade debtor collection period ratio, it is not usual to express the average trade creditor payment period ratio as a percentage.

An upward trend in the average level of trade creditors would suggest that the entity is having some difficulty in finding the cash to pay its creditors. Indeed, it might be a warning that it is running into financial difficulties.

Investment ratios

The various ratios examined in the previous sections are probably of interest to all users of accounts, such as shareholders, managers, creditors or employees. There are, however, some other ratios which are primarily (although not exclusively) of interest to investors. These are known as *investment* ratios, and the main ones are outlined below.

Dividend yield

The first investment ratio which might be found useful is the *dividend yield*. It may be calculated as follows:

$$\text{Dividend yield} = \frac{\text{Nominal value per share}}{\text{Market price per share}} \times \text{Declared dividend rate}$$

The dividend yield measures the rate of return investors would get by purchasing the shares at the current market rate on the basis of a declared dividend rate. If investors buy, for example, 100 £1 ordinary shares at a market rate of £2 per share, and the next declared dividend rate was 10%, their yield would be 5% (£1/2 × 10%). As far as the company is concerned, although they have invested £200 (100 × £2 per share), they will be registered as holding a nominal amount of £100 (100 shares × £1). They are, therefore, entitled to a dividend of £10, which means that they are getting a return of £10 on £200 (or 5%). Dividends are received net of income tax, so some accountants prefer to calculate the *gross* dividend yield. This involves calculating the income tax *assumed* to have been deducted from the dividend and then adding it back. If a shareholder, for example, receives a dividend of £75 and the basic rate of income tax is 25%, the tax assumed to have been deducted will be £25 (£75 × 25/75; *check:* £100 × 25% = £25).

Dividend cover

Another useful investment ratio is the *dividend cover*:

$$\text{Dividend cover} = \frac{\text{Net profit after tax and preference dividend}}{\text{Paid and proposed ordinary dividends}}$$

This ratio gives some idea of the proportion that the ordinary dividends bear to the earnings available for distribution to the ordinary shareholders. The dividend is usually described as being so many times covered by the profits. Thus if the dividend is covered twice, the company would be distributing half of its earnings as dividends for that year.

Earnings per share

Another important investment ratio is that known as *earnings per share* (EPS). This ratio makes it possible to put the profit into context and to avoid looking at it purely in absolute terms. It may be calculated as follows:

$$\text{Earnings per share} = \frac{\substack{\text{Net profit after tax and preference dividend} \\ \text{but before extraordinary items}}}{\text{Number of ordinary shares in issue during the year}}$$

It is customary to calculate this ratio by taking the net profit after tax (although there is no reason why it could not be taken before tax). Preference dividends are deducted because they have to be paid before ordinary shareholders can receive a dividend out of the available earnings. Extraordinary items are excluded because they are items that are not expected to recur, and so their inclusion would distort the year's earnings.

This ratio makes a fair comparison possible between one year's earnings and another, and at the same time relates the earnings to something meaningful, i.e. the number of shares in issue.

Price/earnings ratio

Another common investment ratio is the *price/earnings* ratio (or P/E ratio). It is calculated as follows:

$$\text{Price/earnings ratio} = \frac{\text{Market price per share}}{\text{Earnings per share}}$$

The P/E ratio makes a comparison possible between the earnings per share (as defined above) and the market price. Effectively, it means that the market price is a multiple of the earnings. In theory, the higher the P/E ratio, the greater the demand for the shares (presumably because of the earnings), but a low P/E ratio could also mean that there was little demand for the company's shares even though its earnings were high.

Capital gearing ratio

Capital gearing refers to the proportion that the preference share capital and long-term loans bear to the shareholders' funds plus long-term loans. It may be calculated as follows:

$$\text{Capital gearing ratio} = \frac{\text{Preference shares} + \text{Long-term loans}}{\text{Shareholders' funds} + \text{Long-term loans}} \times 100$$

It should be noted that there are alternative ways of calculating the capital gearing ratio.

A company that has financed itself by a high proportion of borrowing (whether in the form of preference shares or long-term loans) is known as a high geared company. Conversely, a company with a low level of borrowing is regarded as being low geared. A high geared company is potentially a higher risk investment, because before the company can pay any ordinary dividend, it has to earn sufficient profit to cover the interest payments and the preference dividend. This should not be a problem when profits are rising, but if they fall, then the earnings may not be sufficient to pay an ordinary dividend.

Summary of the main ratios

A considerable number of accounting ratios have now been examined. They are summarized below for convenience.

Profitability ratios

$$\text{ROCE} = \frac{\text{Net profit before tax}}{\text{Shareholders' funds}} \times 100$$

$$\text{ROCE} = \frac{\begin{array}{c}\text{Net profit after tax and preference dividend}\\ \text{but before extraordinary items}\end{array}}{\text{Shareholders' funds less preference shares}} \times 100$$

$$\text{ROCE} = \frac{\text{Profit before tax and interest}}{\text{Shareholders' funds plus long-term loans}} \times 100$$

$$\text{ROCE} = \frac{\text{Profit after tax and before extraordinary items}}{\text{Shareholders' funds}} \times 100$$

$$\text{Gross profit ratio} = \frac{\text{Gross profit}}{\text{Total sales revenue}} \times 100$$

$$\text{Mark up ratio} = \frac{\text{Gross profit}}{\text{Cost of goods sold}} \times 100$$

$$\text{Net profit ratio} = \frac{\text{Net profit before tax}}{\text{Total sales revenue}} \times 100$$

Liquidity ratios

$$\text{Current assets ratio} = \frac{\text{Current assets}}{\text{Current liabilities}}$$

$$\text{Acid test ratio} = \frac{\text{Current assets} - \text{Stocks}}{\text{Current liabilities}}$$

Efficiency ratios

$$\text{Stock turnover} = \frac{\text{Cost of goods sold}}{\text{Average stock}}$$

$$\text{Fixed assets turnover} = \frac{\text{Total sales revenue}}{\text{Fixed assets at net book value}}$$

$$\text{Trade debtor collection period} = \frac{\text{Average trade debtors}}{\text{Total credit sales}} \times 365 \text{ days}$$

$$\text{Trade creditor payment period} = \frac{\text{Average trade creditors}}{\text{Total credit purchases}} \times 365 \text{ days}$$

Investment ratios

$$\text{Dividend yield} = \frac{\text{Nominal value per share}}{\text{Market price per share}} \times \text{Declared dividend rate}$$

$$\text{Dividend cover} = \frac{\text{Net profit after tax and preference dividend}}{\text{Paid and proposed ordinary dividends}}$$

$$\text{Earnings per share} = \frac{\text{Net profit after tax and preference dividend but before extraordinary items}}{\text{Number of ordinary shares in issue during the year}}$$

$$\text{Price/earnings ratio} = \frac{\text{Market price per share}}{\text{Earnings per share}}$$

$$\text{Capital gearing} = \frac{\text{Preference shares} + \text{Long-term loans}}{\text{Shareholders' funds} + \text{Long-term loans}} \times 100$$

The 18 ratios listed above form only a small sample of the total number of ratios that could be produced. Used in isolation, they are not particularly helpful. However, when they form part of a detailed analysis, they give a much greater understanding of the company's results than can be obtained from referring simply to the financial accounts.

An illustrative example

This section illustrates the use of these ratios in interpreting a set of accounts. In order to establish a reasonable trend, the results of a company really need to be analysed over something like a five year period, and it is also useful to compare them with similar companies over the same period (there are commercial organizations that provide such comparative data).

Such a long period would obscure the basic procedures, and so in Exhibit 8.1 the data are limited to a single company for a two year period.

Exhibit 8.1

You are provided with the following summarized information relating to Gill Limited for the year to 31 March 19X3:

Gill Limited
Trading, profit and loss account for the year to 31 March 19X3

	19X2		19X3	
	£000	£000	£000	£000
Sales		160		180
Less: Cost of goods sold:				
Opening stock	10		14	
Purchases	100		130	
	110		144	
Less: Closing stock	14	96	24	120
Gross profit		64		60
Less: Expenses:				
Administration	18		24	
Loan interest	1		1	
Selling and distribution	12	31	16	41
Net profit before taxation		33		19
Taxation		15		6
Net profit after taxation		18		13
Dividends: preference (paid)	2		2	
ordinary (proposed)	8		5	
		10		7
Retained profit for the year c/f		8		6

	£000	£000	£000	£000
Retained profit for the year b/f			8	6
Retained profits brought forward			4	12
Retained profits carried forward			£12	£18

GILL LIMITED
Balance sheet at 31 March 19X3

	19X2				19X3	
	£000 Cost	£000 Depreci- ation	£000 Net book value	£000 Cost	£000 Depreci- ation	£000 Net book value
Fixed assets						
Freehold property	60	–	60	60	–	60
Vehicles	42	14	28	48	22	26
	£102	£14	88	£108	£22	86
Current assets						
Stocks		14			24	
Trade debtors		20			60	
Bank		3			1	
		37			85	
Less: current liabilities						
Trade creditors	10			62		
Taxation	15			6		
Proposed dividend	8	33	4	5	73	12
			£92			£98
Capital and reserves						
Authorized, issued and fully paid ordinary shares of £1 each		40			40	
Preference shares (10%)		20			20	
Profit and loss account		12			18	
Shareholders' funds		72			78	
Loans						
Debenture stock (5%)		20			20	
		£92			£98	

Additional information:
1 Purchases and sales are made evenly throughout the year.
2 All purchases and all sales are made on credit terms.
3 You may assume that price levels are stable.

4   The company only sells one product: in 19X2 it sold 40,000 units and in 19X3 60,000 units.
5   There were no sales of fixed assets during the year.
6   The market value of the ordinary shares was estimated to be worth £2.30 per share at 31 March 19X2 and £1.80 per share at 31 March 19X3.

Required:
(a) Compute significant ratios for the two years to 31 March 19X2 and 19X3 respectively; and
(b) using the ratios which you have calculated in part (a) of the question, comment upon the results for the year to 31 March 19X3.

Answer to Exhibit 8.1

(a) Significant ratios   GILL LIMITED

	19X2	19X3

Profitability ratios:

Return on capital employed (ROCE)

$$\frac{\text{Net profit before tax}}{\text{Shareholders' funds}} \times 100 \qquad = \frac{33,000}{72,000} \times 100 \qquad = \frac{19,000}{78,000} \times 100$$

$$= 45.83\% \qquad\qquad = 24.36\%$$

Gross profit

$$\frac{\text{Gross profit}}{\text{Total sales revenue}} \times 100 \qquad = \frac{64,000}{160,000} \times 100 \qquad = \frac{60,000}{180,000} \times 100$$

$$= 40.00\% \qquad\qquad = 33.33\%$$

Mark up

$$\frac{\text{Gross profit}}{\text{Cost of goods sold}} \times 100 \qquad = \frac{64,000}{96,000} \times 100 \qquad = \frac{60,000}{120,000} \times 100$$

$$= 66.67\% \qquad\qquad = 50.00\%$$

Net profit

$$\frac{\text{Net profit before tax}}{\text{Total sales revenue}} \times 100 \qquad = \frac{33,000}{160,000} \times 100 \qquad = \frac{19,000}{180,000} \times 100$$

$$= 20.63\% \qquad\qquad 10.56\%$$

Liquidity ratios:

Current assets

$$\frac{\text{Current assets}}{\text{Current liabilities}} \qquad = \frac{37,000}{33,000} \qquad = \frac{85,000}{73,000}$$

$$= 1.12 \text{ to } 1 \qquad\qquad = 1.16 \text{ to } 1$$

Acid test

$$\frac{\text{Current assets} - \text{Stocks}}{\text{Current liabilities}} \qquad = \frac{37,000 - 14,000}{33,000} \qquad = \frac{85,000 - 24,000}{73,000}$$

$$= 0.70 \text{ to } 1 \qquad\qquad = 0.84 \text{ to } 1$$

	19X2	19X3

Efficiency ratios:

Stock turnover

$$\frac{\text{Cost of goods sold}}{\text{Average stock*}} = \frac{96,000}{\frac{1}{2}(10,000+14,000)} = \frac{120,000}{\frac{1}{2}(14,000+24,000)}$$
$$= 8.0 \text{ times} \qquad = 6.3 \text{ times}$$

* ½ (Opening stocks + Closing stocks)

Fixed assets turnover

$$\frac{\text{Total sales revenue}}{\text{Fixed assets at net book value}} = \frac{160,000}{88,000} = \frac{180,000}{86,000}$$
$$= 1.82 \text{ times} \qquad = 2.09 \text{ times}$$

Trade debtor collection period

$$\frac{\text{Closing trade debtors*}}{\text{Total credit sales}} = \frac{20,000}{160,000} \times 365 = \frac{60,000}{180,000} \times 365$$
$$= 46 \text{ days} \qquad = 122 \text{ days}$$

*Opening trade debtors have not been given for 19X2, so closing trade debtors have been used.

Trade creditor collection period

$$\frac{\text{Closing trade creditors*}}{\text{Total credit purchases}} \times 365 = \frac{10,000}{100,000} \times 365 = \frac{62,000}{130,000} \times 365$$
$$= 37 \text{ days} \qquad = 175 \text{ days}$$

*Opening trade creditors have not been given for 19X2, so closing trade creditors have been used.

Investment ratios:

Dividend yield

$$\frac{\text{Nominal value per share}}{\text{Market price per share}} \times \frac{\text{Declared}}{\text{dividend rate}} = \frac{1.00}{2.30} \times 20\%* = \frac{1.00}{1.80} \times 12.5\%**$$
$$= 8.70\% \qquad = 6.94\%$$

$$* \frac{8,000}{40,000} \times 100 \qquad ** \frac{5,000}{40,000} \times 100$$
$$= 20\% \qquad = 12.5\%$$

Dividend cover

$$\frac{\text{Net profit after tax and preference dividend}}{\text{Paid and proposed ordinary dividends}} = \frac{18,000-2,000}{8,000} = \frac{13,000-2,000}{5,000}$$
$$= 2.00 \text{ times} \qquad = 2.20 \text{ times}$$

Earnings per shares (EPS)

$$\frac{\text{Net profit after tax and preference dividend}}{\text{Number of ordinary shares in issue during the year}} = \frac{18,000-2,000}{40,000} = \frac{13,000-2,000}{40,000}$$
$$= 40.00p \qquad = 27.50p$$

Price/earnings (P/E) ratio

$$\frac{\text{Market price per share}}{\text{Earnings per share}} = \frac{2.30}{0.40} = \frac{1.80}{0.275}$$
$$= 5.75 \qquad = 6.55$$

	19X2	19X3

Capital gearing

$$\frac{\text{Preference share} + \text{Long-term loans}}{\text{Shareholders' funds} + \text{Long-term loans}} \times 100 = \frac{20,000 + 20,000}{72,000 + 20,000} \times 100 = \frac{20,000 + 20,000}{78,000 + 20,000} \times 100$$

$$= 43.48\% \qquad = 40.82\%$$

(b) Comments on the ratios

Profitability

1 The selling price of the product in 19X2 must have been £4.00 per unit since the company sold 40,000 units and its total sales revenue was £160,000 (£160,000 + 40,000). In 19X3 the company sold 60,000 units and its total sales revenue was £180,000. The selling price per unit must, therefore, have been £3.00. It would appear that Gill Limited deliberately reduced its selling price per unit by 25% (£1.00 × 100/£4.00 = 25%). There was thus a 50% increase in sales volume (from 40,000 units to 60,000), but its total sales revenue only increased by £20,000 (or 12.5%).

2 The relatively modest increase in sales revenue did not help to increase the gross profit (down from £64,000 to £60,000), largely because the reduction in mark-up (down from 66.67% to 50%) did not generate sufficient extra sales.

3 The large increase in sales volume also affected overall profitability. The net profit on sales was reduced from 20.63% to 10.56%, partly because of the reduction in gross profit and partly because other expenses increased by £10,000. Consequently, the return on capital employed was much reduced: from 45.83% to 24.36%. This is still a favourable rate of return when compared with alternative forms of investment, but the company's management must view the downward trend with some concern.

Liquidity

1 Gill's current assets position does not appear to have been greatly affected by the overall decline in profitability. In fact the current assets ratio has increased slightly, from 1.12 to 1 to 1.16 to 1. The current assets are in excess of current liabilities in both years, so provided that receipts from trade debtors can be kept in step with payments to trade creditors, the company would appear not to have an immediate liquidity problem.

2 If stocks are excluded from current assets, however, the position is a little more worrying. The acid test ratio was 0.71 to 1 in 19X2, and 0.84 to 1 in 19X3, so there has been an improvement in Gill's immediate liquidity position. Even so, by the end of 19X3 the company did not have sufficient cash to pay its proposed dividend, so it was dependent on either being able to obtain overdraft facilities from the bank, or on cash receipts from its trade debtors (note that there was a similar situation in 19X2). Fortunately, the tax would probably not have to be paid until 1 January 19X4 (i.e. nine months after the year end).

Efficiency

1 Gill was not as efficient in trading in 19X3 as it had been in 19X2. Its stock turnover was down from 8.0 to 6.3, which means that it was not turning over its stocks as quickly in 19X3 as it did in 19X2.

2 The company's investment in fixed assets (as measured by its sales activity) has improved from 1.82 times in 19X2 to 2.09 times in 19X3. This arose largely because the purchase of new assets only increased the gross book value of

its fixed assets by £6,000, whereas the depreciation charge for the year reduced the total net book value by £8,000, a net difference of £2,000.

3   The extra sales generated during 19X3 were made at some cost to its potential liquidity position. At the end of 19X2 its outstanding trade debtors represented 46 days' sales, but at the end of 19X3, they represented 122 days' sales. This suggests that Gill encouraged a greater sales volume by reducing both its selling prices and by offering more generous credit terms. It is also possible that the company was so busy coping with the increased operational activity that it did not have time to control its debtor position.

4   Gill appears to have been fortunate in 19X3 in not having to pay its trade creditors as promptly as it did in 19X2. At the end of 19X2, its trade creditors represented about 37 days' purchases, but at the end of 19X3 they represented 175 days' purchases (or nearly six months' purchases). If Gill had had to pay its creditors as quickly in 19X3 as it had done in 19X2, its total trade creditors at the end of 19X3 would have amounted to about £13,000 (£130,000 × 37/365), instead of the £62,000 actually owing at that date. By paying its trade creditors more quickly, Gill would probably have had a bank overdraft of some £48,000 ((£62,000 – £13,000) = £49,000 – £1,000), instead of the favourable balance of £1,000.

Investment

1   Gill Limited is a private company, so its shares would not be freely available on a recognized stock exchange. The market price of the shares given in the question is bound to be rather a questionable one, and it probably does not reflect the earnings potential of the company.

2   The dividend yield has fallen from 8.7% in 19X2 to 6.94% in 19X3. Compared with the yield currently available from other investments, these yields are about average, although the reduction in the dividend for 19X3 could be the start of a downwards trend.

3   Whilst the reduction in the dividend from 20% in 19X2 to 12.5% in 19X3 is worrying, the dividend is well covered by the earnings. Indeed, the company could have paid the same dividend in 19X3 as it did in 19X2, and the dividend would still have been covered 1.38 times (£13,000 – 2,000/8,000). It would appear that the company's policy is to pay less than half of its earnings as dividend, even if it means reducing the dividend. This would not matter as much to a private company as it would to a public one. In a public company a reduction in dividend can result in a fall in the market value of its shares, thus reflecting the reduction in confidence that the market has in the company.

4   No new shares were issued during the year. Thus as a result of the reduction in profits, the earnings per share declined from 40.00p to 27.50p.

5   The increase in the price earnings ratio (up from 5.75 to 6.55) is surprising. It was probably caused by the market's view (albeit a rather restricted one) that the company's future is a reasonably good one, notwithstanding the reduction in the company's profit. However, this company is a private one, so we cannot be certain how the market price of its shares has been determined.

6   Gill Limited is a fairly high geared company. In 19X2, nearly 44% of its financing had been raised in the form of fixed interest stock, but in 19X3 this was reduced to just under 41%. By financing itself in this way, the company is committed to making annual payments of £3,000 (£2,000 of preference dividend + £1,000 of debenture interest). In absolute terms, this amount is not large, and so although it is a relatively high geared company, its earnings should be sufficient to cover its interest commitments.

Summary

1 In 19X3 Gill Limited achieved its presumed objective of increasing its sales. It did this partly by reducing its unit selling price, and partly by offering extended credit terms to its customers. The effect of this policy has been to reduce gross profit by £4,000 and its net profit by £14,000.

2 The new policy did not affect its liquidity position, largely because the extended credit terms (leading to delays in the settlement of its trade debts) were offset by similar delays in paying its trade creditors.

3 As a result of the reduction in its profits for 19X3, the company reduced its dividend, although its earnings were still sufficient for it to maintain the same dividend as in 19X2.

4 The market (such as it is) does not seem to agree that the reduction in the profit or of the dividend is serious. Indeed, it can be argued the company's future is healthy provided that it can persuade its trade debtors to pay their debts more promptly.

You are now recommended to work through Exhibit 8.1 again most carefully. Make sure that you know how to calculate the ratios, and that you know what they mean. Then try and list your own views on Gill Limited's progress during 19X3. The comments listed above are only brief ones, and much more could have been written about the company. However, the exhibit demonstrates that ratios enable a great deal more information to be extracted from the traditional profit and loss account and balance sheet than is sometimes appreciated.

Ratios help to put the information into context, but it must be emphasized that they must then be used as part of a detailed overall analysis.

The next section outlines how you would undertake such an analysis.

Analysing the accounts

As explained earlier, a considerable number of people will be interested in the affairs of a company. Analysts, creditors, employees, central and local government, investors, journalists, management, shareholders, trade unions and the general public will all have some interest to a greater or a lesser degree in the performance of a particular company. Some of these groups may want to know everything that there is to know about the company, while other groups may only be interested in a fairly limited amount of information.

If you are asked to analyse a set of accounts, therefore, the amount of work you undertake will depend upon the reasons for your investigation. If your own company is considering making a take-over bid for another company, for example, you will probably need all the information that you can get. However, if you are a creditor, your main interest will probably be in finding out whether the company is in a position to pay you what you are owed.

Nonetheless, it is possible to recommend a general procedure that can be followed irrespective of the reasons for the investigation. This procedure is summarized in the following sub-sections.

Obtaining information

You are recommended to find out as much about the company as you can and how it compares with similar companies in the same industry. It would also be useful to examine its future and that of the industry in a national and international context.

It is not usually difficult to obtain information if you search for it. You can start with the company's annual accounts (Part 4 of the book explains how to use such accounts). Even the company's own public relations department may be willing to supply you with a great deal of information about the company. There are also a number of commercial agencies that specialize in obtaining company information, and other sources include journals, magazines and newspapers.

Assimilating such information about the company from a wide range of sources will help you interpret the company's accounts much more meaningfully.

Calculating trends and ratios

It has been explained earlier that it is desirable to examine a company's accounts over a number of years. As a general rule, it is suggested that you choose a period of some three to five years. Too short a period will not enable you to establish much of a trend, and too long a period could mean that you are using information that is somewhat out-of-date.

Once you have collected a set of accounts, the next step is to calculate a number of representative trends and ratios. The exact number and type will depend upon the purpose of your investigation, and you may need to calculate some specialist ratios. If you were examining the accounts of a hotel, for example, you might want to calculate the rooms occupied as a proportion of the rooms in the hotel, or in the case of a retailing organization, the salesmen's salaries as a proportion of sales revenue.

You can begin to assess the trends and calculate the ratios by using a number of different techniques. The four main techniques are summarized below:

1 *Horizontal analysis.* This technique requires a line-by-line comparison to be made between the company's annual accounts over the period chosen for the investigation.
2 *Trend analysis.* Trend analysis is similar to horizontal analysis, except that the first accounts in the series are given a weighting of 100, subsequent accounts in the series then being related to the base of 100.

3 *Vertical analysis.* This technique requires both the profit and loss account and balance sheet items respectively to be expressed as a percentage of the total items.

4 *Ratio analysis.* Accounting ratios have already been dealt with in some detail. As has been emphasized, it is possible to produce a great many ratios, so depending upon your purpose, you may want to convert each item in the accounts into a ratio and compare it with similar ratios for previous periods.

If you had adopted all of these techniques, you would by now have collated a great deal of information, and you would be in a position to compare each year's accounts on a similar basis. However, it is unlikely that the accounts you have obtained will have been adjusted for inflation, so to make a fairer comparison between them you should make some allowance for this factor. This subject is covered further in Chapter 20, but as a rough guide, remember that with an inflation rate of 5% per annum, prices double over a period of 15 years or increase by about 30% over a five year period.

Besides calculating trends and ratios specifically for the company that you are investigating, you might also have been able to obtain similar statistics for other companies in the same industry. You are now, therefore, in a position to try to work out what all the information means.

Interpreting the accounts

The last and most difficult step after collating all the information that you have collected is to explain or to interpret it. What guides are available to help you come to a decision about the company? Much, of course, depends upon the reason for your investigation, but in general it is suggested that you ask the following questions:

1 *The market for the company's products.* Has this expanded or contracted in recent years, and how has the company coped with the changes in market conditions? What will the market be like over (say) the next five years? How will it be affected by general demographic, economic, political and social factors? Does the company seem attuned to these possible changes?

2 *Sales and profits.* Have these increased or decreased over the period? If there has been any growth, has it been because of internal expansion or because of acquisition? Does the management seem keen enough to pursue growth or is the company stagnating?

3 *Capital investment.* What capital investment has there been and what is planned? How would future investment be financed? What retained reserves has the company built up?

4 *Management.* What is the record of its management? Are the senior

managers near retirement? Are they young enough to seek change? Are they ambitious? How well do they seem to have managed the company's resources? Is its liquidity position secure? How good are they at portraying a favourable public image of the company?

5 *Employees and industrial relations.* Does the company appear to have a stable work-force? Has it had any industrial disputes? What is its attitude and relationship like to the trade unions? How does the output and profit record per employee compare with other companies?

6 *Generally.* Having found out a great deal about the company, does it inspire you with some confidence about its future? Is it likely to survive and expand both in the short term and in the long term?

The above questions are not exhaustive, but there is no doubt that having extensively researched a company's history and examined its future, you will already have formed a provisional view before you come to make your recommendations. All that remains for you to do is to set them down on paper. At that stage you may well find that you are expected to produce a brief report, so you have the difficult task of summarizing the main features of the company in just a few pages. You will probably find that producing such a summary is almost as difficult as carrying out the initial investigation!

Conclusion

This chapter concludes the first main part of the book. By now, you should know something about the nature of accounting information, where it comes from, and how it is used.

As has been argued throughout this book, the traditional techniques adopted by accountants are open to some criticism, so it is only right that some reservations should be made about the reliability of accounting information. However, no one has yet devised a better method of accounting, and until they do, you will have to make the best of the present one. As a non-accountant, you are now in an excellent position to make the best use of accounting information while at the same time being able to allow for its deficiencies.

The next part of the book deals with cost and management accounting. This is a most important branch of accounting that is of especial interest to non-accountants working in industry, although its techniques can be used elsewhere. However, it can only be fully appreciated if it is first preceded by a study of financial accounting. If you are in any doubt, therefore, about your understanding of the last six chapters, you are recommended to go back and have another attempt at some of the exhibits and questions.

Questions

8.1 The following information has been extracted from the books of account of Betty for the year to 31 January 19X1.

Trading and profit and loss account for the year to 31 January 19X2

	£000	£000
Sales (all credit)		100
Less: Cost of goods sold:		
Opening stock	15	
Purchases	65	
	80	
Less: Closing stock	10	70
Gross profit		30
Administrative expenses		16
Net profit		£14

Balance sheet at 31 January 19X1

	£000	£000
Fixed assets (net book value)		29
Current assets:		
Stock	10	
Trade debtors	12	
Cash	3	
	25	
Less: Current liabilities		
Trade creditors	6	19
		£48
Financed by:		
Capital at 1 February 19X0		40
Add: Net profit	14	
Less: Drawings	6	8
		£48

Required:
Calculate the following accounting ratios:
1 gross profit;
2 net profit;
3 return on capital employed;
4 current ratio;
5 acid test;
6 stock turnover; and
7 debtor collection period.

8.2 You are presented with the following summarized accounts:

JAMES LIMITED
Profit and loss account for the year to 28 February 19X2

	£000
Sales (all credit)	1,200
Cost of sales	600
Gross profit	600
Administrative expenses	(500)
Debenture interest payable	(10)
Profit on ordinary activities	90
Taxation	(30)
	60
Dividends	(40)
Retained profit for the year	£20

JAMES LIMITED
Balance sheet at 28 February 19X2

	£000	£000	£000
Fixed assets (net book value)			685
Current assets			
Stock		75	
Trade debtors		200	
		275	
Less: Current liabilities			
Trade creditors	160		
Bank overdraft	10		
Taxation	30		
Proposed dividend	40	240	35
			£720
Capital and reserves			
Ordinary share capital			600
Profit and loss account			20
Shareholders' funds			620
Loans:			
10% debentures			100
			£720

Required:
Calculate the following accounting ratios:
1 return on capital employed;
2 gross profit;
3 mark-up;
4 net profit;
5 acid test;
6 fixed asset turnover;
7 debtor collection period; and
8 capital gearing.

8.3 You are presented with the following information for each of three companies:

Profit and loss accounts for the year to 31 March 19X3

	Mark Limited £000	Luke Limited £000	John Limited £000
Profit before tax	£64	£22	£55

Balance sheet (extracts) at 31 March 19X3

	Mark Limited £000	Luke Limited £000	John Limited £000
Capital and reserves			
Ordinary share capital of £1 each	100	177	60
Cumulative 15% preference shares of £1 each	–	20	10
Share premium account	–	70	20
Profit and loss account	150	60	200
Shareholders' funds	250	327	290
Loans			
10% debentures	–	–	100
	£250	£327	£390

Required:
Calculate the following accounting ratios:
1 return on capital employed; and
2 capital gearing.

8.4 The following information relates to Helena Limited:

Trading account year to 30 April

	19X1 £000	19X2 £000	19X3 £000	19X4 £000	19X5 £000	19X6 £000
Sales (all credit)	–	130	150	190	210	320
Less: Cost of goods sold:						
Opening stock	–	20	30	30	35	40
Purchases (all in credit terms)	–	110	110	135	145	305
	–	130	140	165	180	345
Less: Closing stock	–	30	30	35	40	100
	–	100	110	130	140	245
Gross profit	–	£30	£40	£60	£70	£75
Trade debtors at 30 April	£40	£45	£40	£70	£100	£150
Trade creditors at 30 April	£20	£20	£25	£25	£30	£60

Required:
Calculate the following account ratios for each of the five years to 30 April 19X2 to 19X6 inclusive: *1* gross profit; *2* mark-up; *3* stock turnover; *4* trade debtor collection period; and *5* trade creditor payment period.

8.5 You are presented with the following information relating to Hedge Public Limited Company for the year to 31 May 19X5:

(a) The company has an issued and fully paid share capital of £500,000 ordinary shares of £1 each. There are no preference shares.
(b) The market price of the shares at 31 May 19X5 was £3.50.
(c) The net profit after taxation for the year to 31 May 19X5 was £70,000.
(d) The directors are proposing a dividend of 7p per share for the year to 31 May 19X5.

Required:
Calculate the following accounting ratios:
1 dividend yield;
2 dividend cover;
3 earnings per share; and
4 price/earnings ratio.

8.6 The following information relates to Style Limited for the two years to 30 June 19X5 and 19X6 respectively:

Trading, profit and loss accounts for the year

	19X5		19X6	
	£000	£000	£000	£000
Sales (all credit)		1,500		1,900
Less: Cost of goods sold:				
Opening stock	80		100	
Purchases (all on credit terms)	995		1,400	
	1,075		1,500	
	100	975	200	1,300
Gross profit		525		600
Less: Expenses		250		350
Net profit		£275		£250

Balance sheet at 30 June

	19X5		19X6	
	£000	£000	£000	£000
Fixed assets (net book value)		580		460
Current assets:				
Stock	100		200	
Trade debtors	375		800	
Bank	25		–	
	500		1,000	
Less: Current liabilities:				
Bank overdraft	–		10	
Trade creditors	80		200	
	80	420	210	790
		£1,000		£1,250

	£000	£000
Capital and reserves:		
Ordinary share capital	900	900
Profit and loss account	100	350
Shareholders' funds	£1,000	£1,250

Required:

(a) Calculate the following accounting ratios for the two years 19X5 and 19X6 respectively;

   1 gross profit;

   2 mark-up;

   3 net profit;

   4 return on capital employed;

   5 stock turnover;

   6 current ratio;

   7 acid test;

   8 trade debtor collection period; and

   9 trade creditor payment period.

(b) Comment upon the company's performance for the year to 30 June 19X6.

Additional questions (without answers)

8.7 The following summarized information relates to Turnbull public limited company.

Year to 31 October	19X2	19X3	19X4	19X5	19X6
	£000	£000	£000	£000	£000
Profit and loss accounts					
Sales (all credit)	5,500	5,600	5,700	6,000	9,300
Cost of sales	(3,030)	(3,050)	(3,000)	(3,250)	(5,400)
Gross profit	2,470	2,550	2,700	2,750	3,900
Distribution costs	(520)	(550)	(600)	(600)	(900)
Administrative expenses	(1,500)	(1,500)	(1,500)	(1,500)	(2,000)
Profit before taxation	450	500	600	650	1,000
Taxation	(60)	(90)	(120)	(150)	(200)
Profit after taxation	390	410	480	500	800
Dividends	(90)	(90)	(100)	(150)	(150)
Transferred to reserves	300	320	380	350	650
Balance sheets at 31 October					
Fixed assets at cost	3,100	3,200	3,900	4,600	6,000
Less: Accumulated depreciation	200	300	400	500	600
c/f	2,900	2,900	3,500	4,100	5,400

		£000	£000	£000	£000	£000
	b/f	2,900	2,900	3,500	4,100	5,400
Current assets						
Stocks		600	700	750	750	2,400
Trade debtors		800	800	900	900	1,600
Cash and bank		100	100	100	150	260
		1,500	1,600	1,750	1,800	4,260
Current liabilities						
Trade creditors		(2,390)	(2,140)	(2,470)	(2,690)	(5,750)
Taxation		(60)	(90)	(120)	(150)	(200)
Dividend		(90)	(90)	(100)	(150)	(150)
		(2,540)	(2,320)	(2,690)	(2,990)	(6,100)
		£1,860	£2,180	£2,560	£2,910	£3,560
Capital and reserves						
Called up share capital						
(ordinary shares of £1 each)		500	500	500	500	500
Profit and loss account		1,360	1,680	2,060	2,410	3,060
		£1,860	£2,180	£2,560	£2,910	£3,560

Notes:
(1) Stock at 1 November 19X1: £550,000
(2) All purchases are obtained on credit terms.

Required:
Prepare a report for the Board of Directors of Turnbull plc examining the financial performance of the company during the five year period 1 November 19X1 to 31 October 19X6.

8.8 The following information relates to three companies all operating in the same industry.

	Begg plc £000	Chow plc £000	Doyle plc £000
Profit and loss accounts for the year to			
30 November 19X1			
Turnover	11,200	11,500	13,000
Cost of sales	(5,600)	(4,800)	(7,100)
Gross profit	5,600	6,700	5,900
Operating expenses	(4,000)	(3,300)	(4,700)
Profit before taxation	1,600	3,400	1,200
Taxation	(600)	(1,100)	(550)
Profit after taxation	1,000	2,300	650
Dividends	(600)	(200)	(300)
Retained profit	400	2,100	350

	£000	£000	£000
Balance sheets at 30 November 19X1			
Fixed assets at cost	2,600	2,700	2,800
Less: Accumulated depreciation	1,000	700	1,400
	1,600	2,000	1,400
Current assets			
Stocks	1,700	1,300	1,300
Trade debtors	2,900	5,200	2,000
Debtors	300	1,800	300
Cash and bank	400	50	2,200
	5,300	8,350	5,800
Current liabilities			
Trade creditors	(1,300)	(1,200)	(1,500)
Other creditors	(1,000)	(1,400)	(1,450)
Taxation	(600)	(1,100)	(550)
Dividends	(600)	(200)	(300)
	(3,500)	(3,900)	(3,800)
	£3,400	£6,450	£3,400
Capital and reserves			
Called up share capital			
(ordinary shares of £1 each)	500	2,000	750
Profit and loss account	2,900	4,450	2,650
	£3,400	£6,450	£3,400
Market price of shares at			
30 November 19X1	£22.20	£1.90	£7.40

Required:

Assume that you were a trainee investment analyst in a firm of stockbrokers.

Prepare a report for your section manager comparing and contrasting the financial performance of the three companies.

Part 3

Cost and management accounting

9 Basic costing principles

Learning objectives_____

1 describe the nature and purpose of cost and management accounting;

2 appreciate the need for planning and control;

3 summarize the procedure for implementing a cost and management accounting system;

4 outline the steps taken in building up the cost of a product.

Part 2 of this book was concerned with *financial* accounting. This part of the book covers the other main branch of accounting – *cost and management accounting*. For convenience, it will be referred to as *costing*, although as explained in Chapter 1, there are some technical differences between costing (or cost accounting) and management accounting.

Costing is a routine procedure concerned with establishing the detailed costs of individual products and processes. Accountants need costing information in order to help them make recommendations to management for use in decision-making. This should strictly be referred to as management accounting. Accountants, however, do not adhere rigidly to any of these terms, and they are often interchangeable.

The distinction between costing and management accounting is similar to the one between book-keeping and financial accounting. Book-keeping is concerned with the recording of basic accounting information. Financial accounting summarizes that information for the benefit of those groups who have a need or a use for it, especially those outside the entity.

Costing information is similar to financial accounting information in that it has also to be collected, recorded, stored, and eventually extracted. It then needs to be summarized in a format that will help management in decision-making.

This chapter examines the background to costing. Chapters 10 and 11 cover absorption costing, while Chapter 12 looks briefly at the subject of cost book-keeping. Chapter 13 investigates marginal costing, and Chapters 14 and 15 deal with the subject of budgeting and standard costing. Chapter 16 examines capital investment appraisal.

Historical review

As explained in earlier chapters, accounting evolved out of a need for information about how well a business was doing, how much it owed, and how much was owing to it. As businesses became more complex, and as ownership gradually became separated from managerial control, some documentary information became essential both for owners and management. Over the last 150 years, the law has increasingly protected the rights of company shareholders by insisting that a minimum amount of information be supplied to them annually.

The information supplied is usually extracted from company records kept specially for that purpose. These records may also be used to supply the management of the company with information in order to help it plan and control the day-to-day activities of the company. Indeed, sometimes the records that are kept for external reporting purposes are the only major documentary source of information for management.

In such circumstances, management will only be supplied with any detailed information after the company's annual accounts have been prepared. It may only be then that the management appreciates that urgent action needs to be taken, for example, over an impending liquidity crisis. The management ought to know, of course, from their specialist knowledge of the business and their daily contact with it, that some problems are beginning to build up. However, they can sometimes be so involved in dealing with routine matters that unless advised, they are not aware of long-term trends. By the time that they do become aware of them, it might be too late to do much about them. In any case, the annual accounts are not designed for management reporting purposes.

It is not surprising, therefore, to find that with increasing industrialization, management began to demand more information. In particular, it needed to be specially designed, and to be supplied much more frequently than once a year.

In responding to this demand, accountants initially set up a different set of records from those required for financial reporting purposes (even though much of the data were common to both systems). A costing system which is kept quite separate from a financial reporting system is known as an *interlocking* system. Nowadays, it is much more common to find that both systems are kept within one single system. This is known as an *integral* system of costing.

The collection of information specifically for management accounting purposes and its separation from the financial records gradually evolved over a long period of time. Indeed, costing as a major branch of accounting is a relatively recent development. It was not practised very widely in the United Kingdom before 1914, and while the increased industrial activity caused by the two world wars of 1914–18 and 1939–45 encouraged the demand for more information, it was not until about 1960 that the practice of costing began to grow on any scale. Even in the 1990s management in many companies still rely on inadequate information for decision-making purposes. It can be argued very strongly that better information should be supplied to management so that managers can both plan and control the company's activities more effectively. This is the subject of the next section.

Planning and control

If an entity is to be run efficiently, management must know what is expected of it. It is important, therefore, that the entity lays down its basic objectives. These might be quite straightforward, for example, to achieve the maximum return on its capital employed, to provide a service that the public wants, or to provide a healthy environment in which employees can work.

Once the objectives have been established, management has then to work out how best to achieve them. In other words, it has to do some planning before it puts the plans into action. Thereafter, it must ensure that the plans are being carried out by detailed control of the actual events.

Costing information can play a most important part in this process. Unlike financial accounting information, a costing system has been specially designed to help management plan and control, and it has several advantages over financial accounting. These may be summarized as follows:

1 it can be produced frequently and regularly;
2 it is very detailed;
3 it is up-to-date;
4 it does not depend entirely on historical information; and
5 it encourages a forward looking approach.

These are substantial claims, and they will be proved in subsequent chapters. In the meantime, the next section explains how a costing system may be implemented.

Implementation procedure

In order to operate a costing system, a clear organizational structure must be established, and sufficient information must be available in documentary form. These two requirements will be considered separately.

Organizational structure

Planning and control can best be achieved by establishing clear lines of managerial responsibility. This may require a careful examination of the way in which the entity is structured and what responsibility is given to individuals within it.

In large organizations this may involve setting up a considerable number of interrelated departments and subdepartments that range from production departments at the lowest level of the structure to the board of directors at the highest level. This may be described as the pyramid format, and it is shown in a diagrammatic format in Exhibit 9.1.

Exhibit 9.1: Organizational structure: the pyramid format

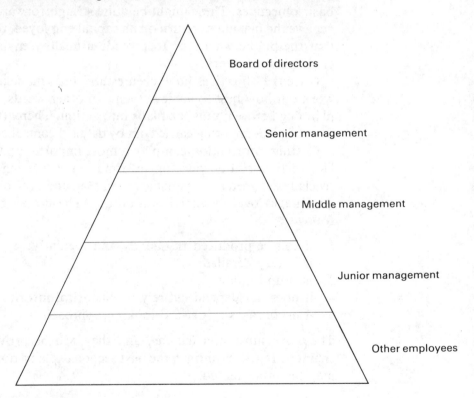

In large companies it is not uncommon for the organizational structure to be of a divisional nature, perhaps based on products or geographical areas in which the company operates. Within each division there may be a number of factories (or works). Each factory may be divided into functions (for example, administration, distribution and production), and each function into departments (for example, machine shop, stores control and wages). The organizational structure of a typical manufacturing company is shown in Exhibit 9.2.

Exhibit 9.2: Organizational structure of a manufacturing company

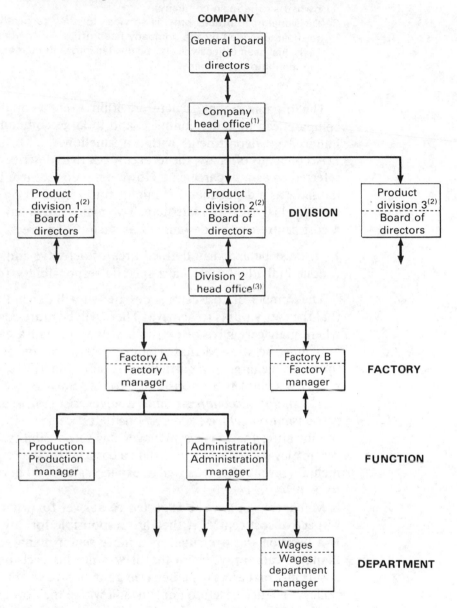

Notes:

1   The company's head office co-ordinates overall company policy. It also provides assistance and guidance generally throughout the company. The head office itself will be divided into a number of functions, such as accounting, marketing

and personnel. Within each function there will probably be a number of departments, such as cash, taxation and salaries.

2 Divisions will usually be managed by a divisional board of directors, the board being answerable to the general board. Divisions often operate as separate limited liability companies in their own right (although all their shares may be owned by the main company).

3 Divisional head offices provide services for their respective divisions, similar to those provided by the company head office for the company as a whole. Divisional head offices will also be divided into a number of functions, and each function into departments.

The organizational structure within even a small manufacturing company can be quite complex, and in large companies there may be hundreds of departments within a function.

Accountants often use the term *cost centre* to describe what is ordinarily referred to as a department. However, a cost centre is not necessarily the same as a department. It might, for example, be a machine or even an individual, such as a salesman. Two main criteria have to be met before a cost centre can be designated as such. They are:

1 it must be a clearly defined area of activity; and
2 one individual must have specific responsibility for it.

The number of cost centres designated will depend upon the control that the entity wants to achieve. There will be more cost centres in cases where managers have responsibility over a small area.

It must be stressed that whatever the organizational structure, the manager in charge of a particular division, function or cost centre must be given complete responsibility for it. Such a system is known as *responsibility accounting*, and it gives rise to what are known as *responsibility centres*. A responsibility centre is any part of an organization for which a manager has responsibility. A responsibility centre may cover a wider area than a cost centre. If a responsibility centre includes revenue items as well as expenses, it would normally be referred to as a *profit centre*.

Managers can only be expected to answer for what goes on in their respective cost centres if they are responsible for any decisions taken. If a decision was overruled by a more senior manager, the cost centre manager can always claim that it was not his decision. Consequently, cost centre managers must be given guidance on what is overall company policy, and then be left to implement it within their own areas. The theory (and practice) suggests that if individual units are all autonomously managed, they will be better managed, because individuals work better if they are left to work on their own. It can then be argued that if each individual unit is well managed there will be a collective benefit for the entity as a whole.

Documentation

The type of organizational structure described above is clearly highly complex. By instituting a considerable number of largely autonomous cost centres, there are formidable problems in managing it as a co-ordinated unit. The charging of costs to cost centres, for example, becomes a major exercise. It is not only necessary to report to each cost centre manager in some detail, but to do so frequently and regularly.

It is essential that all the relevant accounting information is carefully documented, and that the cost of each transaction is charged to the correct cost centre. If this is not done, incorrect decisions may eventually be taken by the managers because they have based their decisions on inaccurate or incomplete data.

In operating a costing system, the following procedure should be implemented:

1 All transactions should be documented.
2 Verbal instructions (for example, orders placed over the telephone) should not be accepted unless they are later confirmed in writing.
3 All documents should be specially designed to suit the particular transaction.
4 There should be a separate document for each type of transaction.
5 Designated documents should only be supplied to authorized users.
6 All transactions should be approved and signed by authorized personnel.

A costing system usually involves so much documentation that if each transaction is to be charged to the correct cost centre, it is usually necessary to have a coding system. This is almost certainly the case if the entity uses a computerized system of accounting. Unfortunately, codes can become very cumbersome, and it is very easy to make a mistake in coding a document (just as it is when dialling a telephone number). Furthermore, coding may be done by relatively junior members of staff who often do not understand why it is important to code documents correctly.

In a large organization, where the accounting may be centralized using a common code, each document may need to be coded with a code of many digits if the transaction is to be charged to the correct cost centre. Such a code might be built-up as follows:

Responsibility centre	*Number of digits required*
Division	000
Factory	000
Cost centre	000
Type of expense	0000
Total digits required	13

Suppose, for example, that the Glasgow factory (code 123) is part of the fibres division (code 015), and it has a maintenance department (code 666). During a particular period, it purchases some raw materials (code 5432). When the invoice is eventually received from the supplier, it will be coded as follows:

$$015/123/666/5432$$

It would obviously be possible to reduce the number of digits depending upon the number of responsibility centres and the degree of analysis required. If possible, codes with few digits should be introduced, although even short codes lend themselves very easily to errors.

A costing system will not work properly unless its purpose has been explained to the staff, and they understand its importance. Operating a costing system is expensive. There is no point in having one if the information that it provides is considered either inaccurate or irrelevant. Indeed, costing systems that are imposed without any consultation or agreement are usually not effective.

The costing procedure will now be examined in some detail.

Costing procedure

In practice, it is not always easy to decide where the responsibility of one manager should end and the responsibility of another manager should begin. It follows, therefore, that it is sometimes difficult to decide which manager should be responsible for a certain cost.

Consider business rates as an example. They are a form of local taxation levied on business property located in a particular area. No one cost centre manager is responsible for the rates charged on the building as a whole (presumably the general or divisional board of directors originally approved the purchase or construction of the building), so which cost centre should be responsible for the rates? In such circumstances, it is tempting to charge the rates to a general or miscellaneous cost centre for which no one manager is directly responsible. It has to be accepted that even the factory manager does not have any real control over rates, because he has probably not got the authority to close the factory down, and hence avoid the rates charge. This would appear to be an argument in favour of using a sundry cost centre.

Accountant do not, however, recommend the use of sundry cost centres. The use of such centres tends to defeat one of the main objectives of responsibility accounting, that is, to make sure that *all* costs are controlled by designated managers. In practice, sundry cost centres tend to attract more and more costs, because by using that cost centre, managers do not have to take a difficult decision. The best advice that can be given is to suggest that the most appropriate cost centre should be chosen, no matter how remote the real control a manager has over a particular cost. Thus business rates might be charged to a legal department cost centre, since that department is probably best placed to conduct the negotiations if there is any dispute about the charge. However, it must be recognized that the legal department manager does not have any formal control over rates, and this must be taken into account when requiring the manager to answer for his departmental costs.

If it is possible to charge all costs to specific cost centres without having too much difficulty in deciding which cost centre to choose, such costs may be described as *direct* costs. This term was examined in Chapter 5. Thus a direct cost in this context is a cost that is easy to identify with a particular cost centre. Costs charged to sundry cost centres are probably *indirect* costs because it has proved difficult to identify them with particular cost centres. All such costs will eventually have to be apportioned to those cost centres that benefit indirectly from the service that they provide. Such an apportionment needs to be undertaken because ultimately all costs will need to be charged to individual products.

Once all the costs have been charged to specific cost centres, some of them may then become *indirect* costs. All the factory canteen costs, for example, may have been collected in one cost centre. As far as the canteen cost centre is concerned, those costs are direct. However, they will not be easy to identify with the products that are being manufactured in the factory, so they will be indirect *product* costs.

Similarly, in a production department manufacturing specific production units, all costs charged to that department will be classified as direct costs, but some of the costs may be difficult to identify with specific units of production. Thus as far as those units are concerned, they will be classified as indirect costs. The total of indirect costs is often referred to as *overhead*.

Cost centres that deal directly with the actual manufacturing and production of units (or processes) are known as *production* cost centres. Those cost centres that provide support services for the production cost centres are known as *service* cost centres.

From the above analysis, it can be ascertained that the cost of a particular unit (for convenience, it will be referred to as a unit cost, but the same applies to industries where there is no identifiable single unit) is comprised of three main elements:

1   direct production costs;
2   indirect production costs; and
3   service costs.

By building up the cost of a unit in this way, it is possible to calculate the total cost of producing a specific unit. If a percentage is added to the cost in order to allow something for profit, it should be possible to determine its selling price. In practice, it may not be possible to fix selling prices using this method, because selling prices will also have to bear some relationship to market prices.

The cost structure of a specific unit is shown in more detail in Exhibit 9.3.

Exhibit 9.3: Unit cost structure: the elements of cost (1)

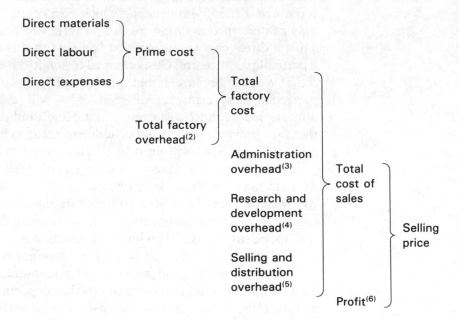

Notes:

1 The structure of the elements of cost is very similar to the structure that was used in Chapter 5 in the preparation of manufacturing accounts.
2 Factory overhead includes indirect production costs and other factory costs that are not easy to identify with production.
3 Administration overhead will include the non-factory cost of operating the company.
4 Research expenditure includes the cost of working on new products and processes. Development costs relate to costs incurred in developing existing products and processes.
5 Selling and distribution overhead includes the cost of promoting the company's product and the cost of distributing them to its customers.
6 A profit loading may be added to the total cost of sales in order to arrive at the unit's selling price.

From Exhibit 9.3 it would appear that the company should base its selling prices on the total unit cost. In some industries, this may be possible. In the construction industry, for example, tender prices are usually built up using the structure shown in Exhibit 9.3. However, as argued above, in many industries there is so much competition that a company is not free to fix its selling prices on a cost-plus basis (that is, on the basis of taking the total unit cost and adding something to it for profit). The company has to charge a price similar to that of its competitors, but at the same time, try to ensure that its total costs will not be in excess of its total sales revenue.

In summary, therefore, the detailed costing procedure described above is important for two main reasons:

1 it is necessary in those industries where selling prices are fixed on a cost-plus basis; and
2 where the company is restrained in fixing its own selling prices, it enables it to control its total costs so that they are not in excess of its total sales revenue.

The method outlined above in explaining how to arrive at the total cost of a unit is known as *total absorption costing*. This method is the one most commonly adopted, and it will be considered again in more detail in Chapter 11.

It is sufficient for the present purpose merely to note that there are a considerable number of problems to be overcome in building up the total cost of a unit in the way that has been described. By definition, direct costs should be easy to *allocate* (allocation is the process of charging whole costs to cost centres or units) to respective cost centres or units, but as has been seen, this is not always the case. Direct costs will be considered in more detail in the next chapter.

The treatment of indirect costs poses even more problems, especially those that are not incurred at the factory level. For this reason, some companies adopt an *absorption costing* system. This means that they do not try to absorb non-factory overhead into product costs. If their selling prices are based on total cost, it is not easy to decide how such overheads should be absorbed into total cost. For control purposes, it is not necessary, since absorption is largely an arithmetical procedure that is undertaken mainly for pricing purposes.

One other problem arises in dealing with absorption costing. Some costs, for example, rent and rates, tend to remain unchanged irrespective of the level of activity in the factory. Such costs are known as *fixed* costs. Those costs that *do* change with activity such as materials used directly in production, are known as *variable* costs. If the fixed costs are shared out on the basis of activity, then the more units that the factory produces, the lower the fixed costs per unit. Conversely, the fewer units that the factory produces, the higher the fixed costs per unit. It follows that if the unit selling price is based on cost, the selling price will vary, depending upon how many units have been produced. This could result in widely fluctuating selling prices. Selling prices that change frequently are not likely to help the company increase its sales.

The problem of fixed costs has given rise to the important costing technique of *marginal costing*. This will be dealt with in Chapter 12.

Conclusion

Cost and management accounting (referred to for convenience as *costing*) is now a very important branch of accounting. It assists management to achieve better planning and more efficient control of resources. Costing has evolved out of financial accounting, and its language and basic methods are similar to those found in financial accounting.

Essentially, costing provides management with a great deal more information than can be obtained from a financial accounting system. In order to implement a costing system, a clear organizational structure needs to be established that gives management specific responsibilities within carefully defined limits. Such limits are usually designated as cost centres. A cost centre is usually similar to a department, but it can be extended to a sub-unit within a department, or even to an individual. Once delineated, those costs for which respective managers are responsible will be charged to their cost centre. Responsibility centres are those areas for which responsibility has been given to specific managers, and profit centres are those responsibility centres that may have revenues charged to them. In order to ensure that costs are charged correctly to cost centres, all information of an accounting nature should be documented. To assist the charging of costs to cost centres, a coding system may have to be adopted.

The most common method of costing is absorption costing, a technique that attempts to share out the total costs of the entity among those units that it has manufactured. This method is useful for planning and control purposes, but it is also necessary when selling prices are based on total cost. However, the technique can give rise to some problems when the entity's total cost contains an element of fixed costs. For this reason marginal costing is used in those circumstances where absorption costing would be inappropriate.

Both of these techniques are considered in later chapters.

Questions

9.1 Briefly describe the differences between financial accounting and management accounting.

9.2 List the categories into which costs may be classified.

9.3 Into what main categories might the organizational structure of a manufacturing entity be classified?

9.4 What is a cost centre?

Additional questions (without answers)

9.5 Write a report for your managing director examining the main types of information that may be obtained from a cost and management accounting system.

9.6 Business organizations are usually based on some form of authoritative organizational structure.

Required:
(a) Outline the main principles to be adopted in developing a business organizational structure;

and

(b) explain why such a structure is necessary for the successful implementation of a cost and management accounting system.

10 Direct costs

Learning objectives_____

1 identify costs that relate directly to production;

2 examine the main methods of charging direct material costs to production;

3 calculate direct material costs using a variety of recognized charging methods;

   and

4 appreciate the significance of direct labour costs and other direct expenses in product costing.

In the last chapter it was suggested that the principal objectives of costing are to help management plan and control an entity's operations. These objectives can be achieved by laying down a clear organizational structure of responsibility, and then leaving the respective managers to operate within that structure with as much autonomy as possible. Overall control is maintained by regular monitoring of each department's progress. In production departments, this may include details about the cost of producing each unit in that particular department.

As was outlined in Chapter 9, the total cost of a specific unit can be broken down into two main parts: direct costs and indirect costs. Direct costs are those costs that are easily identified with that unit, while indirect costs are those costs that are not easy to identify with it.

The definition of a direct cost is fairly imprecise, so that if any difficulty is experienced in deciding whether a cost is a direct cost or not, then by definition it must be an indirect cost. Classifying costs into direct costs and indirect costs is not easy, so that if the definition is taken too literally, hardly any cost at all would be classified as a direct cost. In practice, there are some costs that are generally recognized as being direct because they are *relatively* easy to identify with specific units. It follows that the charging out of direct costs involves some degree of subjectivity.

As will be seen in the next chapter, there is even more subjectivity in dealing with indirect costs, so the entire process of trying to build up the total cost of a particular unit has to be based on a number of arguable assumptions. This means that normally there is no possibility of ever being able to calculate the *exact* cost of a particular unit, because the cost of that unit will depend upon the assumptions that the accountant makes in determining it.

In this chapter, the problems involved in dealing with *direct* costs will be examined.

Direct materials

Direct materials comprise those raw materials and component parts that can be easily and readily identified with particular units of production. If a table, for example, was being assembled, the wood and metal parts used in assembling it would be treated as direct materials, because it would normally be easy to identify them with that particular table. However, the screws needed to hold the parts together would probably not be treated as a direct material cost (even though they are used directly in production). This is because it may be both difficult and impracticable to isolate the cost of a few screws. They would, therefore, be treated as an indirect material cost.

Even if it is relatively easy to identify the physical quantity of goods used in manufacturing a particular unit, it is not always easy to determine the exact cost of that material. Those products that contain liquids, for example, are often quite difficult to cost, because liquids are usually stored in containers. The containers will contain stock purchased at various times. As the liquid is gradually issued to production, it will be replaced with new stock. The new stock may have been purchased at a different price from the old stock, but by keeping all of the liquid in one container, there is no means of determining the *actual* price of the liquid being issued to production. Consequently, any liquid issued to production will have been purchased at a variety of prices. Thus although it may be relatively easy to calculate the actual *quantity* of material issued to production, it is not necessarily very easy to *cost* it accurately.

In these circumstances, the accountant may have to estimate the actual cost of direct materials. If the actual cost of direct materials used in production is known, the accountant will, of course, use that cost, otherwise one of a number of recognized stock valuation methods must be chosen. Some of the main methods are outlined in the following subsections.

Specific identification

It has already been suggested that if the actual price of material is known, the accountant will use that price in charging out the cost of direct materials to production. This is known as the *specific identification* method. In many instances, however, it is quite difficult to identify material purchased at various dates at varying prices, and so other pricing methods may have to be adopted.

First in, first out (FIFO)

It is good practice to issue the oldest stock to production first, followed by the next oldest and so on, and this should be done wherever possible. This method of storekeeping means that old stock is not kept in store for very long, thus avoiding the possibility of deterioration or obsolescence. However, as explained above, some material may be stored in such a way that it is a mixture of old and new stock, and it may not be possible to identify each separate purchase. As far as pricing is concerned, it would still seem logical to charge production with the oldest prices first, followed by the next oldest and so on, and indeed it is a very common method: it is known as the first in, first out (FIFO) method.

It follows, of course, that the prices attached to the physical issue of goods to production are not necessarily the same as those paid for the actual purchases of those goods. Indeed, if it had been possible to identify specific receipts with specific issues, the specific identification method would have been used.

An example of the FIFO prices method is shown in Exhibit 10.1.

Exhibit 10.1: The FIFO pricing method

The following information relates to the receipt and issue of material X into stock during January 19X1:

Date	Receipts into stores			Issues to production
	Quantity Units	Price £	Value £	Quantity Units
1.1.X1	100	10	1,000	
10.1.X1	150	11	1,650	
15.1.X1				125
20.1.X1	50	12	600	
31.1.X1				150

Required:
Using FIFO (first in, first out) method of pricing the issue of goods to production, calculate the following:
(a)   the issue prices at which goods will be charged to production; and
(b)   the closing stock value at 31 January 19X1.

Answer to Exhibit 10.1

(a)   The issue price of goods to production:

Date of issue	Tutorial note	Calculation	£
5.1.X1	(1)	100 units × £10 =	1,000
	(2)	25 units × £11 =	275
		125	£1,275
31.1.X1	(3)	125 units × £11 =	1,375
	(4)	25 units × £12 =	300
		150	£1,675

(b) Closing stock:

25 units × £12 =	£300

Check:

Total receipts (£1,000 + £1,650 + £600) =	3,250
Total issues (£1,275 + £1,675) =	2,950
Closing stock =	£300

Tutorial notes

1   The goods received on 1 January 19X1 are now assumed to have all been issued.
2   This leaves 125 units in stock out of the goods received on 10 January 19X1.
3   All the goods purchased on 10 January 19X1 are now assumed to have been issued.
4   There are now 25 units left in stock out of the goods purchased on 20 January 19X1.

Exhibit 10.1 is a simple example, but it can be seen that the FIFO method may involve using a considerable number of different prices if the amount issued to production comprises a whole series of different purchases.

Last in, first out (LIFO)

An alternative method to FIFO is to adopt LIFO, whereby the *latest* prices are used to charge the issue of goods out to production. The physical quantity of the issue is identified, and the latest price paid for the last receipt of goods is determined. The goods are then charged out at that price. If more goods are being issued than were received at that price, the next oldest price will be used, and so on. As with FIFO, if there is a large issue of goods to production, the total value of the issue could comprise a considerable number of prices.

The method is illustrated in Exhibit 10.2.

Exhibit 10.2: The LIFO pricing method

The same data are used as in Exhibit 10.1.

Required:

Using LIFO (last in, first out) method of pricing the issue of goods to production, calculate the following:

(a) the issue prices at which goods will be issued to production; and

(b) the value of closing stock at 31 January 19X1.

Answer to Exhibit 10.2

(a) The issue price of goods to production:

Date of issue	Tutorial notes	Calculation	£
15.1.X1	(1)	125 units × £11 =	£1,375
31.1.X1	(2)	50 units × £12 =	600
		25 units × £11 =	275
		75 units × £10 =	750
		150	£1,625

(b) Closing stock value:

25 units × £10 =	£250

Check:

Total receipts (£1,000 + £1,650 = £600) =	3,250
Total issues (£1,375 + £1,625) =	3,000
Closing stock =	£250

Tutorial notes

1 This was the latest price at 15 January 19X1.
2 The latest price at 31 January 19X1 was £12, but only 50 units were purchased. The next oldest price, therefore, is used, but only 25 units are left at £11, because 125 units were priced out at £11 on 15 January 19X1. The balance is made up of goods purchased for £10 per unit, which also leaves 25 units in stock at that price.

The LIFO method (like FIFO) can involve a great deal of cumbersome arithmetic, but there is a certain logic to it. By using the latest prices, production is being charged with current economic prices. However, the closing stock will be valued at much older prices. Thus by using LIFO in times of rising prices, the gross profit tends to be lower than it does under FIFO. The lower profit arises because of a combination of a greater charge to production, and a lower value placed on closing stock (a lower closing stock figure reduces the cost of goods sold, because a smaller amount is being deducted from opening stock + purchases). The reverse applies, of course, when prices are falling.

FIFO is an acceptable method of valuing stock for taxation purposes in the United Kingdom. LIFO is not acceptable, and so it is not a common method as it means extra work. This arises because in computing the company's tax charge, the company's profit has to be recalculated.

Weighted average

In order to avoid the detailed arithmetical calculations that are involved in using both the FIFO and LIFO methods of pricing the issue of goods to production, it is possible to substitute an average pricing method. There are two main types of weighted average methods:

1 periodic weighted average; and
2 continuous weighted average method.

The *periodic* weighted average method involves calculating an average issue price based on all the prices paid for materials purchased during a particular *period*. The goods issued to production during that particular period are all then charged out at that average price. By using this method, it is not possible to charge out goods to production until after the period end, because the issue price cannot be calculated until all the purchase prices for the period are known.

The periodic weighted average method is illustrated in Exhibit 10.3.

Exhibit 10.3: The periodic weighted average pricing method

The same data are used as in Exhibit 10.1.

Required:
Using the periodic weighted average method of pricing the issue of goods to production, you are required to calculate the following:
(a) the issue price for January 19X1; and
(b) the closing stock value as at 31 January 19X1.

Answer to Exhibit 10.3

(a) The issue price of goods to production:

Total value of receipts (£1,000 + £1,650 + £600) =	£3,250
Total number of units received (100 + 150 + 50) =	300
∴ Periodic weighted average price =	£10.83
∴ Issue on 15.1.X1: 125 units × £10.83 =	£1,354
∴ Issue on 31.1.X1: 150 units × £10.83 =	£1,625

(b) Value of closing stock:

	£	£
Total receipts		3,250
Less: Issues − 15.1.X1	1,354	
− 25.1.X1	1,625	2,979
∴ Closing stock value =		£271

The *continuous* weighted average method requires frequent changes to be made to the issue price of goods charged to production. Although this method appears very complicated, it is the easiest one to adopt in practice, especially if the details are kept in a stores ledger account. Such an account would show both the quantity and value of stock in store at any particular moment. By dividing the total value of the stock by the total quantity, the continuous weighted average price may be obtained. A new average will need to be calculated if additional receipts are taken into stock at different purchase prices. Unlike the periodic weighted average price, therefore, the continuous weighted average price may change frequently.

The continuous weighted average method is illustrated in Exhibit 10.4. The data are the same that have been used in the previous three exhibits, but the opportunity is taken to present a little more information so that the continuous weighted average price can be explained more clearly.

Exhibit 10.4: The continuous weighted average price method

You are presented with the following information relating to the receipt and issue of material X into stock during January 19X1:

| Date | Receipts into stores | | | Issues to production | | | Stock balance | |
	Quantity Units	Price £	Value £	Quantity Units	Price £	Value £	Quantity Units	Value £
1.1.X1	100	10	1,000				100	1,000
10.1.X1	150	11	1,650				250	2,650
15.1.X1				125	10.60	1,325	125	1,325
20.1.X1	50	12	600				175	1,925
25.1.X1				150	11.00	1,650	25	275
31.1.X1							25	275

Note:
The company uses the continuous weighted average method of pricing the issue of goods to production.

Required:
Check that the prices of goods issued to production during January 19X1 have been calculated correctly.

Answer to Exhibit 10.4

The issue prices of goods to production during January 19X1 using the continuous weighted average method have been calculated as follows:

15.1.X1 $\dfrac{\text{Total stock value at 10.1.X1}}{\text{Total quantity in stock at 10.1.X1}} = \dfrac{£2,650}{250} = \underline{£10.60}$

25.1.X1 $\dfrac{\text{Total stock value at 20.1.X1}}{\text{Total quantity in stock at 20.1.X1}} = \dfrac{£1,925}{175} = \underline{£11.00}$

Other methods

There are a considerable number of other methods that may be considered suitable for determining the pricing of material issues to production. Most of them are examined in accounting textbooks, but they have little importance in practice. However, there is one other method that ought to be mentioned at this stage. This is the *standard cost method* which will be encountered in detail in Chapter 15.

The standard cost method involves estimating the cost of materials to be purchased during a particular future period of time. This is known as the *planned* price, and it would then be used in charging out the cost of materials during the period in question. The actual price of materials would be ignored in charging out materials to production during that period, although it would be necessary to investigate any difference between the actual prices and the planned prices.

The standard cost method is usually adopted as part of a *standard costing system*. Such systems adopt standard (or planned) costs for all elements of cost. Frequent comparisons have to be made with actual costs, and if there are any discrepancies, immediate action taken to correct them.

Choice of pricing method

It would be helpful at this stage if the advantages and disadvantages of each of the above pricing methods were summarized so that you can come to a decision about the one you would recommend. The summary is shown in the following table.

Method	Advantages	Disadvantages
1 FIFO	1 It is logical	1 It is arithmetically cumbersome.
	2 It matches the physical issue of goods.	2 The cost of production relates to out-of-date prices.
	3 The closing stock is closer to the current economic value.	
	4 The stores ledger account is self-balancing: there are no balancing adjustments to be written-off to the profit and loss account.	
	5 It is acceptable for tax purposes.	

contd

Method	Advantages	Disadvantages
2 LIFO	1 Production is charged with costs that are close to current economic values. 2 The stores ledger account is self-balancing: there are no balancing adjustments to be written-off to the profit and loss account.	1 It is arithmetically cumbersome. 2 The closing stock is valued at much older prices that may bear little relationship to current economic prices. 3 This method is not acceptable for tax purposes.
3 Periodic weighted average	1 It is simple to calculate. 2 The issue price relates both to quantities purchased and to changing prices. 3 It is highly accurate because the price is not calculated until the period has ended. 4 It achieves a compromise between the lowest and highest prices. 5 It is not distorted by the quantities purchased.	1 The price cannot be calculated until the period has ended. 2 Prices in previous periods are ignored. 3 It lags behind current economic prices. 4 It may not relate to any price actually paid. 5 It may be necessary to write-off balancing adjustments to the profit and loss account.
4 Continuous weighted average	1 Previous period prices are taken into account. 2 It is easy to calculate. 3 It relates the price of goods purchased to quantities purchased. 4 It produces a price that is not distorted either by low or high prices paid, or by small or large quantities purchased. 5 A new price is calculated on each receipt of goods, so the price is constantly being updated.	1 It lags behind current economic prices. 2 It may not relate to prices actually paid. 3 It may be necessary to write off balancing adjustments to the profit and loss account.

Precise rules cannot be laid down for the choice of a pricing method. LIFO is largely unsuitable because of its tax disadvantages, and the periodic weighted average method is somewhat impracticable as it can only be used after the period end. FIFO matches the attempt to issue the goods in the order in which they were received. This is a theoretical advantage, however, because where the specific identification method cannot be used, there is no certainty that the goods being issued relate to the order in which they were purchased. Wherever possible, the specific identification method would be adopted. Where the issues of goods cannot be identified with specific purchase prices, the continuous weighted average method would appear to be the one that is most suitable: it is easy to calculate, and it does not result in the use of an extreme range of prices. If a company operates a standard costing system, a standard cost would be used for all issue prices, but this can lead to many problems, as will be explained in Chapter 15.

The need to use an estimated price (irrespective of the method adopted) means that the total cost of the unit must also be an estimated cost. As will be seen in the next chapter, before arriving at the total cost of producing a unit, even more estimates have to be made. Thus it follows that there is no such thing as the *true* cost of a specific unit. Costs can only be accurate in an arithmetical sense. This point will be argued in more detail when dealing with indirect costs.

Direct labour

Labour costs include the cost of employees' remuneration plus other costs associated with the employment of labour, such as employers' national insurance, pension fund contributions, and holiday contributions. Labour costs that can be easily identified with specific units of production will be charged directly to production. Other labour costs that are difficult to identify directly with production will be charged as part of overheads.

Once the total labour cost has been analysed between direct and indirect labour, the charging of direct labour costs to production is a relatively straightforward exercise. Unlike the charging of direct material cost, there is no need to devise elaborate charging methods.

Employees engaged directly on production activities will be required to keep timesheets so that the amount of time that they spend working on each unit can be charged to that unit. Thus the hours worked on that unit by each grade of labour will be multiplied by the respective hourly rates of pay, and a percentage added for the employers' other direct employment costs. The total amount is then charged directly against the specific unit.

It must not be assumed that it is always easy to distinguish between direct and indirect labour costs. Supervisory wages at the factory level, for example, are undoubtedly a direct production cost, but they may not be easy to identify with specific units of production, so they have to be treated as an indirect cost.

Labour costs are usually an important constituent element of total unit cost, especially in manufacturing industry. It is important, therefore, that a careful distinction is made between direct and indirect labour costs, and that they are charged out accurately. Management must explain to their employees the purpose of keeping an accurate record of time spent on each job. It may be rather an irksome task for employees to keep such a record, but its importance in unit pricing cannot be over-emphasized. In this respect it is a vital task of *supervisory* management to ensure that timesheets are accurate, and that they are kept up to date.

Direct expenses

Apart from direct material and direct labour costs, there may be other types of direct expenses. These are, however, relatively rare as it is difficult to identify other expenses very easily with specific units. There may be some special cases. When the company, for example, hires special plant or equipment for work on one specific unit, the hire charge will then be charged out directly to that particular unit.

Although other direct expenses are uncommon, it is important that all indirect expenses are carefully examined to see whether it is possible to reclassify some of them as direct expenses. A low level of indirect costs means that there is less difficulty in charging them to production.

Conclusion

This chapter has dealt specifically with *direct* costs. By definition a direct cost is one that is easy to identify with a specific cost centre or with a specific unit. It must be emphasized that the identification of so called direct costs is not easy. In establishing the level of direct material cost, for example, it is necessary to estimate its cost. Consequently, it is possible to argue that there is no such thing as the true cost of a specific unit. A cost may only be accurate in the arithmetical sense, since normally it has to be calculated on the basis of a number of arguable assumptions.

Direct *labour* costs are not usually too difficult to cost, provided that accurate records are kept of the time spent on each job.

In some cases, there may be other types of direct expenses. They are usually quite rare and they do not normally cause any costing problems.

Questions

10.1 The following stocks were taken into stores as follows:

1.1.X1   1,000 units @ £20 per unit.
15.1.X1   500 units @ £25 per unit.

There were no opening stocks.
On 31.1.X1 1,250 units were issued to production.

Required:
Calculate the amount which would be charged to production on 31 January
19X1 for the issue of material on that date using each of the following methods
of material pricing:

1 FIFO (first in, first out);
2 LIFO (last in, first out); and
3 periodic weighted average.

10.2 The following information relates to material ST 2:

		Units	Unit price £	Value £
1.2.X2	Opening stock	500	1.00	500
10.2.X2	Receipts	200	1.10	220
12.2.X2	Receipts	100	1.12	112
17.2.X2	Issues	400	–	
25.2.X2	Receipts	300	1.15	345
27.2.X2	Issues	250	–	

Required:
Calculate the value of closing stock at 28 February 19X2 assuming that the
continuous weighted average method of pricing materials to production has been
adopted.

10.3 You are presented with the following information for Trusty Limited:

19X3	Purchases (units)	Unit cost £	Issues to production (units)
1 January	2,000	10	
31 January			1,600
1 February	2,400	11	
28 February			2,600
1 March	1,600	12	
31 March			1,000

Note: There was no opening stock.

Required:
Calculate the value of closing stock at 31 March 19X3 using each of the following
methods of pricing the issue of materials to production.

1 FIFO (first in, first out);
2 LIFO (last in, first out); and
3 continuous weighted average.

10.4 The following information relates to a certain raw material taken into stock:

| | Receipts | | Issues to production |
	Units	Value	Units
		£	
1.4.X4	50	350	
3.4.X4	30	213	
5.4.X4			60
9.4.X4	20	139	
11.4.X4			25
14.4.X4			10
18.4.X4	35	252	
23.4.X4	60	423	
26.4.X4			100
30.4.X4	45	315	

The opening stock was 20 units at a total value of £120.

Required:
Using the periodic weighted average method of pricing the issue of materials to production, calculate the value of the closing stock as at 30 April 19X4.

10.5 The following information relates to Steed Limited for the years to 31 May 19X5:

	£
Sales	500,000
Purchases	440,000
Opening stock	40,000
Closing stock value using the following pricing methods:	
1 FIFO (first in, first out)	90,000
2 LIFO (last in, first out)	65,000
3 Periodic weighted average	67,500
4 Continuous weighted average	79,950

Required:
Prepare Steed Limited's gross profit for the year to 31 May 19X5 using each of the above closing stock values.

10.6 Iron Limited is a small manufaturing company. During the year to 31 December 19X2 it has taken into stock and issued to production the following items of raw material, known as XY1:

| Date 19X2 | Receipts into stock | | | Issues to production |
	Quantity (Litres)	Price per unit £	Total value £	Quantity (Litres)
January	200	2.00	400	
February				100
April	500	3.00	1,500	
May				300
June	800	4.00	3,200	
July				400
October	900	5.00	4,500	
December				1,400

Notes:

1 There were no opening stocks of raw materials XY1.
2 The other costs involved in converting raw material XY1 into the finished product (marketed as *Carcleen*) amounted to £7,000.
3 Sales of *Carcleen* for the year to 31 December 19X2 amounted to £20,000.
4 For the purpose of this question, an accounting period is defined as the calendar year.

Required:

(a) Illustrate the following methods of pricing the issue of materials to production:
    1 first in, first out (FIFO);
    2 last in, first out (LIFO);
    3 periodic weighted average;
    4 continuous weighted average.
(b) Calculate the gross profit for the year using each of the above methods of pricing the issue of materials to production.

Additional questions (without answers)

10.7 The following information relates to one of Osprey's stores ledger accounts:

| Date 19X8 | Receipts | | Issues |
	Quantity Kilos	Price per kilo £	Quantity Kilos
January	145	10	100
February	180	9	170
March	240	11	150
April	110	11	250
May	220	12	200
June	150	15	165

Stock at 1 January 19X8: 20 kilos at £11.50 per kilo.

Required:

Calculate the cost of the closing stock of the above material as at 30 June 19X8 using each of the following stock valuation methods:

(a) FIFO (first in, first out);
(b) LIFO (last in, first out); and
(c) continuous weighted average.

10.8 Waters has recorded the following information in one of its stores ledger accounts:

| *19X9* | *Receipts* | | *Sales* |
	Quantity *Units*	*Cost per unit* *£*	*Units*
January	290	6	200
February	580	9	700
March	410	12	300
April	730	15	600
May	290	5	200
June	410	7	600
July	720	11	700
August	600	9	500
September	580	11	600
October	590	7	700
November	840	11	750
December	280	4	300

At 1 January 19X9 there were 60 units in stock at a total estimated value of £300. The selling price was £10 per unit.

Required:

(a) Compare and contrast the gross profit for the year to 31 December 19X9 using each of the following stock valuation methods:
   (i) FIFO (first in, first out);
   (ii) LIFO (last in, first out); and
   (iii) continuous weighted average;

(b) prepare a report for the Board of Directors outlining which stock valuation method you would recommend.

11 Indirect costs

Learning objectives_____

1 describe the nature of indirect production costs;

2 detail the steps involved in absorbing such costs into units of production;

3 appreciate how units may be charged with a share of non-factory overheads;

and

4 assess the usefulness of overhead absorption techniques.

It was emphasized in the last two chapters that the calculation of total unit cost requires costs to be classified into direct and indirect costs, and then the indirect costs to be apportioned among respective units. The last chapter dealt with the identification problems associated with direct costs. In this chapter the treatment of indirect costs will be examined.

Indirect costs comprise indirect material cost, indirect labour cost and other expenses that are not easy to identify with specific units. The total of indirect cost is usually referred to as *overhead*. Overhead arises from two main sources:

1 those costs originally allocated to production cost centres but which thereafter cannot be easily identified with specific units; and

2 those costs allocated to service costs centres, which must, therefore, be indirect costs as far as specific units are concerned.

There is no obvious way of identifying indirect costs with specific units (otherwise there would not be any indirect costs), so if it is necessary to calculate the total cost of producing a particular unit, the indirect costs have to be shared out using some equitable method.

The share out of indirect costs will be examined in subsequent sections.

Factory overhead

It was argued in Chapter 9 that for control purposes it is necessary for all costs within an entity to become the direct responsibility of a designated cost centre manager. This section examines how the total factory overhead eventually gets charged to specific units. It is quite a complicated procedure, so for convenience it is divided into a number of stages.

Stage 1: Allocate all costs to specific cost centres

The importance of allocating all costs to specific cost centres cannot be emphasized too strongly. You will recall that allocation is the process of charging out whole items of cost either to cost centres or cost units, that is, it is possible to make such a charge without having to make an apportionment between a number of cost centres. The allocation of costs to specific units was dealt with in the last chapter. This chapter is concerned with *indirect* costs.

As has been explained, it is not always easy to allocate costs to particular cost centres. Sometimes it is necessary to charge a cost to a particular cost centre, even though the manager of that centre may only be remotely responsible for that cost.

If some costs are left unallocated, then they will have to be apportioned (i.e. shared out using some arithmetical basis) among those cost centres that benefit from their services. Business rates, for example, would probably be apportioned on the basis of floor space. Thus if the rates for the factory amounted to £5,000 and the factory had just two cost centres, one occupying 60% of the total floor space and the other cost centre occupying 40%, the first cost centre would be charged with £3,000 and the second cost centre with £2,000. Once all costs have been either allocated or apportioned to appropriate cost centres, then the factory service centre costs have to be shared out.

Stage 2: Share out the factory service cost centre costs

Factory service centre costs will consist mainly of allocated costs, but they could also include some apportioned costs. By definition, service cost centre costs are not directly related to the production of specific units, and as far as production is concerned, they must all be indirect costs.

The next stage in unit costing, therefore, is to share out the total service centre costs amongst the *production* cost centres. This is usually done by apportioning each service centre's total cost amongst those production cost centres that benefit from the service. The method used to apportion the service cost centre costs may be very simple. A few of the more common methods are as follows:

1   *Numbers of employees.* This method would be used for those service cost centres that provide a service to individual employees, for example the canteen, the personnel department and the wages office. Such cost centres may have their costs apportioned on the basis of the number of employees working in a particular production department compared to the total number of employees in all production cost centres.
2   *Floor area.* This method would be used for such cost centres as cleaning and building maintenance.
3   *Activity.* Examples of where this method might be used include the drawings office (on the basis of drawings made), materials handling (based on the number of requisitions processed) and the transport department (on the basis of vehicle operating hours).

A problem arises in dealing with the apportionment of service cost centre costs when service cost centres provide services for each other. The wages office will presumably provide a service for the canteen staff, and in turn, staff employed in the wages office presumably use the canteen. Before the service cost centre costs can be apportioned amongst the production cost centres, therefore, it would appear necessary to make sure that each service cost centre is charged with its share of the other service cost centre costs.

The problem becomes a circular one, because it is not possible to charge some of the canteen costs to the wages office until the canteen has been charged with some of the wages office costs. Equally, it is not possible to charge out the wages office costs until part of the canteen costs have been charged to the wages office. The treatment of reciprocal service costs (as they are known) can become an involved and time-consuming process unless a clear policy decision is taken about their treatment. There are three main solutions.

1   *Ignore interdepartmental service costs.* If this method is adopted, the respective service cost centre costs are only apportioned among the production cost centres. Any servicing that the service cost centres provide for each other is ignored.
2   *Specified order of closure.* This method requires the service cost centre costs to be closed off in some specified order and apportioned out among the production cost centres and the remaining service cost centres. Eventually, as the service cost centres are gradually closed off, there will be only one service cost centre left. The remaining service cost centre costs will then be apportioned amongst the production cost centres. Some order of closure has to be specified,

and this may be quite arbitrary. It may be based, for example, on those centres that provide a service for the largest number of other service cost centres, or it could be based on the cost centres with the highest or the lowest cost in them prior to any interdepartmental servicing. It could also be based on an estimate of the benefit received by other centres.

3 *Mathematical apportionment.* By using this method, the respective service cost centre costs are apportioned among the production cost centres and the other service cost centres on the basis of the estimated benefit provided by the respective service cost centre to all other cost centres. What happens, however, is that additional amounts keep being charged back to a particular service cost centre as further apportionment takes place. It can take a very long time before there is no more cost to charge out to any of the service cost centres, but when it is reached, there will be no costs remaining in the service cost centres. This method involves a great deal of exhaustive arithmetical apportionment, and it is also very time-consuming, especially where there are a great many service cost centres. Although it is possible to carry out the calculations arithmetically, it is more easily done by computer program.

In choosing one of the above methods, it should be remembered that they all depend upon an estimate of how much benefit one department receives from another. Such an estimate amounts to no more than an informed guess. It seems unnecessary, therefore, to build an involved arithmetical exercise on the basis of some highly questionable data. It is suggested that in most circumstances interdepartmental servicing charging may be ignored.

Some fairly complicated procedures have been examined in dealing with stages 1 and 2, so before moving on to stage 3, they will be illustrated in Exhibit 11.1.

Exhibit 11.1

You are provided with the following indirect cost information relating to the New Manufacturing Company Limited for the year to 31 March 19X5:

	£
Cost centre	
Production 1: indirect expenses (to units)	24,000
Production 2: indirect expenses (to units)	15,000
Service cost centre A: allocated expenses	20,000
Service cost centre B: allocated expenses	8,000
Service cost centre C: allocated expenses	3,000

Additional information:
The estimated benefit provided by the three service cost centres to other cost centres is as follows:

Service cost centre A: Production 1 50%; Production 2 30%; Service cost centre B 10%; Service cost centre C 10%.

Service cost centre B: Production 1 70%; Production 2 20%; Service cost centre C 10%.

Service cost centre C: Production 1 50%; Production 2 50%.

Required:

Calculate the total amount of overhead to be charged to cost centre units for both Production cost centre 1 and Production cost centre 2 for the year to 31 March 19X5.

Answer to Exhibit 11.1

New Manufacturing Company Limited
Overhead distribution schedule for the year to 31 March 19X5

Cost centre	Production		Service		
	1	2	A	B	C
	£	£	£	£	£
Allocated indirect expenses	24,000	15,000	20,000	8,000	3,000
Apportion service cost centre costs:					
A (50:30:10:10)	10,000	6,000	(20,000)	2,000	2,000
B (70:20:0:10)	7,000	2,000	–	(10,000)	1,000
C (50:50:0:0)	3,000	3,000	–	–	(6,000)
Total overhead to be absorbed by specific units	£44,000	£26,000	–	–	–

Tutorial notes

1 Units passing through Production cost centre 1 will have to share total overhead expenditure amounting to £44,000. Units passing through Production cost centre 2 will have to share total overhead expenditure amounting to £26,000. Units passing through both departments may be identical: for example, they might be assembled in cost centre 1 and packed in cost centre 2.

2 The total amount of overhead to be shared amongst the units is £70,000 (£44,000 + £26,000 = £24,000 + £15,000 + £20,000 + £8,000 + £3,000). The total amount of overhead originally collected in each of the five cost centres does not change.

3 This exhibit does involve some interdepartmental re-apportionment of service cost centre costs. However, no problem arises because of the basis upon which the question requires the respective service cost centre costs to be apportioned.

4 The objective of apportioning service centre costs is to charge them out to the production cost centres so that they can be charged to specific units.

Stage 3: Absorption of factory overhead

Once all of the indirect cost has been collected in the production cost centres, the next step is to absorb it into specific units.

The method of absorbing overhead into units is normally a simple one. Accountants recommend a single factor, preferably one that relates as closely as possible to the movement of *overhead*. In other words, an attempt is made to choose a factor that correlates with the amount of overhead expenditure actually incurred. Needless to say, like so much else in accounting, there is no obvious factor to choose. Indeed, if there was a close correlation between overhead expenditure and an appropriate factor, it is doubtful whether it would be necessary to designate any expenditure as an overhead expense.

On the whole, it is believed that overheads tend to move with time. Thus the longer a unit stays in production, it is likely that more expenditure will be incurred in overheads. There are six main methods that could be used for absorbing factory overhead, but only three of them are based on relating overhead to the time that each unit spends in production. The basic equation is as follows:

$$\text{Cost centre overhead absorption rate (OAR)} = \frac{\text{Total cost centre overhead (TCCO)}}{\text{Total cost centre activity}}$$

A different absorption rate will have to be calculated for each production cost centre, so by the time that the total cost of the unit has been calculated, the unit will have been charged with a share of overhead for each of the production cost centres that it has been through.

The six main absorption methods are examined in the following subsections.

Specific units

This method is the simplest to operate. It is calculated as follows:

$$\text{Overhead absorption rate} = \frac{\text{Total cost centre overhead}}{\text{Number of units processed in the cost centre}}$$

The same rate would be applied to each unit. Thus it is only a suitable method if the units are identical.

Direct material cost

$$\text{Overhead absorption rate} = \frac{\text{Total cost centre overhead}}{\text{Cost centre total direct material cost}} \times 100$$

The direct material cost of each unit is then multiplied by the absorption rate in order to determine the amount of overhead to be charged to that particular unit.

It is unlikely that there will be a strong correlation between the direct material cost and the level of overheads. There might be special cases, but they are probably quite unusual; for example, where a company uses a high level of precious metals and its overhead costs strongly reflect the cost of protecting those materials.

Direct labour cost

$$\text{Overhead absorption rate} = \frac{\text{Total cost centre overhead}}{\text{Cost centre total direct labour cost}} \times 100$$

The direct labour cost of each unit is then multiplied by the absorption rate in order to determine the amount of overhead to be charged to that particular unit.

If it is true that overhead expenditure tends to increase the more time that a unit spends in production, then this method may be suitable, since the direct labour cost is a combination of hours worked and rates paid. It may not be suitable, however, where the total direct labour cost consists of a relatively low level of hours worked and of a high labour rate per hour, because the total direct labour cost will not then correlate closely with the *time* that the unit spends in production.

Prime cost

$$\text{Overhead absorption rate} = \frac{\text{Total cost centre overhead}}{\text{Prime cost}} \times 100$$

The prime cost of each unit is then multiplied by the absorption rate in order to determine the amount of overhead to be charged to that particular unit.

This method assumes that there is a close correlation between prime cost and overhead incurred. In most cases this is unlikely to be true. It could also be argued that if there is no close correlation between either direct materials or direct labour and overheads, then it is unlikely that there will be much of a correlation between prime cost and overhead. Hence the prime cost method tends to combine the disadvantages of both the direct materials and the direct labour cost methods. It has no real advantages of its own.

Direct labour hours

$$\text{Overhead absorption rate} = \frac{\text{Total cost centre overhead}}{\text{Cost centre total direct labour hours}}$$

The direct labour hours of each unit are then multiplied by the absorption rate in order to determine the amount of overhead to be charged to that particular unit.

This method is highly acceptable, especially in those cost centres that are labour intensive, since it does relate time spent in production to the cost of overhead incurred.

Machine hours

$$\text{Overhead absorption rate} = \frac{\text{Total cost centre overhead}}{\text{Cost centre total machine hours}}$$

The number of machine hours that each unit took to produce is then multiplied by the absorption rate in order to determine the amount of overhead to be charged to that particular unit.

This is the most appropriate method to use in those departments that are machine intensive. There is probably quite a strong correlation between the amount of machine-time that a unit takes to produce and the amount of overhead incurred.

It is difficult to appreciate the meaning of these absorption methods until they are put into context, so Exhibit 11.2 illustrates the use of all six methods.

Exhibit 11.2

Old Limited is a manufacturing company. The following information relates to the assembling department for the year to 30 June 19X8:

	Assembling department total £000
Direct material cost incurred	400
Direct labour cost incurred	200
Total factory overhead incurred	100
Number of units produced	10,000
Direct labour hours worked	50,000
Machine hours used	80,000

Required:
Calculate the overhead absorption rates for the assembling department using each of the following methods:

1 specific units;
2 direct material cost;
3 direct labour cost;
4 prime cost;
5 direct labour hours; and
6 machine hours.

Answer to Exhibit 11.2

1 Specific units:

$$\text{OAR} = \frac{\text{TCCO}}{\text{Number of units}} = \frac{\pounds100,000}{10,000} = \underline{\underline{\pounds10.00 \text{ per unit}}}$$

2 Direct material cost:

$$OAR = \frac{TCCO}{\text{Direct material cost}} \times 100 = \frac{£100,000}{400,000} \times 100 = \underline{\underline{25\%}}$$

3 Direct labour cost:

$$OAR = \frac{TCCO}{\text{Direct labour cost}} \times 100 = \frac{£100,000}{200,000} \times 100 = \underline{\underline{50\%}}$$

4 Prime cost:

$$OAR = \frac{TCCO}{\text{Prime cost}} \times 100 = \frac{£100,000}{400,000 + 200,000} \times 100 = \underline{\underline{16.67\%}}$$

5 Direct labour hours:

$$OAR = \frac{TCCO}{\text{Direct labour hours}} = \frac{£100,000}{50,000} = \underline{\underline{£2.00 \text{ per direct labour hour}}}$$

6 Machine hours:

$$OAR = \frac{TCCO}{\text{Machine hours}} = \frac{£100,000}{80,000} = \underline{\underline{£1.25 \text{ per machine hour}}}$$

In practice, only one absorption method would be chosen for each production cost centre. The most appropriate absorption rate method to adopt will depend upon individual circumstances. A careful study would have to be made of the correlation between (a) direct materials, direct labour, other direct expenses, direct labour hours, and machine hours; and (b) total overhead expenditure. In most circumstances, it is generally accepted that overhead tends to move with time. Consequently, the longer a unit spends in production, the more overhead that particular unit will incur. As a result, each individual unit ought to be charged with its share of overhead based on the time that it spends in production.

This argument suggests that labour intensive cost centres should use the direct labour hour method of absorbing overhead, and machine intensive departments should use the machine hour rate method.

A comprehensive example

It would now be useful to illustrate overhead absorption in the form of a comprehensive example. It would clearly be impracticable to use an example that involved hundreds of cost centres, and in any case the purpose of the example is to demonstrate the *principles* of absorption costing. Too much data would obscure those principles. Thus, using the minimum amount of data Exhibit 11.3 has been designed to outline the main principles involved in calculating the cost of a specific unit.

Exhibit 11.3

Oldham Limited is a small manufacturing company producing a variety of pumps for the oil industry. It operates from one factory that is geographically separated from its head office. The components for the pumps are assembled in the assembling department; they are then passed through to the finishing department where they are painted and packed. There are three service cost centres: administration, stores and work study.

The following costs were collected for the year to 30 June 19X6:

	£000
Allocated cost centre overhead costs:	
Administration	70
Assembling	25
Finishing	9
Stores	8
Work study	18

Additional information:
1 The allocated cost centre costs are all considered to be indirect costs as far as specific units are concerned.
2 During the year to 30 June 19X6, 35,000 machine hours were worked in the assembling department, and 60,000 direct labour hours in the finishing department.
3 The number of employees working in each department was as follows:

Administration	15
Assembling	25
Finishing	40
Stores	2
Work study	3
	85

4 During the year to 30 June 19X6, the stores received 15,000 requisitions from the assembling department, and 10,000 requisitions from the finishing department. The stores department did not provide a service for any other department.
5 The work study department carried out 2,000 chargeable hours for the assembling department, and 1,000 chargeable hours for the finishing department.
6 One special pump (code named MEA 6) was produced during the year to 30 June 19X6. It took 10 machine hours of assembling time, and 15 direct labour hours were worked on it in the finishing department. Its total direct costs (material and labour) amounted to £100.

Required:
(a) Calculate an appropriate absorption rate for:
  1   the assembling department; and
  2   the finishing department.
(b) Calculate the total factory cost of the special pump.

Answer to Exhibit 11.3

(a)

OLDHAM LIMITED

Overhead distribution schedule for the year to 30 June 19X6

	Production		Service		
Cost centre	Assembling	Finishing	Adminis-tration	Stores	Work study
	£000	£000	£000	£000	£000
Allocated costs (1)	25	9	70	8	18
Apportion administration (2): 25:40:3:2	25	40	(70)	2	3
Apportion stores (3): 3:2	6	4	–	(10)	–
Apportion work study: 2:1	14	7	–	–	(21)
Total overhead to be absorbed	£70	£60	–	–	–

Tutorial notes

1 The allocated costs were given in the question.
2 Administration costs have been apportioned on the basis of employees. Details were given in the question. There were 85 employees in the factory, but 15 of them were employed in the administration department. Administration costs have, therefore, been apportioned on a total of 70 employees, or £1,000 per employee. The administration department is the only service department to provide a service for the other service departments, so no problem of interdepartmental servicing arises.
3 The stores costs have been apportioned on the number of requisitions made by the two production cost centres, that is 15,000 + 10,000 = 25,000, or 3 to 2.
4 The work study costs have been apportioned on the basis of chargeable hours i.e. 2,000 + 1,000 = 3,000, or 2 to 1.

Calculation of chargeable rates:

1 Assembling department:

$$\frac{\text{TCCO}}{\text{Total machine hours}} = \frac{£70,000}{35,000} = \underline{£2.00 \text{ per machine hour}}$$

2 Finishing department:

$$\frac{\text{TCCO}}{\text{Total direct labour hours}} = \frac{£60,000}{60,000} = \underline{£1.00 \text{ per direct labour hour}}$$

It would seem appropriate to absorb the assembling department's overhead on the basis of machine hours because it appears to be a machine intensive department. The finishing department appears more labour intensive, so its overhead will be absorbed on that basis.

(b)   MEA 6: Calculation of total factory cost

	£	£
Direct costs (as given)		100
Add: Factory overhead:		
Assembling department (10 machine hours × £2.00 per MH)	20	
Finishing department (15 direct labour hours × £1.00 per DLH)	15	35
Total factory cost		£135

You are now recommended to work through Exhibit 11.3 again, without reference to the answer.

Non-factory overhead

The chapter so far has concentrated on the apportionment and absorption of *factory* overhead expenditure. Most companies will, however, incur expenditure in areas that are not directly connected with factory activities. There will, for example, be the cost of operating the company's head office, the cost of research and development, and the cost of selling and distributing the product.

As argued in previous chapters, the overall objective in setting up a costing system is to help plan and control the company's activities more effectively. It follows that non-factory overhead cannot be ignored in achieving overall control of the company's costs. It will be necessary to set up a cost centre structure for this type of overhead, and to give managers autonomy for clearly defined areas of responsibility.

If the company's selling prices are based on cost, it will also be necessary to share out non-factory overhead among specific units of production. For pricing purposes, therefore, the factory cost of the unit will have an amount added to it in order to recover the cost of administration, research and development, and selling and distribution overhead. Unfortunately, there is no satisfactory way of absorbing such overhead, because it is difficult to correlate general overhead with any appropriate level of activity.

Sometimes an arbitrary percentage is applied to the total factory cost. This is bound to be a somewhat questionable method, and the effect on tendering or selling prices will have to be examined very carefully. The main methods by which non-factory overhead could be absorbed into unit costs are outlined below.

Administration overhead

The absorption rate for administration overhead can be calculated by relating the total cost of overhead to the total cost of production. The formula is as follows:

$$\text{Overhead absorption rate} = \frac{\text{Total administration overhead}}{\text{Total production cost}} \times 100$$

The absorption rate is then applied to the total factory cost of each particular unit.

If the total sales revenue is known (i.e. selling prices are not based on cost), administration overhead is sometimes apportioned on the basis of sales revenue. The formula is as follows:

$$\text{Overhead absorption rate} = \frac{\text{Total administration overhead}}{\text{Total sales revenue}} \times 100$$

The absorption rate is then applied to the selling price of each particular unit.

Research and development overhead

Like administration overhead, a research and development overhead absorption rate may be calculated on the basis of total production cost, i.e.

$$\text{Overhead absorption rate} = \frac{\text{Total research and development overhead}}{\text{Total production cost}} \times 100$$

The rate is then applied to the total factory cost of each particular unit.

Selling and distribution overhead

The absorption rate for selling and distribution overhead can again be calculated by reference to the total cost of production:

$$\text{Overhead absorption rate} = \frac{\text{Total selling and distribution overhead}}{\text{Total cost of production}} \times 100$$

The rate is then applied to the total factory cost of each particular unit.

It may also be possible to absorb this type of overhead on the basis of total sales revenue if the company does not operate a cost-plus pricing policy. The formula would be as follows:

$$\text{Overhead absorption rate} = \frac{\text{Total selling and distribution overhead}}{\text{Total sales revenue}} \times 100$$

The absorption rate would then be applied to the selling price of each particular unit.

It must be emphasized that the absorption of non-factory overhead among specific units does not help to *control* the total cost of such units. It is largely an arithmetical exercise. Its real value lies only in trying to work out a more accurate selling or tendering price, or in enabling a comparison to be made between the total cost of the company's own products and those of its competitors.

As mentioned in Chapter 9, the absorption of all types of overhead into product cost is known as *total absorption costing*. The absorption of factory overhead only is known simply as *absorption costing*. Absorption costing is more common than total absorption costing, partly because of the difficulty of relating non-factory overhead to specific units, and partly because it is not particularly useful in controlling costs.

A further problem arises in trying to work out an appropriate absorption rate. It must be decided whether the absorption rate should be calculated on the basis of historic cost, or whether to try to work one out in advance. This problem is discussed in the next section.

Pre-determined rates

It has been emphasized throughout this chapter that there is no close correlation between overhead and any particular measure of activity: overhead can only be shared out on some reasonable basis. However, if the total actual overhead incurred is known, it is possible to make sure that it is all charged to specific units, even if it is not clear what relationship it has with any activity level.

To do so, of course, an absorption rate cannot be calculated until both the actual overhead cost and the actual activity (irrespective of how it is measured) are known. In other words, the calculation can only be made on an historic basis.

The adoption of historic absorption rates is not usually very practicable. It is necessary to wait until the actual period is over before calculating an absorption rate, costing the products and invoicing the customers. It would, therefore, normally be desirable to calculate an absorption rate in advance. This is known as a *pre-determined rate*.

In order to calculate a pre-determined absorption rate, it is necessary to estimate both the overhead to be incurred, and the hours that are going to be worked (if hours are to be used as the method of absorbing overhead). If one or other of these estimates turns out to be inaccurate, then the customers could have been either undercharged (if the rate was too low), or overcharged (if the rate was too high).

This situation could be very serious for the company. Low selling prices caused by using a low absorption rate could make the company's products very competitive, but there is not much point in selling a great many units if the company's total sales revenue is not covering its total costs. Similarly, on a cost-plus pricing basis, a high absorption rate may have resulted in a high selling price. The units may not then be competitive. The profit per unit may be high, but not enough units may be sold for the company to be able to recoup its total costs out of its total sales revenue.

The use of pre-determined absorption rates may, therefore, result in an under- or over-recovery of overhead. Overhead may be under- or over-absorbed if the company has under- or over-estimated the actual cost of the overhead, or the actual level of activity (irrespective of how activity is measured). The difference between the actual overhead incurred and the total overhead that the company has charged to production (calculated on a pre-determined basis) gives rise to what is known as a *variance*. If the actual overhead incurred is in excess of the amount charged out, the variance will be *adverse*, that is, the profit will be that much less. However, if the total overhead charged to production was less than was estimated, then the variance will be *favourable*. Other things being equal, a favourable variance gives rise to higher profits, and an adverse variance results in lower profits.

It is a cardinal rule in costing that variances should be written off to the profit and loss account at the end of the costing period in which they were incurred. It is not considered fair to burden the next period's accounts with the previous period's mistakes.

Conclusion

Absorption costing aims to help management plan and control the entity's operations more effectively, but it may also be useful in determining selling prices.

The technique is a highly questionable one, because it is necessary to make a number of arguable assumptions; for example, costs have to be classified into direct and indirect categories, and whereas it is not always easy to charge out direct costs, it is even more difficult to deal with indirect costs.

The technique is carried out in a number of stages. The first stage is to allocate indirect factory costs to appropriate cost centres. The second stage is to apportion service centre costs amongst the relevant production cost centres. The third stage is to absorb the total overhead collected in each production cost centre into specific units.

The apportionment and the absorption stages both depend upon a relationship between the overhead cost and an appropriate measure of activity, even though such a relationship is likely to be somewhat distant. Non-factory overhead is also sometimes absorbed into unit costs, but the relationship between this type of expenditure and production activity is even more distant. For control purposes it is not particularly helpful, although it may sometimes have to be done if selling prices are fixed on a cost-plus pricing basis.

Overhead absorption rates have usually to be pre-determined, because it is impracticable to wait until the period has ended before goods are charged out to production (and hence ultimately to customers). This means that some overhead may be over- or under-absorbed at the period end, and as a result, a favourable or an adverse variance will arise. The variance will be favourable or adverse depending upon whether the estimated cost or estimated level of activity has been over- or underestimated. Such variances should be written off to the profit and loss account for that particular period. They should not be carried forward and charged to the next period's accounts.

In the long run, variances may turn out to have serious consequences. They suggest that the company could be either under- or over-pricing its products. Under-pricing may lead to an under-recovery of total cost, whilst over-pricing could result in a reduction in sales volume. In both cases there will ultimately be a reduction in profitability.

Absorption costing is a technique that must be used with caution. However, as long as managers are aware of its limitations, it can be useful in controlling the company's total costs.

Questions

11.1 Scar Limited has two production departments and one service department. The following information relates to January 19X1:

	£
Allocated expenses	
Production department: A	65,000
B	35,000
Service department	50,000

The allocated expenses shown above are all indirect expenses as far as individual units are concerned.
The benefit provided by the service department is shared amongst the production departments A and B in the proportion 60:40.

Required:
Calculate the amount of overhead to be charged to specific units for both production department A and production department B.

11.2 Bank Limited has several production departments. In the assembly department it has been estimated that £250,000 of overhead should be charged to that particular department. It now wants to charge a customer for a specific order. The data relevant are:

	Assembly department	*Specific unit*
Number of units	50,000	–
Direct material cost (£)	500,000	8.00

	Assembly department	Specific unit
Direct labour cost (£)	1,000,000	30.00
Prime cost (£)	1,530,000	40.00
Direct labour hours	100,000	3.5
Machine hours	25,000	0.75

The accountant is not sure which overhead absorption rate to adopt.

Required:
Calculate the overhead to be absorbed by a specific unit passing through the assembly department using each of the following overhead absorption rate methods:
1 specific units;
2 percentage of direct material cost;
3 percentage of direct labour cost;
4 percentage of prime cost;
5 direct labour hours; and
6 machine hours.

11.3 The following information relates to the activities of the production department of Clough Limited for the month of March 19X3:

	Production department	Order Number 123
Direct materials consumed (£)	120,000	20
Direct wages (£)	180,000	25
Overhead chargeable (£)	150,000	
Direct labour hours worked	30,000	5
Machine hours operated	10,000	2

The company adds a margin of 50% to the total production cost of specific units in order to cover administration expenses and to provide a profit.

Required:
(a) Calculate the total selling price of order number 123 if overhead is absorbed using the following methods of overhead absorption:
  1 direct labour hours;
  2 machine hours.
(b) State which of the two methods you would recommend for the production department.

11.4 Burns Limited has three production departments (processing, assembly and finishing) and two service departments (administration and work study). The following information relates to April 19X4.

	£
Direct material:	
Processing	100,000
Assembling	30,000
Finishing	20,000

Direct labour:
Processing (£4 × 100,000 hours)   400,000
Assembling (£5 × 30,000 hours)   150,000
Finishing (£7 × 10,000 hours) + (£5 × 10,000 hours)   120,000
Administration   65,000
Work study   33,000

Other allocated costs:
Processing   15,000
Assembling   20,000
Finishing   10,000
Administration   35,000
Work study   12,000

Apportionment of costs:

	Process %	Assembling %	Finishing %	Work study %
Administration	50	30	15	5
Work study	70	20	10	–

Total machine hours: Processing 25,000

All units produced in the factory pass through the three production departments before they are put into stock. Overhead is absorbed in the processing department on the basis of machine hours, on the basis of direct labour hours in the assembling department, and on the basis of the direct labour cost in the finishing department.

The following details relate to unit XP6:

	£	£
Direct materials:		
Processing	15	
Assembling	6	
Finishing	1	22
Direct labour:		
Processing (2 hours)	8	
Assembling (1 hour)	5	
Finishing (1 hour × £7 + 1 hour × £5)	12	25
Prime cost		£47

XP6: Number of machine hours in the processing department – 6

Required:
Calculate the total cost of producing unit XP6.

11.5 Outlane Limited's overhead budget for a certain period is as follows:

	£000
Administration	100
Depreciation of machinery	80
Employer's national insurance	10
Heating and lighting	15
Holiday pay	20
Indirect labour cost	10
Insurance: machinery	40
property	11
Machine maintenance	42
Power	230
Rent and rates	55
Supervision	50
	£663

The company has four production departments: L, M, N and O. The following information relates to each department.

Department	L	M	N	O
Total number of employees	400	300	200	100
Number of indirect workers	20	15	10	5
Floor space (square metres)	2,000	1,500	1,000	1,000
Kilowatt hours	30,000	50,000	90,000	60,000
Machine maintenance hours	500	400	300	200
Machine running hours	92,000	38,000	165,000	27,000
Capital cost of machines (£)	110,000	40,000	50,000	200,000
Depreciation rate of machines (on cost)	20%	20%	20%	20%
Cubic capacity	60,000	30,000	10,000	50,000

Previously the company has absorbed overhead on the basis of 100% of the direct labour cost. It has now decided to change to a separate machine hour rate for each department.

The company has been involved in two main contracts during the period, the details of which are as follows:

Department	Contract 1: Direct labour hours and machine hours	Contract 2: Direct labour hours and machine hours
L	60	20
M	30	10
N	10	10
O	–	60
	100	100

Direct labour cost per hour in both departments was £3.00.

Required:
(a) Calculate the overhead to be absorbed by both contract 1 and 2 using the direct labour cost method; and
(b) calculate the overhead to be absorbed using a machine hour rate for each department.

11.6 Sarah Limited has two production cost centres (D and P) and three service cost centres (1, 2, and 3). The following information relates to June 19X6.

Allocated costs	£000
Production cost centres:	
D	45
P	35
Service cost centres:	
1	160
2	71
3	34

All of the above costs are indirect as far as individual production units are concerned.

The service cost centres provide a service both for the production cost centres and for each other. The estimated benefit provided by each service cost to the other cost centres is as follows:

	Production		Service		
	D	P	1	2	3
	%	%	%	%	%
Service: 1	55	20	–	15	10
2	45	40	5	–	10
3	50	10	20	20	–

Required:
Calculate the total amount of overhead to be absorbed by production cost centre D and production cost centre P.

Additional questions (without answers)

11.7 Doyle Limited makes a special type of floor covering. The process involves three production cost centres L, M, and N, and two service cost centres, I and O.

The budgeted overhead expenditure for the year to 31 December 19X7 is as follows:

	Total £000
Canteen expenses	200
Depreciation	300
Heating and lighting	90
Indirect labour production costs	500
Rent, rates and insurance	100
Repairs and maintenance	60
	£1,250

Other information:

	Cost centre				
	L	*M*	*N*	*I*	*O*
Budgeted direct labour hours (000s)	50	50	25	–	–
Budgeted machine hours (000s)	100	50	20	–	
Capital value of plant and machinery (£000)	1,500	1,000	250	200	50
Cubic capacity (metres)	30,000	30,000	20,000	5,000	5,000
Direct allocation: repairs and maintenance (£000)	20	20	10	5	5
Floor areas (sq. metres)	4,000	3,000	1,000	1,000	1,000
Numbers employed	40	30	15	10	5

Required:

(a) Prepare a statement showing the total overhead cost budgeted for each cost centre; and

(b) calculate an appropriate budgeted overhead absorption rate for each of the three production cost centres.

11.8 Greaves Limited has prepared the following budget for the year to 31 March 19X8:

	Production cost centres	
	F	*G*
Costs:	£000	£000
Direct materials	100	30
Direct labour	300	250
Other direct expenses	40	10
Allocated overheads	30	20
Apportioned overheads	50	30
Other information:		
Total budgeted direct labour hours	30,000	25,000
Total budgeted machine hours	40,000	5,000

All units manufactured by Greaves flow through cost centre F and cost centre G.

During the year to 31 March 19X8, the company manufactured a special new unit called 'tacko'. Tacko's actual direct costs per unit were as follows:

	£
Direct materials	90
Direct labour	200
Direct expenses	10

One unit of tacko required 10 direct labour hours and 15 machine hours in cost centre F, and 30 direct labour hours and 5 machine hours in cost centre G.

Required:

(a) Calculate for each cost centre *five* different methods of absorbing production overheads; and

(b) by adopting the most appropriate absorption rates, calculate the total cost of producing one unit of tacko.

12 Recording cost data

Learning objectives

1 compare and contrast financial accounting systems with cost book-keeping systems;

2 examine some basic costing methods;

3 relate such methods to specific industries

and

4 identify and outline some major costing techniques.

In previous chapters, it has been assumed that it is possible to arrive at the cost of a *specific* unit. The discussion has been limited to unit costing, because it is easier to think of costing in this way. In practice, however, it is not always possible to cost individual units, so the costing system has to be adapted in order to cope with different production methods.

This chapter first examines how absorption costing is incorporated into the cost book-keeping system. The main costing methods applied in specific industries are then outlined. Cost book-keeping will not be examined in great detail, however, since it is necessary for non-accountants to have only a general understanding of the procedures that are involved.

Cost book-keeping

As explained in Chapter 9, it is possible for a costing system to be kept quite separate from a financial accounting system. Such systems are known as an interlocking system. Interlocking cost book-keeping systems are rather an unnecessary waste of time and money, because they duplicate a great deal of information that is already contained within the financial accounting system.

In order to avoid as much duplication as possible, it is common to find that cost and financial systems are operated jointly. This type of joint system is known as an integral or an integrated system and is particularly appropriate where the book-keeping is computerized. Since this is the most common form of cost book-keeping, it will be adopted in this chapter in order to explain how such a system works.

Costing information is still subject to the same basic accounting rules as outlined in Chapter 2, irrespective of whether an interlocking or an integral system of costing is operated. The application of the dual aspect rule does, however, require some modification in order to cope with the much more detailed information contained within a costing system.

Books of account (or ledgers) are still used, with each entry being entered in a separate account in a double-entry format. Expenditure continues to be debited to an account and incomes to be credited. The essential difference lies in the number and the type of accounts that are needed to provide management with detailed and up-to-date information.

The cost accounts are grouped according to elements of cost, namely:
1 material;
2 labour; and
3 overheads.

In addition, other accounts will record the incomes, such as sales revenue, dividends receivable and rents receivable. A simplified version of a financial accounting system is shown in Exhibit 12.1. This has been provided so that you can contrast it with a simplified version of an integral cost book-keeping system shown in Exhibit 12.2. Detailed tutorial notes are attached to Exhibit 12.2, and you should consult these notes as you work through the exhibit.

Exhibit 12.1: A simplified financial accounting system

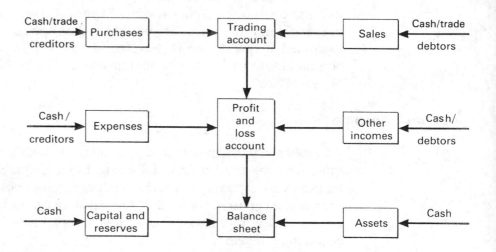

Exhibit 12.2: A simplified cost book-keeping system

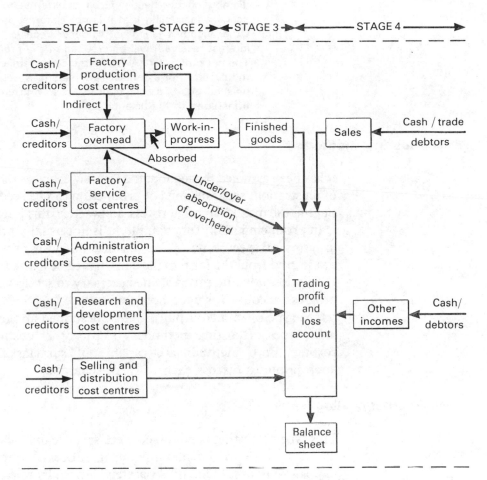

Tutorial notes

Stage 1: The exhibit looks at the system as a whole. Thus each main block of cost centres (factory production, factory service, administration, research and development, and selling and distribution) will be comprised of a considerable number of cost centres.

Stage 2: As a particular unit begins its manufacturing process, a separate work-in-progress account will be opened for each specific unit being manufactured. The work-in-progress account will be debited with (a) the unit's direct costs obtained from the production cost centres, and (b) a share of absorbed factory overhead.

Stage 3: When the unit is completed, it will be transferred at its total factory cost to the finished goods stock account.

Stage 4: (a) The total cost of finished goods sold will be transferred to the trading account and matched with the total sales revenue.

(b) Administration, research and development, and selling and distribution overhead will be transferred to the profit and loss account (assuming that it is not absorbed into product costs).

(c) Other incomes (such as dividends received, rents received and interest received) will be credited to the profit and loss account. The net profit along with all the other remaining balances within the system (for example, raw material stocks, work-in-progress, finished goods stock, debtors, cash and creditors) will then be transferred to the balance sheet.

Basic costing methods

It has been assumed throughout the last few chapters that for the purposes of illustration, separate units of production can be recognized at an early stage in the manufacturing process. In practice, this is not always possible.

In producing milk, for example, it is not usually practicable to think in terms of specific units. For costing purposes, the amount of milk transferred from the farm to the dairy has to be treated as a bulk amount. Otherwise, it would probably be necessary to set up a separate work-in-progress account for each bottle of milk.

The type of input/output problem described above gives rise to two main types of costing methods: specific order costing and operation costing. Both methods are capable of sub-classification, so it is appropriate to discuss each of them separately.

Specific order costing

This type of costing is possible where specific units can be identified at an early stage in the manufacturing process. It may, however, be impossible to cost each *unit* separately, especially when the units are very small, so it may be necessary to cost them in batches. Specific order costing falls into three broad groupings:

1 *Job costing*. This method is used when specific units are produced, such as in an engineering works, or in maintenance or servicing-type jobs, such as decorating, joinery, or plumbing.
2 *Batch costing*. This method is used when specific units are too small to cost individually. It may be used, for example, when producing nuts and bolts, or boots and shoes.
3 *Contract costing*. Here, the specific unit may be very large, such as the construction of a motorway, or of a school.

In specific order costing, each particular method gives rise to its own problems. Basic costing principles are still applied, but the procedure needs some amendment in order to cope with different manufacturing systems.

Operation costing

Operation costing methods are found in those industries where specific units are difficult to identify until a very late stage in the production or assembling process. There are two broad groupings:

1 *Process costing.* Process costing is frequently found in those industries that convert raw materials into a finished product using a process that often requires a chemical change, such as in iron and steel making, and in the chemical and glass industries.
2 *Service costing.* Service costing is found in those industries whose basic objective is to provide a service, such as in local government and in transport undertakings.

Process costing, in particular, gives rise to some very special costing problems. In those processing-type industries where a chemical change takes place during the manufacturing process, for example, it is quite customary to transfer a larger quantity of raw material into the process and to get out a smaller quantity of processed goods. The loss in production arises as a result of the chemical change that has taken place during manufacture. This loss in production is known as a *normal* loss and it can usually be allowed for in costing the product. However, it is not uncommon to find that there is sometimes an *abnormal* gain or loss. It is usual to write off abnormal gains and losses directly to the profit and loss account, and not to charge them against the cost of specific products. Besides different *methods* of costing, there are also a number of *techniques*. These are outlined in the next section.

Costing techniques

The nature of production determines the type of costing method to be adopted. Thereafter, there are a number of costing techniques that can be used in most industries, irrespective of the costing method. The main costing techniques are outlined below.

Absorption costing

Absorption costing has been covered in some detail in earlier chapters. Despite some of the difficulties that were outlined, absorption costing is still the most widely adopted, and most cost book-keeping systems are usually based upon it.

Marginal costing

Marginal costing requires costs to be classified into two broad categories:

fixed costs and variable costs. Fixed costs are those costs that tend to remain constant irrespective of the level of activity. Variable costs are those costs that vary in direct proportion to activity.

The costing books may be kept on the basis of marginal costing, but it is more customary to adopt the technique when dealing with specific decisions. Marginal costing will be covered in more detail in the next chapter.

Superimposed techniques

Both absorption costing and marginal costing are capable of having other techniques *superimposed* upon them. This means that they can be operated independently of any other technique, but it is possible for them to be used in conjunction with the other techniques.

There are two main superimposed techniques. They are outlined briefly below, but they will be encountered again in later chapters.

1 *Budgetary control*. This technique involves preparing detailed plans of future costs and incomes. The plans (or budgets, as they are known) are then compared frequently and regularly with actual results. If necessary, action is then taken to bring the actual results into line with the budgeted results.

2 *Standard costing*. This technique is very similar to budgetary control, except that detailed budgets (or standards) are drawn up for each unit or process. The standards are then compared with the actual result (again, like the budgetary control technique on a frequent and regular basis), and any necessary corrective action is then taken.

Standard costing is used in conjunction with *variance accounting*, a technique that allows detailed arithmetical comparisons to be made between actual and budgeted results. The comparisons are made not only in terms of total cost, but also on the basis of each element of cost.

Conclusion

This chapter has explained briefly how costs are recorded within an absorption costing system. It has also outlined some basic costing methods and techniques.

The costing principles examined in earlier chapters are relevant even in those industries where specific unit costing is not possible, so a basic foundation in costing techniques has now been provided for all non-accountants irrespective of the type of industry in which they work. However, as a result of their widespread application, some of those techniques need to be examined in a little more detail. The next three chapters contain such an examination.

Questions

12.1 What is an integral cost book-keeping system!

12.2 What is an interlocking cost book-keeping system?

12.3 What is meant by the term 'basic costing methods'?

12.4 What is meant by the term 'costing techniques'?

Additional questions (without answers)

12.5 Harper Limited is considering whether it should install an integrated accounting system.

Required:
Prepare a report for your managing director explaining what is meant by such a system, and outlining its advantages.

12.6 Examine the difference between job costing and batch costing.

13 Marginal costing

Learning objectives_____

1 distinguish between fixed and variable costs;

2 assess the relevance of identifying variable costs;

3 apply the marginal costing technique to some simple examples;

4 understand the importance of limiting factors;

and

5 appraise critically the marginal cost technique.

As has been argued in previous chapters absorption costing can provide some misleading information, especially if it is used for short-term decision-making. The main problem arises because absorption costing requires that *all* costs be shared out amongst specific units, irrespective of whether some of those costs are increased or decreased as a result of producing more or less units. The technique that has been devised to cope with this problem is known as *marginal costing*, and it forms the subject of this chapter.

The problem of fixed costs

In absorption costing the distinction between fixed costs and variable costs is not recognized. *Fixed costs* were defined in an earlier chapter as being those costs that tend not to change regardless of the level of activity, and variable costs as those costs that tend to vary in direct proportion to activity.

In absorption costing the fact that some costs (i.e. the fixed costs) will not be affected by making a particular unit is disregarded, and so some of those costs are charged to that unit even though there is no direct relationship. This questionable assumption can best be illustrated by an example.

Suppose that an attempt is being made to estimate the cost of a particular car journey by someone who already owns a fully taxed and insured car. If the car is to be used for the journey, the main cost arising will be that spent on petrol (although there will be a slight increase in its servicing requirements, and it may depreciate a little more quickly). The tax and insurance costs will not be affected by this particular journey: they are fixed costs, no matter how many extra journeys are undertaken. Thus as far as that specific journey is concerned, the only extra cost is the cost of the petrol. The decision to estimate only the *extra* cost of the journey (or for that matter, the extra cost of producing one more unit) gives rise to the technique of marginal costing.

If absorption costing was used to estimate the cost of the journey, all the costs of running the car over (say) a year would be added up and divided by its annual mileage. The average (or absorbed) cost per mile would then be applied to the mileage expected to be incurred on that particular journey. It would clearly be absurd to cost a specific journey in this way: the total cost of running the car is not being affected by the journey. What must be calculated is the marginal (or the extra) cost, and this may then be contrasted with the cost of optional forms of transport, such as travelling by train or by aircraft. Even then, cost may not be the sole criterion in deciding to use the car instead of travelling by train or going by air, because such non-quantifiable factors as comfort and convenience would also need to be taken into account.

In costing the extra cost of a car journey, the *fixed* costs of owning a car are irrelevant. They do form part of the overall cost of car ownership, of course, and they do have to be taken into account when deciding how much it costs to run a car. Otherwise, they should be ignored.

Managers in industry face similar costing decisions. These decisions can also best be solved by using the marginal cost technique. An absorbed cost is not very helpful in deciding upon the outcome of a specific event, for example, in reducing selling prices or in contracting for new work. In taking such specific decisions, the company's fixed costs may not be immediately affected, although in the long run even the fixed costs may change if the company expands (or contracts) on any scale.

Nonetheless, the marginal cost technique is useful for short-term specific decision-making. The next section examines the application of the technique.

The marginal cost technique

As was explained in earlier chapters, costing records are usually kept on the basis of absorption costing. It would be possible to keep them on a marginal costing basis, but this means that in extracting data from such records the effect of fixed costs may not be taken into account. In the long run, of course, the company has to recover all of its costs, even though in the short run, the fixed costs should be ignored in dealing with a specific decision. Most companies use absorption costing for book-keeping purposes, but adapt the data when information for specific decisions is needed.

In theory the marginal costing technique is very easy to adapt, although in practice there are some considerable problems to overcome. These problems largely arise because of the assumptions that have to be made in using the technique. These assumptions are summarized below.

1 Total cost can be analysed into fixed costs and variable costs.
2 Fixed costs tend to remain constant in the short term irrespective of the level of activity.
3 Fixed costs do not bear any relationship whatsoever to the specific units (or processes) being produced, and it is impossible to apportion them amongst specific units because no direct relationship exists.
4 Variable costs tend to vary in *direct* proportion to activity.
5 Some costs are semi-variable, that is, they contain an element of both fixed and variable costs (electricity costs and telephone charges, for example, both contain a fixed rental element, but the variable charge depends upon the use made of the service).

These assumptions are somewhat simplistic but they are useful in helping to arrive at decisions in cases where some costs are not likely to be affected by the decision being taken.

The technique basically requires total cost to be classified into its fixed and variable elements, instead of classifying it into direct and indirect categories, as in absorption costing. Exhibit 13.1 shows a cost statement presented on a marginal cost basis.

Exhibit 13.1: A typical marginal cost statement

	Product			
	A	B	C	Total
	£000	£000	£000	£000
Sales revenue (1)	100	70	20	190
Less: Variable cost of sales (2)	30	40	10	80
Contribution (3)	70	30	10	110
Less: Fixed costs (4)				60
Profit/(Loss) (5)				£50

Tutorial notes

1 The total sales revenue would be analysed into different product groupings (in this example for products A, B and C).
2 The variable costs include direct materials, direct labour costs, other direct expenses and variable overhead. In most cases, direct costs are the same as

variable costs, but there can be some instances of where they are not the same, for example, a machine operator's salary that is fixed under a guaranteed annual wage agreement.

3 The term *contribution* is used to describe the difference between the sales revenue and the variable cost of those sales. A positive contribution helps to pay for the fixed costs.

4 The fixed costs include all the other costs that do not vary in direct proportion to the sales revenue. Fixed costs are assumed to remain constant over a period of time. They do not bear any relationship to the units produced or the sales achieved, and therefore it is not possible to apportion them amongst the individual products. The total of the fixed costs can *only* be deducted from the total contribution.

5 Total contribution less the fixed costs gives the profit (if the balance is positive) or a loss (if the balance is negative).

From Exhibit 13.1 it can be seen that it is possible to arrange the information in the form of a series of equations:

Let S = sales revenue
V = variable costs
C = contribution
F = fixed costs
P = profit
Therefore: $S - V = C$
$C - F = P$
or $C = F + P$
$\therefore S - V = F + P$

The equation $S - V = F + P$ is known as the marginal cost equation, and it captures the essence of the marginal cost technique. The next section explains how it is used.

The application of marginal costing

By using the marginal cost equation it is possible to cost fairly easily any specific decision that management is thinking of taking. Indeed, even if a decision might affect the basic marginal costing assumptions (such as a change in the level of fixed costs), the data can be adapted without any real difficulty.

The data are easy to adapt for two main reasons:

1 It can normally be assumed that fixed costs will remain constant and that they will not be affected by a particular decision.

2 It is possible to calculate the contribution at any level of sales activity, since the variable costs are assumed to vary in direct proportion to the sales revenue.

These points are illustrated in Exhibit 13.2.

Exhibit 13.2: Examples of changes in variable cost and contribution

	One unit	Product 100 units	1,000 units	%
	£	£	£	
Selling price	10	1,000	10,000	100
Less: Variable costs	6	600	6,000	60
Contribution	£4	£400	£4,000	40%

Tutorial notes

1 The variable cost per unit is 60%, and the contribution 40% of the sales revenue.
2 This relationship is assumed to hold good no matter how many units are sold.
3 For every unit sold, the company makes a contribution of £4.
4 The fixed costs are ignored, because they are assumed not to change with the level of activity.

Once all the fixed costs have been covered by the total contribution, each extra unit sold results in an extra amount of profit equal to the contribution earned by that particular unit. Note, however, that profit is not necessarily the same as contribution. This will only be the case once the total contribution has covered the fixed costs. It is only at that stage that any further contribution will be the same as an increase in profit. The point is illustrated in Exhibit 13.3.

Exhibit 13.3: Effect on profit at varying levels of activity

Activity in units:	1,000	2,000	3,000	4,000	5,000
	£	£	£	£	£
Sales	10,000	20,000	30,000	40,000	50,000
Less: Variable costs	5,000	10,000	15,000	20,000	25,000
Contribution	5,000	10,000	15,000	20,000	25,000
Less: Fixed costs	10,000	10,000	10,000	10,000	10,000
Profit (loss)	£(5,000)	–	£5,000	£10,000	£15,000

Tutorial notes

1 The exhibit illustrates five levels of activity: from 1,000 units to 5,000 units.
2 At each level of activity, the fixed costs remain constant.
3 At each level of activity, the variable costs remain in direct proportion to the sales revenue, i.e. 50%. This means that the relationship of contribution to sales is also 50%.

It can be seen from Exhibit 13.3 that only when the fixed costs have been covered by the contribution (at an activity level of 2,000 units), does the increase in contribution thereafter equal the increase in profit. At an activity level of 2,000 units the company's sales revenue is just sufficient to cover its total costs, and at this level it neither makes a profit nor a loss. This is known as its *break-even* position.

The relationship of contribution to sales is known (rather confusingly) as the *profit/volume* (or P/V) *ratio*. Note that it does not mean *profit* in relation to sales, but *contribution* in relation to sales.

The P/V ratio is extremely useful. Once it has been calculated, it can be applied to any level of sales. If the fixed costs are then deducted, the new profit on the amended level of sales can be determined very quickly. Sometimes, of course, the fixed costs will be affected by a change in activity, but if they do change, only a minor amendment is necessary in order to allow for such a change.

The relationships that have been described above may be presented in the form of a chart known as a *break-even graph* (or chart). Accountants believe that it is sometimes much easier to make the point about the relationship between sales, variable costs and fixed costs if it is presented diagrammatically. Exhibit 13.4 illustrates a break-even graph. It is based in the same data as used in Exhibit 13.3.

Exhibit 13.4: A break-even chart

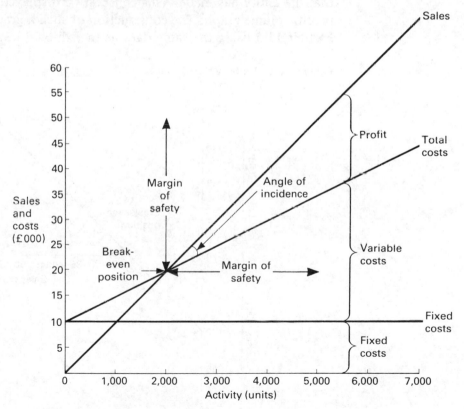

Tutorial notes

1   The total cost line is a combination of the fixed costs and the variable costs. It thus ranges from a total cost of £10,000 (fixed costs only) at a nil level of activity, to £35,000 when the activity level is 5,000 units (fixed costs of £10,000 + variable costs of £25,000).

2   The angle of incidence is the angle formed between the sales line and the total cost line. The wider the angle, the greater the amount of profit. A wide angle of incidence plus a wide margin of safety (see 3 below) indicates a highly profitable position.

3   The margin of safety is the distance between the sales achieved and the sales level needed to break-even. It can be measured either in units (along the x axis) or in sales revenue terms (along the y axis).

4   Activity (measured along the x axis) may be measured either in units, or as a percentage of the theoretical maximum level of activity, or in terms of sales revenue.

Exhibit 13.4 shows quite clearly the relationships that are assumed to exist when the marginal cost technique is adopted. Thus the sales revenue, the variable costs and the fixed costs are all assumed to be linear, i.e. they can all be represented by straight lines from a point where there is no activity right through to infinity.

A break-even chart does not show clearly the amount of profit or loss that the entity has made. This can best be displayed in the form of a profit/volume graph. The construction of such a graph is illustrated in Exhibit 13.5 using the same data as in Exhibit 13.3.

Exhibit 13.5: Profit/ volume graph

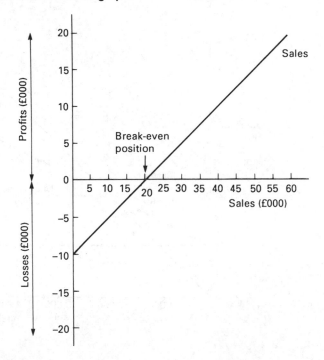

Tutorial notes

1 The *x* axis can be represented either in terms of units, as a percentage of the theoretical maximum level of activity, or in terms of sales revenue.
2 The *y* axis represents profits (positive amounts) or losses (negative amounts).
3 With sales at a level of £50,000, the profit is £15,000. The sales line cuts the *x* axis at the break-even position, and if there are no sales, the losses equals the fixed costs of £10,000.

In practice, the marginal cost relationships are not likely to remain linear over a wide range of activity, and the basic assumptions may only be valid over a fairly narrow range. While this point may appear to create some difficulty in adopting the marginal cost technique, it should be appreciated that wide fluctuations in activity are not normally experienced. Companies usually operate over a fairly narrow range of activity, and the various relationships may be almost linear. The information prepared is only a guide to management. It must not be taken too literally, and there are many other factors that must also be taken into account.

Nonetheless, it would be useful to summarize the criticisms of marginal costing so that you can take them into account when assessing the value of costing information prepared on marginal cost lines. This is the subject of the next section.

Criticisms of marginal costing

The assumptions adopted in preparing marginal cost statements lead to a number of criticisms of the technique:

1 Costs cannot be easily divided into fixed and variable categories.
2 Variable costs do not vary in direct proportion to activity at all levels of activity; for example, the cost of direct materials may increase or decrease because of shortages in supply or because of bulk buying, while the direct labour costs may be fixed in the short run because of the need to give a minimum period of notice before staff can be dismissed.
3 The fixed costs will change (at least to some extent) as activity increases or decreases.
4 It is difficult to decide over what period of time costs will remain fixed: in the long run all costs become variable because the company can avoid them altogether by going into liquidation.
5 A specific decision affecting one product may in turn affect other products, especially if they are complementary, such as a garage that sells oil and petrol.
6 The marginal cost technique does not take into account product mix. A percentage increase or decrease in total sales and total variable costs,

for example, may not have the same percentage effect on individual product ranges.

7   Fixed costs cannot be entirely ignored; in the long run if the company Is to survive its total sales revenue must cover all of its costs.

8   Non-cost factors (such as the security of supplies and the availability of finance) have to be taken into account in arriving at a specific decision.

These are all very severe criticisms of the marginal cost technique. Provided that it is used with caution, that the information is only treated as a *guide* to decision-making, and that other non-cost factors are taken into account, it is still a very useful technique.

Marginal costing formulae

The marginal cost technique requires cost to be classified into fixed and variable categories, and as outlined earlier, the respective relationships can be put in the form of an equation. It is possible to extract a number of other equations from the marginal cost equation, and they can be quite useful in examining specific problems. For convenience these equations are summarized below:

1   Sales − variable cost of sales = contribution: $\qquad$ $S - V = C$

2   Contribution − fixed costs = profit/(loss): $\qquad$ $C - F = P/(L)$

3   Break-even (B/E) position = contribution − fixed costs: $\qquad$ $C - F$

4   B/E in sales value terms $= \dfrac{\text{Fixed costs} \times \text{sales}}{\text{Contribution}}$: $\qquad$ $\dfrac{F \times S}{C}$

5   B/E in units $= \dfrac{\text{Fixed costs}}{\text{Contribution per unit}}$: $\qquad$ $\dfrac{F}{C \text{ per unit}}$

6   Margin of safety (M/S) in value terms $= \dfrac{\text{Profit} \times \text{sales}}{\text{Contribution}}$: $\qquad$ $\dfrac{P \times C}{C}$

7   M/S in units $= \dfrac{\text{Profit}}{\text{Contribution per unit}}$: $\qquad$ $\dfrac{P}{C \text{ per unit}}$

The application of some of these formulae is illustrated in Exhibit 13.6.

Exhibit 13.6: Use of marginal cost formulae

The following information relates to Happy Limited for the year to 30 June 19X8:

		10,000
Number of units sold		

	Per unit	Total
	£	£000
Sales	30	300
Less: Variable costs	18	180
Contribution	12	120
Less: Fixed costs		24
Profit		£96

Required:
In value and unit terms calculate the following:

1 the break-even position; and
2 the margin of safety.

Answer to Exhibit 13.6

1 Break-even position in value terms:

$$\frac{F \times C}{C} = \frac{£24,000 \times £300,000}{120,000} = \underline{£60,000}$$

Break-even in units:

$$\frac{F}{C \text{ per unit}} = \frac{£24,000}{12} = \underline{2,000 \text{ units}}$$

2 Margin of safety in value terms:

$$\frac{P \times S}{C} = \frac{£96,000 \times 300,000}{120,000} = \underline{£240,000}$$

Margin of safety in units:

$$\frac{P}{C \text{ per unit}} = \frac{£96,000}{12} = \underline{8,000 \text{ units}}$$

Check that you understand the significance of the above solutions. You could also use the data to prepare a break-even chart and a profit/volume graph.

An illustrative example

It would now be helpful to examine the technique of marginal costing in the context of a simple example. Exhibit 13.7 summarizes a typical problem with which a board of directors might be faced.

Exhibit 13.7

Looking ahead to the financial year ending 31 March 19X5, the directors of Problems Limited are faced with a budgeted loss of £10,000. This is based on the following data:

Budgeted number of units	10,000
	£000
Sales revenue	100
Less: Variable costs	80
Contribution	20
Less: Fixed costs	30
Budgeted loss	£(10)

The directors would like to aim for a profit of £20,000 for the year to 31 March 19X5. Various proposals have been put forward, none of which require a change in the budgeted level of fixed costs. These proposals are as follows:

1 Reduce the selling price of each unit by 10%.
2 Increase the selling price of each unit by 10%.
3 Stimulate sales by improving the quality of the product; this would increase the variable cost of the unit by £1.50 per unit.

Required:
(a) For each proposal calculate:
     (i)   the break-even position in units and in value terms;
     (ii) the number of units required to be sold in order to meet the profit target.
(b) State which proposal you think should be adopted.

Answer to Exhibit 13.7

Problems Limited
(a) (i) and (ii):

Workings:	£
Profit target	20,000
Fixed costs	30,000
Total contribution required	£50,000

The budgeted selling price per unit is £10 (100,000/10,000).

The budgeted outlook compared with each proposal may be summarized as follows:

Per unit:	Budgeted position	Proposal 1	Proposal 2	Proposal 3
	£	£	£	£
Selling price	10	9	11	10.00
Less: Variable costs	8	8	8	9.50
(a) Unit contribution	£2	£1	£3	£0.50
(b) Total contribution required to break-even (=fixed costs)	£30,000	£30,000	£30,000	£30,000
(c) Total contribution required to meet the profit target	£50,000	£50,000	£50,000	£50,000
∴ no. of units to break-even [(b)/(a)]	15,000	30,000	10,000	60,000
∴ no. of units to meet the profit target [(c)/(a)]	25,000	50,000	16,667	100,000

(b)

Comments:

1 By continuing with the present budget proposals, the company would need to sell 15,000 units to break-even, or 25,000 units to meet the profit target. In order to break-even the company needs to increase its sales by 50%, or by 250% to meet the profit target.
2 A reduction in selling price of 10% per unit would require sales to increase by 300% in order to break-even, or by 500% to meet the profit target.
3 By increasing the selling price of each unit by 10%, the company would only have to sell at the budgeted level to break-even, but its unit sales would have to increase by two-thirds to meet the profit target.
4 By improving the product at an increased variable cost of £1.50 per unit, the company would require a six-fold increase to break-even, or ten-fold to meet the profit target.

Conclusion:

It would appear that increasing the selling price by 10% would be a more practical solution for the company to adopt. In the short run, at least it will break-even, and there is the possibility that sales could be sufficient to make a small profit. In the long run it has a much better chance of meeting the profit target than do the other proposals. Some extra stimulus would be needed, however, to lift sales to this level over such a relatively short period of time. In any case, it is not clear why an increase in price should increase sales, unless the product is one which only sells at a comparatively high price, such as cosmetics and patent medicines. It must also be questioned whether the cost relationships will remain as indicated in the exhibit over such a large increase in activity. In particular, it is unlikely that the fixed costs will remain entirely fixed if there is such a large increase in sales.

Limiting factors

As can be seen in Exhibit 13.7, when optional decisions are considered, the aim will always be to maximize contribution, because the greater the contribution, the more chance there is of covering the fixed costs and hence of making a profit. When managers are faced with a choice, therefore, between (say) producing product A at a contribution of £10 per unit, or of producing product B at a contribution of £20 per unit, they would normally choose product B. Sometimes, however, it may not be possible to produce unlimited quantities of product B because there could be a limit on how many units of B could either be sold or produced.

Such limits are known as *limiting factors* (or *key factors*). Limiting factors may arise for a number of reasons; for example, it may not be possible to sell more than a certain number of units, or there may be production restraints (such as shortages of raw materials, skilled labour, or factory space), or the company may not be able to finance the anticipated rate of expansion.

If there are limits to production and sales, then it is necessary to follow a simple rule in order to decide on which product to concentrate. The rule can be summarized as follows:

> Choose that work which provides the maximum contribution
> per unit of limiting factor employed.

This sounds very complicated, but it is, in fact, quite simple. Suppose that direct materials are a limiting factor, and that only a certain quantity is available. The contribution each unit makes would then be converted into (say) the contribution per kilogram. If the number of direct labour hours were a limiting factor, and a choice had to be made between two jobs, the respective contributions would be converted into the contribution per direct labour hour. The job chosen would be that which earned the most contribution for each direct labour employed on it.

The application of key factors is illustrated in Exhibit 13.8.

Exhibit 13.8

Quays Limited manufactures a product for which there is a shortage of raw materials known as PX. During the year to 31 March 19X7, only 1,000 kilograms of PX will be available. PX is used in manufacturing both product 8 and product 9. The following information is relevant:

Per unit	Product 8	Product 9
	£	£
Selling price	300	150
Less: Variable costs	200	100
Contribution	£100	£50
P/V ratio	33⅓	33⅓
Kilograms required	5	2

Required:
State which product Quays Limited should concentrate on producing.

Answer to Exhibit 13.8

	Product 8	Product 9
	£	£
Contribution per unit	100	50
Limiting factor per unit	5	2
∴ contribution per kilogram	£20	£25

Choice:
Product 9 because it gives the highest contribution per unit of limiting factor.

Check:
Maximum contribution of product 8:

200 units (1,000/5) × contribution per unit = 200 × £100 = £20,000

Maximum contribution of product 9:

500 units (1,000/2) × contribution per unit = 500 × £50 = £25,000

It has been assumed in Exhibit 13.8 that there is only one limiting factor. There could, of course, be many more limiting factors. Suppose, for example, that it is not possible to sell more than 400 units of product 9. The company would then aim to sell all the 400 units. The total contribution would amount to £20,000 (400 × £25). The 400 units would consume 800 units of raw materials (400 × 2 kilograms), leaving 200 kilograms for use in producing product 8. Product 8 requires 5 kilograms per unit of raw materials, so 40 units could be completed at a total contribution of £4,000 (40 × £100). The position can be summarized as follows:

	Product 8	Product 9	Total
Units sold	40	400	
Raw materials (kilograms used)	200	800	1,000
Contribution per unit (£)	100	50	
Total contribution (£)	4,000	20,000	24,000

The £24,000 total contribution compares with the contribution of £25,000 which the company could have made if there was no limiting factor affecting product 9's sales.

Conclusion

Marginal costing is a most important technique. It is particularly useful in the short term, but it is of less value when long-term decisions have to be made.

The technique depends upon two main assumptions:

1 some costs remain fixed, irrespective of the level of activity; and
2 other costs vary in direct proportion to sales.

These assumptions are not usually valid over the long term, but provided that they are used with caution, they can be usefully adopted in the short term.

It should also be remembered that the marginal costing technique is only a *guide* to decision-making, and that other non-cost factors have to be taken into account.

This chapter concludes a study of the basic structure of cost and management accounting. The next two chapters examine the superimposed techniques of budgetary control and standard costing. These techniques can be used in conjunction with a basic costing system.

Questions

13.1 The following information relates to Pole Limited for the year to 31 January 19X2.

	£000
Administration expenses:	
Fixed	30
Variable	7
Semi-variable (fixed 80%, variable 20%)	20
Materials:	
Direct	60
Indirect	5
Production overhead (all fixed)	40
Research and development expenditure:	
Fixed	60
Variable	15
Semi-variable (fixed 50%, variable 50%)	10
Sales	450
Selling and distribution expenditure:	
Fixed	80
Variable	4
Semi-variable (fixed 70%, variable 30%)	30
Wages:	
Direct	26
Indirect	13

Required:
Using the above data, compile a marginal cost statement for Pole Limited for the year to 31 January 19X2.

13.2 You are presented with the following information for Giles Limited for the year to 28 February 19X2.

	£000
Fixed costs	150
Variable costs	300
Sales (50,000 units)	500

Required:
(a) Calculate the following:
    (i) the break-even point in value terms and in units;
    (ii) the margin of safety in value terms and in units.
(b) Prepare a break-even chart.

13.3 The following information applies to Ayre Limited for the two years to 31 March 19X2 and 19X3 respectively:

Year	Sales £000	Profits £000
31.3.19X2	750	100
31.3.19X3	1,000	250

Required:
Assuming that the cost relationships had remained as given in the question,

calculate the company's profit if the sales for the year to 31 March 19X3 had reached the budgeted level of £1,200,000.

13.4 The following information relates to Carter Limited for the year to 30 April 19X3:

Units sold	50,000
Selling price per unit	£40
Net profit per unit	£9
Profit/volume ratio	40%

During 19X4 the company would like to increase its sales substantially, but to do so it would have to reduce the selling price per unit by 20%. The variable cost per unit will not change, but because of the increased activity, the company will have to invest in new machinary which will increase the fixed costs by £30,000 per annum.

Required:
Given the new conditions, calculate how many units the company will need to sell in 19X4 in order to make the same amount of profit as it did in 19X3.

13.5 Puzzled Limited would like to increase its sales during the year to 31 May 19X5. To do so, it has several mutually exclusive options open to it as follows:

1 reduce the selling price per unit by 15%;
2 improve the product resulting in an increase in the variable cost per unit of £1.30;
3 spend £15,000 on an advertising campaign;
4 improve factory efficiency by purchasing more machinery at a fixed extra annual cost of £22,500.

During the year to 31 May 19X4, the company sold 20,000 units. The cost details were as follows:

	£000
Sales	200
Variable costs	150
Contribution	50
Fixed costs	40
Profit	£10

These cost relationships are expected to hold in 19X5.

Required:
State which option you would recommend and why.

13.6 Micro Limited has some surplus capacity. It is now considering whether it should accept a special contract to use some of its spare capacity. However, this contract will use some specialist direct labour which is in short supply.

The following details relate to the proposed contract:

	£
Contract price	50,000
Variable costs:	
Direct materials	10,000
Direct labour	30,000

4,000 direct labour hours would be required in order to complete the contract.

The company's budget for the year during which the contract would be undertaken is as follows:

	£000
Sales	750
Less: Variable costs	500
Contribution	250
Less: Fixed costs	230
Profit	£20

Direct labour hours: 50,000 maximum available during the year.

Required:
State, giving your reasons, whether the special contract should be accepted.

Additional questions (without answers)

13.7 The following information relates to Mere's budget for the year to 31 December 19X7:

Product	K	L	M	Total
	£000	£000	£000	£000
Sales	700	400	250	1,350
Direct materials	210	60	30	300
Direct labour	100	200	200	500
Variable overhead	90	60	50	200
Fixed overhead	20	40	40	100
	420	360	320	1,100
Profit/(loss)	280	40	(70)	250
Budgeted sales (units)	140	20	25	

Note:
Fixed overheads are apportioned on the basis of direct labour hours.

The directors are worried about the loss that product M is budgeted to make, and various suggestions have been made to counteract the loss, viz.:

1 stop selling product M;
2 increase its selling price by 20%;
3 reduce its selling price by 10%;

4 reduce its costs by purchasing a new machine costing £350,000, thereby decreasing the direct labour cost by £100,000 (the machine would have a life of five years; its residual value would be nil).

Required:
Evaluate each of these proposals.

13.8 Temple Limited has been offered two new contracts, the details of which are as follows:

Contract	1	2
	£000	£000
Contract price	1,000	1,500
Direct materials	300	300
Direct labour	300	600
Variable overhead	100	100
Fixed overhead	100	200
	800	1,200
Profit	200	300
Direct materials required (kilos)	50,000	100,000
Direct labour hours required	10,000	25,000

Note:
The fixed overhead has been apportioned on the basis of direct labour cost.

Temple is a one product firm. Its budgeted cost per unit for the year to 31 December 19X8 is summarized below:

	£
Sales	6,000
Direct materials (100 kilos)	700
Direct labour (200 hours)	3,000
Variable overhead	300
Fixed overhead	1,000
	5,000
Profit	1,000

The company would only have the capacity to accept one of the new contracts. Unfortunately, materials suitable for use in all of its work are in short supply, and the company has estimated that only 200,000 kilos would be available during the year to 31 December 19X8.

Even more worrying is the shortage of skilled labour, and only 100,000 direct labour hours are expected to be available during the year.

The good news is that there may be an up-turn in the market for its normal contract work.

Required:
Advise management which contract to accept.

14 Budgetary control

Learning objectives_____

1 describe the nature and purpose of budgeting and budgetary control;

2 outline the steps involved in implementing and operating a system of budgetary control;

   and

3 appreciate the significance of fixed and flexible budgets.

The last five chapters have examined the basic principles of cost and management accounting. For convenience, it has been assumed that most of the costing information has been prepared on an historical basis. However, as was pointed out in Chapter 9, one of the major disadvantages of *financial* accounting is that it is almost entirely concerned with looking back to what has happened. Managers are probably more concerned with what *might* happen.

If the maximum benefits are to be obtained from a cost and management accounting system it ought also to be able to provide management with information that deals with the future, as well as with the past. This can be achieved by incorporating into the cost and management accounting system a technique known as *budgetary control*. Budgetary control is the subject of this chapter.

Budgetary control is known as a *superimposed* technique, that is, it supplements an already existing costing system. Thus while it is possible to operate a costing system without budgetary control, it is particularly advantageous to incorporate budgetary control into it. In this chapter, budgetary control is examined from the point of view of a non-accountant. As will be seen, the preparation of budgets (and their use for control purposes), involves some fairly detailed exercises. Such exercises are usually undertaken by a team of accountants specially employed for the purpose, although the team does, of course, need the assistance of other personnel. Indeed, if the budgetary control system is to work successfully, most employees will need to be heavily involved in the entire process.

This chapter is primarily concerned with those aspects of budgeting that are of particular relevance to the non-accountant. It begins by examining what is meant by budgeting.

The nature of budgeting

The term 'budget' is well understood. In private life, many individuals prepare their own personal budget. Even in an informal sense, everyone does some budgeting at some time or other; for example, by working out what one expects to earn over (say) the next twelve months, and comparing it with what one expects to spend during the same period. Such a budget may not be very precise, and it may not be formally written down. Nonetheless, it contains all the ingredients of what accountants mean by a budget.

The essential features of a budget are summarized below.

1 It lays down policies which are expected to be pursued in order to meet the overall objectives of the entity.
2 It contains both quantitative and financial data.
3 The data are usually formally documented.
4 It is prepared for a future period of time.
5 It covers a defined period of time.

In practice, a considerable number of budgets will be prepared, for example for sales, production and administration. These detailed budgets will then be combined into what is known as a *master* budget.

Once the master budget has been prepared, it will be examined in great detail in order to see whether the overall plan can be accommodated. It could be the case, for example, that the sales budget provides for a large increase in sales. As a result, the production budgets will have been prepared to meet the extra sales demand. However, the cash budget might suggest that the entity cannot finance the extra activity required. Thus additional financing arrangements will have to be made, because obviously no organization would normally turn down the opportunity of improving its profitability.

The detailed preparation of individual budgets is a valuable exercise in its own right, because it forces management to look ahead. It is a natural human tendency always to be looking to the past, but past experience may not always be an adequate preparation for the future. If managers are asked to produce a budget, it does at least encourage them to examine what they *have* been doing in relation to what they *could* do.

Nonetheless, the full benefits of a budgeting system are only realized when it is also used for control purposes. When budgets are used as a form of control, the technique is known as *budgetary control*.

Budgetary control has several important features which may be summarized as follows:

1 Managers' responsibilities have to be clearly defined.
2 Managers' budgets lay down the policies for their own sphere of responsibility.
3 Managers have a responsibility to follow their budget once it has been approved.
4 Managers' actual performances are constantly compared with the planned (or budgeted) results.
5 Corrective action is taken if the actual results differ from the budgeted results.
6 Departures from budget are only permitted if they have been approved by senior management.
7 Variances that are unaccounted for will be subject to individual investigation.

Budgetary control is, therefore, basically a control technique whereby actual results are continuously checked against planned results. All variances should be carefully investigated. The immediate actual performance will be changed if it is judged necessary so that it can be brought into line with the budgeted results, or the budget will be amended to take account of new developments.

Now that the nature of budgeting and budgetary control has been briefly outlined, it is possible to examine how it is operated. This is covered in the next section.

Budget procedure

In practice, the budget procedure may be very detailed and extremely time-consuming. The procedure starts with a determination of the entity's objectives. Once the entity has decided what it is aiming to achieve over the budget period, it will then need to make a forecast of what is likely to happen.

There is a technical difference between a forecast and a budget. A forecast is a prediction of what is *likely* to happen. A budget is a formal written statement of what *should* happen.

In order to make it easier to follow, the budgeting process will be considered in various stages.

The budget period

The main budget period is usually based on a calendar year, although as explained in Chapter 9 it may be shorter or longer depending upon the industry or the type of budget.

Besides determining the main budget period, it is also necessary to prepare sub-period budgets. Sub-period budgets are required for control purposes, because actual results are compared with budgeted results, and this has to be done regularly in order for it to be effective. The sub-budget periods for some functions may need to be very short if tight control is to be exercised over them. The cash budget, for example, may need to be prepared on a weekly basis, whereas the administration budget may only need to be prepared monthly.

Administration

The budget procedure may be administered by a special budget committee, or it may be supervised by the accounting function. It will be necessary for the budget committee to lay down general guidelines in accordance with the entity's objectives, and to ensure that individual departments operate within them. The production department needs to know, for example, what the entity is budgeting to sell so that it can prepare its own budget on the basis of the budgeted level of sales, but the detailed production budget must be left to the production manager to decide.

This principle is in line with the concept of responsibility accounting that was outlined in an earlier chapter. If the control procedure is to work properly, managers must be given responsibility for a clearly defined area of activity, such as a cost centre. Thereafter, they are expected to be fully answerable for all that goes on in their own cost centre. Unless managers are given responsibility they cannot be expected to be answerable for something which is outside their control. This means that as far as budgets are concerned, managers must help prepare, amend and *approve* their own department's budget, otherwise the budgetary control system will not work.

The budgeting process

The budgeting process is illustrated in Exhibit 14.1. Study the exhibit very carefully noting how the various budgets fit together.

Later on in the chapter a calculative example will illustrate how the budgeting process actually works in practice, but for the moment a brief description will be sufficient.

In commercial organizations the first budget to be prepared is usually the sales budget. Once the sales for the budget period (and for each sub-budget period) have been determined, the next stage is to calculate the effect on production. This will then enable an agreed *level of activity* to be determined. The level of activity may be expressed in so many units or as a percentage of the theoretical productive capacity of the entity. Once the level of activity has been established, departmental managers can be instructed to base their budgets on it.

Exhibit 14.1: The budgeting process

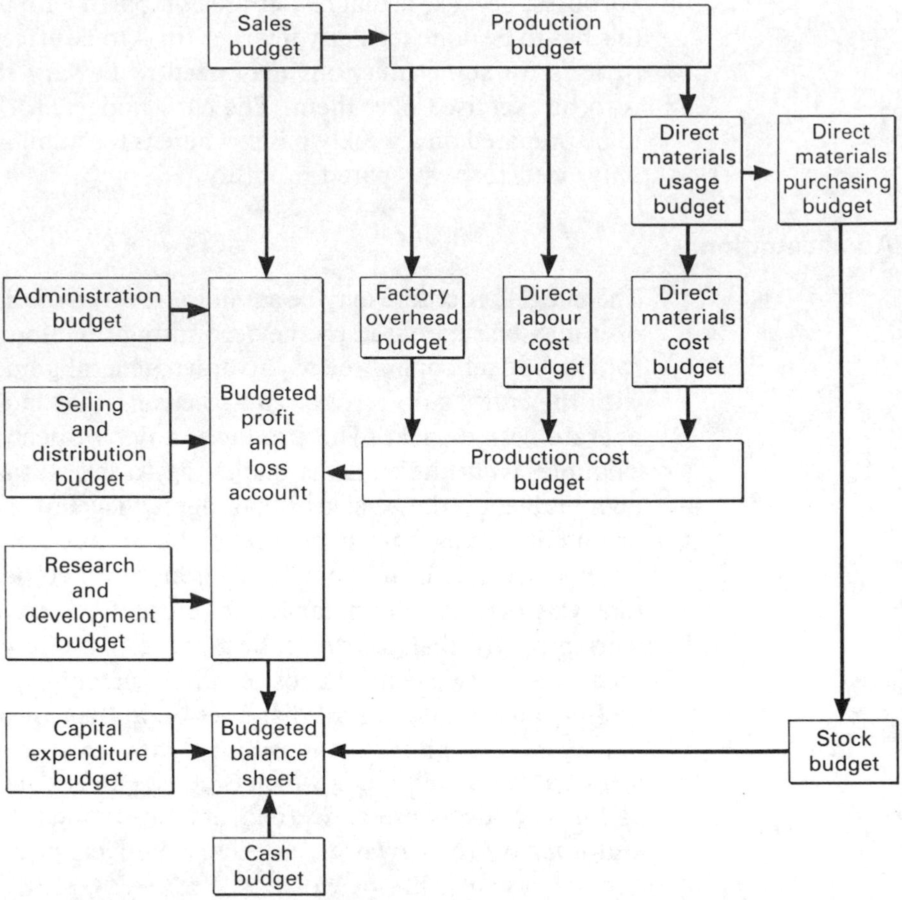

Assume, for example, that it has been agreed that 1,000 units can be sold during a particular budget period. The production department will need this information in order to prepare its budget. This does not necessarily mean that it will budget for a production level of 1,000 units, because it will need to allow for any units it expects to have in stock at the beginning of the budget period, and for the number of units it wants to have in stock at the end of the budget period.

The budgeted production level will then be translated into how much material and labour will be required to meet that particular budgeted level. Similarly, it will be necessary to prepare overhead budgets. Much of the general overhead expenditure of the entity (such as factory administration, general administration, and research and development expenditure) will tend to be fixed expenditure and it will not be directly affected by production levels. However, in some instances, a marked change in activity may lead to changes being made to the overhead budgets.

The sales and distribution overhead budget may be one budget that will not be entirely fixed in nature. An increase in the number of units sold, for example, may require more delivery vans to be purchased, and extra staff employed to operate them.

Functional budgets

A budget prepared for a particular cost centre (or department) is known as a *functional budget*. All the functional budgets will be combined into what was described earlier as the *master budget*. The master budget forms, in effect, a budgeted profit and loss account and a budgeted balance sheet.

Once all the functional budgets have been combined into the master budget, it may not be acceptable to the senior management of the entity. This may be because the entity cannot cope with that particular budgeted level of activity, perhaps because of production or financial constraints. Indeed, one of the most important budgets is the *cash budget*. The cash budget translates all the other functional budgets (including that for capital expenditure) into cash terms. It will show in detail the pattern of cash receipts and expenditure both for the main budget period and for each sub-budget period. If the cash budget shows that the entity will have difficulty in financing a particular budgeted level of activity, it will give management an opportunity to find alternative sources of finance.

This latter point illustrates the importance of being aware of the entity's future commitments, so that something can be done if there are likely to be problems. The master budget usually takes so long to prepare, however, that by the time that it has been completed, it will be almost impossible to make major alterations. It is then tempting for senior management to make changes to the functional budgets without reference to the individual cost centre managers. It is most unwise to do so without consultation, because it is difficult to use such budgets for control purposes if the respective managers have not agreed to the changes. As argued earlier, they can hardly take responsibility for budgets that have been imposed upon them.

As it is difficult to see how all the functional budgets fit together, it would be helpful to demonstrate how they are prepared. An illustrative example is included in the next section.

Functional budgets: an illustrative example

It would obviously be very difficult to observe the basic procedures involved in the preparation of the functional budgets if an extremely detailed example were used. Exhibit 14.2 has, therefore, been especially devised to illustrate the *main* procedures. In practice, there would be very many more steps involved.

Exhibit 14.2

Sefton Limited manufactures one product known as EC2. The following information relates to the preparation of the budget for the year to 31 March 19X9:

1   Sales budget details for product EC2:
 Expected selling price per unit: £100.
 Expected sales in units: 10,000.
 All sales are on credit terms.
2   EC2 requires 5 units of raw material E and 10 units of raw material C. E is expected to cost £3 per unit, and C £4 per unit. All goods are purchased on credit terms.
3   Two departments are involved in producing EC2, machining and assembly. The following information is relevant:

	Direct labour per unit of product (hours)	Direct labour rate per hour £
Machining	1.00	6
Assembling	0.50	8

4   The finished production overhead costs are expected to amount to £100,000.
5   At 1 April 19X8, 800 units of EC2 are expected to be in stock at a value of £52,000, 4,500 units of raw material E at a value of £13,500, and 12,000 units of raw material C at a value of £48,000. Stocks of both finished goods and raw materials are planned to be 10% above the expected opening stock levels as at 1 April 19X8.
6   Administration, selling and distribution overhead is expected to amount to £150,000.
7   Other relevant information:
 (a) Opening trade debtors are expected to be £80,000. Closing trade debtors are expected to amount to 15% of the total sales for the year.
 (b) Opening trade creditors are expected to be £28,000. Closing trade creditors are expected to amount to 10% of the purchases for the year.
 (c) All other expenses will be paid in cash during the year.
 (d) Other balances at 1 April 19X8 are expected to be as follows:

	£	£
(i) Share capital: ordinary shares		225,000
(ii) Retained profits		17,500
(iii) Proposed dividend		75,000
(iv) Fixed assets at cost	250,000	
Less: Accumulated depreciation	100,000	
		150,000
(v) Cash at bank and in hand		2,000

8   Capital expenditure will amount to £50,000 payable in cash on 1 April 19X8.
9   Fixed assets are depreciated on a straight-line basis at a rate of 20% per annum on cost.

Required:

In so far as the information permits, prepare all the relevant budgets for Sefton Limited for the year to 31 March 19X9.

Answer to Exhibit 14.2

Even with a much simplified budgeting exercise, there is clearly a great deal of work involved in preparing the budgets. To make it easier for you to understand what is happening, the procedure will be outlined step by step.

Step 1: Prepare the sales budget

Units of EC2	Selling price per unit	Total sales value
	£	£
10,000	100	1,000,000

Step 2: Prepare the production budget

	Units
Sales of EC2	10,000
Less: Opening stock	800
	9,200
Add: Desired closing stock (opening stock + 10%)	880
Production required	10,080

Step 3: Prepare the direct materials usage budget

Direct material:

E: 5 units × 10,080	50,400 units
C: 10 units × 10,080	100,800 units

Step 4: Prepare the direct materials purchase budget

Direct material	E	C
	(Units)	*(Units)*
Usage (as per Step 3)	50,400	100,800
Less: Opening stock	4,500	12,000
	45,900	88,800
Add: Desired closing stock (opening stock + 10%)	4,950	13,200
	50,850	102,000
	× £3	× £4
∴ Total value of purchase	£152,550	£408,000

Step 5: Prepare the direct labour budget

	Machining	Assembling
Production units (as per Step 2)	10,080	10,080
× direct labour hours required	×1 DLH	× 0.50 DLH
	10,080 DLH	5,040 DLH
× direct labour rate per hour	× £6	× £8
	£60,480	£40,320

Step 6: Prepare the fixed production overhead budget

Given   £100,000

Step 7: Calculate the value of the closing raw material stock

Raw material	Closing stock * (units)	Cost per unit £	Total value £
E	4,950	3	14,850
C	13,200	4	52,800
			£67,650

*Step 4

Step 8: Calculate the value of the closing finished stock

	£	£
Unit cost:		
Direct materials: E – 5 units × £3 per unit	15	
C – 10 units × £4 per unit	40	55
Direct labour: Machining – 1 hour × £6 per DLH	6	
Assembling – 0.50 hours × £8 per DLH	4	10
Total direct cost		£65
× units in stock		× 880
		£57,200

Step 9: Prepare the administration, selling and distribution budget

Given   £150,000

Step 10: Prepare the capital expenditure budget

Given   £50,000

Step 11: Calculate the cost of goods sold

	£
Opening stock (given)	52,000
Manufacturing cost:	
Production units (Step 2) × Total direct cost (Step 3)	
= 10,080 × £65	655,200
	707,200
Less: Closing stock (Step 8: 880 units × £65)	57,200
Cost of goods sold (10,000 units)	£650,000

Step 12: Prepare the cash budget

	£
Receipts	
Opening debtors	80,000
Sales (£1,000,000 × 85%)	850,000
	930,000

Payments

Opening creditors	28,000
Purchases (Step 4: (£152,550 + 408,000) × 90%)	504,495
Wages (Step 5: £60,480 + 40,320)	100,800
Fixed production overhead	100,000
Administration, selling and distribution overhead	150,000
Capital expenditure	50,000
Proposed dividend (19X8)	75,000
	1,008,295
Net receipts	(78,295)
Add: Opening cash	2,000
Budgeted closing cash balance (overdrawn)	£(76,295)

Step 13: Prepare the budgeted profit and loss account

	£	£
Sales (Step 1)		1,000,000
Less: Variable cost of sales (Step 8: 10,000 × £65		650,000
Gross margin		350,000
Less: Fixed production overhead (Step 6)	100,000	
Depreciation ((£250,000 + 50,000) × 20%))	60,000	160,000
Production margin		190,000
Less: Administration, selling and distribution overhead (Step 9)		150,000
Budgeted net profit		£40,000

Step 14: Prepare the budgeted balance sheet

	£	£	£
Fixed assets (at cost)			300,000
Less: Accumulated depreciation			160,000
			140,000
Current assets			
Raw materials (Step 7)		67,650	
Finished stock (Step 8)		57,200	
Trade debtors (15% × £1,000,000)		150,000	
		274,850	
Less: Current liabilities			
Trade creditors (Step 4: 10% × (£152,550 + 408,000))	56,055		
Bank overdraft (Step 12)	76,295	132,350	142,500
			£282,500
Financed by:			
Share capital			
Ordinary shares			225,000
Retained profits (£17,500 + 40,000)			57,500
			£282,500

Exhibit 14.2 is a fairly complicated example, although much detail has been excluded; for example, the company produces only one product, and the value of the opening stocks at 1 April 19X8 is the same as the budgeted costs of manufacture during the year to 31 March 19X9.

You are now recommended to work through Exhibit 14.2 once more. Use the budgeting process guide shown in Exhibit 14.1. It would then be advisable to have another go at Exhibit 14.2, but this time without reference to the solution.

Fixed and flexible budgets

Once the master budget has been agreed, all personnel in the entity are expected to ensure that they adhere to it. However, some entities only use the budgeting process as a planning exercise. Once the master budget has been agreed, there may be no attempt to use it for control purposes. Thus the actual results will not be frequently compared with the budgeted results, and the budget may be virtually ignored. If this is the case, the entity is not getting the best out of the budgeting system.

As suggested earlier, budgets are particularly useful if they are also used as a means of control. The control is achieved if the actual performance is constantly compared with the budgeted results, any variance investigated, and adverse trends are corrected.

The constant comparison of the actual results with the budgeted results may be done either on a *fixed* budget basis or a *flexible* budget basis. If a fixed budget system is operated, then the actual results for a particular period will be compared with the original budgets. A flexible budget system allows for changes that may have taken place since the budgets were prepared. Thus, in certain circumstances, the original budgets will be changed (or in accounting terminology, *flexed*) before they are compared with the actual results.

It may seem a little strange to suggest that the budget may be changed. A budget is a form of measure; to consider changing it would appear to be like having an elastic ruler. If measurements are to be consistent, the ruler has to stay the same length, and the same requirement should apply to budgets.

This argument is very attractive, but if it is accepted for budgetary control purposes, some quite misleading variances may well be produced.

As was explained earlier, managers (especially those directly involved in production) will base their budgets on the budgeted level of activity. If the actual level of activity is greater than the budgeted level, managers will have to allow for more expenditure on direct materials, direct labour and other expenses.

Suppose, for example, that a manager has prepared a cost centre budget on the basis of an anticipated level of activity of 70%. During the actual period, the company is much busier than expected, and the actual level of activity turns out to be 80%. Almost certainly, those cost centres that have been affected by the increased activity will have spent more than they had budgeted.

If the actual performance is then compared with the original budget on a fixed budget basis, it will appear as though the manager has greatly exceeded the budget. There is then a tendency to argue that the variances have been caused by the unexpected increase in activity (which may be outside the control of the manager concerned). While this may be partly true, the increased activity may hide variances which the manager should have been able to control.

This problem may be overcome by *flexing* the budget, that is, revising it on the basis of what it would have been if the manager had budgeted for an activity level of 80% instead of 70%. The other assumptions and calculations made at the time the budget was prepared (such as material prices and wage rates) will not be amended.

If the entity operates a flexible budget system, the original budgets may be prepared on the basis of a wide range of possible activity levels. This method, however, is very time-consuming, and it is unlikely that one will have been prepared that is exactly identical to the actual level of activity. The best method is to wait until the actual level of activity is known, and then take the original budget data and flex (or amend) them accordingly.

The procedure is illustrated in Exhibit 14.3.

Exhibit 14.3: Flexible budget procedure

The following information had been prepared for Carp Limited for the year to 30 June 19X6:

	Budget 50%	Actual 60%
Level of activity		
	£	£
Costs:		
Direct materials	50,000	61,000
Direct labour	100,000	118,000
Variable overhead	10,000	14,000
Total variable cost	160,000	193,000
Fixed overhead	40,000	42,000
Total costs	£200,000	£235,000

Required:
Prepare a flexed budget operating statement for Carp Limited for the year to 30 June 19X6.

Answer to Exhibit 14.3

Carp Limited

Flexed budget operating statement for the year to 30 June 19X6

	Flexed budget	Actual costs	Variance: favourable/ (adverse)
	£	£	£
Direct materials (1)	60,000	61,000	(1,000)
Direct labour (1)	120,000	118,000	2,000
Variable overhead (1)	12,000	14,000	(2,000)
Total variable costs	192,000	193,000	(1,000)
Fixed overhead (2)	40,000	42,000	(2,000)
Total costs (3)	£232,000	£235,000	£(3,000)

Tutorial notes

1   All the budgeted variable costs have been flexed by 20% because the actual activity was 60% compared with a budgeted level of 50% (i.e. a 20% increase).
2   The budgeted fixed costs are not flexed because by definition they ought not to change with activity.
3   Instead of using the total fixed budget cost of £200,000 (as per the question), the total flexed budget costs of £232,000 can be compared more fairly with the total actual cost of £235,000.
4   Note that the terms 'favourable' and 'adverse' (as applied to variances) mean favourable or adverse to profit. In other words, profit will be either greater or less than the budgeted profit.
5   The reasons for the variances between the actual costs and the flexed budget will need to be investigated. The flexed budget shows that even allowing for the increased activity, the actual costs were in excess of the budget allowance.
6   Similarly, it will be necessary to investigate why the actual activity was higher than the budgeted activity. It could have been caused by inefficient budgeting, or by quite an unexpected increase in sales activity. While this would normally be welcome, it might have placed a strain on the productive and financial resources of the entity. If the increase is likely to be permanent, management will need to make immediate arrangements to accommodate the new level of activity.

It should be emphasized that the primary purpose of a budgetary control system is to control as closely as possible the activities of the entity. There will invariably be variances between the actual and the budgeted results no matter how carefully the budgets are prepared. This does not matter unduly, as long as it is possible to find out why the variances occurred, and to take corrective action before it is too late to do anything about them.

Conclusion

This chapter has argued that the full benefits of a cost and management accounting system can best be gained if a budgetary control system is superimposed upon it. The preparation of budgets is a valuable exercise in itself. It forces management to look ahead to what might happen rather than to look back to what did happen, but it is even more valuable if it is also used as a form of control.

Budgetary control enables actual results to be frequently measured against an agreed plan. Departures from that plan can be quickly spotted, and steps taken to correct any unwelcome trends. The comparison of actual results with a fixed budget may not be particularly helpful if the company has operated at a different level of activity from the budgeted level, so it is sometimes preferable to compare actual results with a flexed budget.

It will be necessary for the difference between the actual level of activity and the budgeted level to be carefully investigated. As so many of the functional budgets are based upon the budgeted level of activity, it is vital that it is assessed as accurately as possible, since an error in estimating the level of activity will affect all of the company's financial and operational activities.

The next chapter deals with standard costing. Although standard costing is a technique that is very similar to budgetary control, it involves going into a great deal more detail.

Questions

14.1 You are presented with the following information for Moray Limited.

Budgeted sales units for the six months to 30 June 19X1

January	200
February	250
March	370
April	400
May	500
June	550

Additional information:
1 Opening stock at 1 January 19X1 was expected to be 320 units.
2 Desired closing stock level at 30 June 19X1 was 450 units.

Required:
Calculate the minimum number of units to be produced each month if an even production flow is to be established.

14.2 You have been presented with the following budgeted information relating to Jordan Limited for the six months to 31 December 19X2:

	July	August	September	October	November	December
Sales (units)	70	140	350	190	150	120
Closing stock (units	230	370	200	190	180	100

Additional information:
Opening stock at 1 July 19X2 is expected to be 100 units.

Required:
Calculate the monthly production levels required to meet the above budgeted data.

14.3 The directors of Dalton Limited have been presented with the following budgeted information for the six months to 30 June 19X3:

	January	February	March	April	May	June
Sales (units)	90	150	450	150	130	120

Additional information:
1 The opening stock at 1 January 19X3 is expected to be 100 units.
2 Units are only available for sale in the period following the month in which they were manufactured.

Required:
Calculate the minimum number of units to be produced each month in order to meet the budgeted monthly sales figures assuming that the directors wish to adopt the minimum possible production flow.

14.4 The following information has been prepared for Tom Limited for the six months to 30 September 19X4:

Budgeted production levels Product X

	Units
April	140
May	280
June	700
July	380
August	300
September	240

Product X uses two units of component A6 and three units of component B9. At 1 April 19X4 there were expected to be 100 units of A6 in stock, and 200 units of B9. The desired closing stock levels of each component were as follows:

Month end 19X4	A6	B9
	(units)	(units)
30 April	110	250
31 May	220	630
30 June	560	340
31 July	300	300

31 August	240	200
30 September	200	180

During the six months to 30 September 19X4, component A6 was expected to be purchased at a cost of £5 per unit and component B9 at a cost of £10 per unit.

Required:
Prepare the following budgets for each of the six months to 30 September 19X4:

1 direct materials usage budget; and
2 direct materials purchase budget.

14.5 Don Limited has one major product which requires two types of direct labour to produce it. The following data refer to certain budget proposals for the three months to 31 August 19X5:

Month	Production units
30.6.X5	600
31.7.X5	700
31.8.X5	650

Direct labour hours required per unit:

	Hours	Budgeted rate per hour
		£
Production	3	4
Finishing	2	8

Required:
Prepare the direct labour cost budget for each of the three months to 31 August 19X5.

14.6 Gorse Limited manufactures one product. The budgeted sales for period 6 are for 10,000 units at a selling price of £100 per unit. Other details are as follows:

1 Two components are used in the manufacture of each unit:

Component	Number	Unit cost of each component
		£
XY	5	1
WZ	3	0.50

2 Stocks at the beginning of the period are expected to be as follows:
   (a) 4,000 units of finished goods at a unit cost of £52.50 per unit.
   (b) Component XY: 16,000 units at a cost of £1.
       Component WZ: 9,600 units at a unit cost of £0.50.
3 Two grades of employees are used in the manufacture of each unit:

Employee	Hours per unit	Labour rate per hour
		£
Production	4	5
Finishing	2	7

4 Factory overhead is absorbed into units cost on the basis of direct labour hours. The budgeted factory overhead for the period is estimated to be £96,000.

5 The administration, selling and distribution overhead for the period has been budgeted at £275,000.

6 The company plans a reduction of 50% in the quantity of finished stock at the end of period 6, and an increase of 25% in the quantity of each component.

Required:
Prepare the following budgets for period 6:
1 sales;
2 production quantity;
3 materials usage;
4 materials purchase;
5 direct labour;
6 the budgeted profit and loss account for period 6.

14.7 The following budget information relates to Flossy Limited for the three months to 31 March 19X7.

1 Budgeted profit and loss accounts:

Month	31.1.X7	28.2.X7	31.3.X7
	£000	£000	£000
Sales (all on credit)	2,000	3,000	2,500
Cost of sales	1,200	1,800	1,500
Gross profit	800	1,200	1,000
Depreciation	(100)	(100)	(100)
Other expenses	(450)	(500)	(600)
	(550)	(600)	(700)
Net profit	£250	£600	£300

2 Budgeted balance sheets:

Budgeted balances	31.12.X6	31.1.X7	28.2.X7	31.3.X7
	£000	£000	£000	£000
Current assets:				
Stocks	100	120	150	150
Debtors	200	300	350	400
Short-term investments	60	–	40	30
Current liabilities:				
Trade creditors	110	180	160	150
Other creditors	50	50	50	50
Taxation	150	–	–	–
Dividends	200	–	–	–

3 Capital expenditure to be incurred on 20 February 19X7 was expected to amount to £470,000.

4 Sales of plant and equipment on 15 March 19X7 are expected to raise £30,000 in cash.
5 The cash at bank and in hand on 1 January 19X7 was expected to be £15,000.

Required:
Prepare Flossy Limited's cash budget for each of the three months during the quarter ending 31 March 19X7.

14.8 Chimes Limited has prepared a flexible budget for one of its factories for the year to 30 June 19X8. The details are as follows:

Production capacity	30%	40%	50%	60%
	£000	£000	£000	£000
Direct materials	42	56	70	84
Direct labour	18	24	30	36
Factory overhead	22	26	30	34
Administration overhead	17	20	23	26
Selling and distribution overhead	12	14	16	18
	£111	£140	£169	£198

Additional information:
1 The company is only operating at 45% of its capacity, and an increase in capacity during the year to 30 June 19X8 is unlikely. At that capacity, the sales revenue has been budgeted at a level of £135,500.
2 It would be possible to close the factory down for twelve months, and then re-open it again on 1 July 19X8 when trading conditions were expected to improve. The costs of doing so are estimated to be as follows.

	£000
Redundancy and other closure costs	30
Property and plant maintenance during the year to 30 June 19X8	10
Re-opening costs	20

However, £30,000 would be saved as a result of a reduction in general company and factory fixed overheads.

Required:
Determine whether the factory should be closed during the year to 30 June 19X8.

Additional questions (without answers)

14.9 Avsar limited has extracted the following budget details for the year to 30 September 19X9:

1 Sales: 4,000 units of V at £500 per unit
    7,000 units of R at £300 per unit
2 Materials usage (units):

Raw material

	O1	I2	L3
V	11	9	12
R	15	1	10

3 Raw material costs (per unit)

	£
O1	8
I2	6
L3	3

4 Raw material stocks:

	Units		
	O1	I2	L3
At 1 October 19X8	1,300	1,400	400
At 30 September 19X9	1,400	1,000	200

5 Finished stocks

	Units	
	V	R
At 1 October 19X8	110	90
At 30 September 19X9	120	150

6 Direct labour

	Product	
	V	R
Budgeted hours per unit	10	8
Budgeted hourly rate (£)	12	6

7 Variable overhead

	Product	
	V	R
Budgeted hourly rate (£)	10	5

8 Fixed overhead: £193,160 (to be absorbed on the basis of direct labour hours).

Required:
(a) Prepare the following budgets:
    (i)   sales;
    (ii)   production units;
    (iii) materials usage;
    (iv) materials purchase;
       and
    (v)   production cost;
  and
(b) calculate the total budgeted profit for the year to 30 September 19X9.

14.10 The following budgeted trading, and profit and loss accounts, and balance sheets, relating to the three months to 31 March 19X4, have been prepared for Ramsay Limited:

	January	*February*	*March*
Trading, profit and loss accounts			
	£000	£000	£000
Sales	200	300	400
Opening stock	15	20	30
Purchases	145	220	330
	160	240	360
Less: Closing stock	20	30	80
	140	210	280
Gross profit	60	90	120
Less: Expenses	20	30	40
Profit	40	60	80

Balance sheets	1.1.X4	31.1.X4	28.2.X4	31.3.X4
	£000	£000	£000	£000
Fixed assets at cost	390	400	410	420
Less: Accumulated depreciation	155	160	166	180
	235	240	244	240
Investments	18	50	35	60
Current assets				
Stocks	15	20	30	80
Trade debtors	20	25	45	100
Prepayments	2	2	3	10
Cash and bank	4	3	2	–
	41	50	80	190
Current liabilities				
Bank overdraft	–	–	–	(8)
Trade creditors	(35)	(40)	(50)	(90)
Accruals	(3)	(4)	(3)	(2)
Taxation	(30)	(30)	–	–
Dividends	(20)	(20)	–	–
	(88)	(94)	(53)	(100)
Debenture loans	–	–	–	(4)
	£206	£246	£306	£386
Capital and reserves				
Share capital	200	200	200	240
Profit and loss account	6	46	106	146
	£206	£246	£306	£386

Note:

It is not expected that there will be any disposal of fixed assets during the three months to 31 March 19X4.

Required:

Prepare Ramsay's cash budget for *each* of the three months to 31 March 19X4 respectively.

15 Standard costing

Learning objectives_____

1   outline the nature and purpose of standard costing;

2   summarize the steps involved in implementing and operating a
    standard costing system;

3   calculate simple standard cost ratios and variances;

4   assess the significance of a standard cost operating statement;
    and

5   conduct a variance analysis investigation.

Standard costing is an extension of budgetary control. In standard costing, however, instead of just preparing a budget for a particular department, an attempt is made to prepare a budget for each unit (or each process) that flows through that department. The budgeted unit (or process) cost is referred to as the *standard cost*. The technique is similar to budgetary control in that the standard cost of each unit is compared with the actual unit cost. Immediate action is then taken to correct any adverse trends.

While there are close similarities between budgetary control and standard costing, standard costing goes into much greater detail. The total variance between the actual cost of a particular unit and the standard cost, for example, is calculated and analysed into its constituent elements. The degree of analysis depends partly upon management requirements, and partly upon the type of product being produced. This type of detailed analysis is known as *variance analysis*.

The calculation of the variances is largely a routine arithmetical exercise, and the non-accountant is unlikely to be involved in it. You are more likely to be responsible for investigating the reasons *why* variances have arisen, and it is much easier to do so if you know something about how they have been calculated.

Although budgetary control and standard costing adopt very similar principles, not all entities can incorporate standard costing into their control procedures. Standard costing is really only suitable where the company is producing a product. In order to produce standard costs, it is necessary to prepare cost centre budgets. Thus it is possible to have a budgetary control system without having a standard costing system, but it is impossible to have a standard costing system without having a budgetary control system.

This chapter basically falls into two main parts. The first part outlines the background to standard costing, and the second part examines variance analysis in some depth.

Administration

In the introduction to this chapter, it was explained that standard costing is an extension of a budgetary control system. The responsibility for administering it will either be that of the budget committee or of the accounting function. The detailed procedure is considered in the following subsections.

The standard costing period

The overall period for which the standards are prepared will normally conform with the main and sub-budget periods. It may also be necessary (as it is sometimes with budgeting) to adopt fairly short standard costing periods, for example, where market and production conditions are subject to frequent changes or where it is difficult to plan ahead for very long periods of time. As the selling price charged to customers will usually be based on the standard cost of a particular unit, it would be unwise to fix the selling price based on out-of-date information simply because that was the standard cost for the period, no matter how long ago it was determined.

Types of standard

The preparation of standard costs requires great care and attention to detail. As each element of cost is subject to detailed arithmetical analysis and investigation, it is important that the initial information is accurate. Indeed, the information produced by a standard costing system will be virtually useless if subsequent analyses reveal that the main cause of any variance was inefficient budgeting and standard setting.

In preparing standard costs, management will need to be provided with the level of activity to be used in preparing the standard costs. An activity level should be chosen that is capable of being achieved. It would be possible to choose a standard that was *ideal*, that is, one that represented a performance that could be achieved only under the most favourable of conditions. Such a standard would normally be unrealistic, because it is rare for ideal conditions to be experienced.

A much more practical standard to adopt is an *expected* standard. An expected standard is one that the entity can expect to attain in reasonably efficient working conditions. In other words, it accepts that some delays and inefficiencies will occur, but it assumes that management will attempt to minimize them.

In the short run, it may be necessary to adopt the *current* standard. By accepting the current standard, the entity is accepting that it takes time to eliminate all the obvious inefficiencies, but it will plan on the basis of current conditions until it can move to a reasonably attainable standard. Hence entities should only plan to use current standards for a short time before they move to an expected standard.

Preparation

Standard costing is a sophisticated means of planning and controlling an entity's operations. The standard costs themselves are time-consuming to prepare, costly to produce, and expensive to operate. The technique requires so much detailed information that most employees need to be convinced of its value if it is to work properly. The preparation of standard costs calls for considerable team-work.

There is no point in having a standard costing system if those who are supposed to benefit from it regard it as having no value. If standard costing is to operate effectively its purpose has to be understood by the employees, because they will be responsible for preparing the basic information. If this is done ineffectively or inefficiently, then any decision based upon it will be questionable.

The type of information required to produce standard costs can be summarized as follows:

1 Direct materials: types, quantities and price.
2 Direct labour: grades, numbers and rates of pay.
3 Variable overhead: the total variable overhead cost analysed into various categories such as employee and general support costs.
4 Fixed overhead: the total fixed overhead analysed into various categories such as employee costs, building costs and general administration expenses.

From the above information, it can be seen that the standard cost of a particular unit is comprised four main elements:

1 direct materials;
2 direct labour;
3 variable overhead; and
4 fixed overhead.

In turn, each element comprises two factors, namely quantity and price.

Thus the total standard cost of a specific unit may be built-up as follows:

		£
1	Direct materials:	
	Quantity × price (2 units × £5)	10
2	Direct labour:	
	Hours × hourly rate (5 hours × £10)	50
3	Variable overhead:	
	Hours × variable overhead absorption rate per hour	
	(5 hours × £6)	30
4	Fixed overhead:	
	Hours × fixed overhead absorption rate per hour	
	(5 hours × £3)	15
Total standard cost per unit		£105

Note: The above summary is based on fictitious data. It assumes that the unit cost is calculated on the basis of standard *absorption* costing. This is the most common method of standard costing, although it is possible to adopt a system of standard *marginal* costing.

If the standard costs are prepared on the basis of absorption costing, overhead will be absorbed on the basis of *standard* hours (in a non-standard costing system, you will recall, overhead is absorbed on the basis of actual hours). A standard hour represents the amount of work that should be performed in an hour, given that it is produced in standard conditions, that is, in *planned* conditions. Each unit is given a standard time of so many hours in which it should be produced, and it is against that standard that the actual hours will be compared.

In order to calculate the standard overhead cost of a unit, the standard overhead absorption rate for the period is multiplied by the number of *standard* (not actual) hours that the unit should have taken to produce.

As the standard absorption rate is multiplied by the standard hours, this method is a significant departure from that adopted in a non-standard costing system. This is a most important point, and it will be considered again later on in the chapter.

Some companies also prepare standard costs for sales, although such costs are not as common as cost variances. If sales variances are to be prepared, the difference between the actual sales revenue and the standard revenue is analysed into a number of representative sales variances. A detailed analysis of the budgeted sales will be needed in order to obtain the following information:

1   the range and number of each product to be sold;

2 the selling price of each product;

3 the respective periods in which sales are to take place; and

4 the geographical areas in which they are to be sold.

Control ratios

The main financial accounting ratios were examined in Chapter 8. In a standard costing system it is also possible to extract a number of ratios. There are three important control ratios. These inform management about the level of efficiency that the entity has achieved, and they enable management to spot unfavourable trends so that immediate corrective action can be taken.

Before these three control ratios are examined, one most important point must be emphasized. In standard costing, actual costs are compared with the standard cost of the *actual* level of activity achieved. It is tempting to compare the actual costs with the budgeted cost, but it is not customary to do so in standard costing. By comparing the actual cost with the standard cost of the *actual* production, the budget is effectively being flexed. This means that any variances that do arise can be more realistically assessed, because the same level of activity is then being used to measure the actual costs against the budgeted costs.

Bearing this point in mind, the three control ratios will now be considered in the following subsections.

The productivity (or efficiency) ratio

This ratio compares the total standard (or allowed) hours of units produced with the total actual hours taken to produce those units. It is calculated as follows:

$$\frac{\text{Standard hours of production}}{\text{Actual hours worked}} \times 100$$

The productivity ratio enables management to check whether the company has produced the units in more or less time than had been allowed.

The capacity ratio

The capacity ratio compares the total actual hours worked with the total budgeted hours. It is calculated as follows:

$$\frac{\text{Actual hours worked}}{\text{Budgeted hours}} \times 100$$

This ratio enables management to ascertain whether all of the budgeted hours were used to produce actual units.

The production/volume ratio

This ratio compares the total allowed hours for the work actually produced with the total budgeted hours. It is calculated as follows:

$$\frac{\text{Standard hours of production}}{\text{Budgeted hours}} \times 100$$

The production/volume ratio enables management to compare the work produced (measured in terms of standard hours) with the budgeted hours of work. This ratio gives management some information about how effective the company has been in using the budgeted hours.

The productivity, capacity and production/volume ratios are illustrated in Exhibit 15.1.

Exhibit 15.1

The following information relates to the Frost Production Company Limited for the year to 31 March 19X4:

1   Budgeted direct labour hours: 1,000.
2   Budgeted units: 100.
3   Actual direct labour hours worked: 800.
4   Actual units produced: 90.

Required:
Calculate the following control ratios:
(a)   the productivity ratio;
(b)   the capacity ratio; and
(c)   the production/volume ratio.

Answer to Exhibit 15.1

(a)   The productivity ratio:

$$\frac{\text{Standard hours of production}}{\text{Actual hours worked}} \times 100 = \frac{900^*}{800} \times 100 = \underline{\underline{112.5\%}}$$

*Each unit is allowed 10 standard hours (1,000 hours/100 units), and since 90 units were produced, the total standard hours of production = 900.

It would appear that the company has been more efficient in producing the goods than it did. It was allowed 900 hours to do so, but it produced them in only 800 hours.

(b)   The capacity ratio:

$$\frac{\text{Actual hours worked}}{\text{Budgeted hours}} \times 100 = \frac{800}{1,000} = \underline{\underline{80\%}}$$

In this case, all of the time planned to be available (the capacity) was not utilized, either because it was not possible to work 1,000 direct labour hours, or because the company did not undertake as much work as it could have done.

(c) The production/volume ratio:

$$\frac{\text{Standard hours of production}}{\text{Budgeted hours}} \times 100 = \frac{900^*}{1,000} \times 100 = \underline{\underline{90\%}}$$

*As calculated for the productivity ratio.

It appears that if the 90 units had been produced in standard conditions, another 100 hours would have been available (10 units × 10 hours). In fact, since the 90 units only took 800 hours to produce, at least another 20 units could have been produced in standard conditions

$$\frac{1,000 - 800}{10} = \underline{\underline{20 \text{ units}}}$$

Comment on the results

The budget allowed for 100 units to be produced and each unit was expected to take 10 direct labour hours to complete, a total budgeted activity of 1,000 direct labour hours. However, only 90 units were actually produced. If these units had been produced in standard time, they should have taken 900 hours (90 units × 10 direct labour hours). These are the standard hours of production. In fact, the 90 units were completed in 800 actual hours. It appears, therefore, that the units were produced more efficiently than had been expected. The management will still need, of course, to investigate why only 90 units were produced and not the 100 budgeted units.

Variance analysis

As outlined earlier, any difference between actual costs and standard costs is comprised of two main variances: price and quantity. As far as profit is concerned, these variances may either be favourable (F) to profit or adverse (A). This means that the actual prices paid or costs incurred can be either less than was anticipated (favourable to profit) or more than anticipated (adverse to profit).

Similarly, the quantities used in production can result in less being used (favourable to profit) or more than expected (adverse to profit).

It is possible to analyse each element of cost into price and quantity variances (although they are not always referred to as such). The main cost variances may be summarized as follows:

1　Direct material total variance = Direct material price variance + Direct material usage variance.
2　Direct labour total variance = Direct labour rate variance + Direct labour efficiency variance.
3　Variable production overhead total variance = Variable overhead expenditure variance + Variable overhead efficiency variance.

4   Fixed production overhead variance = Fixed production expenditure variance + Fixed production volume variance. The Fixed production volume variance may be sub-analysed as follows: Fixed production volume variance = Fixed production capacity variance + Fixed production productivity variance.

The main variances are shown in diagrammatic form in Exhibit 15.2.

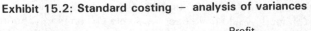

Exhibit 15.2: Standard costing – analysis of variances

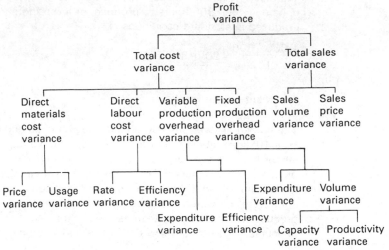

Variance analysis formulae

It would be useful at this stage to summarize the basic formulae for use in later exhibits.

The formulae used are as follows.

Direct materials

1   Cost variance = (Actual price per unit × Actual quantity used) – (Standard price per unit × Standard quantity for actual production).

2   Price variance = (Actual price per unit – Standard price per unit) × Total actual quantity used.

3   Usage variance = (Total actual quantity used – Standard quantity for actual production) × Standard price.

Direct labour

1   Cost variance = (Actual hourly rate × Actual hours) – (Standard hourly rate × Standard hours for actual production).

2 Rate variance = (Actual hourly rate − Standard hourly rate) × Actual hours worked.

3 Efficiency variance = (Actual hours worked − Standard hours for actual production) × Standard hourly rate.

Variable production overhead

1 Variable production overhead total variance = Actual variable production overhead − [Standard hours of production × Variable production overhead absorption rate (V.OAR)].

2 Expenditure variance = Actual variable overhead expenditure − (Actual hours worked × V.OAR).

3 Efficiency variance = (Standard hours of production − Actual hours worked) × V.OAR.

Fixed production overhead

1 Fixed production overhead variance = Actual fixed production overhead − [Standard hours of production × Fixed overhead absorption rate (F.OAR)].

2 Expenditure variance = (Actual fixed overhead expenditure − Budgeted fixed overhead expenditure).

3 Capacity variance = Budgeted fixed overhead expenditure − (Actual hours worked × F.OAR).

4 Productivity variance = (Actual hours worked − Standard hours for actual production) × F.OAR.

5 Volume variance = Budgeted fixed overhead expenditure − (Standard hours for actual production × F.OAR).

NB: Capacity variance = Productivity variance + Volume variance.

An illustrative example

The calculation of the main cost variances is illustrated in Exhibit 15.3.

Exhibit 15.3

The following information has been extracted from the records of the Frost Production Company Limited for the year to 31 March 19X4:

Budgeted costs per unit: £
Direct materials (15 kilograms × £2 per kilogram)   30
Direct labour (10 hours × £4 per direct labour hour)   40
Variable overhead (10 hours × £1 per direct labour hour)   10
Fixed overhead (10 hours × £2 per direct labour hour)   20

Total budgeted cost per unit   £100

The following budgeted data are also relevant:
1   The budgeted production level was 100 units.
2   The total standard direct labour hours amounted to 1,000.
3   The total budgeted variable overhead was estimated to be £1,000.
4   The total budgeted fixed overhead was £2,000.
5   The company absorbs both fixed and variable overhead on the basis of direct
    labour hours.

Actual costs: £
Direct materials   2,100
Direct labour   4,000
Variable overhead   1,000
Fixed overhead   1,600

Total actual costs   £8,700

Note: 90 units were produced in 800 actual hours, and the total actual quantity
of direct materials consumed was 1,400 kilograms.

Required:
Calculate the direct materials, direct labour, variable overhead and fixed overhead
cost variances.

Answer to Exhibit 15.3

To begin the answer to this question, first summarize the total variance for each
element of cost:

Actual units produced	*Actual costs*(1)	*Total standard cost for actual production*		*Variance*	
	£	£		£	
Direct materials	2,100	2,700	(1)	600	(F)
Direct labour	4,000	3,600	(2)	400	(A)
Variable overhead	1,000	900	(3)	100	(A)
Fixed overhead	1,600	1,800	(4)	200	(F)
Total	£8,700	£9,000		£300	(F)

Notes:
(a) F = favourable to profit; A = adverse to profit.
(b) The numbers in brackets refer to the tutorial notes below.

Tutorial notes

1   The standard cost of direct materials for actual production = the actual units
    produced × the standard direct material cost per unit, i.e. 90 × £30 = £2,700.

2   The standard cost of direct labour for actual production = the actual units produced × standard direct labour cost per unit, i.e. 90 × £40 = £3,600.
3   The standard variable cost for actual performance = the actual units produced × variable overhead absorption rate per unit, i.e. 90 × £10 = £900.
4   The fixed overhead cost for the actual performance = the actual units produced × fixed overhead absorption rate, i.e. 90 × £20 = £1,800.

It can be seen from Exhibit 15.3 that the total actual cost of producing the 90 units was £300 less than the budget allowance. An investigation would need to be held in order to find out why only 90 units were produced when the company had budgeted for 100 units. Furthermore, although the 90 units have cost £300 less than might have been expected, a number of other variances have contributed to the overall variance. Assuming that these variances are considered significant, they would need to be carefully investigated in order to find out what caused them. Both the direct materials and the fixed overhead, for example, cost £600 and £200 respectively less than the budget allowance, while the direct labour cost £400 and the variable overhead £100 more than might have been expected.

As a result of calculating the variances for each element of cost, it should be easier for management to investigate why the actual production cost was £300 less than might have been expected. However, the accountant can provide even greater guidance by analysing the variances into their major causes. This may be achieved by examining each element of cost. The calculation of the respective variances will first be demonstrated, and then a brief explanation of their possible causes will be given.

Direct materials

1   Direct materials price variance = (Actual price per unit – Standard price per unit) × Total actual quantity used.
∴ The price variance = (£1.50 – 2.00) × 1,400 kg
= £700 (F)

The actual price per unit was £1.50 (£2,100/1,400) and the standard price was £2.00 per unit. There was, therefore, a total saving (as far as the price of the materials is concerned) of £700 (£0.50 × 1,400).

2   Direct materials usage variance = (Total actual quantity used – Standard quantity for actual production) × Standard price.
∴ The usage variance = (1,400 – 1,350) × £2.00
= £100 (A)

In producing 90 units, Frost should have used 1,350 kilograms (90 × 15 kg), instead of the 1,400 kilograms actually used. If this extra usage is valued at the standard price (the difference between the actual price and the standard price has already been allowed for), there is an adverse usage variance of £100 (50 kg × £2).

3   Direct materials cost variance = Price variance + Usage variance
$$= £700 \text{ (F)} + £100 \text{ (A)}$$
$$= \underline{£600 \text{ (F)}}$$

The £600 favourable cost variance was shown earlier in the cost summary on page 292. This variance might have arisen because Frost purchased cheaper materials. If this was the case, then it probably resulted in a greater wastage of materials because the materials were of an inferior quality.

Direct labour

1   Direct labour rate variance = (Actual labour hourly rate − Standard labour hourly rate) × Actual hours worked.
∴ The rate variance = (£5.00 − 4.00) × 800 DLH
$$= \underline{£800 \text{ (A)}}$$

The actual hourly rate is £5.00 per DLH (£4,000/800). Every extra actual hour worked, therefore, results in an adverse variance of £1.00, or £800 in total (£1.00 × 800).

2   Direct labour efficiency variance = (Actual hours worked − Standard hours for actual production) × Standard hourly rate.
∴ The efficiency variance = (800 − 900) × £4 per hour
$$= \underline{£400 \text{ (F)}}$$

The actual hours worked were 800. However, 900 hours would have been allowed for the 90 units actually produced (90 × 10 DLH). If these hours are valued at the standard hourly rate, a favourable variance of £400 arises. The favourable efficiency variance has arisen because the 90 units took less time to produce than allowed for in the budget.

3   Direct labour cost variance = Rate variance + Efficiency variance
$$= £800 \text{ (A)} + £400 \text{ (F)}$$
$$= \underline{£400 \text{ (A)}}$$

The £400 adverse variance was shown earlier in the cost summary on page 292. It arises because the company paid more per direct labour hour than had been budgeted, although this was offset by the units being produced in less time than the budgeted allowance. This variance could have been caused by using a higher grade of labour than had been intended, but the higher labour rate per hour was not completely offset by greater efficiency.

Variable production overhead

Not all accountants consider it necessary to analyse the variable production overhead total variance into sub-variances. The adverse variance of £100 (A) (as shown earlier in the summary of variances on page 292) arises because the variable overhead absorption rate was calculated on the basis of a budgeted cost of £10 per unit. In fact the absorption rate ought to have been £11.11 per unit (£1,000/90), because the total actual variable cost was £1,000. There would, of course, be no variable production overhead cost for the ten units that were not produced.

If the variable production overhead total variance is analysed into sub-variances, the result would be as follows.

1　Expenditure variance = Actual variable overhead expenditure − (Actual hours worked × V.OAR).
∴ Expenditure variance = £1,000 − (800 × £1.00)
= £200 (A)

2　Efficiency variance = (Standard hours of production − Actual hours worked) × V.OAR.
∴ Efficiency variance = (900 − 800) × £1.00
= £100 (F)

3　Variable production overhead total variance = Expenditure variance + Efficiency variance = £200 (A) + £100 (F) = £100 (A)

Fixed production overhead

1　Fixed overhead expenditure variance = Actual fixed overhead expenditure Budgeted fixed overhead expenditure.
∴ Expenditure variance = £1,600 − £2,000
= £400 (F)

The actual expenditure was £400 less than the budgeted expenditure. This means that the fixed production overhead absorption rate (F.OAR) was £400 higher than it needed to have been if there had not been any other fixed overhead variances.

2　Fixed production volume variance = Budgeted fixed overhead − (Standard hours of production × F.OAR).
∴ Volume variance = £2,000 − (900 × £2.00)
= £200 (A)

As a result of producing fewer units than expected, £200 *less* overhead has been absorbed into production.

3 Fixed production overhead capacity variance = Budgeted fixed overhead expenditure − (Actual hours worked × F.OAR).

∴ Capacity variance = £2,000 − (800 × £2.00)
= £400 (A)

The capacity variance shows that the actual hours worked were less than the budgeted hours. Other things being equal, therefore, not enough overhead would have been absorbed into production. It should be noted that the capacity variance will be *favourable* when the actual hours are in excess of the budgeted hours. This might seem odd, but it would mean that the company had worked more hours than it had originally budgeted. As a result, it should have been able to produce more units, thereby absorbing more overhead into production. This variance links with the capacity ratio demonstrated earlier in the chapter. The capacity ratio showed that only 80% of the budgeted capacity had been utilized, so probably not as much overhead was absorbed into production as had been originally expected.

4 Fixed production overhead productivity variance = (Actual hours worked − Standard hours for actual production) × F.OAR.

∴ Productivity variance = (800 − 900) × £2.00
= £200 (F)

This variance shows the difference between the 900 standard hours that the work is worth (90 × 10 = 900 hours), compared with the amount of time that it took to produce those units (i.e. 800 hours). As explained earlier, in a standard costing system, overhead is absorbed on the basis of *standard* hours. Assuming that the budgeted fixed overhead expenditure had been equal to the actual fixed overhead expenditure, production would have been charged with £200 of extra overhead because the 90 units were produced in less time than the standard allowance. The factory has been *more* efficient in producing the goods than might have been expected. This variance complements the productivity (or efficiency) ratio of 112.5% which was illustrated earlier in the chapter.

Remember:

Capacity variance + Productivity variance = Volume variance.

∴ Volume variance = £400 (A) + £200 (F)
= £200 (A)

(See also 2 above.)

5 Fixed production overhead variance. This variance was calculated earlier (shown on the summary of variances on page 292). The basic formula is as follows:

$$\text{Overhead variance} = \text{Expenditure variance} + \text{Volume variance}$$
$$= £400 \text{ (F)} + £200 \text{ (A)}$$
$$= \underline{\underline{£200 \text{ (F)}}}$$

The actual activity was less than the budgeted activity. Thus less fixed overhead was absorbed into production. However, the overhead expenditure was budgeted at a level of £2,000, but the actual expenditure was only £1,600. The overestimate of expenditure, therefore, compensated for the overestimate of activity. This means that the 90 units actually produced were charged £200 more of overhead than was necessary. If the selling price is based on standard costs, it is possible that this overestimate could make their eventual selling price less competitive. In this case the variance would appear to be very small.

A considerable number of variances have now been worked through. Using the formulae listed on pp. 290–291, you are recommended to work through Exhibit 15.2 without reference to the solution.

Sales variances

It was suggested earlier that sales variances are not common in practice, but if adopted, there is a choice between two different types: (1) variances based on sales value; and (2) variances based on sales margin. Sales value variances are based on actual and budgeted selling prices. Sales margin variances allow for the cost of selling the goods, the margin being defined as the difference between the sales revenue of units sold and the *standard* cost of those sales. The standard cost may be based either on absorption costing or marginal costing.

If the entity decides to use sales variances, it is recommended that the sales margin method be adopted, as this method highlights the effect of sales on profit. In this section, both types of variances will be examined.

The formulae used in calculating sales variances are summarized in the subsections below. The summary is in two parts: the first part shows the formulae for sales value variances, and the second part the formulae for sales margin variances. (See Exhibit 15.4.)

Sales value variances

1 Sales value total variance:
   Total variance = (Actual selling price per unit × Actual quantity) − (Standard selling price per unit × Budgeted quantity).

2 Sales value selling price variance:
   Price variance = (Actual selling price per unit − Standard selling price per unit) × Total quantity of units sold.

3   Sales value volume variance:
    Volume variance = (Total actual quantity of units sold − Total budgeted quantity) × Standard selling price.

4   Note that the Total variance (1) = Price (2) + Volume (3).

Sales margin variances

1   Sales margin operating profit due to sales variance:
    Operating profit variance = [(Actual selling price per unit − Standard cost per unit) × Actual quantity] − (Standard margin × Budgeted quantity).

2   Sales margin due to selling price variance:
    Selling price variance = [(Actual selling price per unit − Standard cost per unit) × Actual quantity] − (Standard margin per unit × Actual quantity).

3   Sales margin due to sales volume variance:
    Sales volume variance = (Actual quantity − Budgeted quantity) × Standard margin.

4   Note that the Operating profit due to sales variance (1) = Due to selling price (2) + Due to sales volume (3).

The use of these formulae is illustrated in Exhibit 15.4.

Exhibit 15.4

The following data relate to Frozen Limited for the year to 31 July 19X9:

	Budget/standard	Actual
Sales	100 units	90 units
Selling price per unit	£10	£10.50
Standard absorption cost per unit	£7	−

Required:
Calculate the following sales variances:
1   sales value variances; and
2   sales margin variances.

Answer to Exhibit 15.4

1   *Sales value variances*
(a) Sales value selling price variance:
     Price variance = (Actual selling price per unit − Standard selling price per unit) × Total actual quantity of units sold.
     ∴ Selling price variance = (£10.50 − 10.00) × 90
                              = £45 (F)

The actual selling price per unit was £0.50 more than the standard selling price, so an overall total favourable variance arises. Other things being equal, profit would have been £45 higher than had been anticipated.

(b) Sales volume variance:
Volume variance = (Total actual quantity of units sold − Total budgeted quantity) × Standard selling price per unit.
∴ Volume variance = (90 − 100) × £10.00
= £100 (A)

Ten fewer units were sold than had been envisaged, and so the effect on sales revenue (ignoring any price variance) would be to reduce the total sales revenue by £100.

(c) Sales value total variance. The sales value total variance can be calculated either by adding together the price variance and the volume variance (£45 (F) + £100 (A) = £55 (A)), or by using the detailed formula:
Total variance = (Actual selling price per unit × Actual quantity) − (Standard selling price per unit × Budgeted quantity).
∴ Total variance = (£10.50 × 90) − (£10.00 × 100)
= £945 − £1,000
= £55 (A)

The £55 adverse variance arises partly because the number of units sold was only 90 compared with a budgeted quantity of 100 units. However, the reduction in volume (which caused an adverse variance) was compensated by an increase in the selling price of each unit. It is possible that the price increase caused the sales volume to drop, but this point would need to be carefully investigated.

2   *Sales margin variances*
(a) Sales margin variance due to selling price:
Price variance = [(Actual selling price per unit − Standard cost per unit) × Actual quantity] − (Standard margin per unit × Actual quantity).
∴ Price variance = [(£10.50 − 7.00) × 90] − [(£10.00 − 7.00) × 90]
= £315 − £270
= £45 (F)

The sales margin variance due to selling price should be exactly the same as that calculated by the sales value method.

(b) Sales margin variance due to sales volume:
Volume variance = (Actual quantity − Budgeted quantity) × Standard margin.
∴ Volume variance = (100 − 90) × (£10.00 − £7.00)
= £30 (A)

This margin variance arises because the number of units sold fell below the budgeted level, thereby affecting the overall amount of profit (or margin) achieved.

(c) Sales margin operating profit due to sales variance. This variance is the total of the selling price variance and the sales volume variance, i.e. £45 (F) + £30 (A) = £15 (F). It may also be calculated by formula:
Operating profit variance = [(Actual selling price per unit − Standard cost per unit) × Actual quantity] − (Standard margin × Budgeted quantity).
∴ Operating profit variance = [(£10.50 − £7.00) × 90] − (£3 × 100)
= £15 (F)

The favourable selling price variance of £45 (or £0.50 per unit) helped to offset the adverse volume variance of £30 caused by selling ten fewer units. It should be noted that the *standard* cost is used in calculating sales margin variances. Any variance between actual costs and standard costs will be extracted as part of the cost analysis.

You are now recommended to work through Exhibit 15.4 without reference to the answer, although you may need to refer to the sales variance formulae listed on page 297–298.

Operating statements

The calculation of standard cost variances is obviously a complex arithmetical process. The process can become even more complicated if the variances outlined in the preceding sections are analysed into sub-variances. Fortunately for non-accountants, it is unlikely that they will have to calculate such variances. It is important, however, to have some knowledge of how they are calculated in order to be in a better position to investigate their causes. Indeed, the non-accountant's main role in variance analysis will probably be to carry out such an investigation, and then to take any necessary corrective action.

Once all the variances have been calculated, they may usefully be summarized in an operating statement. There is no standardized format for such statements, but the one shown in Exhibit 15.5 is reasonably representative.

Exhibit 15.5 Preparation of a standard cost operating statement

Exhibit 15.3 gave some information relating to the Frost Production Company Limited for the year to 31 March 19X4. The cost data used in that exhibit will now be used in Exhibit 15.5, but some additional information is required.

Additional information
1   Assume that the budgeted sales were 100 units at a selling price of £150 per unit.
2   90 units were sold at £160 per unit.
3   Actual non-production overhead expenditure was as follows:

	£
Administration	750
Research and development	150
Selling and distribution	300

Required:
Prepare a standard cost operating statement for the year to 31 March 19X4.

Answer to Exhibit 15.5

Frost Manufacturing Company Limited standard cost operating statement for the year to 31 March 19X4:

			£
Budgeted profit [100 × (£150 − 100)]			5,000
Sales volume variance (1)			(500)
Standard margin of actual sales			4,500
Sales price variance (2)			900
Actual margin of actual sales			5,400

Cost variances: (3)	Adverse	Favourable	
	£	£	
Direct materials:			
Price		700	
Usage	100		
Direct labour:			
Rate	800		
Efficiency		400	
Variable production overhead			
Expenditure	200		
Efficiency		100	
Fixed production overhead			
Expenditure		400	
Capacity	400		
Productivity		200	
	1,500	1,800	300
Operating profit			5,700
Less: Actual non-production overhead:			
Administration		750	
Research and development		150	
Selling and distribution		300	1,200
Actual profit			£4,500

Tutorial notes

1 Sales margin due to sales volume
   = (Actual quantity − Budgeted quantity) × Standard margin
   = (90 − 100) × £50 = £500 (A)

2 Sales margin due to selling price
   = [(Actual selling price per unit − Standard cost per unit) × Actual quantity]
      (Standard margin per unit × Actual quantity)
   = [(£160 − 100) × 90] − (£50 × 90) = £900 (F)

3 Details of cost variances were shown in the answer to Exhibit 15.3 on pages 292–297.

The above format is particularly valuable because it shows in detail the link between the budgeted profit and the actual profit. Thus management can trace the main causes of sales and cost variances. In practice, the statement would also show the details for each product.

The operating profit statement will help management to decide where to begin an investigation into the causes of the respective variances. It is unlikely that they will all need to be investigated. It may be company policy, for example, to investigate only those variances that are particularly significant, irrespective of whether they are favourable or adverse variances. In other words, only *exceptional* variances would be investigated, and a policy decision would have to be taken on how 'exceptional' should be defined.

Conclusion

This has been a long and complex chapter. You may have found that it has been difficult to understand just how standard cost variances are calculated. It is unlikely, however, that you will have to calculate them for yourself. It is sufficient for your purpose to understand their meaning and to have *some* idea of the arithmetical foundation upon which they are built.

The non-accountant's main responsibility will be to investigate the causes of the variances, and to take action if there are any unwelcome trends. A standard costing system is supposed to help management plan and control the entity much more tightly than can be achieved in the absence of such a system, but it can only be of real benefit if it is accepted by those managers whom it is supposed to help. It can hardly help management if all it does is produce a lot of incomprehensible data. Comprehension comes with understanding and knowledge. It is hoped that this chapter has helped in that respect.

The next chapter deals with the problems of capital investment. Such problems may come to light as a result of trying to match the sales forecasts with the production capacity. Thus the budgeting and standard costing exercises may lead to a review of capital investment requirements.

Questions

15.1 You are presented with the following information for X Limited:

Standard price per unit: £10.
Standard quantity for actual production: 5 units.
Actual price per unit: £12.
Actual quantity: 6 units.

Required:
Calculate the following variances:
1   direct materials cost variance;
2   direct materials price variance; and
3   direct materials usage variance.

15.2 The following information relates to Malcolm Limited.

Budgeting production: 100 units.

Unit specification (direct materials): 50 kilograms × £5 per kilogram = £250.
Actual production: 120 units.
Direct materials used: 5,400 kilograms at a total cost of £32,400.

Required:
Calculate the following variances:
1 direct materials cost;
2 direct materials price; and
3 direct materials usage.

15.3 The following information relates to Bruce Limited:

Actual hours: 1,000.
Actual wage rate per hour: £6.50.
Standard hours for actual production: 900.
Standard wage rate per hour: £6.00.

Required:
Calculate the following variances:
1 direct labour cost;
2 direct labour rate; and
3 direct labour efficiency.

15.4 You are presented with the following information for Duncan Limited:

Budgeted production: 1,000 units.
Actual production: 1,200 units.
Standard specification for one unit: 10 hours at £8 per direct labour hour.
Actual direct labour cost: £97,200 in 10,800 actual hours.

Required:
Calculate the following variances:
1 direct labour cost;
2 direct labour rate; and
3 direct labour efficiency.

15.5 The following overhead budget has been prepared for Anthea Limited:

Actual fixed overhead: £150,000.
Budgeted fixed overhead: £135,000.
Fixed overhead absorption rate per hour: £15.
Actual hours worked: 10,000.
Standard hours of production: 8,000.

Required:
Calculate the following fixed overhead variances:
1 fixed production overhead variance;
2 expenditure variance;
3 volume variance;
4 capacity variance; and
5 productivity variance.

15.6   Using the data contained in the previous question, calculate the following control ratios:

1   efficiency.
2   capacity; and
3   activity.

15.7   The following information relates to Osprey Limited:

Budgeted production: 500 units.
Standard hours per unit: 10.
Actual production: 600 units.
Budgeted fixed overhead: £125,000.
Actual fixed overhead: £120,000.
Actual hours worked: 4,900.

Required:
Calculate the following fixed overhead variances:
1   fixed production overhead;
2   expenditure;
3   volume;
4   capacity; and
5   productivity.

15.8   Using the data from the previous question, calculate the following control ratios:

1   efficiency;
2   capacity; and
3   activity.

15.9   Milton Limited has produced the following information:

Total actual sales: £99,000.
Actual quantity sold: 9,000 units.
Budgeted selling price per unit: £10.
Standard variable cost per unit: £7.
Total budgeted units: 10,000 units.

Required:
Calculate the following sales margin variances:
1   operating profit due to sales;
2   selling price; and
3   sales volume.

15.10   You are presented with the following information for Doe Limited:

Budget sales	100 units
Per unit:	
Budget selling price	£30
Less: Budget variable cost	£20
Contribution	£10

| Actual sales | 120 units |
| Actual selling price per unit | £28 |

Required:
Calculate the following sales variances:
(a) Sales margin variances:
    1 operating profit variance due to sales;
    2 selling price; and
    3 sales volume
(b) Sales value variances:
    1 total sales volume variance;
    2 selling price; and
    3 sales volume.

15.11 The following data relate to Judith Limited:

Budget specification

Production at sales budget		2,000 units
Per unit:	£	£
Selling price		150
Less: Variable costs:		
Direct materials (7 kilos × £10 per kilo)	70	
Direct wages (5 DLH × £5 per DLH)	25	
Fixed overhead (5 DLH × £6 F.OAR)	30	125
Budgeted profit per unit		£25
Actual production and sales		2,200 units
Actual selling price per unit		£145
Actual cost.		
Direct material (8 kilos × £9 per kilo)		£72 per unit
Direct wages (4 DLH × £6 per DLH)		£24 per unit
Total actual fixed overhead		£65,000

Required:
(a) Calculate the following control ratios:
    1 efficiency.
    2 capacity; and
    3 activity

(b) Calculate the following variances:
    1 sales margin operating profit due to sales;
    2 sales margin selling price;
    3 sales margin sales volume;
    4 direct materials cost;
    5 direct materials price;
    6 direct materials usage;
    7 direct labour cost;
    8 direct labour rate variance;
    9 direct labour efficiency;

10 fixed production overhead;
11 fixed production overhead expenditure;
12 fixed production overhead volume;
13 fixed production overhead capacity; and
14 fixed production overhead productivity.

(c) Prepare the standard cost operating statement for the period.

Additional questions (without answers)

15.12 The budgeted selling price and standard cost of a unit manufactured by Smillie Limited is as follows:

	£
Selling price	30
Direct materials (2.5 kilos)	5
Direct labour (2 hours)	12
Fixed production overhead	8
	25
Budgeted profit	5

Total budgeted sales: 400 units

During the period to 31 December 19X2, the actual sales and production details were as follows:

	£
Sales (420 units)	13,440
Direct materials (1,260 kilos)	2,268
Direct labour (800 hours)	5,200
Fixed production overhead	3,300
	10,768
Profit	2,672

Required:
Prepare a standard cost operating statement for the period to 31 December 19X2.

15.13 Mean Limited manufactures a single product, and the following information relates to the actual cost of the product for the four weeks to 31 March 19X3:

	£000
Sales (50,000 units)	2,250
Direct materials (240,000 litres)	528
Direct labour (250,000 hours)	1,375
Variable production overhead	245
Fixed production overhead	650
	2,798
Loss	(548)

The budgeted selling price and standard cost of each unit was as follows:

	£
Selling price	55
Direct materials (5 litres)	10
Direct labour (4 hours)	20
Variable production overhead	5
Fixed production overhead	15
	50
Budgeted profit	5

Total budgeted production: 40,000 units.

Required:
Prepare a standard cost operating statement for the four weeks to 31 March 19X3, utilizing as many variances as the data permit.

16 Capital investment

Learning objectives

1 outline the main accounting techniques used in assessing project profitability;

2 make simple calculations using such techniques;

3 assess the significance of capital investment appraisal techniques;

and

4 describe the main sources of funds available for financing capital investment projects.

During the period when the budgets and standard costs are being prepared, it may become apparent that the entity needs to provide for additional capital investment. The sales forecast, for example, may show that there is likely to be an increase in demand for the company's products, but a review of the productive capacity may confirm that the company cannot meet that forecast unless there is further investment.

Given that the sales forecast is accurate, there should be every incentive to prepare the sales and production budgets to meet that particular forecast. This may be very difficult to achieve in the short term, although every opportunity should be taken to do so (perhaps by working overtime). In the long term, the company may have to expand its productive capacity.

Two main problems arise in deciding whether to undertake further capital investment:

1 how to assess the profitability of the prospective investment; and
2 how to finance it.

These problems are examined briefly in this chapter. Accountants now use some fairly sophisticated techniques to assess project profitability, but as these are beyond the scope of this book, the following sections are merely intended to give some idea of what is involved.

Project profitability

There are three basic methods accountants use in deciding whether a project is likely to be profitable. Each method is considered in the following subsections.

Payback

The payback method compares the cost of the investment with the time that it would take for the investment to pay for itself. The investment return is measured in terms of net cash flow. Net cash flow is the difference between the total amount of cash received during a particular period and the total amount of cash paid out during the same period.

Exhibit 16.1: The payback method

Miln Limited is considering investing in some new machinery. The following information has been prepared to support the project:

	£000	£000
Cost of machinery		20
Expected net cash flow:		
Year 1	1	
2	4	
3	5	
4	10	
5	10	30
Net profitability		£10

Required:
Calculate the prospective investment's payback period.

Answer to Exhibit 16.1

The payback period is as follows:

	£000
Cumulative net cash flow:	
Year 1	1
2	5
3	10
4	20
5	30

Thus the investment will have paid for itself at the end of the fourth year. At that stage £20,000 will have been received back from the project in terms of net cash flow, and that sum would be equal to the original cost of the project.

As can be seen from Exhibit 16.1, the payback method is very simple to operate, but it does have several disadvantages. These are as follows:

1   It is difficult to calculate the net cash flow and to estimate the periods in which cash will be received or paid.
2   The project with the shortest payback period would normally be chosen, even though other projects with longer payback periods may eventually prove more profitable.
3   The total amount of the investment is ignored and comparisons made between different projects may lead, therefore, to a misleading conclusion. Thus a project with an initial investment of £10,000 may have a shorter payback period than one with an initial investment of £100,000, although in the long run, the larger investment may prove more profitable.
4   The timing of the cash flows is ignored. A project with a short payback period may recover most of its investment towards the end of its payback period, while another project with a longer payback period may recover most of the original investment in the very early stages. There is clearly less risk in accepting a project that recovers most of its cost very quickly than there is accepting one where the benefits are much more long term.

Notwithstanding these disadvantages, the payback method has something to recommend it. Whilst it may appear rather simplistic, it does help managers compare projects, and to think in terms of how long it takes for a project to pay for itself.

Accounting rate of return

The accounting rate of return method assesses project profitability by relating the average net profit of the project to the cost of the original investment. The relationship is usually expressed in the form of a percentage. The method is illustrated in Exhibit 16.2.

Exhibit 16.2: The accounting rate of return method

Bridge Limited is considering investing in a new project, the details of which are as follows:

Project life		5 years
	£000	£000
Project cost		50
Estimated net profit:		
Year 1	12	
2	18	
3	30	
4	25	
5	5	
Total net profit	£90	

Required:
Calculate the accounting rate of return of the proposed new project.

Answer to Exhibit 16.2

The accounting rate of return would be calculated as follows:

$$\frac{\text{Average annual net profits}}{\text{Cost of the investment}} \times 100$$

Average annual net profits = £18,000 (£90,000/5)

$$\therefore \text{Accounting rate of return} = \frac{£18,000}{50,000} \times 100 = \underline{\underline{36\%}}$$

The accounting rate of return method (like the payback method) also has several disadvantages:

1   *The definition of profit.* Net profit could mean either net profit *before* allowing for depreciation on the project, or net profit *after* allowing for the project's depreciation.
2   *The cost of the project.* There is some doubt whether the original cost of the investment should be used, or whether it is more appropriate to use the average amount of capital invested in the project.
3   *The rate of return.* The method gives no guidance on what is an acceptable rate of return.
4   *Timing of returns.* The advantage of earning a high proportion of the total profit in the early years of the project is not taken into account.

The accounting rate of return method may be used where very similar short-term projects are being considered.

Discounted cash flow

An increasingly common method of project appraisal is that known as discounted cash flow (DCF). There are two main methods of incorporating DCF into project appraisal: (1) the net present value method (NPV); and (2) the internal rate of return method (IRR). These two methods will be examined in the following sub-sections.

1   The net present value method

The NPV method recognizes that cash received today might be worth more than cash receivable in the future. A smaller sum might be available now, but if it is invested, its total value might eventually be greater than any sum receivable in the future. Thus if £90.91 is available now, and it can be invested at a rate of interest of 10% per annum, it will be worth £100 in one year's time (£90.91 + £9.09). In these circumstances, it is clearly preferable to have £90.91 now, rather than to be offered less than £100 in a year's time.

This concept is known as the *time value of money*, and it can be incorporated into project appraisal. As cash receivable in the future might not be worth as much when it is received as cash that is available now, it would be fairer to compare them in terms of their present value. To do so, the future net cash flows must be estimated, and then brought back to their present value. Hence this method involves the use of *discounting*, and it is necessary to choose an appropriate rate of interest. The rate of interest chosen might be similar to that which can be obtained by opting for an alternative investment.

It should be noted that future net cash flows are not necessarily worth less because of the effect of inflation (although the declining purchasing power of the monetary unit will be taken into account in assessing future net cash flows). In DCF calculations, cash receivable in the future is considered to be worth less than cash received now, because cash that is available now can be used, i.e. invested.

By adopting the NPV method, optional projects can be more fairly assessed, since the total of their respective net present values can be compared. The project with the highest NPV is likely to be the most profitable, although there are other factors to be taken into account, such as the investment in projects that are necessary for safety reasons.

To help with DCF calculations a discount table is included in Appendix 2. To work out what the value of £100 receivable in twelve months' time is worth at the present time, for example, assuming that it is invested at a rate of return of 10% per annum, simply consult the discount table. Look along the top line for the appropriate rate of interest: in this case it is 10%. Work down the 10% column until you come to the line opposite the year (shown in the left-hand column) in which the cash would be received. In this example, the cash is going to be received in one year's time, so it is only necessary to look down to the first line. The present value of £1 receivable in a year's time is, therefore, £0.9091, or £90.91 if £100 is to be received in a year's time. This calculation can be checked by adding 10% (£9.09) to the £90.91. It is correct, because £9.09 + £90.91 equals the £100 receivable in a year's time.

An example of the NPV method is shown in Exhibit 16.3.

Exhibit 16.3: The net present value method

Rage Limited is considering two capital investment projects. The details are outlined below.

Project	1	2
Estimated life	3 years	5 years
Commencement date	1.1.X1	1.1.X1
	£000	£000
Project cost at 1.1.X1	100	100
Estimated net cash flows:		
Year to: 31.12.X1	20	10
31.12.X2	80	40
31.12.X3	40	40
31.12.X4	–	40
31.12.X5	–	20

The company expects a rate of return of 10% per annum on its capital employed.

Required:
Using the net present value method of project appraisal, assess which project would be more profitable.

Answer to Exhibit 16.3

RAGE LIMITED

Project appraisal:

Year	Net cash flow	Project 1 Discount factor	Present value	Net cash flow	Project 2 Discount factor	Present value
	£	10%	£	£	10%	£
31.12.X1	20,000	0.9091	18,182	10,000	0.9091	9,091
31.12.X2	80,000	0.8264	66,112	40,000	0.8264	33,056
31.12.X3	40,000	0.7513	30,052	40,000	0.7513	30,052
31.12.X4	–	–	–	40,000	0.6830	27,320
31.12.X5	–	–	–	20,000	0.6209	12,418
Total present value			114,346			111,937
Less: Initial cost			100,000			100,000
Net present value			£14,346			£11,937

Tutorial note

The discount factors have been obtained from the discount table shown in Appendix 1.

Although both projects have a positive NPV, project 1 should be chosen in preference to project 2 because its NPV is higher.

Two main problems arise in adopting the NPV method:

1   It is difficult to calculate the net cash flows for each year during the life of the project (a difficulty that is common to other methods of project appraisal).

2   It is not easy to select an appropriate rate of interest. One rate that could be chosen is that rate which the company could earn if it decided to invest the funds outside the business (the external rate of interest). Alternatively, an internal rate of interest could be chosen. This rate would be based on an estimate of what return the company expects to earn on its existing investments. In the long run, if its internal rate of return is lower than the external rate, then it would appear more profitable to liquidate the company and invest the funds elsewhere.

Notwithstanding these problems, the NPV method does take into account the timing of the net cash flows, the project's profitability and the return of the original investment.

2   Internal rate of return method

An alternative method of investment appraisal based on discounted cash flow is the internal rate of return method (IRR). This method requires the calculation of a rate of return that would discount the future net cash flows back to a net present value equal to the original cost of the project. A project would be accepted if the IRR produced a total net present value that was equal to or in excess of the cost of the project. The project would not be accepted if it produced a negative rate of return.

The method is illustrated in Exhibit 16.4.

Exhibit 16.4: The internal rate of return method

Bruce Limited is considering whether to invest £50,000 in a new project. The project's expected net cash flows would be as follows:

Year	£000
1	7
2	25
3	30
4	5

Required:
Calculate the internal rate of return for the proposed new project.

Answer to Exhibit 16.4

BRUCE LIMITED

Calculation of the internal rate of return:

Step 1: Select two discount rates
The first step is to select two discount rates, and then calculate the net present value of the project. The two rates usually have to be chosen quite arbitrarily, although they should preferably cover a narrow range. One of the rates should produce a positive rate of return, and the other rate a negative rate of return. As

far as this question is concerned, rates of 10% and 15% will be chosen to illustrate the method.

Year	Net cash flow	Discount factors		Present value	
		10%	15%	10%	15%
	£			£	£
1	7,000	0.9091	0.8696	6,364	6,087
2	25,000	0.8264	0.7561	20,660	18,903
3	30,000	0.7513	0.6575	22,539	19,725
4	5,000	0.6830	0.5718	3,415	2,859
Total present values				52,978	47,574
Initial cost				50,000	50,000
Net present value				£2,978	£(2,426)

The project is expected to cost £50,000. If the company expects a rate of return of 10%, the project will be accepted, because the NPV is positive. However, if the required rate of return is 15% it will not be accepted, because its NPV is negative. The maximum rate of return that will ensure a positive rate of return must, therefore, lie somewhere between 10% and 15%, so the next step is to calculate the rate of return at which the project would just pay for itself.

Step 2: Calculate the rate of return
To do so, it is necessary to interpolate between the rates used in Step 1. This can be done by using the following formula:

$$IRR = \text{Positive rate} + \left(\frac{\text{Positive NPV}}{\text{Positive NPV} - \text{Negative NPV*}} \times \text{Range of rates} \right)$$

* The negative sign is ignored.

Thus:
$$IRR = 10\% + \left(\frac{2,978}{(2,978 + 2,426)} \times (15\% - 10\%) \right)$$
$$= 10\% + (0.5511 \times 5\%)$$
$$= 10\% + 2.76\%$$
$$= 12.76\%$$

The project will be profitable provided that the company does not require a rate of return in excess of about 13%. Note that the method of calculation used above does not give the precise rate of return (because the formula is only an approximation), but it is adequate enough for decision-making purposes.

It can be seen from Exhibit 16.4 that the IRR method is similar to the NPV method. Future net cash flows have to be estimated and then using discount tables, discounted to their net present value. After calculating the net cash flows, the main problem in using the IRR method is to calculate the internal rate of return. An approximate rate can, however, be calculated by trial and error.

A company would not necessarily go ahead with a project, of course, simply because a project appraisal suggested that it was likely to be profitable. Indeed, there will probably be so many competing projects that they will have to be ranked in order of profitability. In addition, there may well be other projects that have to be undertaken even though they are not revenue earning, for example, projects involving health and safety, such as the provision of car parks and sports grounds. These types of projects may only provide an indirect benefit to the company, but obviously health and safety matters cannot be ignored.

Once the company has decided which project to support, it is then necessary to decide how to finance it. This problem is considered in the next section.

Source of funds

In project appraisal, there is another most important factor to consider: the financing of the project. Basically, there are five main sources of funds available to a company:

1   *From retained profits.* This is probably the main source of funds for most companies.
2   *By issuing more shares for cash.* This can be an expensive operation. If preference shares are issued the company is committing itself to paying a preference dividend. If it issues ordinary shares, it will have to pay out a larger amount of ordinary share dividend even if the amount per share is not increased. If its profits do not match its expectations, the company may have difficulty in meeting a higher amount of dividend.
3   *By long-term borrowing.* The company could issue debentures to pay for its capital investment programme. The debenture interest would be allowable against corporation tax, but the company could become very high geared if it issued more long-term debt. This might cause a problem if profits began to decline, and it was committed to paying out more debenture interest.
4   *By short-term borrowing.* This may be achieved by delaying payments to trade creditors, or by obtaining overdraft facilities at the bank. Capital investments financed by short-term borrowings are clearly very risky: the loan may be called in at short notice, and it may not be renewable.
5   *By leasing and hire purchase contracts.* In the last twenty years, leasing has been a popular way of financing the purchase of fixed assets, probably because of the tax advantages that the method has attracted. These tax advantages have now been much reduced, and leasing as a form of financing is not quite as popular as it was. Hire purchase is also quite a common form of financing, but it is an expensive method of financing the purchase of fixed assets since a high rate of interest is usually charged on such arrangements.

Capital investment appraisal is part of the budgeting process. The budget will have identified what projects need to be undertaken. Usually there are so many competing projects that the company has to rank them in order of priority, including those projects that are necessary on health, social or welfare grounds. A capital expenditure programme will be matched with the available finance in order to ensure that sufficient funds are available at the implementation stage. In most circumstances, the company will finance its capital expenditure programme out of retained earnings, but with large projects it might have to issue more shares or engage in long-term borrowing.

Conclusion

Capital investment appraisal is a complex and time-consuming exercise. It is not possible to be absolutely certain about the profitability of individual projects, but it is possible to make a reasoned comparison between them.

Managers tend to be very enthusiastic about their own sphere of responsibility. Thus the marketing manager may be *sure* that additional sales will be possible, the production director *certain* that a new machine will pay for itself, while the data processing manager is *convinced* that a new computer is essential.

In choosing between such competing projects, the accountant's role is to try to assess the cost of such projects and compare them with the possible benefits. Once a choice has been made, it is then necessary to ensure that the necessary finance will be available to implement them. Capital investment appraisal should not be used as a means of blocking new projects. It is no different from all the other accounting techniques. It is meant to provide additional guidance to management, and it is the responsibility of management to ensure that other factors are taken into account.

Capital investment appraisal concludes this part of the book. The two main branches of accounting (financial accounting and cost and management accounting) have now been examined in some detail. The book has concentrated on examining techniques for *internal* management purposes. The final part of the book will investigate the information prepared largely for *external* reporting purposes.

Questions

16.1 Prospect Limited is considering investing in a new project. The project would cost £100,000 to implement, it would last 5 years and it would then be sold for £50,000. The following are the relevant profit and loss accounts for each year during the life of the project:

Year to 31 March	19X1	19X2	19X3	19X4	19X5
	£000	£000	£000	£000	£000
Sales	2,000	2,400	2,800	2,900	2,000
Less: Cost of goods sold					
Opening stock	–	200	300	450	350
Purchases	1,600	1,790	2,220	1,960	1,110
	1,600	1,990	2,520	2,410	1,460
Less: Closing stock	200	300	550	350	50
	1,400	1,690	1,970	2,060	1,410
Gross profit	600	710	830	840	590
Less: Expenses	210	220	240	250	300
Depreciation	190	190	190	190	190
	400	410	430	440	490
Net profit	200	300	400	400	100
Taxation	40	70	100	100	10
Retained profits	£160	£230	£300	£300	£90

Additional information:
1 All sales are made and all purchases are obtained on credit terms.
2 Outstanding trade debtors and trade creditors at the end of each year are expected to ɔe as follows:

Year	Trade debtors	Trade creditors
	£000	£000
19X1	200	250
19X2	240	270
19X3	300	330
19X4	320	300
19X5	400	150

3 Expenses would all be paid in cash during each year in question.
4 Taxation would be paid on 1 January following each year end.
5 Half the project would be paid for in cash on 1 April 19X0, and the remaining half (also in cash) on 1 January 19X1. The resale value of £50,000 will be received in cash on 31 March 19X6.

Required:
Calculate the annual net cash flow arising from this project.

16.2 Buchan Limited is considering investing in a new machine. The machine will be purchased on 1 January 19X1 and at a cost of £50,000. It is estimated that it would last for 5 years, and it will then be sold at the end of the year for £2,000 in cash. The respective net cash flows estimated to be received by the company as a result of purchasing the machine during each year of its life are as follows:

Year	£	
1	8,000	(excluding the initial cost)
2	16,000	
3	40,000	
4	45,000	
5	35,000	(exclusive of the project's sale proceeds)

Required:
Calculate the payback period for the project.

16.3 Lender Limited is considering investing in a new project. It is estimated that it will cost £100,000 to implement, and that the expected net profit after tax will be as follows:

Year	£
1	18,000
2	47,000
3	65,000
4	65,000
5	30,000

Required:
Calculate the accounting rate of return of the proposed project.

16.4 The following net cash flows relate to Lockhart Limited in connection with a certain project which has an initial cost of £2,500,000:

Year	Net cash flow £000	
1	800	(excluding the initial cost)
2	850	
3	830	
4	1,200	
5	700	

The company's required rate of return is 15%.

Required:
Calculate the net present value of the project.

16.5 Moffat Limited has calculated the following net cash flows for a proposed project costing £1,450,000:

Year	Net cash flow £000	
1	230	(excluding the initial cost)
2	370	
3	600	
4	650	
5	120	

Required:
Calculate the internal rate of return generated by the project.

16.6 Marsh Limited has investigated the possibility of investing in a new machine. The following data have been extracted from the report relating to the project:

Cost of machine on 1 January 19X6: £500,000.
Life: 4 years to 31 December 19X9.
Estimated scrap value: Nil.
Depreciation method: Straight-line.

Year	Accounting profit after tax £000	Net cash flows £000
1	100	50 (excluding the initial cost)
2	250	200
3	250	225
4	200	225
5	–	100

The company's required rate of return is 15%.

Required:
Calculate the return the machine would make using the following investment appraisal methods:
1 payback;
2 accounting rate of return;
3 net present value; and
4 internal rate of return.

Additional questions (without answers)

16.7 Nicol Limited is considering investing in a new machine. The machine would cost £500,000. It would have a life of five years, and a nil residual value. The company uses the straight line method of depreciation.

It is expected that the machine will earn the following extra profits for the company during its expected life:

Year	Profits £000
1	200
2	120
3	120
4	100
5	60

The above profits also represent the extra net cash flows expected to be generated by the machine (i.e. they exclude the machine's initial cost and the annual depreciation charge).

The company's cost of capital is 18%.

Required:
(a) Calculate:
   (i) the machine's payback period; and
   (ii) its net present value
   and
(b) advise management as to whether the new machine should be purchased.

16.8 Hewie Limited has some capital available for investment, and is considering two projects, only one of which can be financed. The details are as follows:

	Project 1	Project 2
Expected life (years)	4	3
	£000	£000
Initial cost	600	500
Expected net cash flows (excluding the initial cost)		
Year		
1	10	250
2	200	250
3	400	50
4	50	–
Residual value	Nil	Nil

Required:
Advise management on which project to accept.

Part 4

Annual reports

17 Disclosure of information

Learning objectives

1 appreciate the need for some minimum disclosure requirements; and

2 list the main contents of a limited liability company's annual report.

Chapter 6 examined how a set of company accounts was constructed. The type of accounts considered in that chapter are compiled largely for the benefit of management. All limited liability companies, however, have to supply their shareholders with a copy of their annual accounts. Such accounts (often referred to as the *published* accounts) are an abbreviated version of those prepared for management purposes. It might seem strange that the owners of the company (i.e. the shareholders) are only supplied with a *summary* of the annual accounts, but by law they are only entitled to the *minimum* amount of information as laid down in the Companies Act 1985.

In this chapter, the legal position will be reviewed with regard to the disclosure of information, along with the additional requirements demanded by the various professional accountancy bodies and by the Stock Exchange. In later chapters the contents of an annual report will be considered in much greater detail.

Minimum disclosure requirements

During the last 50 years, there has been a gradual increase in the minimum amount of information that companies must disclose to their shareholders, and even the minimum disclosure requirements now result in some very complex accounts being prepared for shareholders. Until 1981, Parliament had only laid down broad guidelines that had to be followed in disclosing information to shareholders, and it had been left largely to each individual company to decide how and in what form it should be presented. The 1981 Companies Act went much further than earlier Companies Acts and laid down precise formats for the presentation of the profit and loss account and the balance sheet. The 1981 Act was later consolidated into the Companies Act 1985 (along with the Companies Acts of 1948, 1967, 1976 and 1980). The 1985 Act still retains the prescribed formats although it has now been amended by the Companies Act 1989.

The six major accountancy bodies also insist upon certain additional information being included in the published accounts. As explained earlier in this book, these requirements are contained within Statements of Standard Accounting Practice (SSAPs). The first statement was issued in 1971, and 25 have now been issued, although three have been withdrawn.

SSAPs do not lay down precise guidelines. It is recognized that individual circumstances vary considerably, and it would be impossible to insist upon a rigid interpretation of the methods advocated in the standards. Professionally qualified accountants are, however, supposed to adopt the recommendations when they are preparing published accounts. The standards do not apply exclusively to companies, since it is believed that the principles and methods can be applied to most entities. Nonetheless, some standards are fairly specialist, such as SSAP 21 which deals with leasing and hire purchase accounting.

Besides the Companies Act 1985 and professional accountancy requirements, listed companies have also to comply with a number of Stock Exchange disclosure requirements. Many of these have now been incorporated into the 1985 Act, and they are not quite as significant as they used to be.

Besides supplying a copy of their annual accounts to shareholders, all companies (irrespective of whether they are public or private companies) have to file a copy of their accounts with the Registrar of Companies at Companies House in Cardiff or in Edinburgh. This means that on payment of a small fee the accounts of limited liability companies are open to public inspection. Thus the same information that is available to shareholders is available to any member of the general public.

The Companies Act 1985 does, however, allow some concessions to private companies depending upon the size of the company. All public companies must file the same set of accounts that they submit to their shareholders. Private companies may file abbreviated accounts if they meet two out of the three following criteria:

	Company	
Criteria	*Small*	*Medium*
	Not more than:	Not more than:
Turnover	£2 million	£8 million
Gross assets	£975,000	£3.9 million
Employees	50	250

Notwithstanding this concession, small and medium-sized companies must still supply a detailed set of accounts to their shareholders that comply with the minimum disclosure requirements of the Companies Act 1985.

The only accounts that most employees of public companies are likely to see are the published accounts prepared for the shareholders. Sometimes, employees are supplied with a copy of the shareholders' accounts (although they have no legal right to such a copy), or they might obtain one by applying to the company secretary.

Employees of private companies may only have the option of inspecting the accounts at Companies House (there are various agencies that will make the inspection on behalf of an applicant). If they are employed in small or medium-sized companies, they may only be able to consult the abbreviated version.

In recent years, there has been a tendency for both private and public companies to prepare accounts specially for their employees. Although successive governments have prepared legislation that has encouraged this trend, employees are still not as well provided for as shareholders. Nonetheless, many companies do now supply some fairly detailed information to their employees, and it would appear that the practice is beginning to become much more common.

Although th's part of the book is only concerned with the *minimum* disclosure requirements, it must be appreciated that an annual report is still a fairly long and complicated document. Shareholders who have no knowledge of accounting are probably quite mystified by the contents of such a report, but students who have worked through this book should have no difficulty.

Contents of an annual report

The contents of an annual report extend now to much more than a summary of the internal profit and loss account and balance sheet of a company. Besides containing some promotional material, they often contain a number of other detailed reports and statements.

It is, however, possible to break down a fairly typical report into four main sections. These may be summarized as follows:

Promotional material

Companies usually take the opportunity to include details of their products in their annual report. Shareholders are consumers, of course, so it is beneficial to the company if it can persuade its own shareholders to buy its products.

As this type of information does not form part of the accounting function, it is beyond the scope of this book.

Specialist reports

The annual report will usually include the following specialist reports:

1 the chairman's report;
2 the directors' report; and
3 the auditors' report.

These may be referred to as the *principal* reports, and they form the subject of the next chapter.

The main financial statements

The main financial statements consist of the following:

1 the profit and loss account;
2 the balance sheet; and
3 a statement of source and application of funds.

These statements will be examined in Chapter 19.

Supplementary statements

A number of other reports and statements are usually included in an annual report. The exact number and type depend upon the company and a number of typical examples will be considered in Chapter 20.

Conclusion

As a non-accountant it is unlikely that you will be involved in the detailed preparation of your company's annual report, although you may have to provide information that might be used for that purpose. In fact, the only times that you are likely to see the published version of your company's accounts are if the company supplies you with a copy, or you own shares in the company.

An annual report will probably not mean much to you unless you have had some specialist training in financial accounting. This book has provided that training, and the remaining chapters will make good use of it.

Note: An assignment covering the material in this chapter will be found at the end of Chapter 20.

18 The principal reports

Learning objectives_____

1 list three principal reports contained within a limited liability company's annual report;

and

2 summarize the main contents of such reports.

The annual accounts of a company have to be circulated to every shareholder at least 21 days before the general meeting at which those accounts are to be considered. This requirement also applies to both the auditors' report and the directors' report. It is also usual for the chairman to provide a report for the shareholders. The chairman's report, the directors' report and the auditors' report form the subject of this chapter.

The chairman's report

There is no statutory or professional accounting requirement for the chairman to report to the shareholders, although most annual reports do contain a chairman's report. The chairman's report is usually presented in an early part of the annual report, often immediately after a list of the board of directors and a brief summary of some key statistics.

The report may be very long, although most chairmen manage to limit their comments to one or two pages. As there are no formal requirements covering the contents of such a report, chairmen are quite free to include almost anything that they like. Whilst the auditors may check the contents (especially those elements containing financial data), there is no obligation for them to make any comment about the report. Nonetheless, the chairman will be mindful of the effects that any remarks are likely to have on the company's share price. A great deal of embarrassment could be caused if any comments were eventually proved to be unjustified.

A chairman's report may include the following items:

1 A review of the company's overall results for the year, including some information on divisional, product and sectional performance.
2 A very brief summary of the financial results for the year, especially a comment about the net profit for the year compared with the previous year's net profit.
3 A brief statement of the company's paid and proposed dividends for the year.
4 An explanation of what steps have been taken to improve the company's efficiency and productivity.
5 Details of major acquisitions and disposals of shares in other companies.
6 Some information about the board of directors, for example, about new members, resignations, retirements, achievements and honours.
7 Details about employees, such as those retiring after exceptionally long service.
8 A tribute to fellow directors, employees and other personnel involved in the company.
9 Some comments about the company's prospects.

The directors' report

The directors' report usually follows the chairman's report. It is a statutory requirement that the directors should *attach* a copy of their report to the set of accounts that are sent to the shareholders.

A directors' report now contains a great deal of information, so all that it is possible to do in this section is to summarize the main contents.

Activities

This section may include details of the following:

1 principal activities of the company and any changes in them during the year;
2 a review of developments during the year and a statement of future ones;
3 research and development activities;
4 important events that have happened during the year;
5 the recommended dividend; and
6 the amount set aside or withdrawn from reserves.

Auditors

The auditors have to be re-appointed annually by the shareholders, so it is necessary to state in the report that the auditors are seeking election (or otherwise).

Directors

All the names of those individuals who have been directors during the year should be stated. Those directors who are still directors at the end of the year must have their share and loan capital holdings listed. Any director who does not hold any shares or debentures must disclose that fact.

Donations

If the company has made certain charitable and political donations during the year which *together* exceed £200, then the separate total for both the charitable and the political donations must be stated. If a particular political donation exceeds £200, both the amount and the name of the recipient must be reported.

Employment policy

The company's employment policy towards disabled persons, their training and their career development should be stated.

Fixed assets

Any major changes in fixed assets or any significant difference between the market value and the book value of land and buildings should be outlined.

Share capital

Information about changes in the company's share capital will be given in the accounts, but any such changes should also be referred to in the directors' report.

The directors' report should be signed by one director (or the company secretary) and stated as being signed 'on behalf of the board'. The name of the person signing the report should be stated.

The auditors' report

The auditors' report will normally be quite short. Most auditors' reports will be fairly similar. A typical one would read as follows:

Report of the auditors to the members of Caen plc.
We have audited the financial statements on pages 14 to 30 in accordance with Auditing Standards.

In our opinion the financial statements give a true and fair view of the state of affairs of the Company and the Group at 31 March 19X5 and of the profit and source and application of funds of the Group for the year then ended and have been properly prepared in accordance with the Companies Act 1985.
Cope & Co
Chartered Accountants
31 May 19X5

An auditors' report such as the one outlined above, would be regarded as being an *unqualified* audit report. This means that in the opinion of the auditors, the accounts give a true and fair view, and that they have nothing further to say about them. A *qualified* audit report is supposed to draw the attention of the shareholders to certain aspects of the accounts that do not appear to give a true and fair view, for example, because of the method used to value stocks. The qualification may arise only as a result of a minor point, but even a major qualification (such as that the accounts do *not* represent a true and fair view) is supposed to be very serious.

There is some uncertainty about the importance and relevance of a qualified audit report, particularly if the qualification appears to be a minor one. It used to be rare for audit reports to be qualified, but in recent years it has become quite common. The effect of a qualified audit report ought, at the very least, to result in some searching questions being put to the directors at the general meeting. If the explanation appears unsatisfactory, then the shareholders should consider dismissing the directors. Such an event is comparatively rare.

The auditors' report may come before or after the main financial statements. These will be considered in the next chapter.

Conclusion

This chapter has outlined the contents of the three main reports that are contained within a typical annual report. First, the chairman's report was examined. This report is not required either by statute or by professional accounting requirements. Next the contents of a directors' report were summarized; this type of report is now a major source of much statutory and professional accounting information. And finally, the contents of a typical auditors' report were outlined. This is one of the shortest reports to be found in the annual report.

Note: An assignment covering the material in this chapter will be found at the end of Chapter 20.

19 The main financial statements

Learning objectives_____

1　list the main financial statements contained within a limited liability company's annual report;

　and

2　summarize and identify the main items disclosed in such statements.

The main financial statements considered in this chapter are the profit and loss account, the balance sheet, and a statement of source and application of funds. Annual reports usually contain other types of statements, and these will be examined in the next chapter.

The background to published accounts

The structure and format of profit and loss accounts, balance sheets and statements of source and application of funds for internal management purposes have already been examined in previous chapters. In practice, the information contained in such statements can be extremely complex. The Companies Act 1985 recognizes that it would be impracticable to expect a company to supply a similar amount of information to all its shareholders, so only a certain minimum amount of information has to be disclosed to shareholders. However, when additional professional accounting and Stock Exchange requirements are also included, the total amount is still quite considerable.

Additional features

There are certain features of published financial statements that have not been encountered before. These are summarized below.

Group accounts

Most published annual accounts will contain the results for a *group* of companies. There are a few examples of public companies that are not part of a group, but they are comparatively rare.

A group is like a family. The company (say Company A) may buy shares in another company (say Company B). When Company A owns more than 50% of the voting shares in Company B, B becomes a *subsidiary* of A. If A owned more than 20% of the voting shares in B but less than 50%, B might be referred to as an *associated* or *related* company of A. In effect B is considered to be the off-spring of A, and in turn B might have children of its own (say Company C and Company D). C and D then become part of the family, i.e. they become part of the group structure. It should be noted that the Companies Act 1985 (as amended by Companies Act 1989) uses the terms *group undertaking* for a subsidiary company, and *undertakings in which the company has a participating interest* for an associated or related company.

The significance of these relationships is that the published accounts will be prepared for the group as a whole. Even though B, C and D are companies in their own right (and might therefore be expected to prepare accounts for themselves), the entity becomes part of the group, and any inter-group relationships between them are ignored when preparing the accounts.

When inspecting a set of published accounts, therefore, you will usually see a *group* profit and loss account, a *group* balance sheet, and a *group* statement of source and application of funds. The Companies Act 1985 (as amended) requires a parent company (Company A in this example) to prepare *consolidated* accounts comprising a consolidated profit and loss account and a consolidated balance sheet. Statements of source and application of funds are not required by law, but normally a group funds' statement would also be prepared.

In order to prepare such accounts, it is necessary to add together (or consolidate) all of the company accounts that form part of the group. As a result, all the subsidiary and associated company results are absorbed into the holding company's accounts (although some specific information about such companies has still to be disclosed). The preparation of group accounts can be an enormous and highly specialist task. Indeed, it is something of a specialism even among professional accountants.

Notes to the accounts

Another additional feature of group accounts is that they will probably be accompanied by many pages of notes. These notes provide even more information about the items disclosed in the accounts themselves. Such notes form an integral part of the accounts, although they usually contain so much detail that it is sometimes difficult to find the required information.

Comparative figures

The 1985 Companies Act requires the current year's accounts to be accompanied by comparisons with the previous year's results. This adds to the amount of information given in the accounts, although it is advantageous, of course, to be able to compare the current year with the previous year.

The remaining sections of this chapter examine published accounts in a little more detail.

The group profit and loss account

The Companies Act 1985 lays down a choice of two types of structural format for the presentation of the profit and loss account. These are as follows:

1   the horizontal format, whereby the expenditure is listed on the left-hand side of the page, and the income on the right-hand side; and
2   the vertical format, whereby the income and expenditure is displayed on a line-by-line basis.

In this book, the vertical format has been almost exclusively adopted. This format has been deliberately chosen because it is one used by most companies, and it is, therefore, the one that is most likely to be met in practice.

Besides permitting a choice of structural formats, the Act also permits the expenditure to be displayed according to its *type*. There are two types of format permitted by the Act:

1   the operational format; and
2   the type of expenditure format.

These formats are illustrated in Exhibit 19.1 using fictitious data.

As can be seen from Exhibit 19.1, the type of expenditure format is very much more detailed than the operational format. Both types are used in the United Kingdom, but it is possible that the operational format is more popular, probably because it is a little easier to follow. A similar format has, in fact, been adopted in earlier chapters.

Exhibit 19.1: The vertical profit and loss account expenditure formats

1 *Operational format*		2 *Type of expenditure format*		
	£000		£000	£000
Turnover	9,000	Turnover		9,000
Cost of sales	(5,500)	Changes in stocks		
Gross profit	3,500	of finished goods		
		and work-in-progress		200
		Own work		
		capitalized		50
		Other operating		
		income		100
				9,350
Distribution costs	(1,000)	Raw materials and		
		consumables	(4,000)	
Administration expenses	(1,600)	Other external		
Operating profit	900	charges	(400)	
		Staff costs	(3,000)	
		Depreciation and		
		other amounts		
		written off tangible		
		and intangible		
		fixed assets	(900)	
Other operating income	100	Other operating		
		charges	(50)	(8,350)
Operating profit	£1,000	*Operating profit*		£1,000

Note: After the operating profit stage the two formats are identical.

You should now be in a position to examine a published profit and loss account in some detail, such as the one outlined in Exhibit 19.2.

Exhibit 19.2: Example of a published profit and loss account

ENERGY PUBLIC LIMITED COMPANY
Group profit and loss account for the year to 31 March 19X2

	Notes to the accounts (1)	19X2 £000	19X1 £000
Turnover (2)	2	49,000	34,000
Cost of sales (3)		(40,000)	(26,000)
Gross profit (4)		9,000	8,000
Distribution costs (5)		(4,000)	(3,000)
Administrative expenses (5)		(2,000)	(1,500)
Other operating income (6)		20	20
Operating profit (7)		3,020	3,520
Income from shares in participating interests (8)		100	50
Income from other fixed asset investments (9)		150	130
c/f		3,270	3,700

		b/f		3,270	3,700
Other interest receivable and other income (10)				45	40
Interest payable and similar charges (11)				(260)	(90)
Profit on ordinary activities before taxation (12)		2/3		3,055	3,650
Tax on profit on ordinary activities (13)		4		(100)	(600)
Profit on ordinary activities after taxation (14)				2,955	3,050
Minority interests (15)				(110)	(200)
Profit before extraordinary items attributable to members of the holding company (16)				2,845	2,850
Extraordinary items (17)		5		(45)	(250)
Profit for the financial year (18)		6		2,800	2,600
Dividends paid and proposed (19)		7		(2,400)	(2,300)
Retained profit for the year (20)				£400	£300
Earnings per share (21)		8		2.85p	2.85p

Note: The numbers in brackets shown after each narration relate to the tutorial notes given below. The amounts are presented only for illustrative purposes.

Tutorial notes

1 The formal notes to the accounts have not been presented with this exhibit, as most of the items will be considered as part of these tutorial notes. It will be noticed that Note (1) to the accounts is missing. This is because the first formal note to the accounts is often a statement of accounting policies. This statement lists the accounting policies that have been adopted in drawing up that particular set of accounts.

2 Turnover is usually defined as being sales to customers outside the group, less returns by customers, exclusive of trade discounts and value added tax.

3 The detailed calculation for the cost of goods sold does not have to be disclosed. It is not defined in the Companies Act 1985.

4 The gross profit may not be identical to that shown in the internal accounts, because of the definition used for cost of sales.

5 The 1985 Companies Act does not define what is meant by distribution costs or administrative expenses.

6 Other operating income will include income from rentals and royalties.

7 This is the point at which the operational and type of expenditure formats become identical.

8 This includes the group's share of profits or losses in associated or related companies.

9 Income from other fixed asset investments may include dividends received from non-group companies.

10 Other interest receivable and similar income includes interest received on loans.

11 Interest payable and similar charges will include interest payable on bank and other short-term borrowings.

12 The profit on ordinary activities before taxation will require a detailed formal note to the accounts. It will include such information as the auditors' remuneration, directors' emoluments (as they are called), details of wages and

salaries (in total), depreciation charges (in total), and social security and pension costs.

13 The tax on the profit on ordinary activities will include the company's corporation tax for the year.

14 The amount shown for profit on ordinary activities after taxation is simply a sub-total. It illustrates what could be paid in dividends if all of the after-tax profit was to be distributed.

15 A proportion of the after-tax profits may be due to shareholders outside the group if the holding company has not purchased all of the shares in a subsidiary company.

16 The amount of profit available to group members before extraordinary items is a sub-total. It shows the amount of after-tax profit for the year that could be distributed to group members.

17 Extraordinary items are incomes (or expenditures) that (a) are material; (b) arise outside the ordinary course of business; and (c) are not expected to recur frequently or regularly. If such items were not separately disclosed, they would distort the ordinary results.

18 The profit for the financial year is the total amount of net profit for the year available for distribution to group members.

19 The dividends paid and proposed to be paid will include dividends paid or payable on all types of shares.

20 The retained profit for the year will be transferred to the revenue reserves shown in the balance sheet. It will be used to help finance the future expansion of the company.

21 The definition of earnings per share was given in Chapter 8.

As can be seen from Exhibit 19.2, the amount of information that it is necessary to disclose in a published profit and loss account is quite formidable. It should also be remembered that examples of the *formal* notes attached to the profit and loss account have not been reproduced. For a large company, such notes might extend to about twelve pages of closely printed material.

The group balance sheet

The Companies Act 1985 allows a choice of balance sheet format. The choice is as follows:

1 a horizontal format, whereby the assets are laid out on the left-hand side of the page, and the capital on the right-hand side; and

2 a vertical format, whereby the assets are listed before the liabilities.

In this book, the vertical format has almost exclusively been adopted, because in the United Kingdom, vertical balance sheets are very popular.

A published balance sheet will not look very different from one prepared for internal purposes. As noted earlier, however, it will probably be prepared for a group, comparative figures will be given, and there will be many formal notes attached to it.

A typical published balance sheet is shown in Exhibit 19.3.

Exhibit 19.3: Example of a published balance sheet

ENERGY PUBLIC LIMITED COMPANY
Group balance sheet at 31 March 19X2

	Notes to the accounts (1)	Group 19X2 £000	Group 19X1 £000	Company 19X2 £000	Company 19X1 £000
Fixed assets (2)					
Intangible assets (3)	9	90	60	—	—
Tangible assets (4)	10	1,400	1,350	1,300	1,200
Investments (5)	11	70	50	1,300	1,200
		1,560	1,460	2,600	2,400
Current assets (7)					
Stocks (8)	12	6,500	3,800	3,300	1,350
Debtors (9)	13	7,500	4,500	4,800	1,800
Investments (10)	14	60	50	—	—
Cash at bank and in hand (11)		700	130	20	10
(12)		14,760	8,480	8,120	3,160
Creditors: amounts falling due within one year (13)	15	(8,500)	(3,800)	(7,000)	(2,900)
Net current assets (14)		6,260	4,680	1,120	260
Total assets less current liabilities (15)		7,820	6,140	3,720	2,660
Creditors: Amounts falling due after more than one year (16)	16	(3,000)	(1,700)	—	—
Provisions for liabilities and charges (17)		(1,200)	(1,500)	—	—
(17)		£3,620	£2,940	£3,720	£2,660
Capital and reserves (19)					
Called-up share capital (20)	17	1,000	1,000	1,000	1,000
Share premium account (21)	18	500	500	500	500
Revaluation reserve (22)	19	600	600	900	900
Other reserves (23)	20	360	100	300	60
Profit and loss account (24)	21	1,040	640	1,020	200
(25)		3,500	2,840	3,720	2,660
Minority interests (26)		120	100	—	—
(27)		£3,620	£2,940	£3,720	£2,660

Approved by the board on XX June 19X2 (28)

. . . . Director

(29)

Note: The number in brackets after each narration relates to the tutorial notes. The amounts are presented only for illustrative purposes.

Tutorial notes

1 Formal notes have not been attached to this exhibit as most of the items will be considered as part of these tutorial notes. The first formal balance sheet note begins at (9), because it is a continuation of the profit and loss account notes shown in the previous section. In order to comply with the Companies Act 1985 both the group and the holding company's own balance sheets are shown.

2 The net book value must be shown under the three headings of (a) intangible assets, (b) tangible assets, and (c) investments.

3 Intangible assets are those assets that are not of a physical nature, such as goodwill, patents and development costs.

4 Tangible assets include land and buildings, plant and machinery, fixtures, fittings, tools and equipment.

5 Fixed asset investments are those that are intended to be held for the long term, i.e. in excess of twelve months.

6 This line is the total net book value of all the fixed assets.

7 Current assets have also to be analysed into a number of categories.

8 Stocks must be disclosed under a number of categories, e.g. raw materials and consumables, work-in-progress, finished goods and payments on account.

9 Debtors have also to be analysed under such headings as trade debtors, other debtors, prepayments and accrued income.

10 Current asset investments are those investments held for the short term, i.e. for normally less than twelve months.

11 Cash at bank and in hand. This will be the same amount that appears in the balance sheet prepared for internal purposes.

12 This line represents the total of current assets.

13 Creditors have to be analysed between short-term creditors (i.e. those payable within the next twelve months), and long-term creditors (i.e. those that do not have to be paid for at least twelve months). Both short- and long-term creditors have to be analysed into a number of categories, such as trade creditors, other creditors, and accruals and deferred income.

14 The net current assets line is a sub-total (Current assets (12) *less* Creditors: Amounts falling due within one year (13)).

15 This is another sub-total (Fixed assets (6) *plus* Net current assets (14)).

16 See tutorial note 13 above.

17 Provisions for liabilities and charges include provisions for pensions and similar obligations, taxation (including deferred taxation), as well as other provisions (not specified in the Companies Act 1985).

18 This line represents the balance sheet total.

19 The capital and reserves section is the other main part of the balance sheet. It explains how the net assets (18) have been financed.

20 The called-up share capital represents all of the shares that have been issued, details of which will be shown in a formal balance sheet note.

21 The share premium account records the extra amount on top of the nominal value of their shares that shareholders were willing to pay when they bought their shares. It does not attract a dividend, and there are very few uses to which it can be put.

22 Sometimes fixed assets, such as land and buildings, will be revalued. The difference between the revalued amount and the net book value will be credited to a revaluation reserve account. The reserve cannot be distributed to shareholders as dividend.

23 Other reserves. This balance may include a number of other reserve accounts both of a capital nature (i.e. reserves that cannot be distributed to shareholders) and of a revenue nature (i.e. amounts that may be distributed to shareholders).

24 This is the total of all the profits that have not been distributed to shareholders, less those that have been put in special reserve accounts.

25 This is the total of the capital and reserves section of the balance sheet. It represents shareholders' funds.

26 The minority interests represent that proportion of the net assets of subsidiary companies owned by shareholders outside the group.

27 This line should balance with line (18).

28 The balance sheet should be signed by a director.

29 It is possible that other formal notes will be attached to the balance sheet.

Study Exhibit 19.3 very carefully. Its basic layout should be reasonably familiar to you, although there is a lot more detail in it than you have been used to in earlier examples.

Group statements of source and application of funds

The construction of a statement of source and application of funds has already been considered in some detail in Chapter 7. Published funds statements differ little from the format that was used in that chapter, apart from reflecting the activities of a *group* of companies, and the inclusion of comparative figures.

Unlike the profit and loss account and the balance sheet, funds statements do not have any statutory backing, but the accountancy profession considers them so important that they can be considered as one of the main financial statements. Indeed, SSAP 10 requires any entity with a turnover in excess of £25,000 per annum to prepare such a statement. However, as argued earlier, there is some doubt whether they do mean much to the layman.

Exhibit 19.4 gives an example of a statement of source and application of funds for a group of companies. You will see that apart from more detail, its format is reasonably familiar.

Exhibit 19.4: Example of a group statement of source and application of funds

ENERGY PUBLIC LIMITED COMPANY
Statement of source and application of funds for the year to 31 March 19X2

	19X2			19X1		
	£000	£000	£000	£000	£000	£000
Source of funds						
Profit before tax and extra-ordinary items, less minority interest (1)		2,945			3,450	
Extraordinary items (2)		(45)			(250)	
c/f		2,900			3,200	

	£000	£000	£000	£000	£000	£000
b/f			2,900			3,200
Adjustments for items not involving the movement of funds:						
Minority interests in the retained profits for the year (3)			110			200
Depreciation			180			160
Profits retained in undertakings in which the company has a participating interest (4)			(50)			(130)
Total generated from operations			3,140			3,430
Funds from other sources (5)						
Shares issued in part consideration of the acquisition of a subsidiary			40			20
Capital raised under executive option scheme			15			10
			3,195			3,460
Application of funds						
Dividends paid		(1,200)			(1,500)	
Tax paid		(100)			(700)	
Purchase of fixed assets		(250)			(200)	
Purchase of goodwill on acquisition of a subsidiary (6)		(100)			(350)	
Debentures redeemed		(50)	(1,700)		(50)	(2,800)
			1,495			660
Increase in working capital						
Increase in stocks		2,700			900	
Increase in debtors		3,000			200	
Increase in creditors — excluding taxation and dividends		(4,785)			(470)	
Movement in net liquid funds:						
Increase (decrease) in cash balances	570			30		
Increase (decrease) in short-term investments	10	580		–	30	
			1,495			660

Note: The figures in brackets after some of the narrations refer to the tutorial notes given below. The amounts are presented only for illustrative purposes.

Tutorial notes

1 This line links with the various items in the published profit and loss account.
2 Extraordinary items can either be a source of funds or an application of funds.
3 The minority interests share of the retained profits do not belong to the group, but they are still a source of funds because the share has not been paid out.
4 The group only receives dividends from undertakings in which the company has a participating interest and not the whole of its profits. The undertaking's profits have, therefore, to be added back because they are not a source of funds.

5 Funds from other sources are just illustrative examples.
6 The cost of purchasing goodwill in a subsidiary will be the difference between the total amount paid for the shares and the value of the investment.

The format of Exhibit 19.4 is based on the example given in the appendix to SSAP 10. This format is not mandatory, and the student may well come across examples of different formats.

Conclusion

You are now recommended to study most carefully the format of a published profit and loss account, a published balance sheet and a published statement of source and application of funds. The basic structures have been given in this chapter, but you should obtain copies of published accounts so that you can compare them.

Although the 1985 Companies Act has done much to standardize the format of published accounts, you will still find that some companies have their own style. However, the basic features examined in this chapter will be common to most companies, and you should now be able to work your way through almost any set of published accounts.

Note: An assignment covering the material in this chapter will be found at the end of Chapter 20.

Since the second edition of this book was prepared, the ASB has withdrawn SSAP 10 and replaced it with Financial Reporting Standard (FRS) No. 1 – Cash Flow Statements. The main aim of FRS 1 is to show the cash position of an entity much more clearly than was the case with SSAP 10.

Students should note that while the FRS 1 format is somewhat different from SSAP 10, many of the adjustments required to compile the Cash Flow Statement are very similar.

---

20 Supplementary statements and reports

Learning objectives

1 outline the effect of inflation on a set of accounts prepared under the historic cost convention;

2 identify the main items that need to be adjusted in order to counteract the effect of inflation;

3 summarize the various techniques that may be used in preparing a set of inflation adjusted accounts;

and

4 detail the nature and purpose of a number of other reports that may be contained within a limited liability company's annual report.

Annual reports usually contain other statements and reports besides the ones examined in the previous two chapters. There are no legal or professional accounting requirements that make it necessary to produce additional statements, although at various times the Accounting Standards Committee (now the Accounting Standards Board) has given much encouragement to the publication of a variety of reports.

The amount, type and format of additional statements varies enormously. In this chapter four of the more common types of supplementary statements and reports will be examined. These are as follows:

1 inflation adjusted reports;
2 value added statements;
3 statistical summaries; and
4 employee reports.

Inflation adjusted reports

In recent years the accountancy profession has produced a number of proposals that would allow for the effect of inflation on accounts prepared on the basis of the historic cost convention. All of these proposals have been abandoned, largely because it is not easy to gain acceptance for any new method of accounting that would replace one that has been in existence for centuries. Before examining these proposals it is necessary to explain something about the nature of inflation, and what effect it has on accounts prepared under the *historic cost* convention.

Inflation and its effect

There is no satisfactory definition of inflation. For the purpose of this text, it can be regarded as either an upward movement in prices, or a downwards movement in the purchasing power of the monetary unit. In other words, during a period of inflation, £100 available in cash in 19X1 will purchase fewer goods in 19X2 than £100 would purchase in 19X1. Thus in order to purchase the same amount of goods in 19X2 as were purchased in 19X1, more than £100 would have to be paid.

As far as accounting is concerned, the effect of inflation on the traditional historic cost accounts can be stated quite simply: it tends to overstate profit. The proprietors may then withdraw the profit in cash. As a result, it may be difficult to pay for new stocks and to replace the fixed assets. If it cannot find alternative sources of finance, then the entity may have to reduce its operating activities.

The main effects of inflation on historic cost accounts may be summarized as follows:

1 *Closing stock value.* The closing stock usually has a higher value than goods purchased in earlier periods. A high closing stock figure tends to overstate the gross profit (because the closing stock is *deducted* from the opening stock + purchases). However, when the stock is eventually sold it will probably cost more to replace than it did when it was purchased.
2 *Depreciation understated.* Depreciation is usually based on the historic cost of the asset. Assets will usually be replaced at a greater cost, so insufficient resources will have been set aside if the depreciation charge is based on the historic cost.
3 *Loss on loans.* If the entity has put some of its funds into short- or long-term loans (such as in a bank deposit account or into debenture stock), such loans will lose value in a period of inflation. The entity might have invested (say) £10,000 in debenture stock in 19X1 that will be repaid in 19X5. In 19X5 the entity will receive £10,000, but £10,000 received in 19X5 will not purchase the same amount of goods as £10,000 did in 19X1. Consequently, the entity loses by investing in an investment that is fixed in money terms.
It also loses by allowing credit to its customers. Such debts will

be fixed in money terms, so that when the cash is eventually received it will purchase fewer goods.

4 *Gains on borrowings.* An entity does not always lose during a period of inflation. It benefits if it borrows money on a short-term or on a long-term basis. Goods purchased on credit terms, for example, will be settled in *money* terms, but the monetary payment will then be worth less than it was when it was originally incurred. Similarly, by borrowing money through issuing debentures, it will eventually have to pay back less money in *real* terms than it borrowed.

The accountancy profession's answer

In trying to cope with the effect of inflation on historic cost accounts, two main schools of thought have evolved. These are as follows:

The current purchasing power school

This school argues that the historic cost accounts should be adjusted on the basis of some suitable inflation index. In the United Kingdom, the index usually recommended is known as the *retail price index* (RPI). The RPI suffers from two main disadvantages:

1 it measures the effect of inflation on retail consumption; and
2 it does not necessarily measure the effect of inflation on a specific company.

Nonetheless, the current purchasing power (CPP) method of allowing for inflation is relatively easy to adopt, and it has the advantage of still retaining the historic cost accounting rule. Each transaction (or collection of transactions) is measured against the index at the time that it was purchased, and compared with the index at the end of the relevant accounting period. The historic cost of the transaction is adjusted by multiplying it by the closing index and dividing it by the opening index. Take, for example, the following information:

	£	RPI
Fixed asset purchased on 1.1.X1:	1,000	100
Historic cost accounts prepared on 31.12.X1		120

∴ In the current purchasing power accounts the fixed asset would be shown as:

$$\frac{(£1,000 \times 120)}{100} = £1,200$$

It is possible that many tables and charts in an annual report have been adjusted on a current purchasing power (CPP) basis, although it is unlikely that the main financial statements have been indexed in this way.

The current value school

In the United Kingdom, the CPP school was much in favour until about 1975, but since then it has lost out to the current value school. There are several versions of current value accounting. Essentially, the current value method requires fixed assets and stocks to be included in the accounts at their current value, rather than at their historic cost.

The main version of current value accounting used in the United Kingdom is known as *current cost accounting* (CCA). CCA became the subject of an accounting standard in 1980 (SSAP 16). Like all standards, it was supposed to be mandatory, but it became so unpopular that it was withdrawn at the end of 1985.

SSAP 16 was a very complicated statement (probably one reason for its unpopularity). Basically, what it tried to do was to reduce the level of the historic cost profit in order to allow for the effect of inflation. Thus the entity would always be able to retain sufficient funds in the business to be able to continue operating at the same level that it had done in the past. In other words, it could maintain its *operating capability*.

The statement required four main adjustments to be made to the historic cost profit and loss account, and two to the balance sheet. Each of these adjustments will be considered separately, so that you may judge for yourself whether they meet the problems of accounting for inflation that were outlined earlier. The profit and loss account adjustments may be summarized as follows:

1   *A cost of sales adjustment (COSA).* This adjustment required both the opening and closing stock to be adjusted (normally by indexing, using a method similar to that adopted in CPP accounting) to a value which represented the average value of stock for the period. Hence both the opening and the closing stock was put on the same price base as the purchases made during the period.

2   *An additional depreciation adjustment (ADA).* This adjustment meant that the depreciation charge for the year was normally based on the *replacement* cost of the asset, rather than on its historic cost.

3   *A monetary working capital adjustment (MWCA).* Monetary working capital is basically the difference between trade debtors and trade creditors. SSAP 16 required an adjustment to be made for monetary working capital for the reasons outlined earlier, i.e. in times of inflation, entities gain by borrowing and lose by lending. This adjustment made an allowance for such gains and losses. The adjustment was made by adjusting both the opening net monetary

working capital and the closing net monetary working capital so that they were measured on the same price basis. The opening and closing values were usually indexed so that they both represented the average value for the year. The adjustment was very similar to that adopted for making the cost of sales adjustment.

4 *A gearing adjustment (GA).* It is quite customary for a company to finance its operations partly from long-term borrowings, often in the form of debentures. As argued earlier, if a company has borrowed money on a long-term basis during a period of inflation it will benefit, because by the time that the company comes to repay the loan, the purchasing power of the original loan will have declined.

The cost of sales adjustment, the additional depreciation adjustment, and the monetary working capital adjustment all normally reduce the profit available for distribution to the shareholders. It seems only fair, therefore, that if shareholders are also to benefit from inflation as a result of long-term borrowings, then their profit should be increased by a proportion of any inflationary gain.

The gearing adjustment tried to measure the extent of the shareholders' gain. It was a highly complex and controversial adjustment. The total of the three other profit and loss account adjustments (COSA, ADA and MWCA) were reduced by that proportion of the company financed by long-term borrowings. Suppose, for example, that the total of COSA + ADA + MWCA = £10,000, and that the gearing proportion was 20% (i.e. average long-term borrowings amounted to 20% of the average net operating assets), then £2,000 (£10,000 × 20%) would be credited to the profit and loss account. To allow for inflation, the *net* extra cost to the profit and loss account would then be £8,000 (£10,000 − £2,000).

The two balance sheet adjustments required under SSAP 16 were as follows:

1 *Fixed assets.* These were normally to be included at their net replacement cost (i.e. their gross replacement cost less the accumulated depreciation based on that replacement cost). In effect, the gross replacement cost would be what the company would have to pay for similar assets if they had been replaced at the balance sheet date.

2 *Closing stocks.* The closing stocks were also to be included in the balance sheet at their replacement cost as at the date of the balance sheet.

It should be noted that these six adjustments (four in the profit and loss account and two in the balance sheet) would alter the balancing of the accounts. SSAP 16 enabled the double entry to be completed by entering the above adjustments in a corresponding account called the *current cost reserve account.* This account was simply a balancing account, and it was entered in the capital and reserves section of the balance sheet.

The current position

As a result of the abandonment of SSAP 16, most companies do not prepare current cost accounts. Some companies, however, produce summaries of their historic cost accounts adjusted for inflation. They do this in one of two ways:

1 either they index some (if not all) of their historic cost results by adopting a CPP approach; or
2 they adjust both their fixed assets and closing stocks on to a value basis (even if they do not produce a full set of SSAP 16 adjusted accounts).

The non-accountant need not be unduly concerned with the technicalities of accounting for inflation, although you should be *aware* of the misleading impression gained by using summaries based on historic cost accounts.

Ideally, you should also make some allowance for inflation. In the absence of any other information, you should use the retail price index to convert the data on to a current purchasing power basis.

Value added statements

In 1975 the Accounting Standards Committee (its work has now been taken over by the Accounting Standards Board) published a discussion paper called 'The Corporate Report'. The purpose of the study was to re-examine the aims and scope of the published financial reports. The Committee suggested that there was a need for entities to publish a number of additional reports to complement the main financial statements. One of the reports recommended was a *statement of value added* (or a value added statement).

Value added was defined as 'the wealth created by the entity as a result of the collective efforts of capital, employees and management'. It was argued that the statement should show how the value was added (basically, sales revenue less materials and purchased services), and how that value was used (basically to pay employees, shareholders and the government).

As a result of 'The Corporate Report', some companies began to include a value added statement in their annual reports, but they have not become very popular. Nonetheless, they are a useful addition to an annual report. In format, they appear very similar to statements of source and application of funds: the first part of the statement explains where the *value* has come from, and the second part of the statement outlines where it has gone to.

As there are no statutory or professional accountancy requirements supporting the inclusion of a value added statement in an annual report, there is little agreement about their precise format. The format of a value added statement will be illustrated, therefore, by adopting the example used in 'The Corporate Report'. The details are shown in Exhibit 20.1.

Exhibit 20.1: Example of a value added statement

ENERGY PUBLIC LIMITED COMPANY
Group value added statement for the year to 31 March 19X2

	19X2		19X1	
	£000	%	£000	%
Turnover (1)	1,500		1,200	
Brought-in materials and services (2)	(1,000)		(800)	
	500		400	
Other incomes (3)	50		40	
Total value added (4)	£550		£440	
Applied the following ways:				
To pay employees (5)				
Wages, pensions and fringe benefits	300	55	280	64
To pay providers of capital (5)				
Interest on loans	30		25	
Dividends to shareholders	60		55	
	90	16	80	18
To pay government (5)				
Corporation tax payable	45	8	40	9
To provide for maintenance and expansion of capital (5)				
Depreciation	40		35	
Retained profits	75		5	
	115	21	40	9
Total value added (6)	£550	100%	£440	100%

Note: The numbers in brackets after some of the narrations refer to the tutorial notes given below. The amounts have been included purely for illustrative purposes.

Tutorial notes

1 Turnover represents sales to external customers, net of trade discounts, value added tax and other sales taxes.
2 Bought-in materials and services includes the cost of sales.
3 Other incomes include investment income.
4 Total value added is the wealth created during the particular period in question.

5 The disposition of the wealth is shown under four main headings: (a) to pay employees; (b) to pay the providers of capital; (c) to pay the government; and (d) to provide for maintenance and expansion of the assets.
6 The total disposition should agree with the total value added (see tutorial note 4).

The information needed to compile a value added statement comes from the profit and loss account. The statement is simply a rearrangement of the information contained in that account. However, the amount of value added cannot be directly linked with any specific balance in the profit and loss account.

A value added statement has several uses. Some of the main ones are summarized below:

1 It provides additional information about the company's performance.
2 It shows the increase in the company's resources.
3 It highlights the proportion of the value added paid to the employees.
4 It shows the contribution paid to the government.
5 It helps in implementing profit schemes, in encouraging employee participation, and in creating a more co-operative working environment.

A value added statement may be seen, therefore, as something of a political statement. If it is viewed in this light, then it clearly will not achieve some of the benefits claimed for it by its advocates.

Statistical summaries

One of the accounting rules dealt with in Chapter 2 was the *periodicity* rule. It was suggested that in order to provide a report for the owners of the business, it was necessary to establish an accounting period of some consistent length. In most circumstances, entities have tended to adopt an accounting period equivalent to twelve calendar months. Such a period is quite an artificial period of time, especially in the case of those entities that have an unlimited life.

In recent years, companies have begun to realize that it may be misleading to present their results purely in terms of one year's results alongside a comparison of last year's results. As a result, it has now become common for companies to include statistical summaries in their annual reports covering a period well in excess of a calendar year.

There are no legal or professional accounting requirements covering such summaries, and there is no general agreement on what period they should cover. Some companies adopt a five year period, while others prepare them over a ten year period. The contents of such statements are again subject to much variety. The data may include, for example, summaries of sales, profit and dividends, assets employed and cash flow. The basic financial data may be accompanied by key statistics and a number of selected accounting ratios. An example of a five year financial summary is illustrated in Exhibit 20.2.

Exhibit 20.2: Example of a five year financial summary

ENERGY PUBLIC LIMITED COMPANY

	19X1 £m	19X2 £m	19X3 £m	19X4 £m	19X5 £m
Profit summary					
Turnover	9	14	28	52	85
Profit before taxation	1	2	5	8	9
Balance sheet items					
Tangible fixed assets	15	18	20	23	45
Net current assets	180	200	210	220	230
Called up share capital	5	15	15	30	30
Reserves	100	150	180	200	250
Statistics					
Earnings per ordinary share	20p	30p	50p	110p	120p
Dividends per ordinary share	5p	10p	15p	20p	25p
Dividend cover (times)	5	5	6	10	10

Note: The values have been shown purely for illustrative purposes. Some companies produce very detailed summaries.

Statistical summaries that cover a long period of time are helpful in establishing trends, but it is important to put each year's results on to a consistent basis. Legal and professional accounting requirements do change over a five to a ten year period, and the company may also have altered its accounting policies.

If a fair comparison is to be made between the respective periods, it is also essential that some allowance be made for inflation. Remember that at a rate of inflation of 5% per annum, prices increase by about 30% over a five year period, and double over a fifteen year period.

Employee reports

The Companies Act 1985 pays very little attention to the interests of employees. It has been left largely to employment protection legislation to encourage employee reporting, and many companies now prepare reports specifically for their employees. Such information may be included as a special section in the shareholders' annual report, or it may be included in an additional report.

As yet, there is little clear guidance about the form and content of employee reports. There is a tendency for them to be just a simplified and shortened version of the shareholders' report. They sometimes use elaborate charts and diagrams, often in many different types of print, styles and colours. In many cases, they make no attempt to translate accounting terminology into the sort of language that everyone can understand, and sometimes their linguistic style is highly condescending. There is still much work to do before the accountancy profession is in a position to produce an acceptable employee report.

Students are recommended to collect examples of employee reports, and then to decide whether the style and contents may be both appealing and useful to employees.

Conclusion

This chapter has examined a number of supplementary statements and reports that might well be found in a company's annual report. All such reports should contain the main financial statements, namely a profit and loss account, a balance sheet, and a statement of source and application of funds. Beyond that, the number, type, style and variety of reports will vary from company to company.

Some annual reports may contain the absolute minimum amount of statutory and professional accountancy information, while other reports will contain so much information that it is difficult to absorb it all. However, regardless of the exact format of an annual report, the student who has worked his way through this book should now be in an excellent position to make the most of any such report, no matter what it contains.

Assignment

For this assignment, you are required to obtain a copy of the annual report of a public limited liability company. It does not really matter what type of company you choose, although you are recommended to obtain the accounts of a manufacturing company as such companies are more likely to follow the format that has been adopted in this book. You are advised to avoid banks, building societies, insurance companies, investment trusts, and unit trusts, since their accounts will probably be somewhat different from the ones that have been described in the last four chapters.

The purpose of the assignment is to help you become more familiar with the contents of an annual report. By having to find out the answers to some fairly difficult questions, you will have to search through the report most carefully. It is hoped that by doing so, you will soon know where to look for certain types of important information.

Required:

Examine the annual report of a public limited liability company, and then answer the following questions (if the report covers a group of companies, answer for the group):

1 What amount was paid to charity during the year?
2 Were there any exceptional items listed in the profit and loss account? If so, what were they, and for how much?
3 What depreciation method(s) did the company adopt?
4 How much was the chairman paid?
5 What was the total amount of dividends paid and proposed?
6 Were there any extraordinary items? If so, what for, and how much?
7 What was the total net book value of the tangible fixed assets?
8 How much ordinary dividend was paid and payable per share?
9 If the company held assets overseas, what rates of exchange did it adopt for converting overseas currencies into sterling?
10 What amount of political donations were paid during the year, and to whom?
11 What was the profit on ordinary activities for the year before taxation?
12 What was the balance on the deferred taxation account?
13 What was the total amount of the minority interest?
14 What was the turnover for the year?
15 What was the total of the shareholders' funds?
16 What were the auditors' fees?
17 How many directors had the company?
18 What was the dividend cover?
19 What amount was paid for the hire of plant and machinery?
20 What was the total of the directors' emoluments?
21 How many employees had the company?
22 What were the principal activities of the company during the year?
23 Were there any qualifications in the auditors' report? If so, what were they?
24 What method did the company use for valuing its stock?
25 What were the earnings per share?
26 Were the accounts prepared under the historic cost convention?
27 Did the company disclose details of any conditions or events that were uncertain at the balance sheet date? If so, what were these conditions and events? Has the company been able to estimate their financial effects?
28 Did the company produce any supplementary accounting statements? If so, what were they?
29 Did the total of current assets exceed the total of short-term creditors? If so, by how much?
30 What date were the accounts signed, and by whom?

Questions (without solutions)

20.1 The following trial balance has been extracted from the books of Grieve Public Limited Company as at 31 December 19X1:

	Dr £000	Cr £000
Accruals		1,800
Administrative expenses	4,200	
Called up share capital (£1 ordinary shares)		5,600
Cash and bank	200	
Distribution costs	1,800	
Extraordinary income		100
Fixed assets: at cost	5,500	
Accumulated depreciation (at 31 December 19X1)		2,000
Prepayments	300	
Profit and loss account		900
Purchases	11,000	
Sales		18,000
Stock (at 1 January 19X1)	2,000	
Trade creditors		1,600
Trade debtors	5,000	
	£30,000	£30,000

Additional information:
1 Stocks at 31 December 19X1: £3,000,000.
2 Corporation tax based on the profit for the year at a rate of 35% is estimated to be £1,000,000.
3 The corporation tax on the extraordinary income is estimated to be £25,000.
4 Assume that the basic rate of income tax is 25%.
5 The company proposes to pay an ordinary dividend of 10p per share.

Required:
Insofar as the information permits, prepare Grieve's profit and loss account for the year to 31 December 19X1 and a balance sheet as at that date in accordance with the Companies Act 1985 and related statements of standard accounting practice.

20.2 On 1 April 19X2, Duff Limited purchased an 80% holding in Ruff Limited. The following extracts relate to the financial year ending 31 March 19X3:

		Duff Ltd £000	Ruff Ltd £000
Profit and loss accounts			
Sales		1,400	400
Cost of sales		(640)	(280)
Gross profit	c/f	760	120

		£000	£000
	b/f	760	120
Distribution costs		(50)	(20)
Administrative expenses		(550)	(40)
Profit before taxation		160	60
Taxation		(20)	(30)
Profit after taxation		140	30
Dividends		(120)	(10)
Retained profits		£ 20	£ 20

Balance sheets

	£000	£000
Fixed assets at net book value	450	150
Investment		
Ruff Limited	150	—
Current assets		
Stocks	160	30
Debtors	1,000	60
Cash and bank	30	10
	1,190	100
Current liabilities		
Creditors	(430)	(50)
Taxation	(20)	(30)
Dividend	(120)	(10)
	(570)	(90)
	£1,220	£160
Capital and reserves		
Called up share capital (£1 ordinary shares)	800	100
Profit and loss account	420	60
	£1,220	£160

Additional information:
1 Ruff's profit and loss account at 1 April 19X2 was £40,000.
2 Ignore advance corporation tax.
3 Any goodwill arising on acquisition should be written off immediately at the time of acquisition.

Required:
Prepare the Duff Group of Companies consolidated profit and loss account for the year to 31 March 19X3, and a consolidated balance sheet as at that date. (Ignore the detailed disclosure provisions of the Companies Act 1985.)

Appendix 1 Further reading

Lecturers may want to encourage students to expand on some of the exhibits and questions used in this book by reference to other accounting works. Although this book contains sufficient accounting material for most first year courses in accounting, some students may want to add to their knowledge of the subject.

There are many accounting books available for *accounting* students, but they usually go into considerable technical and specialist detail, so they must be used with caution. Lecturers will need to be very careful, therefore, that non-accounting students do not become totally confused if they begin to use such texts.

Bearing this point in mind, the following books are worth considering.

Financial accounting

Jennings, A. R.: *Financial Accounting*, DPP Publications, London, 1990.
This book will be helpful to students for reference purposes.

Laughlin, R. C. and Gray, R. H.: *Financial Accounting – method and meaning*, Van Nostrand Reinhold, London, 1988.
This book is aimed at the first and second year undergraduate market, so it is probably safe to use.

Wood, F.: *Business Accounting*, Volumes 1 and 2, 5th e., Pitman, 1989.
Wood is the master accounting text-book writer. His books can be recommended with absolute confidence.

Management accounting

Drury, C.: *Management and Cost Accounting*, 2nd e., Van Nostrand Reinhold, 1988.
This book is an advanced book that has become the established British text on the subject. It will prove a valuable reference book, but non-accountants must use it with very great care.

Wilson, R. M. S. and Chua, W. F.: *Managerial Accounting – method and meaning*, Van Nostrand Reinhold, London, 1988.
This book is aimed at the first and second year undergraduate market. Non-accounting students will probably find it easier to follow than Drury.

Exercises

Dyson, J. R.: *Case Studies in Basic Accounting*, Pitman, London, 1990.
This is the companion volume to *Accounting for non-accounting students*.

Dyson, J. R.: *Intermediate Accounting*, DPP Publications, London, 1989.
This book covers both basic and intermediate financial accounting. It contains
a great many questions suitable for non-accounting students.

Appendix 2 Discount table

Present value of £1 received after n years discounted at $i\%$

i	1	2	3	4	5	6	7	8	9	10
n										
1	.9901	.9804	.9709	.9615	.9524	.9434	.9346	.9259	.9174	.9091
2	.9803	.9612	.9426	.9246	.9070	.8900	.8734	.8573	.8417	.8264
3	.9706	.9423	.9151	.8890	.8638	.8396	.8163	.7938	.7722	.7513
4	.9610	.9238	.8885	.8548	.8227	.7921	.7629	.7350	.7084	.6830
5	.9515	.9057	.8626	.8219	.7835	.7473	.7130	.6806	.6499	.6209
6	.9420	.8880	.8375	.7903	.7462	.7050	.6663	.6302	.5963	.5645

i	11	12	13	14	15	16	17	18	19	20
n										
1	.9009	.8929	.8850	.8772	.8696	.8621	.8547	.8475	.8403	.8333
2	.8116	.7929	.7831	.7695	.7561	.7432	.7305	.7182	.7062	.6944
3	.7312	.7118	.6931	.6750	.6575	.6407	.6244	.6086	.5934	.5787
4	.6587	.6355	.6133	.5921	.5718	.5523	.5337	.5158	.4987	.4823
5	.5935	.5674	.5428	.5194	.4972	.4761	.4561	.4371	.4190	.4019
6	.5346	.5066	.4803	.4556	.4323	.4104	.3910	.3704	.3521	.3349

Appendix 3 Answers to questions

Chapter 1

1.1 (a) To keep a record of the company's day-to-day progress.
   (b) To prepare the company's annual financial accounts.
   (c) To supply information to the management for decision-making and control.
   (d) To operate a system of internal auditing.
   (e) To minimize the company's tax liabilities.

1.2 It is required by law. External auditors report to the shareholders on whether the accounts represent a true and fair view (the discovery of fraud is only incidental to this purpose).

1.3 Accountants collect a great deal of information about a company's activities and then translate it into monetary terms — a language that everyone understands. The information that is collected can help non-accountants do their job more effectively because it provides them with better guidance upon which to take decisions, but the decision is still theirs. Furthermore, all managers must be aware of the statutory accounting obligations to which their company has to adhere if they are to avoid taking part in unlawful acts.

1.4 No. The preparation of management accounts is for the company to decide if it believes that they serve a useful purpose.

1.5 Yes. These are contained in the Companies Act 1985. In addition, listed companies have to abide by certain Stock Exchange requirements, and qualified accountants are also bound by a great many mandatory professional requirements.

1.6 To collect and store detailed information about an entity's activities, and then to abstract it and summarize it in the most effective way for whatever purpose it is intended to be used.

Chapter 2

2.1 *1* Matching.
   2 Historic cost.
   3 Quantitative.
   4 Periodicity.

      5 Prudence.
      6 Going-concern.

2.2 *1* Relevance.
      2 Entity.
      3 Consistency.
      4 Materiality.
      5 Historic cost.
      6 Realization.

2.3 *1* Entity.
      2 Objectivity.
      3 Periodicity.
      4 Prudence.
      5 Dual aspect.
      6 Realization.

2.4 *1* (a) Prudence.
         (b) The long-term services obtained from a professional footballer are highly unpredictable.
      2 (a) Realization.
         (b) Although it may appear somewhat imprudent to do so, the risk is usually small in taking profit prior to the receipt of cash.
      3 (a) Entity.
         (b) The company does not have a legal title to the house.
      4 (a) Prudence.
         (b) The profit cannot be known for sometime (although in some cases a proportion may be claimed if the final outcome is reasonably certain).
      5 (a) Materiality.
         (b) It would be unduly pedantic to insist on matching the cost of small stocks of stationery purchased in an earlier period with the revenue of a future period.
      6 (a) Prudence.
         (b) The improvement work may never result in a more successful revenue earning drug. (NB: In certain specific instances, earlier period costs on development work may be matched with revenues earned after the work has been completed.)

Chapter 3

3.1 Adam's books of account:

	Account	
	Debit	*Credit*
1	Cash	Capital
2	Purchases	Cash
3	Van	Cash

4	Rent	Cash
5	Cash	Sales
6	Office machinery	Cash

3.2 Brown's books of account:

		Account
	Debit	*Credit*
1	Bank	Cash
2	Cash	Sales
3	Purchases	Bank
4	Office expenses	Cash
5	Bank	Sales
6	Motor car	Bank

3.3 Corby's books of account:

		Account
	Debit	*Credit*
1	Purchases	Smith
2	Cash	Capital
3	Cash	Sales
4	Purchases	Cash
5	Bank	Cash
6	Machinery	Cash

3.4 Davies' books of account:

		Account
	Debit	*Credit*
1	Bank	Capital
2	Purchases	Swallow
3	Cash	Sales
4	Purchases	Cash
5	Dale	Sales
6	Motoring expenses	Bank

3.5 Edgar's books of account:

		Account
	Debit	*Credit*
1	Purchases	Gill
2	Ash	Sales
3	Cash	Sales
4	Purchases	Cash
5	Gill	Bank
6	Cash	Ash

3.6 Ford's books of account:

	Debit	Credit
1	Cash	Sales
2	Purchases	Carter
3	Holly	Sales
4	Purchases	Cash
5	Sales returns	Holly
6	Carter	Purchases returns

3.7 Gordon's books of account:

	Debit	Credit
1	Purchases	Watson
2	Cash	Sales
3	Moon	Sales
4	Watson	Bank
5	Watson	Discounts received
6	Cash	Moon
7	Discounts allowed	Moon
8	Purchases	Cash

3.8 Harry's books of account:

	Debit	Credit
1	Cash	Capital
2	Bank	Cash
3	Rent	Bank
4	Purchases	Paul
5	Van	Bank
6	Cash	Sales
7	Purchases	Nancy
8	Motoring expenses	Cash
9	Nancy	Purchases returns
10	Mavis	Sales
11	Drawings	Cash
12	Purchases	Cash
13	Sales return	Mavis
14	Nancy	Bank
15	Cash	Mavis
16	Nancy	Discounts received
17	Discounts allowed	Mavis
18	Petty cash	Bank

3.9 Ivan's ledger accounts:

Cash Account

		£			£
1.9.X9	Capital	10,000	2.9.X9	Bank	8,000
12.9.X9	Cash	3,000	3.9.X9	Purchases	1,000

Capital Account

					£
			1.9.X9	Cash	10,000

Bank Account

		£			£
2.9.X9	Cash	8,000	20.9.X9	Roy	6,000
30.9.X9	Norman	2,000			

Purchases Account

		£			£
3.9.X9	Cash	1,000			
10.9.X9	Roy	6,000			

Roy's Account

		£			£
20.9.X9	Bank	6,000	10.9.X9	Purchases	6,000

Sales Account

		£			£
			12.9.X9	Cash	3,000
			15.9.X9	Norman	4,000

Norman

		£			£
15.9.X9	Sales	4,000	30.9.X9	Bank	2,000

3.10 Jones' ledger accounts.

Bank Account

		£			£
1.10.X1	Capital	20,000	10.10.X1	Petty cash	1,000
			25.10.X1	Lang	5,000
			29.10.X1	Green	10,000

Capital Account

					£
			1.10.X1	Bank	20,000

Van Account

		£			£
2.10.X1	Lang	5,000			

Lang's Account

		£			£
25.10.X1	Bank	5,000	2.10.X1	Van	5,000

Purchases Account

		£			£
6.10.X1	Green	15,000			
20.10.X1	Cash	3,000			

Green's Account

		£			£
28.10.X1	Discounts received	500	6.10.X1	Purchases	15,000
29.10.X1	Bank	10,000			

Petty Cash Account

		£			£
10.10.X1	Bank	1,000	22.10.X1	Miscellaneous Expenses	500

Sales

		£			£
			14.10.X1	Haddock	6,000
			18.10.X1	Cash	5,000

Haddock

		£			£
14.10.X1	Sales	6,000	30.10.X1	Discounts allowed	600
			31.10.X1	Cash	5,400

Cash Account

		£			£
18.10.X1	Sales	5,000	20.10.X1	Purchases	3,000
31.10.X1	Haddock	5,400			

Miscellaneous Expenses

		£		£
22.10.X1	Petty cash	500		

Discounts Received Account

	£			£
		28.10.X1	Green	500

Discounts Allowed Account

		£		£
30.10.X1	Haddock	600		

3.11 Ken's ledger accounts:

Cash Account

		£			£
1.11.X2	Capital	15,000	2.11.X2	Bank	14,000
27.11.X2	Sales	5,000	28.11.X2	Purchases	4,000
			30.11.X2	Bank	1,000

Capital Account

		£			£
			10.11.X2	Cash	15,000

Bank Account

		£			£
2.11.X2	Cash	14,000	3.11.X2	Rent	1,000
30.11.X2	Main	1,000	26.11.X2	Office expenses	2,000
30.11.X2	Pain	2,000	29.11.X2	Ace	4,000
30.11.X2	Vain	3,000	29.11.X2	Mace	5,000
30.11.X2	Cash	1,000	29.11.X2	Pace	6,000

Rent Account

		£		£
3.11.X2	Bank	1,000		

Purchases Account

		£		£
4.11.X2	Ace	5,000		
4.11.X2	Mace	6,000		
4.11.X2	Pace	7,000		
25.11.X2	Ace	3,000		
25.11.X2	Mace	4,000		
25.11.X2	Pace	5,000		
28.11.X2	Cash	4,000		

Ace's Account

		£			£
29.11.X2	Bank	4,000	4.11.X2	Purchases	5,000
30.11.X2	Discounts received	200	25.11.X2	Purchases	3,000

Mace's Account

		£			£
29.11.X2	Bank	5,000	4.11.X2	Purchases	6,000
30.11.X2	Discounts received	250	25.11.X2	Purchases	4,000

Pace's Account

		£			£
15.11.X2	Purchases returns	1,000	4.11.X2	Purchases	7,000
29.11.X2	Bank	6,000	25.11.X2	Purchases	5,000
30.11.X2	Discounts received	300			

Sales Account

		£			£
			10.11.X2	Main	2,000
			10.11.X2	Pain	3,000
			10.11.X2	Vain	4,000
			27.11.X2	Cash	5,000

Main's Account

		£			£
10.11.X2	Sales	2,000	30.11.X2	Bank	1,000
			30.11.X2	Discounts allowed	100

Pain's Account

		£			£
10.11.X2	Sales	3,000	22.11.X2	Sales return	2,000
			30.11.X2	Bank	2,000
			30.11.X2	Discounts allowed	200

Vain's Account

		£			£
10.11.X2	Sales	4,000	30.11.X2	Bank	3,000
			30.11.X2	Discounts allowed	400

Purchases Returns Account

		£			£
			15.11.X2	Pace	1,000

Sales Returns Account

		£			£
22.11.X2	Pain	2,000			

Office Expenses Account

		£			£
26.11.X2	Bank	2,000			

Discounts Received Account

	£			£
		30.11.X2	Ace	200
		30.11.X2	Mace	250
		30.11.X2	Pace	300

Discounts Allowed Account

		£		£
30.11.X2	Main	100		
30.11.X2	Pain	200		
30.11.X2	Vain	400		

3.12 (a), (b) and (c) Pat's ledger accounts:

Bank Cash Account

		£			£
1.12.X3	Capital	10,000	24.12.X3	Office expenses	5,000
29.12.X3	Fog	4,000	31.12.X3	Grass	6,000
29.12.X3	Mist	6,000	31.12.X3	Seed	8,000
			31.12.X3	Balance c/d	1,000
		£20,000			£20,000
1.1.X4	Balance b/d	1,000			

Capital Account

		£			£
			1.12.X3	Cash	10,000

Purchases Account

		£			£
2.12.X3	Grass	6,000			
2.12.X3	Seed	7,000			
15.12.X3	Grass	3,000			
15.12.X3	Seed	4,000	31.12.X3	Balance c/d	20,000
		£20,000			£20,000
1. 1.X4	Balance b/d	20,000			

Grass's Account

		£			£
12.12.X3	Purchases returns	1,000	2.12.X3	Purchases	6,000
31.12.X3	Cash	6,000	15.12.X3	Purchases	3,000
31.12.X3	Balance c/d	2,000			
		£9,000			£9,000
			1. 1.X4	Balance b/d	2,000

Seed's Account

		£			£
12.12.X3	Purchases returns	2,000	2.12.X3	Purchases	7,000
31.12.X3	Cash	8,000	15.12.X3	Purchases	4,000
31.12.X3	Balance c/d	1,000			
		£11,000			£11,000
			1. 1.X4	Balance b/d	1,000

Sales Account

		£			£
			10.12.X3	Fog	3,000
			10.12.X3	Mist	4,000
			20.12.X3	Fog	2,000
31.12.X3	Balance c/d	12,000	20.12.X3	Mist	3,000
		£12,000			£12,000
			1. 1.X4	Balance b/d	12,000

Fog's Account

		£			£
10.12.X3	Sales	3,000	29.12.X3	Cash	4,000
20.12.X3	Sales	2,000	31.12.X3	Balance c/d	1,000
		£5,000			£5,000
1. 1.X4	Balance b/d	1,000			

Mist's Account

		£			£
10.12.X3	Sales	4,000	29.12.X3	Cash	6,000
20.12.X3	Sales	3,000	31.12.X3	Balance c/d	1,000
		£7,000			£7,000
1. 1.X4	Balance b/d	1,000			

Purchases Returns Account

		£			£
			12.12.X3	Grass	1,000
31.12.X3	Balance c/d	3,000	12.12.X3	Seed	2,000
		£3,000			£3,000
			1. 1.X4	Balance b/d	3,000

Office Expenses Account

		£		£
24.12.X3	Cash	5,000		

Tutorial note

It is unnecessary to balance off an account and bring down the balance if there is only a single entry in it.

(d)

PAT
Trial Balance at 31 December 19X3

	£ Dr	£ Cr
Cash	1,000	
Capital		10,000
Purchases	20,000	
Grass		2,000
Seed		1,000
Sales		12,000
Fog	1,000	
Mist	1,000	
Purchases returns		3,000
Office expenses	5,000	
	£28,000	£28,000

3.13 (a) Vale's books of account:

Bank Account

		£			£
1. 1.X3	Balance b/d	5,000	31.12.X3	Dodd	29,000
31.12.X3	Fish	45,000	31.12.X3	Delivery van	12,000
31.12.X3	Cash	3,000	31.12.X3	Balance c/d	12,000
		£53,000			£53,000
1. 1.X4	Balance b/d	12,000			

Capital Account

		£			£
			1. 1.X3	Balance b/d	20,000

Cash Account

		£			£
1. 1.X3	Balance b/d	1,000	31.12.X3	Purchases	15,000
31.12.X3	Sales	20,000	31.12.X3	Office expenses	9,000
31.12.X3	Fish	7,000	31.12.X3	Bank	3,000
			31.12.X3	Balance c/d	1,000
		£28,000			£28,000
1. 1.X4	Balance b/d	1,000			

Dodd's Account

		£			£
31.12.X3	Bank	29,000	1. 1.X3	Balance b/d	2,000
31.12.X3	Balance c/d	3,000	31.12.X3	Purchases	30,000
		£32,000			£32,000
			1. 1.X4	Balance b/d	3,000

Fish's Account

		£			£
1. 1.X3	Balance b/d	6,000	31.12.X3	Bank	45,000
31.12.X3	Sales	50,000	31.12.X3	Cash	7,000
			31.12.X3	Balance c/d	4,000
		£56,000			£56,000
1. 1.X4	Balance b/d	4,000			

Furniture Account

		£		£
1. 1.X3	Balance b/d	10,000		

Purchases Account

		£			£
31.12.X3	Cash	15,000			
31.12.X3	Dodd	30,000	31.12.X3	Balance c/d	45,000
		£45,000			£45,000
1. 1.X4	Balance b/d	45,000			

Sales Account

		£			£
			31.12.X3	Cash	20,000
31.12.X3	Balance c/d	70,000	31.12.X3	Fish	50,000
		£70,000			£70,000
			1. 1.X4	Balance b/d	70,000

Office Expenses Account

		£		£
31.12.X3	Cash	9,000		

Delivery Van Account

		£		£
31.12.X3	Bank	12,000		

(b)

VALE

Trial balance at 31 December 19X3

	Dr £	Cr £
Bank	12,000	
Capital		20,000
Cash	1,000	
Dodd		3,000
Fish	4,000	
Furniture	10,000	
Purchases	45,000	
Sales		70,000
Office expenses	9,000	
Delivery van	12,000	
	£93,000	£93,000

3.14 (a) Brian's ledger accounts:

Bank Account

		£			£
1.1.X4	Capital	25,000	2.1.X4	Rent	2,000
23.1.X4	Cash	6,000	25.1.X4	Petty cash	500
26.1.X4	Ann	5,500	29.1.X4	Savoy Motors	4,000
31.1.X4	Capital	5,000	30.1.X4	Linda	8,000
			30.1.X4	Sydney	2,000
			31.1.X4	Rent	2,000
			31.1.X4	Balance c/d	23,000
		£41,500			£41,500
1.2.X4	Balance b/d	23,000			

Capital Account

		£			£
			1.1.X4	Bank	25,000
31.1.X4	Balance c/d	30,000	31.1.X4	Bank	5,000
		£30,000			£30,000
			1.2.X4	Balance b/d	30,000

Rent Account

		£			£
2.1.X4	Bank	2,000			
31.1.X4	Bank	2,000	31.1.X4	Balance c/d	4,000
		£4,000			£4,000
1.2.X4	Balance b/d	4,000			

Purchases Account

		£			£
3.1.X4	Linda	5,000			
5.1.X4	Sydney	3,000			
15.1.X4	Linda	10,000	31.1.X4	Balance c/d	18,000
		£18,000			£18,000
1.2.X4	Balance b/d	18,000			

Linda's Account

		£			£
22.1.X4	Purchases return	2,000	3.1.X4	Purchases	5,000
30.1.X4	Bank	8,000	15.1.X4	Purchases	10,000
30.1.X4	Discounts received	700			
31.1.X4	Balance c/d	4,300			
		£15,000			£15,000
			1.2.X4	Balance b/d	4,300

Motor Car Account

		£			£
4.1.X4	Savoy Motors	4,000			

Savoy Motors Account

		£			£
29.1.X4	Bank	£4,000	4.1.X4	Motor car	£4,000

Sydney's Account

		£			£
30.1.X4	Bank	2,000	5.1.X4	Purchases	3,000
30.1.X4	Discounts received	100			
31.1.X4	Balance c/d	900			
		£3,000			£3,000
			1.2.X4	Balance b/d	900

Cash Account

		£			£
10.1.X4	Sales	£6,000	23.1.X4	Bank	£6,000

Sales Account

		£			£
			10.1.X4	Cash	6,000
31.1.X4	Balance c/d	14,000	20.1.X4	Ann	8,000
		£14,000			£14,000
			1.2.X4	Balance b/d	14,000

Ann's Account

		£			£
20.1.X4	Sales	8,000	24.1.X4	Sales return	1,000
			26.1.X4	Bank	5,500
			26.1.X4	Discounts allowed	500
			31.1.X4	Balance c/d	1,000
		£8,000			£8,000
1.2.X4	Balance b/d	1,000			

Purchases Returns Account

		£			£
			22.1.X4	Linda	2,000

Sales Returns Account

		£			£
24.1.X4	Ann	1,000			

Petty Cash Account

		£			£
25.1.X4	Bank	500	28.1.X4	Office expenses	250
			31.1.X4	Balance c/d	250
		£500			£500
1.1.X4	Balance b/d	250			

Discounts Allowed Account

		£			£
26.1.X4	Ann	500			

Office Expenses Account

		£			£
28.1.X4	Petty cash	250			

Discounts Received Account

		£			£
			30.1.X4	Linda	700
31.1.X4	Balance c/d	800	30.1.X4	Sydney	100
		£800			£800
			1.2.X4	Balance b/d	800

(b)

BRIAN
Trial balance at 31 January 19X4

	Dr £	Cr £
Bank	23,000	
Capital		30,000
Rent	4,000	
Purchases	18,000	
Linda		4,300
Motor car	4,000	
Sydney		900
Sales		14,000
Ann	1,000	
Purchases return		2,000
Sales return	1,000	
Petty cash	250	
Discounts allowed	500	
Office expenses	250	
Discounts received		800
	£52,000	£52,000

3.15

FIELD
Trial balance at 28 February 19X5

	Dr £	Cr £
Bank	13,000	
Cash	2,000	
Capital		15,000
Creditors		4,000
Debtors	10,000	
Drawings	5,000	
Electricity	4,000	
Furniture	7,000	
Office expenses	3,000	
Purchases	50,000	
Sales		100,000
Wages	25,000	
	£119,000	£119,000

3.16

TRENT

Corrected trial balance at 31 March 19X4

	Dr £	Cr £
Bank (overdrawn)		2,000
Capital		50,000
Discounts allowed	5,000	
Discounts received		3,000
Dividends received		2,000
Drawings	23,000	
Investments	14,000	
Land and buildings	60,000	
Office expenses	18,000	
Purchases	75,000	
Sales		250,000
Rates	7,000	
Vans	20,000	
Van expenses	5,000	
Wages and salaries	80,000	
	£307,000	£307,000

3.17

SEVERN

Trial balance at 30 April 19X7

	Dr £000	Cr £000
Advertising	14	
Bank (current)	5	
Bank (deposit)	50	
Bank interest received		1
Capital		100
Cash	8	
Creditors		12
Debtors	30	
Discounts allowed	5	
Discounts received		2
Drawings	45	
Fees received		10
Furniture and fittings	18	
Land and buildings	40	
Motor cars	22	
Motor car expenses	4	
Plant and equipment	37	
c/f	278	125

		£000	£000
	b/f	278	125
Purchases		300	
Purchases returns			15
Rents received			5
Sales			500
Sales returns		20	
Telephone		3	
Wages		44	
		£645	£645

Chapter 4

4.1

ETHEL

Trading, profit and loss account for the year to 31 January 19X1

	£
Sales	35,000
Less: Purchases	20,000
Gross profit	15,000
Less: Expenses:	
Office expenses	11,000
Net profit	£4,000

ETHEL

Balance sheet at 31 January 19X1

Fixed assets	£	£
Premises		8,000
Current assets		
Debtors	6,000	
Cash	3,000	
	9,000	
Less: Current liabilities		
Creditors	3,000	6,000
		£14,000
Financed by:		
Capital		
Balance at 1 February 19X0		10,000
Net profit for the year		4,000
		£14,000

4.2

MARION

Trading, profit and loss account for the year to 28 February 19X2

	£000	£000
Sales		400
Less: Purchases		200
Gross profit		200
Less: Expenses:		
Heat and light	10	
Miscellaneous expenses	25	
Wages and salaries	98	133
Net profit		£67

MARION
Balance sheet at 28 February 19X2

	£000	£000
Fixed assets		
Buildings		50
Current assets		
Debtors	30	
Bank	4	
Cash	2	
	36	
Less: Current liabilities		
Creditors	24	12
		£62
Financed by:		
Capital		50
Balance at 1 March 19X2		
Net profit for the year	67	
Less: Drawings	55	12
		£62

4.3

GARSWOOD
Trading, profit and loss account for the year to 31 March 19X3

	£	£
Sales (£63,000 − £3,000)		60,000
Less: Purchases (£21,400 − £1,400)		20,000
Gross profit		40,000
Add: Other incomes:		
Discounts received	600	
Investment income received	400	1,000
c/f		41,000

		£	£
	b/f		41,000
Less: Expenses:			
Advertising		2,300	
Discounts allowed		100	
Electricity		1,300	
Stationery		900	
Wages		38,700	43,300
			£(2,300)

GARSWOOD
Balance sheet at 31 March 19X3

	£	£	£
Fixed assets			
Machinery			20,000
Office equipment			10,000
			30,000
Investments			4,000
Current assets			
Trade debtors		6,500	
Other debtors		1,500	
Bank		300	
Cash		100	
		8,400	
Less: Current liabilities			
Trade creditors	5,200		
Other creditors	800	6,000	2,400
			£36,400
Financed by:			
Capital			
Balance at 1 April 19X2			55,700
Less: Net loss for the year		(2,300)	
Add: Drawings		(17,000)	(19,300)
			£36,400

4.4 (a)

LATHOM
Trading account for the year to 30 April 19X4

	£	£
Sales		60,000
Less: Cost of goods sold:		
Opening stock	3,000	
Purchases	45,000	
	48,000	
Less: Closing stock	4,000	44,000
		£16,000

(b) Under current assets as the first item.

4.5 (a)

RUFFORD

Trading account for the year to 31 March 19X5

Stock method	1		2		3	
	£	£	£	£	£	£
Sales (£82,000 – £4,000)		78,000		78,000		78,000
Less: Cost of goods sold						
Opening stock	4,000		4,000		4,000	
Purchases (£48,000 – £3,000)	45,000		45,000		45,000	
	49,000		49,000		49,000	
Less: Closing stock	8,000	41,000	16,000	33,000	4,000	45,000
Gross profit		£37,000		£45,000		£33,000

(b) For the year to 31 March 19X6, other things being equal, method 1 would result in a *higher* gross profit than by using method 2 (whereas the reverse is true for the year to 31 March 19X5).

4.6

STANDISH

Trading, profit and loss account for the year to 31 May 19X6

	£	£
Sales		79,000
Less: Cost of goods sold:		
Opening stock	7,000	
Purchases	52,000	
	59,000	
Less: Closing stock	12,000	47,000
Gross profit		32,000
Less: Expenses:		
Heating/light	1,500	
Miscellaneous	6,700	
Wages and salaries	17,800	26,000
Net profit		£6,000

STANDISH

Balance sheet at 31 May 19X6

	£	£
Fixed assets		
Furniture and fittings		8,000
Current assets		
Stock	12,000	
Debtors	6,000	
Cash	1,200	
	19,200	
c/f		8,000

		£000	£000
	b/f	19,200	8,000
Less: Current liabilities			
Creditors		4,300	14,900
			£22,900
Financed by:			
Capital			
Balance at 1 June 19X5			22,400
Net profit for the year		6,000	
Less: Drawings		5,500	500
			£22,900

4.7

WITTON
Trading, profit and loss account for the year to 30 June 19X7

	£	£
Sales		30,000
Less: Cost of goods sold:		
Purchases	14,000	
Less: Closing stock	2,000	12,000
Gross profit		18,000
Less: Expenses:		
Office expenses	8,000	
Motor car: depreciation (20% × £5,000)	1,000	9,000
Net profit		£9,000

WITTON
Balance sheet at 30 June 19X7

	£	£
Fixed assets		
Motor car		5,000
Less: Depreciation		1,000
		4,000
Current assets		
Stocks	2,000	
Debtors	3,000	
Cash	500	
	5,500	
Less: Current liabilities		
Creditors	1,500	4,000
		£8,000
Financed by:		
Capital		
At 1 July 19X6		3,000
Net profit for the year	9,000	
Less: Drawings	4,000	5,000
		£8,000

4.8

CROXTETH
Trading, profit and loss account for the year to 31 July 19X8

	£	£	£
Sales			85,000
Less: Cost of goods sold:			
Opening stock		4,000	
Purchases		70,000	
		74,000	
Less: Closing stock		14,000	60,000
Gross profit			25,000
Less: Expenses:			
Depreciation: delivery vans (30%			
×£40,000)	12,000		
shop equipment (10%			
×£8,000)	800	12,800	
Shop expenses		7,200	20,000
Net Profit			£5,000

CROXTETH
Balance sheet at 31 July 19X8

	£	£	£
Fixed assets	Cost	*Accumulated depreciation*	*Net book value*
Delivery vans	40,000	24,000	16,000
Shop equipment	8,000	3,200	4,800
	£48,000	£27,200	£20,800
Current assets			
Stock		14,000	
Bank		2,000	
		16,000	
Less: Current liabilities			
Creditors		4,800	11,200
			£32,000
Financed by:			
Capital			
Balance at 1 August 19X7			35,000
Net profit for the year		5,000	
Less: Drawings		8,000	(3,000)
			£32,000

Tutorial note

Accumulated depreciation:

Delivery vans: £12,000 (b/f) + £12,000 = £24,000.

Shop equipment: £2,400 (b/f) + £800 = £3,200.

4.9 (a) Calculation of the depreciation charge for the year to 31 August 19X9:

	£	£	£	£
1 Land				—
2 Buildings: 2% × £150,000			=	3,000
3 Plant at cost	55,000			
Less: Residual value	5,000			
	50,000 × 5%		=	2,500
4 Vehicles at cost		45,000		
Less: Accumulated depreciation at				
31 August 19X8		28,800		
		16,200 × 40%	=	6,480
5 Furniture at cost		20,000		
Less: Residual value		2,000		
		18,000 × 10% = 1,800		
Additions at cost		3,000		
Less: Residual value		300		
		2,700 × 10% =	270	2,070

Total amount of depreciation (charged to the profit and loss account
for the year to 31 August 19X9) £14,050

(b)

BARROW
Balance sheet (extract) at 31 August 19X9

Fixed assets	*Cost*	*Accumulated depreciation*	*Net book value*
	£	£	£
Land	200,000	—	200,000
Buildings	150,000	63,000	87,000
Plant	55,000	40,000	15,000
Vehicles	45,000	35,280	9,720
Furniture	23,000	14,670	8,330
	£473,000	£152,950	320,050

4.10

PINE
Trading, profit and loss account for the year to 30 September 19X2

		£	£
Sales			40,000
Less: Cost of goods sold:			
Purchases		21,000	
Less: Closing stock		3,000	18,000
Gross profit	c/f		22,000

		£	£
	b/f		22,000
Less: Expenses:			
Depreciation: furniture (15% × £8,000)		1,200	
General expenses		14,000	
Insurance (£2,000 − £200)		1,800	
Telephone (£1,500 + £500)		2,000	19,000
			£3,000

PINE

Balance sheet at 30 September 19X2

	£	£	£
Fixed asset			
Furniture			8,000
Less: Depreciation			1,200
			6,800
Current assets			
Stock		3,000	
Debtors		5,000	
Prepayments		200	
Cash		400	
		8,600	
Less: Current liabilities			
Creditors	5,900		
Accrual	500	6,400	2,200
			£9,000
Financed by:			
Capital			
At 1 October 19X1			6,000
Net profit for the year			3,000
			£9,000

4.11

DALE

Trading, profit and loss account for the year to 31 October 19X3

	£	£	£
Sales			350,000
Less: Cost of goods sold:			
Opening stock		20,000	
Purchases		240,000	
		260,000	
Less: Closing stock		26,000	234,000
Gross profit			116,000
Less: Expenses:			
Depreciation: office equipment	7,000		
vehicles	4,000	11,000	
	c/f	11,000	116,000

	£	£	£
b/f		11,000	116,000
Heating and lighting (£3,000 + £1,500)		4,500	
Office expenses		27,000	
Rates (£12,000 − £2,000)		10,000	
Wages and salaries		47,000	99,500
Net profit			£16,500

DALE
Balance sheet at 31 October 19X3

	£ Cost	£ Accumulated depreciation	£ Net book value
Fixed assets			
Office equipment	35,000	21,000	14,000
Vehicles	16,000	8,000	8,000
	£51,000	£29,000	22,000
Current assets			
Stocks		26,000	
Trade debtors		61,000	
Prepayments		2,000	
Bank		700	
		89,700	
Less: Current liabilities			
Trade creditors	21,000		
Accruals	1,500	22,500	67,200
			£89,200
Financed by:			
Capital			
At 1 November 19X2			85,000
Net profit for the year		16,500	
Less: Drawings		12,300	4,200
			£89,200

4.12 (a)

ASTLEY
Adjustments for accruals and prepayments for the year to 30 November 19X4

	Electricity £	Gas £	Insurance £	Rates £	Telephone £	Wages £
Cash paid during the year	26,400	40,100	25,000	16,000	3,000	66,800
Add: Prepayments at 1 December 19X3	—	—	12,000	4,000	—	—
	26,400	40,100	37,000	20,000	3,000	66,800
Less: Accruals at 1 December 19X3	5,200	—	—	—	1,500	1,800
c/f	21,200	40,100	37,000	20,000	1,500	65,000

	b/f	21,200	40,100	37,000	20,000	1,500	65,000
Add: Accruals at 30 November 19X4		8,300	—	—	6,000	—	—
		29,500	40,100	37,000	26,000	1,500	65,000
Less: Prepayments at 30 November 19X4		—	4,900	14,000	—	200	—
Charge to the profit and loss account for the year to 30 November 19X4		£29,500	£35,200	£23,000	£26,000	£1,300	£65,000

(b)   Balance sheet at 30 November 19X4

	£
Current assets	
Prepayments (£4,900 + £14,000 + £200)	19,100
Current liabilities	
Accruals (£8,300 + £6,000)	14,300

4.13

DUXBURY

Trading, profit and loss account for the year to 31 December 19X3

	£	£
Sales		95,000
Less: Cost of goods sold:		
Purchases	65,000	
Less: Closing stock	10,000	55,000
Gross profit		40,000
Less: Expenses:		
Depreciation: delivery van (20% × £20,000)	4,000	
Office expenses (£12,100 + £400 − £500)	12,000	
Provision for doubtful debts (5% × £32,000)	1,600	17,600
Net profit		£22,400

DUXBURY

Balance sheet at 31 December 19X3

	£	£	£
Fixed assets			
Delivery van at cost			20,000
Less: Depreciation			4,000
			16,000
Current assets			
Stocks		10,000	
Trade debtors	32,000		
Less: Provision for doubtful debts	1,600	30,400	
	c/f	40,400	16,000

		£	£	£
	b/f	40,400	16,000
Prepayment		500		
Cash		300		
		41,200		
Current liabilities				
Trade creditors	5,000			
Accrual	400	5,400	35,800
			£51,800

Financed by:
Capital

	£	£
Balance at 1 January 19X3		40,000
Net profit	22,400	
Less: Drawings	10,600	11,800
		£51,800

4.14 (a) BEECH

Balance sheet (extracts) at	19X4	19X5	19X6	19X7
	£	£	£	£
Current assets				
Trade debtors	60,000	55,000	65,000	70,000
Less: provision for doubtful debts (10%)	6,000	5,500	6,500	7,000
	54,000	49,500	58,500	63,000

(b) Profit and loss accounts: increase/decrease in provision for doubtful debts:

	£	£	
Year to:			
31 January 19X4		6,000	(New)
31 January 19X5	5,500		
Less: Provision at 31 January 19X4	6,000	500	(Decrease)
31 January 19X6	6,500		
Less: Provision at 31 January 19X5	5,500	1,000	(Increase)
31 January 19X7	7,000		
Less: Provision at 31 January 19X6	6,500	500	(Increase)

4.15 ASH
Trading, profit and loss account for the year to 31 March 19X5

	£	£
Sales		150,000
Less: Cost of goods sold:		
Opening stock	10,000	
Purchases	80,000	
	c/f 90,000	150,000

		£	£
	b/f	90,000	150,000
Less: Closing stock		15,000	75,000
Gross Profit			75,000
Less: Expenses:			
Bad debt		6,000	
Depreciation: furniture (10% × £9,000)		900	
Electricity (£2,000 + £600)		2,600	
Increase in provision for doubtful debts (£21,000 − £6,000 = £15,000 × 10%) − £1,200		300	
Insurance (£1,500 − £100)		1,400	
Miscellaneous expenses		65,800	77,000
Net loss			£(2,000)

ASH

Balance sheet at 31 March 19X5

	£	£	£
Fixed assets			
Furniture at cost			9,000
Less: Accumulated depreciation (£3,600 + £900)			4,500
			4,500
Current assets			
Stocks		15,000	
Trade debtors (£21,000 − £6,000)	15,000		
Less: Provision for doubtful debts	1,500	13,500	
Prepayment		100	
		28,600	
Less: Current liabilities			
Trade creditors	20,000		
Accrual	600		
Bank overdraft	4,000	24,600	4,000
			£8,500
Financed by:			
Capital			
Balance at 1 April 19X4			20,500
Less: Net loss for the year		(2,000)	
Add: Drawings		(10,000)	(12,000)
			£8,500

4.16 ELM
Trading, profit and loss account for the year to 30 June 19X6

	£	£	£
Sales (£820,000 − £4,000)			816,000
Less: Cost of goods sold:			
Opening stock		47,000	
Purchases (£645,000 − £2,000)		643,000	
		690,000	
Less: Closing stock		50,000	640,000
Gross profit			176,000
Add: Other incomes:			
Discounts received		500	
Interest on investments		800	
Decrease in provision for doubtful debts (£42,000 × 5% − £2,300)		200	1,500
			177,500
Less: Expenses:			
Advertising		3,000	
Depreciation: Furniture (15% × £12,000)	1,800		
vehicles (£35,000 − £7,000 × 20%)	5,600	7,400	
Discounts allowed		400	
Electricity (£3,200 + £300)		3,500	
General expenses		28,900	
Rates (£6,000 − £1,000)		5,000	
Telephone		1,300	
Wages and salaries		77,600	127,100
Net profit			£50,400

ELM
Balance sheet at 30 June 19X6

	£ Cost	£ Accumulated depreciation	£ Net book value
Fixed assets			
Furniture	12,000	3,600	8,400
Vehicles	35,000	12,600	22,400
	£47,000	£16,200	30,800
Investments at cost			5,000
Current assets			
Stocks		50,000	
Trade debtors	42,000		
Less: Provision for doubtful debts	2,100	39,900	
		89,900	35,800
c/f			

		£	£
b/f		89,900	35,800
Prepayment		1,000	
Bank		400	
Cash		100	
		91,400	
Less: Current liabilities			
Trade creditors	13,000		
Accrual	300	13,300	78,100
			£113,900

Financed by:
Capital

Balance at 1 July 19X6			73,500
Net profit for the year		50,400	
Less: Drawings		10,000	40,400
			£113,900

4.17   LIME
Trading, profit and loss account for the year to 30 September 19X7

	£	£
Sales		372,000
Less: Cost of goods sold:		
Opening stock	36,000	
Purchases	320,000	
	356,000	
Less: Closing stock	68,000	288,000
Gross profit		84,000
Less: Expenses:		
Bad debts	13,000	
Depreciation: office equipment (£44,000 − £4,000 × 25%)	10,000	
Insurance (£1,800 − £200)	1,600	
Loan interest	7,500	
Loss on disposal of office equipment (£4,000 − £3,000 − £500	500	
Miscellaneous expenses	57,700	
Provision for doubtful debts (10% × £93,000 − £13,000 − £2,000) (increase)	6,000	
Rates (£10,000 + £2,000)	12,000	108,300
Net loss		£(24,300)

LIME
Balance sheet at 30 September 19X7

	£	£	£
Fixed assets			
Office equipment at cost (£44,000 − £4,000)			40,000
Less: Accumulated depreciation (£22,000 − £3,000 + £10,000)			29,000
	c/f		11,000

	b/f	£	£	£
				11,000
Current assets				
Stocks			68,000	
Trade debtors (£93,000 – £13,000)		80,000		
Less: Provision for doubtful debts		8,000	72,000	
Prepayment			200	
			140,200	
Less: Current liabilities				
Trade creditors		105,000		
Accrual		2,000		
Bank overdraft		15,200	122,200	18,000
				£29,000
Financed by:				
Capital				
Balance at 10 October 19X6				19,300
Less: Net loss for the year			(24,300)	
Add: Drawings			(16,000)	(40,300)
				(21,000)
Loan (from Cedar)				50,000
				£29,000

4.18 TEAK

Trading, profit and loss account for the year to 31 December 19X8

	£	£
Sales		164,000
Less: Cost of goods sold:		
Opening stock	2,800	
Purchases (£83,000 – £6,000)	77,000	
	79,800	
Less: Closing stock	15,800	64,000
Gross profit		100,000
Add: Incomes:		
Building society interest (£700 + £800)	1,500	
Dividends (£100 + £600)	700	
Interest from Gray	500	2,700
		102,700
Less: Expenses:		
Depreciation: plant & equipment (30%		
× £50,000)	15,000	
vehicles (£64,000 – £16,000)		
× 25%	12,000	
Office expenses (£39,000 + £1,200 – £9,000)	31,200	
Vehicle expenses	12,600	70,800
Net profit		£31,900

TEAK
Balance sheet at 31 December 19X8

	£ Cost	£ Accumulated depreciation	£ Net book value
Fixed assets			
Plant and equipment	50,000	45,000	5,000
Vehicles	64,000	28,000	36,000
	£114,000	£73,000	41,000
Investments at cost			5,000
Current assets			
Stocks		15,800	
Short-term loan		10,000	
Trade debtors		13,200	
Debtors (£800 + £600)		1,400	
Building society deposit		20,000	
Cash at bank and in hand		400	
		60,800	
Less: Current liabilities			
Trade creditors	22,200		
Accrual	1,200	23,400	37,400
			£83,400
Financed by:			
Capital			
Balance at 1 January 19X8			66,500
Net profit for the year		31,900	
Less: Drawings (£6,000 + £9,000)		15,000	16,900
			£83,400

Chapter 5

5.1   MEGG
Manufacturing account for the year to 31 January 19X1

	£000	£000
Direct material:		
Stock at 1 February 19X0	10	
Purchases	34	
	44	
Less: Stock at 31 January 19X1	12	
Materials consumed		32
Direct wages		65
Prime cost	c/f	97

	£000	£000
b/f		97
Factory overhead expenses:		
Administration	27	
Heat and light	9	
Indirect wages	13	49
		146
Add: Work-in-progress at 1 February 19X0		17
		163
Less: Work-in-progress at 31 January 19X1		14
Manufacturing cost of goods produced		£149

5.2   MOOR

Manufacturing, trading, and profit and loss account for the year to
28 February 19X2

	£	£	£
Sales			250,000
Cost of sales:			
Direct materials consumed:			
Stock at 1 March 19X1	13,000		
Purchases	127,500		
	140,500		
Less: Stock at 28 February 19X2	15,500	125,000	
Direct labour		50,000	
Prime cost		175,000	
Factory overheads		27,700	
		202,700	
Add: Work-in-progress at 1 March 19X1		8,400	
		211,100	
Less: Work-in-progress at 28 February 19X2		6,300	
Manufacturing cost		204,800	
Add: Stock of finished goods at 1 March 19X1		24,000	
		228,800	
Less: Stock of finished goods at 28 February 19X2		30,000	198,800
Gross profit			51,200
Administration expenses		33,000	
Selling and distribution expenses		10,200	43,200
Net profit			£8,000

5.3

STUART
Manufacturing, trading, and profit and loss account for the year to 31 March 19X3

	£000	£000	£000
Sales			1,932
Cost of sales:			
Direct materials consumed:			
Stock at 1 April 19X2	38		
Purchases	1,123		
	1,161		
Less: Stock at 31 March 19X3	44	1,117	
Direct labour		330	
Prime cost		1,447	
Factory overheads		230	
		1,677	
Work-in-progress: at 1 April 19X2	29		
at 31 March 19X3	42	(13)	
Manufacturing cost		1,664	
Finished stock: at 1 April 19X2	67		
: at 31 March 19X3	65	2	1,666
Gross profit			266
Administration expenses		112	
Miscellaneous expenses		16	128
Net profit for the year			£138

STUART
Balance sheet at 31 March 19X3

	£000	£000	£000
Fixed assets			
Plant and machinery at cost			594
Less: Accumulated depreciation			199
			395
Current assets			
Stocks: raw materials	44		
work-in-progress	42		
finished goods	65	151	
Debtors		184	
Bank		7	
		342	
Less: Current liabilities			
Creditors		335	7
			£402
Financed by:			
Capital			
At 1 April 19X2			264
Add: Net profit for the year			138
			£402

5.4   THE DAVID AND PETER MANUFACTURING COMPANY
Manufacturing, trading, and profit and loss account for the year to
30 April 19X4

	£000	£000	£000
Sales			420
Cost of sales:			
Direct materials consumed:			
Stock at 1 May 19X3	12		
Purchases	100		
	112		
Less: Stock at 30 April 19X4	14	98	
Direct labour		70	
Prime cost		168	
Factory overhead expenses:			
General factory expenses	13		
Heat and light (¾ × £52,000)	39		
Rent and rates (⅔ × £42,000)	28		
Depreciation of equipment (15% × £360,000)	54	134	
		302	
Work-in-progress: At 1 May 19X3	18		
At 30 April 19X4	16	2	
Manufacturing cost		304	
Finished goods: At 1 May 19X3	8		
At 30 April 19X4	22	(14)	290
Gross profit			130
Administration salaries		76	
General office expenses		9	
Heat and light (¼ × £52,000)		13	
Rent and rates (⅓ × £42,000)		14	112
Net profit for the year			£18

THE DAVID AND PETER MANUFACTURING COMPANY
Balance sheet at 30 April 19X4

	£000	£000	£000
Fixed assets			
Equipment at cost			360
Less: Accumulated depreciation (£180 + £54)			234
			126
Current assets			
Stocks:			
Raw materials	14		
Work-in-progress	16		
Finished goods	22	52	
Debtors		116	
Cash		18	
c/f		186	126

	£000	£000
b/f	186	126
Current liabilities		
Creditors	102	84
		£210
Financed by:		
Capital		
At 1 May 19X3		218
Net profit for the year	18	
Less: Drawings	26	(8)
		£210

5.5   JEFFREY

Manufacturing, trading, and profit and loss account for the year to 31 May 19X5

	£000	£000	£000
Sales			693
Cost of sales:			
Direct materials:			
Stock at 1 June 19X4		17	
Purchases		180	
		197	
Less: Stock at 31 May 19X5		20	
		177	
Direct labour		200	
Prime cost		377	
Factory overhead expenses:			
General expenses	60		
Plant depreciation (20% × £160,000)	32	92	
		469	
Work-in-progress: At 1 June 19X4	21		
At 31 May 19X5	30	(9)	
Manufacturing cost		460	
Manufacturing profit (20%)		92	
Market value of goods produced		552	
Purchases of finished goods		55	
		607	
Finished goods stock: At 1 June 19X4	26		
At 31 May 19X5	29	(3)	604
Gross profit on trading			89
Gross profit on manufacture			92
			181
Office expenses		127	
Office equipment depreciation (10% × £30,000)		3	130
Net profit for the year			£51

JEFFREY
Balance sheet at 31 May 19X5

	£000 Cost	£000 Depreciation	£000 Net book value
Fixed assets			
Plant	160	102	58
Office equipment	30	12	18
	£190	£114	76
Current assets			
Stocks:			
Raw materials	20		
Work-in-progress	30		
Finished goods	29	79	
Debtors		89	
Bank		6	
		174	
Less: Current liabilities			
Creditors		156	18
			£94
Financed by:			
Capital			
At 1 June 19X4			58
Add: Net Profit for the year		51	
Less: Drawings		15	36
			£94

5.6   **CLARICO**
Manufacturing, trading and profit and loss account for the year to 30 June 19X6

	£000	£000	£000
Sales			1,570
Cost of sales:			
Direct materials consumed:			
Stock at 1 July 19X5		120	
Purchases	450		
Carriage inwards	22	472	
		592	
Less: Stock at 30 June 19X6		102	
		490	
Direct labour		142	
Prime cost	c/f	632	1,570

		£000	£000	£000
	b/f		632	1,570
Factory overhead expenses:				
Electricity ((£16 + £4) × 80%)		16		
Plant depreciation (20% × £110)		22		
Rent and rates ((£70 + £15 − £25) × 60%)		36		
Indirect wages		48	122	
			754	
Work-in-progress: At 1 July 19X5		40		
At 30 June 19X6		74	(34)	
Manufacturing cost			720	
Manufacturing profit (10%)			72	
Market value of goods produced			792	
Purchases of finished goods			30	
			822	
Finished goods stock: At 1 July 19X5		48		
At 30 June 19X6		76	(28)	794
Gross profit on trading				776
Gross profit on manufacture				72
				848
Administration expenses:				
General		39		
Electricity ((£16 + £4) × 20%)		4		
Rent and rates ((£70 + £15 − £25) × 40%)		24		
Wages		26	93	
Selling and distribution expenses:				
Sales expenses		56		
Wages		18		
Delivery van expenses (£12 + £3 − £2)		13		
Delivery van depreciation (25% × £36)		9	96	
Other expenses				
Increase in provision for doubtful debts ((10% × £800) − £55)			25	214
Net profit for the year				£634

CLARICO
Balance sheet at 30 June 19X6

	£000	£000	£000
	Cost	Depreciation	Net book value
Fixed assets			
Plant	110	62	48
Delivery vans	36	27	9
	£146	£89	57
c/f			57

	£000	£000	£000
b/f			57
Current assets			
Stocks:			
Raw materials	102		
Work-in-progress	74		
Finished goods	76	252	
Trade debtors	800		
Less: Provision for doubtful debts (10%)	80	720	
Prepayments (£25 + £2)		27	
Cash		7	
		1,006	
Less: Current liabilities			
Trade crditors	265		
Accruals (£4 + £15 + £3)	22	287	719
			£776
Financed by:			
Capital			
At 1 July 19X5			252
Add: Net profit for the year		634	
Less: Drawings		110	524
			£776

Chapter 6

6.1

MARGO LIMITED
Profit and loss account for the year to 31 January 19X1

	£000
Profit for the financial year	10
Tax on profit	3
	7
Proposed dividend (10p × £50)	5
Retained profit for the year	£2

MARGO LIMITED
Balance sheet at 31 January 19X1

	£000	£000	£000
Fixed assets			
Plant and equipment at cost			70
Less: Accumulated depreciation			25
	c/f		45

	£000	£000	£000
b/f			45
Current assets			
Stocks		17	
Trade debtors		20	
Cash at bank and in hand		5	
		42	
Less: Current liabilities			
Trade creditors	12		
Taxation	3		
Proposed dividend	5	20	22
			£67

Capital and reserves	*Authorized*	*Issued and fully paid*
	£000	£000
Share capital (ordinary shares of £1 each)	75	50
Profit and loss account (£15 + £2)		17
		£67

6.2
HARRY LIMITED
Profit and loss account for the year to 28 February 19X2

	£000	£000
Gross profit for the year		150
Administrative expenses (£65 + (10% × £60))	71	
Distribution costs	15	86
Profit for the year		64
Taxation		24
Dividends: Ordinary proposed	20	40
Preference paid	6	26
Retained profit for the year		£14

HARRY LIMITED
Balance sheet at 28 February 19X2

	£000	£000	£000
Fixed assets			
Furniture and equipment at cost			60
Less: Accumulated depreciation			42
			18
Current assets			
Stocks		130	
Trade debtors		135	
Cash at bank and in hand		10	
c/f		275	18

	£000	£000	£000
b/f		275	18
Less: Current liabilities			
Trade creditors	25		
Taxation	24		
Proposed dividend	20	69	206
			£224

Capital and reserves	*Authorized, issued and fully paid*
	£000
Ordinary shares of £1 each	100
Cumulative 15% preference shares of £1 each	40
	140
Share premium account	20
Profit and loss account (£50 + £14)	64
	£224

6.3   JIM LIMITED
Trading and profit and loss account for the year to 31 March 19X3

	£000	£000	£000
Sales			270
Less: Cost of goods sold:			
Opening stock		16	
Purchases		124	
		140	
Less: Closing stock		14	126
Gross profit			144
Less: Expenses:			
Advertising		3	
Depreciation: Furniture and fittings (15% × £20)	3		
Vehicles (25% × £40)	10	13	
Directors' fees		6	
Rent and rates		10	
Telephone and stationery		5	
Travelling		2	
Wages and salaries		24	63
Net profit			81
Corporation tax			25
			56
Proposed dividend			28
Retained profit for the year			£28

JIM LIMITED
Balance sheet at 31 March 19X3

	Cost £000	Accumulated depreciation £000	Net book value £000
Fixed assets			
Vehicles	40	20	20
Furniture and fittings	20	12	8
	£60	£32	28
Current assets			
Stocks		14	
Debtors		118	
Bank		11	
		143	
Less: Current liabilities			
Creditors	12		
Taxation	25		
Proposed dividend	28	65	78
			£106

	Authorized £000	Issued and fully paid £000
Capital and reserves		
Ordinary shares of £1 each	100	70
Profit and loss account (£8 + £28)		36
		£106

6.4
CYRIL LIMITED
Trading, profit and loss account for the year to 30 April 19X4

	£000	£000	£000
Sales			900
Less: Cost of goods sold:			
Opening stock		120	
Purchases		480	
		600	
Less: Closing stock		140	460
Gross profit			440
Add: Income:			
Investment income			5
	c/f		445

	£000	£000	£000
b/f			445
Less: Expenses:			
Advertising		2	
Auditors' remuneration		6	
Bank interest		4	
Directors' remuneration		30	
Depreciation: Buildings	28		
Vehicles	9	37	
General expenses		15	
Repairs and renewals (£4 – £2)		2	
Wages and salaries		221	317
Net profit			128
Corporation tax			60
			68
Dividends: Proposed ordinary			
(10p per share)		50	
Preference paid		15	65
Retained profit for the year			£3

CYRIL LIMITED
Balance sheet at 30 April 19X4

	Cost	Accumulated depreciation	Net book value
	£000	£000	£000
Fixed assets			
Freehold land and buildings	800	130	670
Motor vehicles	36	27	9
	£836	£157	679
Investments at cost (Market value £35,000)			30
Current assets			
Stocks		140	
Debtors		143	
Prepayment		2	
		285	
Less: Current liabilities			
Bank overdraft	20		
Creditors	80		
Accrual	6		
Taxation	60		
Proposed dividend	50	216	69
			£778

	Authorized, issued and fully paid £000
Capital and reserves	
Ordinary shares of £1 each	500
Cumulative 10% preference shares of £1 each	150
	650
Share premium account	25
Profit and loss account (£100 + £3)	103
	£778

6.5 NELSON LIMITED
Trading, profit and loss account for the year to 31 May 19X5

	£000	£000
Sales		800
Less: Cost of goods sold:		
Opening stock	155	
Purchases	400	
	555	
Less: Closing stock	195	360
Gross profit		440
Add: Income:		
Investment income		22
		462
Less: Expenses:		
Administrative expenses (£257 + £13)	270	
Auditors' fees	10	
Debenture interest (12% × £100)	12	
Directors' remuneration	60	
Depreciation: Furniture and fittings (12.5% × £200)	25	
Wages and salaries (£44 − £4)	40	417
Net profit		45
Corporation tax		8
		37
Dividends: Ordinary − interim	20	
− proposed	5	
Preference (paid and payable)	10	35
Retained profit for the year		£2

NELSON LIMITED
Balance sheet at 31 May 19X5

	£000	£000	£000
Fixed assets			
Furniture and fittings at cost			200
Less: Accumulated depreciation			
(£48 + £25)			73
			127
Investments at cost (market value £340,000)			335
Current assets			
Stock		195	
Debtors		225	
Prepayment		4	
Cash at bank and in hand		5	
		429	
Less: Current liabilities			
Creditors	85		
Accruals (£13 + £6)	19		
Corporation tax	8		
Proposed dividends: Ordinary	5		
Preference	5	122	307
			£769

Capital and reserves		Authorized	Issued and fully paid
		£000	£000
Ordinary shares of £1 each		500	400
Cumulative 5% preference shares of £1 each		200	200
		£700	600
Share premium account			50
Profit and loss account (£17 + £2)			19
Shareholders' funds			669
Loans:			
12% Debentures			100
			£769

6.6 KEITH LIMITED

Trading, profit and loss account for the year to 30 June 19X6

	£000	£000
Sales		2,100
Less: Cost of goods sold:		
Opening stock	134	
Purchases	1,240	
c/f	1,374	2,100

		£000	£000
	b/f	1,374	2,100
Less: Closing stock		155	1,219
			881
Add: Income:			
Investment income			4
			885
Less: Expenses:			
Advertising		30	
Auditors' remuneration		12	
Debenture interest (10% × £70)		7	
Directors' remuneration		55	
Electricity		28	
Insurance (£17 − £3)		14	
Depreciation: Machinery (20% × £420)		84	
Vehicles (25% × £80)		20	
Increase in provision for doubtful debts ((5% × £300) − £8)		7	
Office expenses		49	
Rent and rates		75	
Wages and salaries		358	739
Net profit			146
Corporation tax			60
			86
Dividends: Proposed ordinary (400,000 × 10p)		40	
Preference		4	44
Retained profit for the year			£42

KEITH LIMITED
Balance sheet at 30 June 19X6

	Cost £000	Accumulated depreciation £000	Net book value £000
Fixed assets			
Machinery	420	236	184
Vehicles	80	60	20
	£500	£296	204
Investments (market value £30,000)			28
Current assets			
Stock		155	
Trade debtors	300		
Less: Provision for doubtful debts (5%)	15	285	
Prepayment		3	
Bank		7	
c/f		450	232

		£000	£000	£000
	b/f		450	232
Less: Current liabilities				
Creditors		69		
Accruals (£7 + £12)		19		
Corporation tax		60		
Proposed dividend		40	188	262
				£494

	Authorized	Issued and fully paid
	£000	£000
Capital and reserves		
Ordinary shares of £0.50 each	300	200
Cumulative 8% preference shares of £1 each	50	50
	£350	250
Profit and loss account (£132 + £42)		174
Shareholders' funds		424
Loans:		
10% Debentures		70
		£494

Chapter 7

7.1   DENNIS LIMITED
Statement of source and application of funds for the year
to 31 January 19X2

	£	£
Source of funds		
Profit before tax (£60 − £26)		34
Issue of shares for cash (£800 − £700)		100
		134
Application of funds		
Purchase of land (£700 − £600)		(100)
		34
Increase/decrease in working capital:		
Increase in stocks (£120 − £100)	20	
Increase in debtors (£250 − £200)	50	
(Increase) in creditors (£220 − £180)	(40)	
Movement in net liquid funds:		
Cash (£10 − £6)	4	34

7.2   FRANK LIMITED
Statement of source and application of funds for the year to 28 February 19X2

	£	£
Source of funds		
Profit before tax (£40 – £30)		10
Adjustments for items not involving the movement of funds:		
Depreciation (£100 – £80)		20
Total generated from operations		30
Funds from other sources:		
Issue of debentures		60
		90
Application of funds		
Purchase of investments		(100)
		(10)
Increase/decrease in working capital:		
Increase in stocks (£190 – £160)	30	
Decrease in debtors (£220 – £110)	(110)	
Decrease in creditors (£160 – £200)	40	
Movement in net liquid funds:		
Increase in cash balances (£10 + £20)	30	(10)

7.3   STARTER
Statement of source and application of funds for the year to 31 March 19X3

	£	£
Source of funds		
Profit		4,000
Adjustment for item not involving the movement of funds:		
Depreciation		2,000
Total generated from operations		6,000
Funds from other sources		
Capital introduced		20,000
		26,000
Application of funds:		
Purchase of van		(10,000)
		16,000
Increase/decrease in working capital:		
Increase in stock	1,000	
Increase in trade debtors	5,000	
(Increase) in trade creditors	(2,500)	
Movement in net liquid funds:		
Increase in bank balance	12,500	16,000

7.4 GREGORY LIMITED

Statement of source and application of funds for the year to 30 April 19X4

	£000	£000
Source of funds		
Profit before tax		75
Adjustments for items not involving the movement of funds:		
Depreciation (£180 – £100)		80
		155
Funds from other sources		
Issue of loans		50
		205
Application of funds		
Dividends paid	(35)	
Tax paid	(18)	
Purchase of plant (£550 – £400)	(150)	(203)
		2
Increase/decrease in working capital		
Increase in stocks (£90 – £50)	40	
Decrease in debtors (£50 – £70)	(20)	
(Increase) in creditors (£55 – £45)	(10)	
Movement in net liquid funds:		
(Decrease) in cash balances (£2 – £10)	(8)	2

7.5 PILL LIMITED

Statement of source and application of funds for the year to 31 May 19X5

	£000	£000
Source of funds		
Profit before tax		580
Adjustments for items not involving the movement of funds:		
Depreciation (£60 + £40)		100
Total generated from operations		680
Funds from other sources:		
Issue of shares for cash (£550 – £500)		50
		730
Application of funds		
Dividends paid (£150 + £250 – £100)	(300)	
Tax paid (£170 + £150 – £220)	(100)	
Purchase of fixed assets ((£800 – £600) + (£250 – £200))	(250)	
Repayment of loans (£190 – £40)	(150)	(800)
c/f		(70)

	£000	£000
b/f		(70)

Increase/decrease in working capital

Increase in stocks (£540 – £400)	140	
Increase in debtors (£200 – £180)	20	
(Increase) in creditors (£300 – £270)	(30)	
Movement of net liquid funds:		
(Decrease) in cash balances (£320 – £120)	(200)	(70)

7.6   BRIAN LIMITED

Statement of source and application of funds for the year to 30 June 19X6

	£000	£000
Source of funds		
Profit before tax		115
Adjustments for items not involving movement		
of funds:		
Depreciation	35	
Loss on sale of vehicle	3	
Increase in provision for doubtful debts	1	39
Total generated from operations		154
Funds from other sources:		
Sale of vehicle		12
		166
Application of funds		
Dividends paid	(20)	
Tax paid	(52)	
Purchase of vehicles	(75)	(147)
		19
Increase/decrease in working capital		
Decrease in stocks (£60 – £50)	(10)	
Increase in debtors (£100 – £80)	20	
Decrease in creditors (£53 – £60)	7	
Movement in net liquid funds:		
Increase in cash balances (£8 – £6)	2	19

Chapter 8

8.1 BETTY

Accounting ratios year to 31 January 19X1:

1 Gross profit ratio:

$$\frac{\text{Gross profit}}{\text{Total sales revenue}} \times 100 = \frac{£30}{£100} \times 100 = \underline{\underline{30\%}}$$

2 Net profit ratio:

$$\frac{\text{Net profit}}{\text{Sales}} \times 100 = \frac{£14}{£100} \times 100 = \underline{\underline{14\%}}$$

3 Return on capital employed:

$$\frac{\text{Net profit}}{\text{Average capital}} \times 100 = \frac{£14}{\frac{1}{2}(£40+48)} \times 100 = \underline{\underline{31.8\%}}$$

4 Current ratio:

$$\frac{\text{Current assets}}{\text{Current liabilities}} = \frac{£25}{£6} = \underline{\underline{4.2 \text{ to } 1}}$$

5 Acid test:

$$\frac{\text{Current assets} - \text{stock}}{\text{Current liabilities}} = \frac{£25 - £10}{£6} = \underline{\underline{2.5 \text{ to } 1}}$$

6 Stock turnover:

$$\frac{\text{Cost of goods sold}}{\text{Average stock}} = \frac{£70}{\frac{1}{2}(£15+10)} = \underline{\underline{5.6 \text{ times}}}$$

7 Debtor collection period:

$$\frac{\text{Trade debtors}}{\text{Credit sales}} \times 365 = \frac{12}{100} \times 365 = \underline{\underline{43.8 \text{ days}}}$$

8.2 JAMES LIMITED

Accounting ratios year to 28 February 19X2:

1 Return on capital employed:

$$\frac{\text{Net profit before taxation and dividends}}{\text{Shareholders' funds}} \times 100 = \frac{£90}{\frac{1}{2}(£600+620)} \times 100$$
$$= \underline{\underline{14.8\%}}$$

2 Gross profit:

$$\frac{\text{Gross profit}}{\text{Sales}} \times 100 = \frac{£600}{£1,200} \times 100 = \underline{\underline{50\%}}$$

3 Mark-up:

$$\frac{\text{Gross profit}}{\text{Cost of goods sold}} \times 100 = \frac{£600}{£600} \times 100 = \underline{\underline{100\%}}$$

4 Net profit:

$$\frac{\text{Net profit before taxation and dividends}}{\text{Sales}} \times 100 = \frac{£90}{£1,200} \times 100$$
$$= \underline{\underline{7.5\%}}$$

5 Acid test:

$$\frac{\text{Current assets} - \text{stocks}}{\text{Current liabilities}} = \frac{\pounds 275 - \pounds 75}{\pounds 240} = \underline{\underline{0.83 \text{ to } 1}}$$

6 Fixed assets turnover:

$$\frac{\text{Sales}}{\text{Fixed assets (NBV)}} = \frac{\pounds 1,200}{\pounds 685} = \underline{\underline{1.75 \text{ times}}}$$

7 Debtor collection period:

$$\frac{\text{Trade debtors}}{\text{Credit sales}} \times 365 = \frac{\pounds 200}{\pounds 1,200} \times 365 = \underline{\underline{60.8 \text{ days}}}$$

8 Capital gearing:

$$\frac{\text{Long-term loans}}{\text{Shareholders' funds and long-term loans}} \times 100 = \frac{\pounds 100}{\pounds 720} \times 100$$
$$= \underline{\underline{13.9\%}}$$

8.3 Accounting ratios year to 31 March 19X3:

	Mark Limited	Luke Limited	John Limited
1 Return on capital employed: $\dfrac{\text{Net profit before taxation and dividends}}{\text{Shareholders' funds}} \times 100$	$\dfrac{\pounds 64}{\pounds 250} \times 100$ $= \underline{\underline{25.6\%}}$	$\dfrac{\pounds 22}{\pounds 327} \times 100$ $= \underline{\underline{6.7\%}}$	$\dfrac{\pounds 55}{\pounds 290} \times 100$ $= \underline{\underline{19.0\%}}$
2 Capital gearing: $\dfrac{\text{Preference shares} + \text{Long-term loans}}{\text{Shareholders' funds} + \text{Long-term loans}} \times 100$	No preference shares or long-term loans	$\dfrac{\pounds 20}{\pounds 327} \times 100$ $= \underline{\underline{6.1\%}}$	$\dfrac{\pounds 10 + 100}{\pounds 390} \times 100$ $= \underline{\underline{28.2\%}}$

8.4 HELENA LIMITED
Accounting ratios 19X2 to 19X6:

	19X2	19X3	19X4	19X5	19X6
1 Gross profit: $\dfrac{\text{Gross profit}}{\text{Sales}} \times 100$	$\dfrac{£30}{£130} \times 100$ $= 23.1\%$	$\dfrac{£40}{£150} \times 100$ $= 26.7\%$	$\dfrac{£60}{£190} \times 100$ $= 31.6\%$	$\dfrac{£70}{£210} \times 100$ $= 33.3\%$	$\dfrac{£75}{£320} \times 100$ $= 23.4\%$
2 Mark-up: $\dfrac{\text{Gross profit} \times 100}{\text{Cost of goods sold}}$	$\dfrac{£30}{£100} \times 100$ $= 30\%$	$\dfrac{£40}{£110} \times 100$ $= 36.4\%$	$\dfrac{£60}{£130} \times 100$ $= 46.2\%$	$\dfrac{£70}{£140} \times 100$ $= 50\%$	$\dfrac{£75}{£245} \times 100$ $= 30.6\%$
3 Stock turnover: $\dfrac{\text{Cost of goods sold}}{\text{Average stock}}$	$\dfrac{£100}{\frac{1}{2}(£20+£30)}$ $= 4 \text{ times}$	$\dfrac{£110}{\frac{1}{2}(£30+£30)}$ $= 3.7 \text{ times}$	$\dfrac{£130}{\frac{1}{2}(£30+£35)}$ $= 4 \text{ times}$	$\dfrac{£140}{\frac{1}{2}(£35+£40)}$ $= 3.7 \text{ times}$	$\dfrac{£245}{\frac{1}{2}(£40+£100)}$ $= 3.5 \text{ times}$
4 Trade debtor collection period: $\dfrac{\text{Average trade debtors}}{\text{Credit sales}} \times 365$	$\dfrac{\frac{1}{2}(£45+40)}{£130} \times 365$ $= 119.3 \text{ days}$	$\dfrac{\frac{1}{2}(£40+45)}{£150} \times 365$ $= 103.4 \text{ days}$	$\dfrac{\frac{1}{2}(£70+40)}{£190} \times 365$ $= 105.7 \text{ days}$	$\dfrac{\frac{1}{2}(£100+70)}{£210} \times 365$ $= 147.7 \text{ days}$	$\dfrac{\frac{1}{2}(£150+100)}{£320} \times 365$ $= 142.6 \text{ days}$
5 Trade creditor payment period: $\dfrac{\text{Average trade creditors}}{\text{Credit purchases}} \times 365$	$\dfrac{\frac{1}{2}(£20+20)}{£110} \times 365$ $= 66.4 \text{ days}$	$\dfrac{\frac{1}{2}(£25+20)}{£110} \times 365$ $= 74.7 \text{ days}$	$\dfrac{\frac{1}{2}(£25+25)}{£135} \times 365$ $= 67.6 \text{ days}$	$\dfrac{\frac{1}{2}(£30+25)}{£145} \times 365$ $= 69.2 \text{ days}$	$\dfrac{\frac{1}{2}(£60+30)}{£305} \times 365$ $= 53.9 \text{ days}$

8.5 HEDGE PLC

Accounting ratios:

1 Dividend yield:

$$\frac{\text{Nominal value per share}}{\text{Market price per share}} \times \frac{\text{Declared}}{\text{dividend rate}} = \frac{£1}{£3.5} \times 7\% = \underline{\underline{2\%}}$$

2 Dividend cover:

$$\frac{\text{Net profit after taxation}}{\text{Ordinary dividends}} = \frac{£70,000}{£35,000} = \underline{\underline{2 \text{ times}}}$$

3 Earnings per share:

$$\frac{\text{Net profit after taxation}}{\text{Number of ordinary shares in issue}} = \frac{£70,000}{500,000} = \underline{\underline{14p}}$$

4 Price/earnings ratio:

$$\frac{\text{Market price per share}}{\text{Earnings per share}} = \frac{£3.50}{£0.14} = \underline{\underline{25}}$$

8.6 (a)

STYLE LIMITED

Accounting ratios:

		19X5	19X6
1	Gross profit: $\dfrac{\text{Gross profit}}{\text{Sales}} \times 100$	$\dfrac{£525}{£1,500} \times 100 = \underline{\underline{35\%}}$	$\dfrac{£600}{£1,900} \times 100 = \underline{\underline{31.6\%}}$
2	Mark-up: $\dfrac{\text{Gross profit}}{\text{Cost of goods sold}} \times 100$	$\dfrac{£525}{£975} \times 100 = \underline{\underline{53.8\%}}$	$\dfrac{£600}{£1,300} \times 100 = \underline{\underline{46.2\%}}$
3	Net profit: $\dfrac{\text{Net profit}}{\text{Sales}} \times 100$	$\dfrac{£275}{£1,500} \times 100 = \underline{\underline{18.3\%}}$	$\dfrac{£250}{£1,900} \times 100 = \underline{\underline{13.2\%}}$
4	Return on capital employed: $\dfrac{\text{Net profit}}{\text{Shareholders' funds}} \times 100$	$\dfrac{£275 \times 100}{\frac{1}{2}(£900 + 1,000)} = \underline{\underline{28.9\%}}$	$\dfrac{£250 \times 100}{\frac{1}{2}(£900 + 1,250)} = \underline{\underline{23.3\%}}$
5	Stock turnover: $\dfrac{\text{Cost of goods sold}}{\text{Average stock}}$	$\dfrac{£975}{\frac{1}{2}(£80 + 100)} = \underline{\underline{10.8 \text{ times}}}$	$\dfrac{£1,300}{\frac{1}{2}(£100 + 200)} = \underline{\underline{8.7 \text{ times}}}$
6	Current ratio: $\dfrac{\text{Current assets}}{\text{Current liabilities}}$	$\dfrac{£500}{£80} = \underline{\underline{6.3 \text{ to } 1}}$	$\dfrac{£1,000}{£210} = \underline{\underline{4.8 \text{ to } 1}}$

7 Acid test:

$$\frac{\text{Current assets} - \text{stock}}{\text{Current liabilities}}$$

   $$\frac{£500 - 100}{£80} = 5 \text{ to } 1 \qquad \frac{£1,000 - 200}{£210} = 3.8 \text{ to } 1$$

8 Trade debtor collection period:

$$\frac{\text{Trade debtors}}{\text{Credit sales}} \times 365$$

   $$\frac{£375}{£1,500} \times 365 = 92 \text{ days} \qquad \frac{£800}{£1,900} \times 365 = 154 \text{ days}$$

9 Trade creditor payment period:

$$\frac{\text{Trade creditors}}{\text{Purchases}} \times 365$$

   $$\frac{£80}{£995} \times 365 = 30 \text{ days} \qquad \frac{£200}{£1,400} \times 365 = 53 \text{ days}$$

(b) *Brief comments*

The company increased its sales in 19X6 by £400,000 (26.7%). It appeared to achieve this by reducing its profit on goods sold, but the increased activity probably resulted in additional expenses. As a result, even in absolute terms, its net profit was down from £275,000 to £250,000. It should also be noted there is no explanation why an amount was not set aside for taxation or dividends either in 19X5 or 19X6.

Its liquidity position is still healthy, even if its debtor collection period (based on year-end figures) has increased substantially (as has the time taken to pay the creditors). This may be a deliberate policy to stimulate sales or it may be that it has been too busy to encourage its customers to settle their debts.

Not surprisingly, the cash position has deteriorated and at the end of 19X6 the company was in overdraft.

Increased trading activity does not always guarantee survival if the company cannot settle its debts as they fall due. Unless it becomes more efficient in this respect, the company's long-term future could be uncertain.

Chapter 9

9.1 *Financial accounting* is mainly concerned with supplying information to the external users of an entity.

Management accounting is concerned with producing information for use within an entity.

9.2 *1* Elements
       2 Units
       3 Direct and indirect
       4 Fixed and variable
       5 Controllable and non-controllable
       6 Relevant and irrelevant
       7 Responsibility
       8 Normal and abnormal

9.3 *1* General board of directors
2 Divisions
3 Factories or works
4 Functions
5 Cost centres

9.4 A clearly defined area of responsibility that is charged with its own identifiable operating costs. A cost centre may take the form of a department, an area, a machine or an individual (such as a salesman).

Chapter 10

10.1 1 FIFO:

			£
1,000 units	@£20	=	20,000
250 units	@£25	=	6,250
Charge to production			£26,250

2 LIFO:

			£
500 units	@£25	=	12,500
750 units	@£20	=	15,000
Charge to production			£27,500

3 Periodic weighted average:

Units	Value
	£
1,000 @ £20	20,000
500 @ £25	12,500
1,500	£32,500

$$\text{Average} = \frac{£32,500}{1,500} = £21.67$$

Charge to production $= 1,250 \times £21.67 = £27,088$

10.2 MATERIAL ST 2

	Stock	Units	Total stock value	Average unit price
			£	£
1.2.X2	Opening	500	500	1.00
10.2.X2	Receipts	200	220	
		700	720	1.03
12.2.X2	Receipts	100	112	
		800	832	1.04
17.2.X2	Issues	(400)	(416)	
	c/f	400	416	

				£	£
		b/f	400	416	
25.2.X2	Receipts		300	345	
			700	761	1.09
27.2.X2	Issues		(250)	(273)	
28.2.X2	*Closing stock*		£450	£488	

10.3 Closing stock calculations:

1 FIFO:

800 units   @ £12   =   £9,600

2 LIFO:

			£
600 units	@ £12	=	7,200
200 units	@ £10	=	2,000
800			£9,200

3 Continuous weighted average:

		Total stock		*Average unit*
	Stock	Units	Value	price
			£	£
1.1.X3	Purchases	2,000	20,000	10
31.3.X3	Issues	(1,600)	(16,000)	
		400	4,000	
1.2.X3	Purchases	2,400	26,400	
		2,800	30,400	10.86
28.2.X3	Issues	(2,600)	(28,236)	
		200	2,164	
1.3.X3	Purchases	1,600	19,200	
		1,800	21,364	11.87
31.3.X3	Issues	(1,000)	(11,870)	
		800	£9,494	

10.4 Calculation of closing stock:

	Units	Value
		£
Total receipts:	240	1,692

Periodic weighted average price: $\dfrac{£1,692}{£240} = £7.05$

Total issues: 195 units – all issued at £7.05 = £1,375

	£	Units
In stock at 30.4.X4 *Less:* Issues:		
£1,692 − £1,375 =	317	45 (240 − 195)
Add: Stock at 1.4.X4	120	20
Closing stock at 30.4.X4	£437	65

10.5

STEED LIMITED
Trading Account for the year to 31 May 19X5

	FIFO	LIFO	Periodic weighted average	Continuous weighted average
	£	£	£	£
Sales	500,000	500,000	500,000	500,000
Less: Cost of goods sold:				
Opening stock	40,000	40,000	40,000	40,000
Purchases	440,000	440,000	440,000	440,000
	480,000	480,000	480,000	480,000
Less: Closing stock	90,000	65,000	67,500	79,950
	390,000	415,000	412,500	400,050
Gross profit	£110,000	£85,000	£87,500	£99,950

10.6 IRON LIMITED

(a) Pricing the issue of materials to production

1 First in, first out (FIFO):
Total receipts   =   2,400 litres
Total issues   =   2,200 litres
Therefore closing stock = 200 litres @ £5 per litre = £1,000

2 Last in, first out (LIFO):
Closing stock position at 31 December 19X4:

		£
October receipts:	All issued in December	
June receipts:	400 litres issued in July	
	400 litres issued in December	
April receipts:	300 litres issued in May	
	leaving	
	100 litres in stock @ £3.00	
	per litre =	300
January receipts:	100 litres issued in February	
	leaving	
	100 litres in stock @ £2.00	
	per litre =	200
Closing stock value:		£500

3   *Periodic weighted average:*
Total value of receipts = £9,600
Total receipts = 2,400 litres
Therefore periodic weighted average price per litre = £4.00.
Value of stock = £4 × 200 litres = £800

4   *Continuous weighted average:*

Month	Quantity	Value	Stock balance Average price per litre in stock	Issued at per litre
	(litres)	£	£	£
January	200	400	2.00	
February	(100)	(200)		2.00
	100	200		
April	500	1,500		
	600	1,700	2.83	
May	(300)	(849)		2.83
	300	851		
June	800	3,200		
	1,100	4,051	3.68	
July	(400)	(1,472)		3.68
	700	2,579		
October	900	4,500		
	1,600	7,079	4.42	
December	(1,400)	(6,188)		4.42
	200	£891		

(b)   Calculation of gross profit

Method	(1) FIFO	(2) LIFO	(3) Periodic weighted average	(4) Continuous weighted average
	£	£	£	£
Sales	20,000	20,000	20,000	20,000
Less: Cost of goods sold:				
Purchases	9,600	9,600	9,600	9,600
Less: Closing stock	1,000	500	800	891
	8,600	9,100	8,800	8,709
Conversion costs	7,000	7,000	7,000	7,000
Manufacturing cost	15,600	16,100	15,800	15,709
Gross profit	£4,400	£3,900	£4,200	£4,291

Chapter 11

11.1 SCAR LIMITED
Overhead apportionment January 19X1:

	Production Department		Service Department
	A	B	
	£000	£000	£000
Allocated expenses	65	35	50
Apportionment of services department's expenses in the ratio 60:40	30	20	(50)
Overhead to be charged	£95	£55	—

11.2 BANK LIMITED
Assembly department – overhead absorption methods:

1 Specific units:

$$\frac{\text{Total cost centre overhead}}{\text{Number of units}} = \frac{£250,000}{50,000} = \underline{\underline{£5 \text{ per unit}}}$$

2 Direct materials:

$$\frac{\text{Total cost centre overhead}}{\text{Direct materials}} \times 100 = \frac{£250,000}{500,000} \times 100 = 50\%$$

Therefore 50% of £8 $= \underline{\underline{£4 \text{ per unit}}}$

3 Direct labour:

$$\frac{\text{Total cost centre overhead}}{\text{Direct labour}} \times 100 = \frac{£250,000}{1,000,000} \times 100 = 25\%$$

Therefore 25% of £30 $= \underline{\underline{£7.50 \text{ per unit}}}$

4 Prime cost:

$$\frac{\text{Total cost centre overhead}}{\text{Prime cost}} \times 100 = \frac{£250,000}{1,530,000} \times 100 = 16.34\%$$

Therefore 16.34% of £40 $= \underline{\underline{£6.54 \text{ per unit}}}$

5 Direct labour hours:

$$\frac{\text{Total cost centre overhead}}{\text{Direct labour hours}} = \frac{£250,000}{100,000} = £2.50 \text{ per direct labour hour}$$

Therefore £2.50 of 3.5 DLH $= \underline{\underline{£8.75 \text{ per unit}}}$

6 Machine hours:

$$\frac{\text{Total cost centre overhead}}{\text{Machine hours}} = \frac{£250,000}{25,000} = £10 \text{ per machine hour}$$

Therefore £10 of 0.75 $= \underline{\underline{£7.50 \text{ per unit}}}$

11.3   CLOUGH LIMITED

(a)   Overhead absorption for March 19X3 – Production department:

1   Direct labour hours:

$$\frac{\text{Total cost centre overhead}}{\text{Direct labour hours}} = \frac{£150,000}{30,000} = £5 \text{ per DLH}$$

Therefore for order number 123: £5 × 5 = £25

2   Machine hours:

$$\frac{\text{Total cost centre overheads}}{\text{Machine hours}} = \frac{£150,000}{10,000} = £15 \text{ per MH}$$

Therefore for order number 123: £15 × 2 = £30

Selling price of order number 123	*Direct labour hours*	*Machine hours*
	£	£
Direct materials	20	20
Direct wages	25	25
Prime costs	45	45
Overhead	25	30
Total cost	70	75
Administration + profit (50%)	35	37.50
Selling price	£105	£112.50

(b)   As the department appears more labour intensive than machine intensive, use the direct labour hour method.

11.4   BURNS LIMITED

Overhead absorption schedule – April 19X4:

	Processing	Assembling	Finishing	Administration	Work study
	£	£	£	£	£
Direct labour	—	—	—	65,000	33,000
Allocated costs	15,000	20,000	10,000	35,000	12,000
				100,000	
Apportion:					
Administration (50:30:15:5)	50,000	30,000	15,000	(100,000)	5,000
					50,000
Work study (70:20:10)	35,000	10,000	5,000	—	(50,000)
Overhead to be absorbed	£100,000	£60,000	£30,000	—	—

Calculation of absorption rates:

Processing department: $\dfrac{\text{TCCO}}{\text{Machine hours}} = \dfrac{£100,000}{25,000} = £4 \text{ per MH}$

Assembling department: $\dfrac{\text{TCCO}}{\text{Direct labour hours}} = \dfrac{£60,000}{30,000} = £2 \text{ per DLH}$

Finishing department: $\dfrac{\text{TCCO}}{\text{Direct labour cost}} \times 100 = \dfrac{£30,000}{£120,000} \times 100 = \underline{\underline{25\%}}$

Total cost of producing unit XP6:

	£	£
Prime cost		47
Overhead:		
Processing (£4 × 6 MH)	24	
Assembling (£2 × 1)	2	
Finishing (25% × £12)	3	29
Total cost		£76

11.5 OUTLANE LIMITED

(a) *Overhead charge – direct labour cost method:*

	Contract 1	Contract 2
Direct labour cost:		
DLH × rate per hour = 100 × £3.00	£300	£300
Therefore overhead to be absorbed (100%) =	£300	£300

(b) *Overhead charge – machine hour rate method:*

Overhead absorption schedule

		Department			
	Apportionment method	*L* £000	*M* £000	*N* £000	*O* £000
Administration	Total number of employees	40	30	20	10
Depreciation of machinery	Depreciation rate	22	8	10	40
Employer's National Insurance	Total number of employees	4	3	2	1
Heating and lighting	Cubic capacity	6	3	1	5
Holiday pay	Total number of employees	8	6	4	2
Indirect labour cost	Number of indirect employees	4	3	2	1
Insurance: machinery	Capital cost	11	4	5	20
property	Floor space	4	3	2	2
Machine maintenance	Maintenance hours	15	12	9	6
Power	Kilowatt hours	30	50	90	60
Rent and rates	Floor space	20	15	10	10
Supervision	Total number of employees	20	15	10	5
Overhead to be absorbed		184	152	165	162

	£000	£000	£000	£000
Overhead to be absorbed b/f	184	152	165	162
÷ Machine hours	92	38	165	27
= Overhead absorption rate	£2	£4	£1	£6

Department	Contract 1			Contract 2		
	Machine hours	Absorption rate	Total	Machine hours	Absorption rate	Total
		£	£		£	£
L	60	2	120	20	2	40
M	30	4	120	10	4	40
N	10	1	10	10	1	10
O	—	—	—	60	6	360
Total overhead to be absorbed			£250			£450

11.6   SARAH LIMITED

Overhead absorption schedule for June 19X6:

Cost centre	Production		Service		
	D	P	1	2	3
	£000	£000	£000	£000	£000
Method 1: specified order of closure					
Allocated costs	45	35	160	71	34
Apportion the service cost centre costs in the following order (different orders are possible):					
1 (55:20:15:10)	88	32	(160)	24	16
				95	
2 (45:40: – :10)	45	40		(95)	10
3 (50:10)	50	10			(60)
Overhead to be absorbed	£228	£117	—	—	—
Method 2: Ignore inter department servicing					
Allocated costs	45	35	160	71	34
Apportion the service cost centre costs as follows:					
1 (55:20)	117	43	(160)	—	—
2 (45:40)	38	33	—	(71)	—
3 (50:10)	28	6	—	—	(34)
Overhead to be absorbed	£228	£117	—	—	—

Chapter 12

12.1 One that contains both financial and cost accounts.

12.2 One in which the cost accounts are kept quite separate from the financial accounts, and there is little double-entry connection between them.

12.3 A method of costing designed to suit the particular circumstances in which goods are manufactured or services provided.

12.4 An application of costing methods devised to suit the circumstances in which information is presented to management.

Chapter 13

13.1

POLE LIMITED
Marginal cost statement for the year to 31 January 19X2

	£000	£000
Sales		450
Less: Variable costs:		
Direct materials	60	
Direct wages	26	
Administration expenses: variable (£7 + £4)	11	
Research and development expenditure: variable (£15 + £5)	20	
Selling and distribution expenditure: variable (£4 + £9)	13	
		130
Contribution		320
Less: Fixed costs:		
Administration expenses (£30 + £16)	46	
Materials: indirect	5	
Production overhead	40	
Research and development expenditure (£60 + £5)	65	
Selling and distribution expenditure (£80 + £21)	101	
Wages: indirect	13	270
Profit		£50

13.2 GILES LIMITED

(a) (i) *Break-even point*

In value terms:

$$\frac{\text{Fixed costs} \times \text{sales}}{\text{Contribution}} = \frac{£150}{(£500 - £300)} \times £500 = \underline{\underline{£375,000}}$$

In units:

	£
Selling price per unit (£500 ÷ 50)	10
Less: Variable cost per unit (£300 ÷ 50)	6
Contribution per unit	£4

$$\frac{\text{Fixed costs}}{\text{Contribution per unit}} = \frac{£150,000}{£4} = 37,500 \text{ units}$$

(ii) *Margin of safety*

In value terms:

$$\frac{\text{Profit} \times \text{sales}}{\text{Contribution}} = \frac{£50 \times 500}{£200} = £125,000$$

In units:

$$\frac{\text{Profit}}{\text{Contribution per unit}} = \frac{£50,000}{£4} = 12,500 \text{ units}$$

12.2 (b) Break-even chart

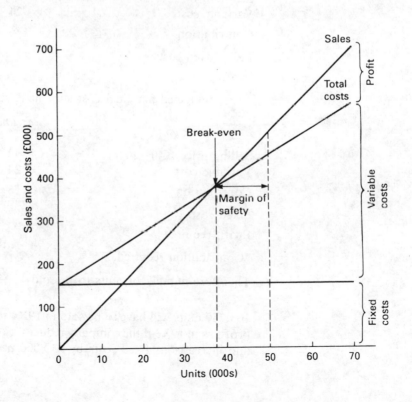

13.3 **AYRE LIMITED**

Since the company makes a profit of £100,000 on sales of £750,000, all the fixed costs must have been covered. A rise in sales, therefore, of £250,000 (£1,000,000 − £750,000) giving an increase in profit of £150,000 (£250,000 − £100,000) means that the increased variable cost was £100,000. Therefore the profit/volume ratio is 60% (150/250 × 100) and the variable cost of sales must be 40%.

Year to 31 March 19X3	Budget	Actual
	£000	£000
Budget sales	1,200	1,000
Less: Variable costs (40%)	480	400
Contribution	720	600
Less: Fixed costs (60% × £1,000 − profit of £250)	350	350
Budget profit	£370	£450

13.4 **CARTER LIMITED**

Marginal cost statement year to 30 April 19X3

	Per unit	Total (50,000 units)
	£	£000
Selling price	40	2,000
Variable cost	24	1,200
Contribution	£16	800
Less: Fixed costs		350
Profit		£450

Budgeted marginal cost statement year to 30 April 19X4

	Per unit	Total £000
Selling price (£40 − 20%)	32	
Variable costs	24	
Contribution	£8	830*
Fixed costs		380
Profit required		£450

*Contribution required.

Therefore number of units to be sold $= \dfrac{830,000}{8} = 103,750$ units.

103,750 units will have to be sold in 19X4 to make the same amount of profit as in 19X3 if the company reduces its selling price per unit by 20% and increases its fixed costs by £30,000 per annum.

13.5 PUZZLED LIMITED

Option 1 Reduce the selling price by 15%:

	£
New selling price per unit	8.50
Variable cost per unit	7.50
Contribution per unit	£1.00

$$\text{Therefore break-even} = \frac{\text{Fixed costs}}{\text{Contribution per unit}} = \frac{£40,000}{£1.00} = 40,000 \text{ units}$$

Option 2 Improve the product:

	£
Selling price per unit	10.00
New variable cost per unit	8.80
Contribution per unit	£1.20

$$\text{Therefore break-even} = \frac{\text{Fixed costs}}{\text{Contribution per unit}} = \frac{£40,000}{£1.20} = 33,333 \text{ units}$$

Option 3 Advertising campaign:

	£
Selling price per unit	10.00
Variable cost per unit	7.50
Contribution per unit	£2.50

$$\text{Therefore break-even} = \frac{\text{Fixed costs}}{\text{Contribution per unit}} = \frac{£40,000 + £15,000}{£2.50}$$
$$= 22,000 \text{ units}$$

Option 4 Improve factory efficiency:

$$\text{Break-even} = \frac{\text{Fixed costs}}{\text{Contribution per unit}} = \frac{£40,000 + £22,500}{£2.50}$$
$$= 25,000 \text{ units}$$

Conclusion

The advertising campaign would require fewer extra units to be sold in 19X5 compared with 19X4 in order to break even: 22,000 units compared with 16,000 (£40,000 ÷ £2.50).

This would require an increase of 10% on the current year's sales just to break even, although it is fewer than the other options. To make the same profit as in 19X4, 30,000 units would have to be sold (30,000 × £2.50 = £75,000, to cover the fixed costs of £55,000 + the profit of £20,000). Would the campaign also have to be repeated in future years? Has the company got the immediate cash resources in order to carry out the campaign? Can the sales be increased by the required amount simply by advertising?

13.5 MICRO LIMITED

Budgeted contribution per unit of limiting factor for the year:

$$\frac{£250,000}{50,000} = £5 \text{ per direct labour hour}$$

Contribution per unit of limiting factor for the special contract:

	£	£
Contract price		50,000
Less: Variable costs:		
Direct materials	10,000	
Direct labour	30,000	40,000
Contribution		£10,000

Therefore contribution per unit of limiting factor:

$$\frac{£10,000}{4,000} = £2.50 \text{ per direct labour hour}$$

Conclusion

The special contract earns less contribution per unit of limiting factor than does the *average* of ordinary budgeted work. It may be profitable to accept the contract if either it displaces less profitable work or surplus direct labour hours are available. A careful assessment should be undertaken to ascertain whether much more profitable work would be found than is the case with the contract already being considered. It would be unwise to accept the special contract if it will displace other more profitable contracts that could arise in the near future.

Chapter 14

14.1 MORAY LIMITED

	Units
Total budgeted sales: January–June 19X1	2,270
Add: Desired stock at 30 June 19X1	450
	2,720
Less: Opening stock at 1 January 19X1	320
∴ Required production units	2,400

$$\text{Monthly average production} = \frac{2,400}{6} = 400 \text{ units}$$

14.2 JORDAN LIMITED

Budgeted production for the six months to 31 December 19X1:

19X2		Sales (units)	Production (units)	Balance (units)
1.7	Balance b/f	—	—	100
31.7	Sales	70	—	30
	Production	—	200	230
31.8	Sales	140	—	90
	Production	—	280	370
30.9	Sales	350	—	20
	Production	—	180	200
31.10	Sales	190	—	10
	Production	—	180	190
30.11	Sales	150	—	40
	Production	—	140	180
31.11	Sales	120	—	60
	Production	—	40	<u>100</u>

14.3 DALTON LIMITED

	Units
Total budgeted sales: January to June 19X3	1,090
Less: Expected opening stock at 1 January 19X3	100
	990

Average monthly production required $\therefore = 165$ (990/6)
Note that: Opening stock − sales = stock remaining + monthly
production = closing stock.

19X3	O/stock	− sales =	stock remaining	+ monthly production	= c/stock
January	100	− 90 =	10	+ 165	= 175
February	175	− 150 =	25	+ 165	= 190
March	190	− 450 =	(260)		

165 units produced in both January and February will not enable the
company to meet its monthly budgeted sales figure for March 19X3. In
order to do so, it could produce 295 units (165 + 260/2) in both January
and February, and produce 150 units per month in March, April, May
and June. This would enable the company to meet its budgeted April
sales figures, and to achieve a reasonably smooth production flow.
However, it would mean that by the end of June 19X3, the budgeted
closing stock will be 200 units compared with 100 units at 1 January 19X3.
    The calculations are as follows:

19X3	O/stock	− sales =	stock remaining	+ monthly production	= c/stock
January	100	− 90 =	10	+ 295	= 305
February	305	− 150 =	155	+ 295	= 450
March	450	− 450 =	0	+ 150	= 150
April	150	− 150 =	0	+ 150	= 150

19X3	O/stock	− sales	= stock remaining	+ monthly production	= c/stock
May	150	− 130 =	20	+ 150	= 170
June	170	− 120 =	50	+ 150	= 200

Whether the company would wish to adopt this policy is debatable. It might wish, for example, to keep a minimum number of units in stock (perhaps 100 units) at any one time. This would mean increasing the number of units produced in 19X2, because according to the above figures, the company would be left with only 10 units ready for sale at the end of January 19X3. Another 295 units would, however, be immediately ready for sale in February 19X3.

14.4 TOM LIMITED

1 Direct materials usage budget:

| Month | Number of units | | | | | | |
	30.4.X4	31.5.X4	30.6.X4	31.7.X4	31.8.X4	30.9.X4	Six months to 30.9.X4
Component:							
A6 (2 units for X)	280	560	1,400	760	600	480	4,080
B9 (3 units for X)	420	840	2,100	1,140	900	720	6,120

2 Direct materials purchase budget:

Component A6	30.4.X4	31.5.X4	30.6.X4	31.7.X4	31.8.X4	30.9.X4	Six months to 30.9.X4
Material usage (as above)	280	560	1,400	760	600	480	4,080
Add: Desired closing stock	110	220	560	300	240	200	200
	390	780	1,960	1,060	840	680	4,280
Less: Opening stock	100	110	220	560	300	240	100
Purchases (units)	290	670	1,740	500	540	440	4,180
Price per unit	£5	£5	£5	£5	£5	£5	£5
Total purchases	£1,450	£3,350	£8,700	£2,500	£2,700	£2,200	£20,900

Component B9	30.4.X4	31.5.X4	30.6.X4	31.7.X4	31.8.X4	30.9.X4	Six months to 30.9.X4
Material usage (as above)	420	840	2,100	1,140	900	720	6,120
Add: Desired closing stock	250	630	340	300	200	180	180
	670	1,470	2,440	1,440	1,100	900	6,300
Less: Opening stock	200	250	630	340	300	200	200
Purchases (units)	470	1,220	1,810	1,100	800	700	6,100
Price per unit	£10	£10	£10	£10	£10	£10	£10
Total purchases	£4,700	£12,200	£18,100	£11,000	£8,000	£7,000	£61,000

14.5 DON LIMITED

Direct labour cost budget:

	Quarter 30.6.X5	31.7.X5	31.8.X5	*Three months to* 31.8.X5
Grade:				
Production (units)	600	700	650	1,950
Direct labour hours per unit	3	3	3	3
Total direct labour hours	1,800	2,100	1,950	5,850
Budgeted rate per hour (£)	4	4	4	4
Production cost (£)	7,200	8,400	7,800	23,400
Finishing (units)	600	700	650	1,950
Direct labour hours per unit	2	2	2	2
	1,200	1,400	1,300	3,900
Budgeted rate per hour (£)	8	8	8	8
Finishing cost (£)	9,600	11,200	10,400	31,200
Total budgeted direct labour cost	£16,800	£19,600	£18,200	£54,600

14.6 GORSE LIMITED

1 Sales budget:

Quantity	*Selling price* £	*Sales volume* £
10,000	100	1,000,000

2 Production quantity budget:

Sales budget (units)	*Closing stock (units)*	*Opening stock (units)*	*Production required (units)*
10,000	2,000	(4,000)	8,000

3 Materials usage budget:

Component	*Component usage*	*Production (units)*	*Total component usage (units)*
XY	5	8,000	40,000
WZ	3	8,000	24,000

4 Materials purchase budget:

	Component XY	WZ	*Total* £
Budget usage	40,000	24,000	
Stock increase (25%)	4,000	2,400	
Purchase quantities	c/f 44,000	26,400	

		£
b/f 44,000	26,400	

Cost price per unit b/f	£1	£0.50	£0.50
Purchase values	£44,000	£13,200	£57,200

5 Direct labour budget:

Grade	Production budget	Budgeted hours per unit	Total budgeted hours	Budget labour rate per hour £	Total direct labour cost £
Production	8,000	4	32,000	5	160,000
Finishing	8,000	2	16,000	7	112,000
			48,000		£272,000

6 Budgeted profit and loss account:

	Per unit £	Total £
Sales units		10,000
Sales revenue	100.00	1,000,000
Less: costs:		
Production (see workings)	52.50	525,000
Total factory cost	£47.50	475,000
Administration, selling and distribution		275,000
Budgeted profit for period 6		£200,000

	£	£
Workings:		
Unit cost:		
Direct materials:		
Component XY:5 × £1	5.00	
WZ:3 × £0.50	1.50	6.50
Direct labour:		
Production: 4 × £5	20.00	
Finishing: 2 × £7	14.00	34.00
		40.50
Production overhead:		
$\dfrac{£96,000}{48,000} = £2$ per DLH × 6		12.00
		£52.50

14.7

FLOSSY LIMITED
Cash budget for the three months to 31 March 19X7

	January £000	February £000	March £000
Receipts:			
Debtors (Workings 1)	1,900	2,950	2,450
Sales of plant and equipment	—	—	30
Sale of short-term investments	60	—	10
	£1,960	£2,950	£2,490
Payments:			
Trade creditors (Workings 2)	1,150	1,850	1,510
Other creditors	450	500	600
Capital expenditure	—	470	—
Short-term investments	—	40	—
Tax	150	—	—
Dividends	200	—	—
	£1,950	£2,860	£2,110
Monthly net cash flow	10	90	380
Opening balance	15	25	115
Closing balance	£25	£115	£495
Workings:			
1 Trade debtors			
Sales	2,000	3,000	2,500
Add: Opening debtors	200	300	350
	2,200	3,300	2,850
Less: Closing debtors	300	350	400
Cash from trade debtors	£1,900	£2,950	£2,450
2 Purchases			
Cost of goods sold	1,200	1,800	1,500
Add: Closing stock	120	150	150
	1,320	1,950	1,650
Less: Opening stock	100	120	150
Purchases for each quarter	1,220	1,830	1,500
Add: Opening trade creditors	110	180	160
	1,330	2,010	1,660
Less: Closing trade creditors	180	160	150
Cash to trade creditors	£1,150	£1,850	£1,510

14.8 **CHIMES LIMITED**

Option 1 Keep the factory open

	£000	45% £000
Production capacity		
Sales revenue		135.5
Less: Variable cost of sales:		
Direct materials	63	
Direct labour	27	
Variable overhead:		
Factory	18	
Administration	13.5	
Selling and distribution	9	130.5
		5
Contribution		
Less: Fixed costs:		
Factory	10	
Administration	8	
Selling and distribution	6	24
Budgeted loss		£(19)

Option 2 Close the factory

	£000
Costs:	
Redundancy and other closure costs	(30)
Property and plant maintenance	(10)
Re-opening costs	(20)
	(60)
Less: Saving in fixed overheads	30
Net cost of closure	£(30)

Decision

As the factory will still make a contribution during the year to 30 June 19X8, it should be kept open. However, there may be other non-cost factors also to take into account.

Chapter 15

15.1 **X LIMITED**

	£
1 Direct materials cost variance:	
Actual price per unit × Actual quantity = £12 × 6:	72
Less: Standard price per unit × Standard quantity	
for actual production = £10 × 5:	50
	£22(A)

2 Direct materials price variance:
(Actual price − Standard price) × Actual quantity
= (£12 − £10) × 6:   £12(A)

3 Direct materials usage variance:
(Actual quantity − Standard quantity) × Standard
price = (6 − 5) × £10:   £10(A)

15.2 MALCOLM LIMITED

		£
_1_	Direct materials cost variance:	
	Total actual cost	32,400
	Less: Standard quantity for actual production ×	
	Standard price = (50 × 120) × £5:	30,000
		£2,400(A)

2 Direct materials price variance:
(Actual price − Standard price) × Actual quantity =
(£6* − £5) × 5,400:   £5,400(A)

$$*\frac{£32,400}{5,400}$$

3 Direct materials usage variance:
(Actual quantity − Standard quantity) × Standard
price = (5,400 − 6,000*) × £5:   £3,000(F)

*(120 units × 50 kilograms)

15.3 BRUCE LIMITED

		£
_1_	Direct labour cost variance:	
	Actual hours × Actual hourly rate = 1,000 × £6.50:	6,500
	Less: Standard hours for actual production ×	
	Standard hourly rate = 900 × £6.00:	5,400
		£1,100(A)

2 Direct labour rate variance:
(Actual hourly rate − Standard hourly rate) × Actual
hours = (£6.50 − 6.00) × 1,000:   £500(A)

3 Direct labour efficiency variance:
(Actual hours − Standard hours for actual production)
× Standard hourly rate = (1,000 − 900) × £6.00:   £600(A)

15.4 DUNCAN LIMITED

		£
_1_	Direct labour cost variance:	
	Actual direct labour cost	97,200
	Less: Standard hours for actual production ×	
	Standard hourly rate = (10 × 1,200) × £8:	96,000
		£1,200(A)

2 Direct labour rate variance:
(Actual hourly rate − Standard hourly rate)
× Actual hours = (£9* − 8) × 10,800:   £10,800(A)

$$*\frac{£97,200}{10,800}$$

3 Direct labour efficiency variance:
(Actual hours − Standard hours for actual
production) × Standard hourly rate
= (10,800 − 12,000*) × £8:   £9,600(F)

*1,200 × 10 DLH = 12,000

15.5 ANTHEA LIMITED

		£
1	Fixed production overhead variance:	
	Actual fixed overhead	150,000
	Less: Standard hours of production × F.OAR = 8,000 × £15	120,000
		£30,000(A)

2 Fixed overhead expenditure variance:
Actual fixed overhead − budgeted fixed overhead =
£150,000 − £135,000:   £15,000(A)

3 Fixed overhead volume variance:
Budgeted fixed overhead − Standard hours of
production × F.OAR) = £135,000 − (8,000 × £15):   £15,000(A)

4 Fixed overhead capacity variance:
Budgeted fixed overhead − (Actual hours worked
× F.OAR) = £135,000 − (10,000 × £15):   £15,000(F)

5 Fixed overhead productivity variance:
Actual hours worked − Standard hours of
production × F.OAR = (10,000 − 8,000)
× £15,000:   £30,000(A)

15.6 ANTHEA LIMITED

Control ratios:
1 Efficiency:

$$\frac{\text{SHP}}{\text{Actual hours}} \times 100 = \frac{8,000}{10,000} \times 100 = 80\%$$

2 Capacity:

$$\frac{\text{Actual hours}}{\text{Budgeted hours*}} \times 100 = \frac{10,000}{9,000} \times 100 = 111.1\%$$

$$*\frac{£135,000}{15}$$

3 Activity:

$$\frac{\text{SHP}}{\text{Budgeted hours}} \times 100 = \frac{8,000}{9,000} \times 100 = \underline{\underline{88.9\%}}$$

15.7 OSPREY LIMITED

1 Fixed production overhead variance: £

Actual fixed overhead   120,000

Less: Standard hours of production × F.OAR =

$$(600 \times 10) \times \left(\frac{£125,000}{500 \times 10}\right):$$ $\underline{150,000}$

                                              $\underline{\underline{£30,000(F)}}$

2 Fixed overhead expenditure variance:

Actual fixed overhead − Budgeted fixed overhead =

£120,000 − £125,000: $\underline{\underline{£5,000(F)}}$

3 Fixed overhead volume variance:

Budgeted fixed overhead − Standard hours of

production × F.OAR = £125,000 − (6,000* × £25): $\underline{\underline{£25,000(F)}}$

4 Fixed overhead capacity variance:

Budgeted fixed overhead − (Actual hours worked

× F.OAR) = £125,000 − (4,900 × £25): $\underline{\underline{£2,500(A)}}$

5 Fixed overhead productivity variance:

(Actual hours worked − Standard hours of

production) × F.OAR = (4,900 − 6,000*) × £25: $\underline{\underline{£27,500(F)}}$

*600 units × 10 standard hours

15.8 OSPREY LIMITED

Control ratios:

1 Efficiency:

$$\frac{\text{SHP}}{\text{Actual hours}} \times 100 = \frac{6,000}{4,900} \times 100 = \underline{\underline{122.4\%}}$$

2 Capacity:

$$\frac{\text{Actual hours}}{\text{Budgeted hours}} \times 100 = \frac{4,900}{5,000} \times 100 = \underline{\underline{98\%}}$$

3 Activity:

$$\frac{\text{SHP}}{\text{Budgeted hours}} \times 100 = \frac{6,000}{5,000} \times 100 = \underline{\underline{120\%}}$$

15.9 MILTON LIMITED

1 Operating profit due to sales variance:

	£
Total actual sales	99,000
Less: Actual quantity × Standard variable cost	
= 9,000 × £7:	63,000
	36,000
Less: Budgeted units × Standard margin	
= 10,000 × £3*:	30,000
	£6,000(F)

*(£10 − 7)

2 Selling price variance:

(Actual selling price × budgeted selling price)
× Actual units sold = (£11* − 10) × 9,000: £9,000(F)

$$*\frac{99,000}{9,000}$$

3 Sales volume variance:

(Actual quantity − Budgeted units) × Standard
margin = (9,000 − 10,000) × £3: £3,000(A)

15.10 DOE LIMITED

(a) *1* Operating profit due to sales variance:

	£
Total actual sales (120 × £28)	3,360
Less: Actual quantity × Standard variable cost	
= 120 × £20:	2,400
	960
Less: Budgeted units × Standard margin	
= 100 × £10:	1,000
	£40(A)

2 Selling price variance:

(Actual selling price − Budgeted selling price)
× Actual units (£28 − 30) × 120 £240(A)

3 Sales volume variance:

(Actual quantity − Budgeted units) × Standard
margin (120 − 100) × £10: £200(F)

(b) *1* Total sales value variance:

(Actual selling price per unit × Actual
quantity) − (Standard selling price per unit
× Budgeted quantity = (120 × £28) −
(100 × £30) = £3,360 − 3,000: £360(F)

2 Selling price variance:
See (a) *1* above: £240(A)

3 Sales volume variance:
(Actual quantity − Budgeted quantity) ×
Budgeted selling price = (120 − 100) × £30: £600(F)

15.11 JUDITH LIMITED

(a) *1* Efficiency ratio:
$$\frac{\text{SHP}}{\text{Actual hours}} \times 100 = \frac{(5 \times 2,200)}{(4 \times 2,200)} \times 100 = \underline{125\%}$$

2 Capacity ratio:
$$\frac{\text{Actual hours}}{\text{Budgeted hours}} \times 100 = \frac{8,800}{5 \times 2,000} \times 100 = \underline{88\%}$$

3 Activity ratio:
$$\frac{\text{SHP}}{\text{Budgeted hours}} \times 100 = \frac{11,000}{10,000} \times 100 = \underline{110\%}$$

(b) *1* Sales margin operating profit variance £
due to sales:
Actual sales = 2,200 × £145: 319,000
Less: Actual quantity × Standard cost
= 2,200 × £125: 275,000
44,000
Less: Budgeted units × Standard margin
= 2,000 × £25: 50,000
£6,000(A)

2 Sales margin selling price variance:
(Actual selling price − Budgeted selling price)
× Actual units = (£145 − 150) × 2,200: £11,000(A)

3 Sales margin sales volume variance:
(Actual quantity − Budgeted units) × Standard
margin = (2,200 − 2,000) × £25: £5,000(F)

4 Direct materials cost variance:
Actual quantity × Actual price = 2,200 × £72: 158,400
Less: Standard quantity for actual production
× Standard price = (7 kilos × 2,200) × £10: 154,000
£4,400(A)

5 Direct materials price variance:
(Actual price − Standard price) × Actual
quantity = (£9 − 10) × (2,200 × 8): £17,600(F)

6 Direct materials usage variance:

(Actual quantity – Standard quantity)
    × Standard price = ((8 × 2,200) –
    (7 × 2,200)) × £10:   £22,000(A)

7 Direct labour cost variance:

Actual hours × Actual hourly rate =
    (4 × 2,200) × £6:   52,800
Less: Standard hours for actual production
    × Standard hourly rate = (2,200 × 5)
    × £5:   55,000
                                                               £2,200(F)

8 Direct labour rate variance:

(Actual hourly rate – Standard hourly rate)
    × Actual hours = (£6 – £5) × (4 × 2,200):   £8,800(A)

9 Direct labour efficiency variance:

(Actual hours – Standard hours for actual
    production) × Standard hourly rate =
    (8,800 – 11,000) × £5:   £11,000(F)

10 Fixed production overhead variance:

Actual fixed overhead: 65,000
Less: Standard hours of production × F.OAR
    = (2,200 × 5) × £6:   66,000
                                                               £1,000(F)

11 Fixed production overhead expenditure variance:

Actual fixed overhead – Budgeted fixed
    overhead = £65,000 – (£30 × 2,000):   £5,000(A)

12 Fixed production overhead volume variance:

Budgeted fixed overhead – (Standard hours of
    production × F.OAR) = £60,000 –
    (11,000 × £6):   £6,000(F)

13 Fixed production overhead capacity variance:

Budgeted fixed overhead – (Actual hours
    worked × F.OAR) = £60,000 – (8,800 × £6):   £7,200(A)

14 Fixed production overhead productivity variance:

(Actual hours worked – Standard hours of
    production) × F.OAR = (8,800 – 11,000)
    × £6:   £13,200(F)

(c)

Standard cost operating statement for the period	£
Budgeted profit (£25 × 2,000)	50,000
Sales volume variance (£25 × 200)	5,000
Standard margin of actual sales	55,000
Sale price variance (£5 × 2,200)	(11,000)
Actual margin of actual sales	44,000

Cost variances:	Adverse £	Favourable £
Direct materials:		
Price		17,600
Usage	22,000	
Direct labour:		
Rate	8,800	
Efficiency		11,000
Fixed production overhead:		
Expenditure	5,000	
Capacity	7,200	
Productivity		13,200
	£43,000	£41,800	(1,200)
Actual profit			£42,800

Chapter 16

16.1 PROSPECT LIMITED

Calculation of net cash flows:

Year to 31 March	19X1 £000	19X2 £000	19X3 £000	19X4 £000	19X5 £000	19X6 £000
Cash receipts						
Trade debtors (Working 1)	1,800	2,360	2,740	2,880	1,920	400
Sale of project	—	—	—	—	—	50
	1,800	2,360	2,740	2,880	1,920	450
Cash payments						
Purchase of project	1,000	—	—	—		
Trade creditors (Working 2)	1,350	1,770	2,160	1,990	1,260	150
Expenses	210	220	240	250	300	—
Taxation	—	40	70	100	100	10
	2,560	2,030	2,470	2,340	1,660	160
Net cash flows	£(760)	£330	£270	£540	£260	£290

	19X1 £000	19X2 £000	19X3 £000	19X4 £000	19X5 £000	19X6 £000
Workings:						
Year to 31 March						
1 Trade debtors						
Sales	2,000	2,400	2,800	2,900	2,000	—
Less: Closing trade						
debtors	200	240	300	320	400	—
	1,800	2,160	2,500	2,580	1,600	—
Add: Opening trade						
debtors	—	200	240	300	320	400
Cash received	£1,800	£2,360	£2,740	£2,880	£1,920	£400
2 Trade creditors						
Purchases	1,600	1,790	2,220	1,960	1,110	—
Less: Closing trade						
creditors	250	270	330	300	150	—
	1,350	1,520	1,890	1,660	960	—
Add: Opening trade						
creditors	—	250	270	330	300	150
Cash purchases	£1,350	£1,770	£2,160	£1,990	£1,260	£150

16.2 BUCHAN LIMITED

Payback period:

Year	Investment outlay	Cash inflow	Net cash flow	Cumulative cash flow
	£	£	£	£
1	(50,000)	8,000	(42,000)	(42,000)
2	—	16,000	16,000	(26,000)
3	—	40,000	40,000	14,000
4	—	45,000	45,000	59,000
5	—	37,000	37,000	96,000

Payback period therefore = 2 years 7.8 months*

*Net cash flow becomes positive in Year 3. Assuming the net cash flow accrues evenly it becomes positive during August: $(26/40 \times 12) = 7.8$ months (i.e. 2 years and 7.8 months).

16.3 LENDER LIMITED

$$\text{Accounting rate of return} = \frac{\text{Average annual net profit after tax}}{\text{Cost of the investment}} \times 100$$

$$= \frac{1/5(£18,000 + £47,000 + £65,000 + £65,000 + £30,000)}{£100,000} \times 100$$

$$= \frac{45,000}{100,000} \times 100$$

$$= 45\%$$

Note: Based on the *average* investment, the ARR

$$= \frac{£45,000}{1/2(£0 + £100,000)} \times 100$$

$$= 90\%$$

16.4 LOCKHART LIMITED

Net present value:

Year	Net cash flow £000	Discount factor @ 15%	Present value £000
1	800	0.8696	696
2	850	0.7561	643
3	830	0.6575	546
4	1,200	0.5718	686
5	700	0.4972	348
Total present value			2,919
Initial cost			2,500
Net present value			£419

16.5 MOFFAT LIMITED

Internal rate of return:

Year	Net cash flow £000	Discount factors 5%	7%	Present value £000 @ 5%	£000 @ 7%
1	230	0.9524	0.9346	219	215
2	370	0.9070	0.8734	336	323
3	600	0.8638	0.8163	518	490
4	420	0.8227	0.7629	346	320
5	110	0.7835	0.7130	86	78
Total present value				1,505	1,426
Initial cost				1,450	1,450
Net present value				£55	£(24)

Internal rate of return

$$= \text{Positive rate} + \frac{\text{Positive NPV}}{\text{Positive NPV} + \text{Negative NPV}} \times \text{Range}$$

$$= 5\% + \frac{55}{55 + 24} \times 2\%$$

$$= 5\% + 1.4\%$$

$$= \underline{\underline{6.4\%}}$$

16.6 MARSH LIMITED

1 Payback

Year	Investment outlay £000	Cash inflow £000	Net cash flow £000	Cumulative cash flow £000
1	(500)	50	(450)	(450)
2	—	200	200	(250)
3	—	225	225	(25)
4	—	225	225	200
5	—	100	100	300

Therefore payback $= 3 \text{ years} + \dfrac{(25 \times 12)}{225} = \underline{\underline{3 \text{ years } 1.3 \text{ months}}}$

2 Accounting rate of return:

$$\frac{\text{Average annual net profit after tax}}{\text{Cost of the investment}} \times 100$$

$$= \frac{£000 \ (100 + 250 + 250 + 200)}{4}$$

$$= \frac{200}{500} \times 100$$

$$= \underline{\underline{40\%}}$$

Note: If the average cost of the investment is used:

$$= \frac{200}{1/2(£0 + 500)} = \frac{200}{250} \times 100 = \underline{\underline{80\%}}$$

3 Net present value:

Year	Net cash flow £000	Discount factor @ 15%	Present value £000
1	50	0.8696	43
2	200	0.7561	151
3	225	0.6575	148
4	225	0.5718	129
5	100	0.4972	50
Total present value			521
Initial cost			500
Net present value			£21

3 Internal rate of return:

Year	Net cash flow £000	Discount factor @ 15%	Discount factor @ 17%	Present value @ 15% £000	Present value @ 17% £000
1	50	0.8696	0.8547	43	43
2	200	0.7561	0.7305	151	146
3	225	0.6575	0.6244	148	140
4	225	0.5718	0.5337	129	120
5	100	0.4972	0.4561	50	46
Total present value				521	495
Initial cost				500	500
Net present value				£21	£(5)

$$IRR = \text{Positive rate} + \frac{\text{Positive NPV}}{\text{Positive NPV} + \text{Negative NPV}} \times \text{Range}$$

$$= 15\% + \frac{22}{21 + 5} \times 2\%$$

$$= 15\% + 1.7\%$$

$$= \underline{\underline{16.7\%}}$$

Index